CONSTRUCTING SINGAPORE

CONSTRUCTING
SINGAPORE

Elitism, Ethnicity and the Nation-Building Project

Michael D. Barr
and
Zlatko Skrbiš

niasPRESS

an imprint of NUS Press, Singapore

First published in 2008 by NIAS Press
Reprinted in 2011
Now an imprint of NUS Press
AS3-01-02, 3 Arts Link, National University of Singapore
Email: nusbooks@nus.edu.sg
Website: https://nuspress.nus.edu.sg

British Library Cataloguing in Publication Data
Barr, Michael D.
    Constructing Singapore : elitism, ethnicity and the
    nation-building project. - (Democracy in Asia series ; no.
    11)
    1. Elite (Social sciences) - Singapore 2. Discrimination -
    Singapore 3. Nation-building - Singapore 4. Singapore -
    Social conditions 5. Singapore - Politics and government
    I. Title II. Skrbis, Zlatko
    305.5'2'095957

ISBN: 978-87-7694-028-7 (hbk)
        978-87-7694-029-4 (pbk)

Typeset by NIAS Press
Printed by Markono Print Media Pte Ltd

To Shamira and Marta

Contents

Acknowledgements   *ix*

Abbreviations   *xi*

1   Introduction: Island, Colony, City, Nation   1

2   The Singapore Story: Constructing a National Myth   18

3   Constructing the Nation: Elitism and Ethnicity   39

4   The Culture of Elite Governance   57

5   Incomplete Assimilation: From Civic Nationalism to Ethno-Nationalism   87

6   Building the 'New' Singaporean and New Elite   112

7   Catching Them Young: Afraid to Fail in Kindergarten   127

8   Grades, *Kiasuism* and Race: Primary School and Beyond   150

9   Sorting the 'Scholars' from the 'Commoners': Secondary School and Junior College   179

10   Winners and Losers: Gender, Race and Class in Elite Selection   208

11   Making a Mandarin: Inside the Administrative Elite   229

12   Conclusion: A Tentative Assessment of Singapore's Nation-Building Project   252

Bibliography   272

Index   297

List of Tables

2.1   Periodisation of Singapore's history   22

8.1   A comparison of the stated objectives of the Primary 1 Maths syllabi, 1980 and 1999   158

10.1   President's Scholars by gender, 1966 to 2007   211

10.2   President's Scholars by race   215

10.3   SAFOS scholarship winners by race   217

10.4   President's Scholars by Secondary School or Junior College, 1970, 1972, 1975, 1981 and 1982   220

10.5   President's Scholars by Secondary School and Junior College, 2001–2007   221

10.6   SAFOS winners by Secondary School and Junior College, 2004–2007   222

List of Figures

2.1   Cover of a secondary history textbook used in Singapore schools, 1984–99   19

5.1   Tudungs, Singapore style   103

6.1   Advertising billboard in Singapore, April 2004   113

6.2   Examination papers for sale, Bedok, March 2004   116

7.1   Life of a pre-schooler, 1992   127

7.2   A PCF kindergarten at Clementi, April 2003   141

8.1   Racial stereotyping in a Primary 1 textbook, 1981   151

8.2   Miss Li, from the *PEP* textbooks   164

8.3   Miss Chen, from the *NESPE* textbooks   166

8.4   Mr Ahmad in *not* a teacher. From *NESPE* textbooks   167

12.1   Flags in HDB estate, Bedok, July 2005   253

Acknowledgements

ACKNOWLEDGING THOSE WHO HAVE ASSISTED in the research and writing of a book is one of the last things that an author does before putting the manuscript in the mail. It is therefore with a mixed sense of achievement, humility and relief that I am pleased to acknowledge the many institutional and personal debts that Zlatko and I have accumulated over the four years during which this book took shape.

Let us first acknowledge our institutional debts: the Australian Research Council for funding my Fellowship and Discovery Grant, which provided most of the funds needed for the project; the University of Queensland for supporting the project with a New Staff Research Start-Up Grant in 2002; the University of Queensland School of History, Philosophy, Religion and Classics for hosting me during the project; the University of Queensland School of Social Science for its institutional support; the Flinders University School of Political and International Studies for its support in the final stages; the National University of Singapore Department of History for hosting me during my 2003 and 2004 research trips; and the Asia Research Institute for hosting me during my 2005 research trip. We are also grateful to the National University of Singapore Central Library, the National Institute of Education Library, the National Archives of Singapore and the Institute of Southeast Asian Studies Library for allowing access to their collections.

Our personal debts of gratitude are legion and include many interviewees who cannot be named, and others (including many academics) who have assisted us in ways of which they are possibly only dimly aware: advice, insights and information conveyed in conversations, seminars and in anonymous feedback on articles submitted to academic journals. We cannot hope to do justice to all those who have contributed to this book, but there are a few who stand out as having been singularly deserving of mention.

First, we want to thank our wives and partners, Shamira and Marta. Shamira read and edited the entire manuscript (some parts more than once) and it would be a gross understatement to say that they both lost a good deal of their husbands' attention during the actual writing. Next we need to thank Professor Carl Trocki and Professor Bob Elson. They each read an almost completed version of the manuscript and provided highly critical feedback. This was a tremendous sacrifice of their time and we are truly grateful for their efforts. I am also very grateful to Professor Wang Gungwu who generously devoted several hours of his precious time to discussing the project with me back in 2003 when its form was still taking shape.

Among the staff of the various libraries that have assisted me, I wish to single out Ms Ch'ng Kim See of the Institute of Southeast Asian Studies, Mr Tim Yap Fuan of the NUS Central Library and Mr Mark Cryle of the University of Queensland Humanities and Social Sciences Library for special thanks.

Thanks also to Dr Kevin Tan, Mr Lim Cheng Tju, Mr Loh Kah Seng, Ms Ayesha Nachiar and Dr Trudy Jacobsen. At the beginning of the project Kevin devoted half a morning of his valuable time to providing me with introductions to his friends so I could approach them for interviews. As it turned out, many of these introductions proved to be of critical importance and helped determine the direction of the research. Cheng Tju and Kah Seng each advised me on translations from Chinese and Ayesha did the same with a Tamil source. Trudy's particular role was to push me out of my comfort zone by challenging me to study elite selection through the prism of gender.

I also wish to acknowledge and thank my able and enthusiastic research assistants: Ms Adaline Lau, Ms Carol Ng, Mr Loh Kah Seng and Mr Laurence Brown.

I should also mention that a version of Chapter 4 has appeared in *Asian Studies Review*, vol. 30, no. 1, 2006 under the title 'Beyond Technocracy: The Culture of Elite Governance in Lee Hsien Loong's Singapore'. A version of Chapter 7 and part of Chapter 8 have appeared in *Asian Ethnicity*, vol. 6, no. 3, 2005 in an article co-authored with Jevon Low entitled 'Assimilation as Multiracialism: The Case of Singapore's Malays'. Part of Chapter 9 has appeared in *Educational Research for Policy and Practice*, vol. 5, no. 1, 2006 under the title, 'Racialised Education in Singapore'. Part of Chapter 10 has appeared in the *Far Eastern Economic Review*, October 2006 under the title, 'The Charade of Meritocracy'. I am grateful to the copyright holders and to Jevon Low for permission to reproduce this material.

MDB

Abbreviations

AMP   Association of Muslim Professionals

CCA   Co-Curricular Activities (formerly ECA)

CCC   Citizen's Consultative Committee (a GRO)

CDAC   Chinese Development Assistance Council

CMIO   Chinese-Malay-Indian-Other (racial quadratomy)

CNA   *Channel NewsAsia*

DSA   Direct School Admission

EA   Eurasian Association

ECA   Extra-Curricular Activities (later CCA)

EDB   Economic Development Board

EM1, EM2, EM3 Primary school streams introduced in 1992

GEP   Gifted Education Programme

GLC   Government-Linked Companies

GRO   Grassroots organisation

HDB   Housing and Development Board

IE   Institute of Education (later NIE)

ISD   Internal Security Department

ITE   Institute of Technical Education

KiFAS   Kindergarten Financial Assistance Scheme

MAS   Monetary Authority of Singapore

MCDS   Ministry of Community Development and Sport (later MCYS)

MCYS   Ministry of Community Development, Youth and Sport (formerly MCDS)

MENDAKI Council for the Development of the Malay-Muslim Community (Council for the Development of Muslim Children before 1989)

MFA   Ministry of Foreign Affairs

MHA   Ministry of Home Affairs

MINDEF Ministry of Defence

MITI   Ministry of International Trade and Industry (Japan)

MOE   Ministry of Education

MOF   Ministry of Finance

MOH   Ministry of Health

MP   Member of Parliament

MTI   Ministry of Trade and Industry

MUIS   Majlis Ugama Islam Singapura; Islamic Religious Council of Singapore

NE   National Education

NIE   National Institute of Education (formerly the IE)

NMP   Nominated MP (appointed by Parliament)

NS   National Service

NTU   Nanyang Technological University

NUS   National University of Singapore

PAP   People's Action Party

PCF   PAP Community Foundation

PMO   Prime Minister's Office

PRC   People's Republic of China

PS   Permanent Secretary

PSC   Public Service Commission

PSD   Public Service Division

PSLE   Primary School Leaving Examination

RC   Residents' Committee (a GRO)

S-Cube   'Survival, Security and Success'

SAF   Singapore Armed Forces

SAFOS   SAF Overseas Scholarship

SAP school Special Assistance Plan school

SINDA   Singapore Indian Development Association

ST   *The Straits Times*

TC   Town Council

ONE

Introduction:
Island, Colony, City, Nation

[Singapore] is a multiracial nation in which we shall all share equally in the good life, in which we shall help each other, in which the more fortunate, the more advanced, shall make it their duty to help the less fortunate, and the less advanced to catch up in order that there can be a more just and equitable society.

Lee Kuan Yew, circa 1966[1]

THROUGHOUT THE LENGTH AND BREADTH of post-war Southeast Asia, hosts of peoples were at various times flush with the excitement of post-colonial independence and assertive statehood. Born in the death throes of the Japanese version of Asian nationalism, decolonisation gave birth to a new nationalist mythology that rode across the boundaries of the new states without pause. People were now citizens rather than subjects, and they were formally equal to Europeans. No longer subservient 'Asiatics', they were proud Asians who bowed to no white man.

Where the nationalist victories were won with blood – most notably in Vietnam and Indonesia – their leaders built personality cults presenting themselves as heroes of their people. Leaders such as Ho Chi Minh and Sukarno were able to use this enviable status to great political effect in winning the loyalty of their new citizens. In Ho's case he not only used it against the French, but also in a Chinese- and Soviet-backed war against other nationalists who were defending an entire rival American-backed state. Sukarno used it to augment his considerable powers of rhetoric, manipulation and forceful leadership, and to identify the national will with his own.

The former British colonies, however, won independence through laborious negotiations between Whitehall and national elites. Without exception the colonial authorities had cultivated these local elites, who had generally

1

been educated in the metropolis. Insofar as blood was shed, it was by those who were to remain outside the new ruling elites: most notably Malayan Chinese radicals and communists who found themselves cast as enemies of independent Malaya, just as they had been enemies of the British and Japanese colonial constructs that preceded it.

This left the post-British ruling elites in a less advantageous rhetorical position than their Indonesian and Vietnamese counterparts, but they enjoyed several critical windfalls that more than compensated for this lack. In British Malaya (including Singapore) these compensations included workable systems of governance and bureaucracy, modicums of intact national and fiscal infrastructure, strong indigenous capitalist classes, a secure (if subordinate) position in global markets, and the promise of ongoing, if conditional, support from the British.

Yet, regardless of the state of leadership or practical infrastructure, all these new states were concerned with a major exercise of 'nation building'. This was a versatile concept that often focused on physical or near-physical acts of building the material fabric to fill the hollow shell of the state. Hence, 'nation building' focused on building roads, buildings, monuments, factories, industries, armies, economies, and institutions of governance. These activities were often pervaded by a sense of youthful freshness and sometimes by grim determination to achieve.

The goal was not a state *per se*, since that had already materialised in the process of decolonisation. They were trying to turn formally delineated states into something both aspirational and real. The monuments, factories, airports and armies were not just utilitarian objects designed to provide beauty, jobs, transport or protection. They were symbols of a much more difficult work of creation – an attempt to build a sense of belonging and to provide a repertoire upon which to build the common foundations for national imagination. The citizens were encouraged to form bonds with the new state, and accept these bonds as an expression of nationhood – something much more appealing and intimate than the mere accident of living within a national boundary imposed by a former colonial power. This metamorphosis of citizens into nationals was performed along the vertical axis between the people and the institutions of government, but it was also built on a problematical, and apparently contradictory imperative – the need to build deep, horizontal bonds across society and to contribute to what Benedict Anderson called a 'horizontal comradeship' in an 'imagined community'.[2] They set out to build national identities, whereby citizens conceived a meaningful bond with their fellow citizens as fellow-members of a nation. This task involved the creation of the emotional and conceptual innards that it was hoped would bind the people to the new polities and to the ruling elites. This two-dimensional bonding was the real heart of the exercise of nation building. The various national ruling elites directed this project utilising both the core tools of the state – executive, legislative and bureaucratic power, the military, the education system – and various ancillary tools over which it was, in many instances, able to exercise practical control – media, ruling party, trade unions, traditional and/or civil society.

Ethnic and Civic Bonds

Just as there were many variations in the details of the material aspects of this work of creation, so were there in the construction of national communities. One indicator of such variation was the shifting importance of the ethnic and cultural elements in the nation-building project, such as race, ethnicity, language or religion, in contrast to more civic elements.[3]

Using the conceptual categories provided by David Brown's recent work, we might view Southeast Asian nationalisms as forming a continuum from 'ethnocultural', through 'multicultural' to 'civic'.[4] Viewing Southeast Asian nation-building projects through this prism, we might place Burma on the furthest extreme of the ethnocultural end of the spectrum, with Thailand not far behind, and Singapore towards the other extreme, with Suharto's Indonesia even further out on the 'civic' end of the spectrum. Malaysia might be placed somewhere in the middle of the spectrum. The basis for painting the spectrum in this fashion would be the official relationship between ethnic and national identity in each of the nation-states, with an itemised justification for this hierarchy of countries running as follows:

- After dallying with a heterogeneous multi-ethnic nation-building programme, Burma resorted to a heavy-handed Burman nationalism based unofficially on the Buddhist religion and Burman ethnicity, resulting in a four-decades-long series of civil wars with minority nations that finally left the Burman centre dominant.[5]

- Nation builders in Thailand consciously created a new, highly inclusionary 'Thai' national ethnicity based on religion, language and kingship. Any groups that were willing and able to become literate in the Thai language, at least acknowledge the pre-eminence of Buddhism (if not become Buddhist), venerate the king, and place the national project ahead of regional and ethnic identities and interests could participate fully in this aspirational nation.[6] This strategy has 'worked' for nearly 90% of the population,[7] but it has isolated various minorities and it eventually provoked a violent reaction from the Muslim south of the country.

- Malaysia used ethnicity based on religion, language and race (in that order of priority) as tools in nation building, excluding non-Malays and non-Muslims from full identification with the aspirational nation, but allowing them to live and prosper in a relatively comfortable communion with the centre.

- Singapore is a multi-racial, multi-religious, multi-lingual secular state that combines a modern concept of citizenship with practices that essentialise and emphasise ethnic identity, thus making it less 'modern' and 'civic' than might appear at first glance.

- Except for the aberration of Sukarno's efforts to build a pan-Malay quasi-state based on supposed ethnic ties, Indonesian nationalism has always based itself explicitly on thoroughly modern concepts of citizenship. Under the New Order, the national ideology (Pancasila) was quasi-secular, and race and ethnicity were not even recognised as legitimate forms of identification. The national language is not the language of the dominant Javanese, but that of one of the smaller minorities.[8]

Thus on the basis of official attitudes to ethnicity as an element national identity, we end up with a figure that looks something like this:

Burma	Thailand	Malaysia	Singapore	Indonesia

←——→

Ethnocultural nation building   *Civic nation building*

Charts such as these have a certain attraction for their simplicity, but they are often as misleading as they are useful. Placing Indonesia at the 'civic' end of the spectrum, for instance, obscures the fact that a refusal by the New Order regime to recognise ethnicity and race disguised the clear ethnic dimension in the transmigration policy, whereby Javanese and Madurese were shipped to outlying provinces where they threatened to turn the locals into second-class citizens in their own communities. The stated purpose of the programme was certainly not to engage in ethnic imperialism, but this was the result. The ethnically 'neutral' New Order government also imposed a variation of the Javanese system of village governance onto the entire rural population of Indonesia without ever mentioning its true inspiration. It was done, not in the name of Javanese cultural supremacy, but in the name of 'uniformity' and efficiency.[9]

States and nations, like the individual people who comprise them, rarely fit neatly into analytical categories. A nation can be sophisticated, modern and secular at the same time as it is working through agendas defined through the prisms of race and ethnicity. It is a major contention of this book that such a description applies to Singapore. Despite the official rhetoric that Singapore follows a civic model of nationhood, we argue that since around 1980 the Singapore nation-building project began moving away from a civic-oriented model (where citizenship is based on a modern, inclusive, 'rational' model free of 'primordial' elements such as race, ethnicity or religion) towards a more ethnic-cum-racial form, with the conceptions of 'Chinese ethnicity' and a peculiarly Singaporean notion of 'Chinese values' assuming increasingly important roles. In this respect, the situation is not dissimilar to that in Malaysia. We suggest that since about 1980, Chinese ethnicity and 'values' have surreptitiously come to occupy a similar place in Singapore society to that which Malay ethnicity occupies openly in Malaysia: it is the basis of full identification with the nation, but allows the other communities to live and prosper in a relatively comfortable communion with the centre.

Singapore in the Context of Southeast Asian Nation Building

Singapore is one of the most intriguing specimens of nation building in Southeast Asia. The government ownership of the nation-building project, its micromanagement of everyday life and the role played by the elite are three fundamental elements in this complex and continuing process of construction of a nation. The intense triangulation of these elements and the pace of change they produce make the Singapore example of special interest.

Despite Singapore having few natural resources, the ruling elite has an impressive record of achievement on all the material aspects of nation building. In its relatively short history, Singapore's economic and social development and transformation are nothing short of remarkable. Singapore is today by far the most successful exemplar of material development in the region and it often finds itself the envy of developed countries. Furthermore over the last three-and-a-half decades the ruling party has presided over the formation of a thriving community of Singaporeans who love their country, and who have immense respect, though not necessarily affection, for the regime that rules it.

Nothing about these processes has been 'natural' in any sense of the word. Much of the country's investment in nation building has in fact gone into the selection, training and formation of a ruling and administrative elite that reflects and will perpetuate this vision of the nation – hence this book's focus on elite formation as part of nation building. The ruling elite micromanages both the material progress and the construction of an imagined community, and it spares no effort to see that every consequence is intended and every nuance is deliberate. At times – particularly under the prime ministership of Lee Kuan Yew (1959–1990) – the elite has appeared to strive for omniscience, if not omnipotence. It has claimed the authority of pure reason and conceived of itself as being above class and sectional interests: a political version of the Archimedean point. In its conceit it thought it could target every incremental change in policy to enact precise, planned consequences. Alas the real world does not behave in such an orderly fashion, and so there had to be corrections – and corrections on corrections – as the elite strove for perfection in its creation. John Clammer wrote a vivid contemporary account of this restlessness in the nation-building project in 1985 when he bewailed the constancy and seeming pointlessness of change:

> ... the education system is changed constantly at all levels; expensive projects are begun, like the upgrading of the international airport which was closed down and rendered obsolete two years hence by the opening of a totally new airport; change, construction, urgency are the keywords. But why? What is the ultimate purpose of all this construction, all this energy spent changing what has just been finished? Nobody quite knows, for the system seems to require that today's solution is tomorrow's problem ... .[10]

In the same year Lee Kuan Yew's friend and long term economic adviser, Albert Winsemius, made a similar point in a more light-heated fashion:

> I don't know if you've ever noticed that Singapore and its government often behave like adolescents in a one-sided way, over-stressing a thing and forgetting the rest; then dropping the subject and focusing, once more one sided, on the next thing (*Sunday Times*, 27 January 1985).

This frenetic and often contradictory activity and mismanagement is the reality of Singaporean nation building, but it stands in severe contradiction of the elite's self-image as nearly omniscient technocrats with mastery over all they purvey.

Government Ownership

Part and parcel of the mythology of the elite is the assumption that the government owns the national project body and soul, and that the government's nation-building project and the evolution of the Singaporean nation are the same thing. This feature of nation building has generated an unfortunate but highly predictable consequence: the official nation-building project has relegated national loyalty to being in part a function of the regime's legitimacy.[11] As a direct consequence of this, many people perceive national loyalty as being linked to the determinants of government popularity, especially economic performance. The then Prime Minister, Goh Chok Tong, assumed and highlighted this linkage in his 2002 National Day Rally Speech when, following the recession of 2001, he berated Singaporean 'quitters' who would pack their bags 'whenever the country runs into stormy weather' (*Straits Times*, 19 August 2002). Over the following days the local newspapers were swamped with nearly 600 letters from people indignant that their loyalty had been questioned (*Agence France-Press*, 23 August 2002), but an ACNielsen survey taken before Goh's speech but released after it suggests that Goh really did have his finger on the pulse. The telephone survey of 1,000 people found that twenty-one per cent of Singaporeans harboured 'a desire to leave the country permanently'. An ACNielsen executive speculated that 'the state of the economy' was the driving force. Interestingly almost half of the potential émigrés were attracted to Australia, precisely because of its proximity to Singapore, suggesting the continuing draw of family and familiarity, even among such would-be 'quitters'.[12]

It seemed that in Goh's mind there is a perception that for many people – especially young people – loyalty to Singapore is ultimately conditional on economic performance and opportunity and the government's success in delivering the good life. Yet the government's reading is in fact more nuanced than this, as is revealed in a questionnaire that (as of the mid-2000s) intending 'quitters' need to complete as part of their emigration process. It asks for the three main reasons for emigration. The ten options suggested on the form include 'High cost of living in Singapore', 'Singapore is too regulated and sti-fling', 'Better and less stressful educational opportunities for your children', 'Do not want your son/s to serve National Service', and 'Uncertain future of Singapore'.[13]

The Enigma of the Singapore Elite

A substantial element in the government's ongoing concern is that there might be a disconnection between ordinary Singaporeans and 'the elite'. Throughout modern history, elites have played an integral role in nationalist projects, but they are rarely given such a central or official role as we find in Singapore. Historically, Anthony Smith distinguishes between two phases of elite involvement in nationalism, and consequently, two types of nation-alism.[14] The first is elite nationalism, which emphasises the importance of charismatic and enlightened individuals, both past and present. The second is mass nationalism, in which masses critically contribute to shaping the nation-alist project. These two nationalisms are ideal types in the Weberian sense, and should not be seen as mutually exclusive, but they help us understand the spectrum of elite involvement in the process of nation building. Depending on an historical moment and place, elites can be a decisive element in the process of national 'awakening', particularly if they have a perceived organic attachment with the nation and the people they are calling into existence.

In the case of Singapore, the nation-building project has been unasham-edly elitist and has run in near-perfect parallel with a process of elite formation and engagement. Barr has argued elsewhere that the Singaporean version of elitism is substantially a product of the mind and imagination of Lee Kuan Yew. Its genesis has its roots in Lee's social experiences: growing up as the privileged and gifted eldest son in a well-to-do Chinese family, his exposure to the English class system in England, his wide extra-curricular reading at Cambridge (particularly his reading of Arnold Toynbee's *A Study of History*) and the negative examples he saw in Europe and Asia of the supposed failure of egalitarianism as a dynamic principle of social organisation.[15] Toynbee's work proved particularly important because it provided the conceptual tool that enabled Lee to link his elitism to a concept of social and civilisational progressivism. Toynbee's 'creative minority' was the driver that could pilot a civilisation (or perhaps a small country?) ever forward, at least until this elite lost its creative edge. Hence his elitism is closely linked with a romantic idea of progressivism.

Elitism sits uncomfortably with the idea of a modern, educated polity that utilises the forms of democracy and extols the importance of citizenship, but the political and administrative elites in Singapore have no concern about trumpeting their leadership role to the amorphous masses, which are known collectively as 'the grassroots'. They still follow Lee Kuan Yew's advice from 1966: that the elite needs to cultivate among its members 'a sense of calculated importance', and regard its members as being 'at the very top of society [and possessing] all the qualities needed to lead'.[16] The concept of 'the elite' is not only a significant reality in Singapore governance, but it is arguably *the* central feature of governance. Thanks to the extraordinarily high levels of government ownership of commercial enterprises in Singapore, and the cross-fertilisation of Cabinet and civil service personnel on government-linked boards, the 'elite' reaches into the bowels of Singapore capitalism.[17] Thanks also to the 'symbiotic relationship' between the governing People's Action Party (PAP) and the trade union movement, and the consequent blending of Cabinet and trade union leadership, 'the elite' also dominates the alternate side of the labour-capital divide. In fact there is barely an expression of civil society or the economy that is not consciously and deliberately permeated by the government-linked elite. In those rare cases where an organisation is free of this direct control, this has been achieved by careful negotiation with the government, complete transparency, and eschewing all links that could be vaguely construed as political.[18]

Elitism and Ethnicity[19]

Yet the use of elitism as a tool of leadership and control is not as enigmatic as its application in nation building. Singapore is a modern, educated, cosmopolitan society that has run its nation-building programme on a principle that is implicitly exclusionist, a feat that is all the more audacious in the light of the problematical relationship between elitism and ethnicity in multiracial Singapore. The myth that Singapore's elite relies solely on meritocratic grounds underpins the ideology of elitism, but this mythology is continually being undermined by modes of communal thought that lock the population into rigid and somewhat artificial ethnic categories. This communalism is an inherent part of another element of Singapore's nation-building mythology: that Singapore is not so much the amalgam of its population of individual persons but rather the sum of the official, sharply delineated ethnic groups.

Every Singaporean is allocated an official racial designation, being Chinese (about three-quarters of the population), Malay, Indian or one of the smaller minorities such as Eurasian or Arab. This designation is a factor in determining the schools they and their children attend; what languages they learn at school; what special help might be available for education; where they live; and which parliamentary constituencies they can contest. Racial classification is the only piece of information on the front of a Singaporean identity card apart from one's name and photograph. In fact, Singaporeans outside the dominant Chinese majority are unlikely to think of themselves as Singaporean without hyphenating their Singaporeanness with their racial marker. Thus an Indian is more likely to think of himself or herself as an Indian-Singaporean than as simply a Singaporean. This feature is in part an inheritance of the colonial construction of a plural society,[20] but it has been perpetuated and reinforced in post-colonial Singapore, even as the government has sought to minimise and ameliorate communal tensions in the republic. The myth of the meritocracy is designed to cut across ethnic communalism, but the government undermines its own efforts in a dozen ways by exercises in ethnic ascription, such as the publication of matriculation and university results according to race. Indeed on Hill and Lian's reading, the government is attracted to ethnic ascription precisely because it emphasises communal bonds and provides balance to the individualism generated by the meritocratic order and capitalist materialism.[21]

The official Singaporean approach to ethnicity is a direct result of the social cognition created by founding Prime Minister Lee Kuan Yew. He appropriated the existing social British- and Chinese-generated racial prejudices of the 1940s and 1950s and developed them into a parody of a sophisticated worldview whereby he saw the world as a hierarchy of races. As recently as the late 1990s Lee was still confidently saying:

> When doing a project [the British] would put the Chinese in the middle and put the Indians at the side, and the Indians were expected to keep the pace of the Chinese. And there was a hell of a problem, because one Chinese would carry one pole with two wicker baskets of earth, whereas two Indians would carry one pole with one wicker basket between them. So it's one quarter. Now that's culture. Maybe it has to do with genetic characteristics. I'm not sure.[22]

Three decades earlier, at the beginning of the nation-building project, he was willing to go much further. In 1967 he told a meeting of university students the following parable in answer to the question, 'What is the X-factor in development?':

> Three women were brought to the Singapore General Hospital, each in the same condition and each needing a blood transfusion. The first, a Southeast Asian [read Malay] was given the transfusion but died a few hours later. The second, a South Asian [read Indian] was also given a transfusion but died a few days later. The third, an East Asian [read Chinese] was given a transfusion and survived. That is the X factor in development.[23]

The two members of the audience who independently reported this meeting to Barr in 1996 said there was no doubt in anyone's mind this was a lesson about the hierarchy of the Chinese, Indian and Malay races. This speech was not publicised, but its assumptions underscored the government's approach to many aspects of government and society, especially education. Malays have underachieved as a group in modern Singapore but are told this is due to their cultural deficiencies and their laziness. This cultural deficit thesis has become so pervasive that even Malay teachers accept it and pass the notions onto their pupils.[24] We argue that ethno-racial hierarchies permeate every aspect of Singapore society even though the official discourse of multiracialism – its ostensible even-handedness, and the avowed opposition to any form of ethnic chauvinism – obscures this reality. The above quotations from Lee are indicative of a deeply ingrained discourse of 'progress and survival'[25] based on the assumption – backed by social statistics – of the special place and superiority of the Chinese. Behind the façade of even-handed multiracialism lurks a methodical and pervasive sensitivity for things racial that asserts the Chinese character of Singapore multiracialism.

Constructing Singapore

Singapore is a nation in perpetual constructionist mode. We understand this constructionist zeal to consist of three key aspects. First, the Singapore government is continuously fixated on tangible acts of material construction of buildings, roads and, through land reclamation, an expansion of the city-state beyond the limits of its geography. This is predicated on the idea that everything in Singapore works and functions. Anything that fails to comply with the ideals of functionality, cleanliness and order is an aberration and doomed to eventual extinction. Cherian George captured this obsession with the memorable metaphor of 'the air-conditioned nation', following Lee Kuan

Yew's famous declaration that the humble air conditioner represents the most important technological invention of the second millennium because it allows the burgeoning of a society in a forbidding tropical climate. Indeed, George argues that, like its air-conditioned buildings, Singapore is 'a society with a unique blend of comfort and central control, where people have mastered their environment, but at the cost of individual autonomy, and at the risk of unsustainability'.[26]

The second way of understanding the notion of 'constructing Singapore' is through what we call a constructionist disposition towards governmental policies. The government subjects almost every aspect of its social, educational and political life to continuous (re)evaluation and (re)construction, often resulting in fundamental shifts in policy foci. Current examples of such strategies are the pushes to support the creative arts, foster 'entrepreneurship' and turn Singapore into a 'global, cosmopolitan city'. All this makes Singapore a society in continuous flux, informed by a supposedly ever-effective bureaucratic rationality. At the moment this project is aimed at constructing the kind of citizenry that can be optimally effective doing business in the international arena.

The third aspect of Singaporean 'constructionism' – and the one that is the principle focus of this book – operates in the realm of ideology, whereby the ruling elite strives to ensure that its vision of the nation, society, the world and itself will be accepted by the population, and will dominate the social cognition of the population at all levels. As the nation-building project has become increasingly outward-looking – moving from being merely export-oriented in the 1960s, to seeking a role as a dynamic node in a network of 'global cities' in the 1990s and 2000s – this exercise has become increasingly sophisticated, finely nuanced and interesting.

About this Book

This book studies Singapore's nation-building project by focusing on two processes: elite formation and elite selection. We give primary attention to the role that ethno-racial ascription plays in these processes, but also consider the input of personal connections, personal power, class and gender. It is a study of the progress of Singapore's state-sponsored nation-building project from origins that are firmly, if imperfectly, rooted in modernity and civic nationalism, to its current state whereby – we argue – a Singaporean version of Chinese ethnonationalism has overwhelmed the discourse on national and Singaporean identity. A major focus of the study is devoted to tracing the construction of this new notion of 'Singaporeanness' through the mechanisms of elite formation: the education system (nursery to university), National Service, the civil service system of bonded scholarships, the civil service itself (specifically the elite Administrative Service) and the Singapore Armed Forces officer corps. The study includes histories of the development of each level of this process from their origins in the late colonial and early independence periods to their current states of sophistication.

Singapore is widely and correctly regarded as one of the success stories of decolonisation, but this book focuses on its shortcomings. In doing so we do not set out to belittle Singapore's achievements, but we do want to contribute to a better understanding of their limits, and the basis of the realities that have both generated and circumscribed them. In this book we do not shy away from expressing our opinions, but the main strength of this book is, we hope, a thorough presentation and analysis of historical evidence derived from years of archival research and many oral history interviews. Now that this corpus of evidence is in the public domain, others are welcome to take this evidence and interpret it differently.

We freely acknowledge that this book raises many questions without coming to firm answers. If 'the Singapore system' contains as many major shortcomings as we claim, why is it so successful? Is it successful despite the 'flaws' or because of them? Should the terms of its success itself be subjected to critical interrogation? If members of Singapore's ethnic minority groups suffer the levels of discrimination depicted in the pages that follow, why is it that most of them are still loyal Singaporeans who love their country and respect their political leaders? We (and others) may pursue these issues further in the future, but the realities of deadlines and word limits have restrained our pursuit of such questions in this book.

The book itself is the result of collaboration between an historian (Barr) and a sociologist (Skrbiš). All the archival and basic research for the book was conducted by Barr and follows the methodology of the historian. The oral history interviews were also conducted by Barr, except for a handful made available by the Oral History Centre of the National Archives of Singapore, which are acknowledged as such whenever they are cited.

The interviewees were identified and contacted through a variety of methods. The first six to be interviewed were Singaporeans studying at either the University of Queensland or Queensland University of Technology in Brisbane. The next ten interviews were conducted with those among the respondents to 1,000 letters sent in December 2002 by Barr to alumni of the University of Singapore and Nanyang University as listed in the A–C section of the *National University of Singapore Alumni Directory, 1996*. (This was the most recent edition at the time.) Some other respondents came as 'snowballing' introductions from these original 16, but many more were friends and academic associates of Barr in Singapore, or were introduced to Barr by such associates. Barr also wrote directly to several people who held or had previously held positions of significance in government, and some of these agreed to be interviewed. The interviews that resulted from this *ad hoc*, somewhat personal process would have been useless to anyone trying to conduct a statistically significant, representative survey, but it was a goldmine for an historical exploration of elite formation, elite selection and nation building over a period that is still in living memory.

In the end Barr conducted 66 formal interviews over 2002, 2003, 2004 and 2005, most of which were conducted in 2003. These formal interviews were supplemented in a general way by interviews conducted for other research projects on Singapore and by many conversations that were often as informative as formal interviews. Most of the interviewees have been de-identified at the request of the interviewee, and in accordance with procedures approved by the Behavioural and Social Sciences Ethical Review Committee of the University of Queensland, but some chose to waive anonymity. The formal interviews conducted specifically for this project included serving and retired civil servants and Permanent Secretaries, an opposition MP, two former Nominated MPs, a cadre member of the PAP, academics, retired teachers, business entrepreneurs, 'scholars', an Army officer, local and overseas university students and 'grassroots' leaders. The vast majority of interviewees were Chinese, but there were six Malays, 12 Indians, two Eurasians, one Arab and a few whose ethnic origins were not made clear. The sample included 10 Muslims.

The primary contribution of Skrbiš was in relation to comparative and theoretical perspectives to the discussions of nation building, ethnicity and elitism, particularly – but not exclusively – in the early chapters of the book.

Plan of the Book

- The first three chapters serve as an extended introduction. Chapter 2 is a critical study of the historical mythmaking of Singaporean nation building, also serving as a cursory introduction to the history of Singapore. Chapter 3 places the Singaporean treatment of elitism and ethnicity in theoretical and comparative contexts.

- Chapters 4 and 5 expound two of the book's main arguments. Chapter 4 explores the current culture of elite governance, with particular attention to distortions arising from the exercise of personal power and personal connections. Chapter 5 argues that the Singaporean ideal of multiracialism has been twisted into an exercise in Chinese ethnonationalism.

- Chapters 6–10 study the education system. Chapters 6–9 follow the history of the education system sequentially from pre-school to junior college, exploring the processes of nation building, elite formation and elite selection, substantially through the prisms of ethnicity and socio-economic background. Chapter 10 focuses exclusively on the process of elite selection, mainly through the prism of the government scholarship system. It considers gender as factor in elite selection, alongside ethnicity and socio-economic background.

- Chapter 11 examines the processes of elite formation inside the elite echelon of the civil service and in the officer corps of the Singapore Armed Forces. It can be regarded as a prequel to Chapter 4 since it concludes on the doorstep of a consideration of elite governance.

- Chapter 12 is an attempt to assess the efficacy of the nation-building project as it stands at the time of writing.

Notes

1 Ministry of Information and the Arts, *Riding the Tiger: The Chronicle of a Nation's Battle Against Communism*, DVD, Singapore: Ministry of Information and the Arts, 2001, in the section, 'The Tiger at Bay'.

2 Benedict Anderson, *Imagined Communities*, London: Verso, 1993, p. 7.

3 For a consideration of these rival foundations of nationalism, see Liah Greenfeld, 'Nationalism in Western and Eastern Europe Compared', in Stephen E. Hanson and Willfried Spohn (eds), *Can Europe Work? Germany and the Reconstruction of Postcommunist Societies*, Seattle and London: University of Washington Press, 1995, pp. 15–23; and

Benedict Anderson, 'Western nationalism and Eastern nationalism: is there a difference that matters?', *New Left Review* vol. 9, 2001, pp. 31–42.

4   David Brown, 'Contending nationalisms in Southeast Asia', Working Paper No. 117, Asia Research Centre, Murdoch University, Perth, January 2005.

5   Tin Maung Maung Than, 'Dreams and nightmares: state building and ethnic conflict in Myanmar (Burma)', in Kusuma Snitwongse and W. Scott Thompson (eds), *Ethnic Conflicts in Southeast Asia*, Singapore: Institute of Security and International Studies; and Institute of Southeast Asian Studies, 2005, pp. 65–108.

6   Chayan Vaddhanaphuti, 'The Thai state and ethnic minorities: from assimilation to selective integration', in Kusuma and Thompson (eds), *Ethnic Conflicts in Southeast Asia*, pp. 151–166.

7   Charles F. Keyes, 'The politics of language in Thailand and Laos', in Michael E. Brown and Šumit Ganguly, *Fighting Words: Language Policy and Ethnic Relations*, Cambridge, Mass. and London: The MIT Press, 2003, p. 193.

8   R.E. Elson explores some of the tensions in early Indonesian nationalism in 'Constructing the nation: ethnicity, race, modernity and citizenship in early Indonesian thought', *Asian Ethnicity*, vol. 6, no. 3, 2005, pp. 145–60.

9   Rizal Sukma, 'Ethnic conflict in Indonesia: causes and the quest for solution', in Kusuma Snitwongse and Thompson (eds), *Ethnic Conflicts in Southeast Asia*, pp. 1–41.

10 John Clammer, *Singapore: Ideology, Society, Culture*, Singapore: Chopmen, 1985, p. 27.

11 See Lily Zubaidah Rahim, 'The political agenda underpinning economic policy formulation in Singapore's authoritarian developmental state', in Uwe Johannen and James Gomez, *Democratic Transitions in Asia*, Singapore: Select Publishing in association with Friedrich Naumann Foundation, 2001, pp. 222, 223.

12 ACNielsen, 'More Singaporeans than ever before looking to migrate overseas', dateline 4 September 2002. Available HTTP <http://www.acnielsen.com.sg/news.asp?newsID=112> Cited 10 September 2002.

13 Singapore Police Force, 'Application for Certificate of No Criminal Conviction (CNCC)'; cited December 2003. Also available from the Singapore Police Force Website at http://www.spf.gov.sg/service/cer1.html

14 Anthony D. Smith, *Chosen Peoples: Sacred Sources of National Identity*, Oxford: Oxford University Press, 2003, pp. 223, 224.

15 Michael D. Barr, *Lee Kuan Yew: The Beliefs Behind the Man*, Richmond, UK: Curzon, 2000, pp. 97–136, 185–210.

16 Lee Kuan Yew, cited in ibid., p. 106.

17 See Ross Worthington, *Governance in Singapore*, London and New York: RoutledgeCurzon, 2003.

18 The most notable example of this phenomenon is the Association of Muslim Professionals (AMP), a Malay–Muslim educational assistance group that operates in rivalry with the official government-sponsored Malay–Muslim educational assistance group, MENDAKI.

19 The contentions made in this section are developed and justified more completely in Chapters 5–10.

20 A 'plural society' is J.S. Furnivall's term for a society with ethnic groups living side by side, but separately; knowing each other not as individuals but primarily through stereotypes and the market place. He coined the term when writing about colonial Burma and Java. See J.S. Furnivall, *Colonial Policy and Practice: A Comparative Study of Burma and Netherlands India*, Cambridge: Cambridge University Press, 1948, p. 304.

21 Michael Hill and Lian Kwen Fee, *The Politics of Nation Building and Citizenship in Singapore*, London and New York: Routledge, 1995, p. 102.

22 Barr, *Lee Kuan Yew*, p. 191.

23 Ibid., p. 185.

24 See Lily Zubaidah Rahim, *The Singapore Dilemma: The Political and Educational Marginality of the Malay Community*, Kuala Lumpur: Oxford University Press, 1998, especially pp. 49–53, 59–61, 188.

25 Barr, *Lee Kuan Yew*, p. 140.

26 Cherian George, *Singapore – The Air-Conditioned Nation: Essays on the Politics of Comfort and Control 1990-2000*, Singapore: Landmark Books, 2000, pp. 14, 15.

TWO

The Singapore Story:
Constructing a National Myth

The Singapore Story is a very special story.

It is the story of our nation – a small island whose success today could not have been imagined yesterday.

We have survived through war and violence, social turmoil and political upheaval. And along the way, we, as a people, have learnt many lessons.

Find out how we lived through the colonial and occupation years before emerging as our own masters. Learn how we battled the twin challenges of communism and communalism to build the cohesive multi-racial society of today. Witness how the sheer will and determination of a people united in adversity can achieve what no one thought was possible.

Join us as we go into the pages of our past, to hear the stories that only history can tell.

From the cover of *The Singapore Story: Overcoming the Odds. An Interactive Media,* CD-ROM, a National Education Project by the Ministry of Information and the Arts, 1999.

SINCE THE LATE 1990s, 'The Singapore Story' has become standard short-hand for the official history of Singapore as projected by the ruling elite's top-down nation-building project. Conceptually it is the product of four men: S. Rajaratnam, C.V. Devan Nair, George Yeo, and Lee Kuan Yew. The first two were 'first generation' politicians with a talent for mythmaking, and are credited by Hong Lysa with establishing the basic template of Singapore's national mythology.[1] George Yeo is a 'third generation' politician who has successfully taken over their mantle, and Lee Kuan Yew, of course, is the 'father of Singapore' whose political craftsmanship since the 1950s, and bio-graphical and semi-biographical output since the late 1990s, has placed him on the centre-stage of Singapore's history-cum-mythmaking. He even named his personal memoirs *The Singapore Story,* removing all doubt about his own perception of his role and cementing the term in the national lexicon.[2]

The Singapore Story comes in various guises. It has taken the form of an interactive exhibition that was visited by almost every school student in 1998 in a national act of secular pilgrimage that finds an echo in the annual National Day parades. Many have read it through Lee Kuan Yew's multi-volume and multi-edition memoirs, but for many young Singaporeans it has come in the form of the CD-ROM cited at the opening of this chapter.[3] It has also been subsumed into a broader entity called 'National Education', which is expressed in part through the History and Social Studies syllabi taught in Singapore's schools. National Education *per se* is given more detailed attention in Chapter 9, but for the moment it is sufficient to identify The Singapore Story as the

Figure 2.1: Cover of a secondary history textbook used in Singapore schools, 1984–99. (See note 9 for details.)

'official' version of Singapore's history, and the centrepiece of the official nation-building project.

As well as being mere history, The Singapore Story is effectively a secular nationalist narrative. Most nationalist projects tend to rely on skilfully constructing the connections between the past (real or imagined), the present and the future [4] and the Singapore nation-building project is no exception. The prime purpose of such narratives is to encourage members of a putative national community to imagine themselves as sharing a special bond and destiny as members of a nation.[5] The starting point for The Singapore Story – as emphasised in the opening line of the passage quoted above – is an emphasis on the 'specialness' of The Singapore Story. It is a story of humble beginnings, a struggle against the odds, which ultimately leads to success in which all Singaporeans can rejoice, regardless of the diversity of their backgrounds. In contrast to many similar stories, however, The Singapore Story does not project a pre-destined future golden age, but rather holds out the prospect of a stark choice between a celebratory future and one of anarchy and flames. It identifies the present as a point of decision – between accepting the benefits bestowed by the efforts of past and present generations, and throwing it all away in a thoughtless act of pique or selfishness. The present as turning point effectively provides legitimacy to the forces of continuity, embedded in the ruling PAP. It endorses and is intended to endorse the *status quo*.

This chapter is a critical survey of Singapore's history as it is represented in The Singapore Story, and we have selected the CD-ROM, *The Singapore Story: Overcoming the Odds* as the basis of our representation and interrogation. It is a trim, self-contained example of mythmaking and is – within some limits that are canvassed below – representative of the mythmaking associated with the official nation-building project. Selectively appropriated pasts are routinely used by dominant elites as building blocks of nationhood and *Overcoming the Odds* provides a useful illustration of this point. The significance of events and processes, the relative contribution of persons and parties, particular interpretations of various losses and victories are selectively laid before the altar of national memory – a process that, as Benedict Anderson reminds us, also involves a considerable amount of selective forgetting.[6] We are particularly interested in interrogating the periodisation projected in this CD-ROM and its selection of important events. To an historian, breaking the past down into historical periods is one of several means by which one can impose one's interpretation on the past – creating and shaping the building blocks that make up a constructed history. Selecting which events to privilege as important and which to relegate to the margins is an even more obvious way of constructing history. The advantage of interpreting the past through these techniques is that opinions can be interpolated into a narrative without having to fully articulate the assumptions and values that lie behind them. Particular events can be given heightened importance by embedding them in a constructed period that gives it this seeming import. Of course it is neither possible nor desirable to avoid periodisation or selectivity when writing about the past, but by the same token, an interrogation of a writer's periodisation and selectivity can reveal much about both intended and unconsciously hidden agendas.[7] The Singapore Story as it appears on *Overcoming the Odds* is a very forceful example of the power of both techniques.

The periodisation presented in this CD-ROM is not followed in every detail in all representations of The Singapore Story, but the commonalities between them are much stronger than their differences, so we have few qualms about using this example as the template for this chapter, and as a device enabling us to place the story of nation building and elite formation in a broader historical context. To illustrate the reasonableness of this proposition, and also to acknowledge its limitations, we lay side by side in Table 2.1 (overleaf) the periodisation and event selection in *Overcoming the Odds* and those presented in Singapore's 2006 Special/Express Stream Lower Secondary History Syllabus.[8] At a glance the two sides of the table appear to present drastically different narratives because of significant differences in the periodisation, but a closer examination of the content reveals that each of them is being faithful to the same narrative, with only incremental differences between them.

For the benefit of readers who are unfamiliar with The Singapore Story, we might simplify it even further so it reads as a five-point narrative:

1. In 1819 Sir Stamford Raffles arrived and established a British trading post where there had been a sleepy Malay village. The trading post became a thriving colony, attracting hundreds of thousands of Chinese immigrants and smaller numbers of Malays and Indians.

2. It was occupied by the Japanese from 1942–45, after which the British tried to implement a painless exit strategy.

Table 2.1: Periodisation of Singapore's history

Years covered	The Singapore Story: Overcoming the Odds	Official overview of History Syllabus for Lower Secondary (Special/Express Course), 2006
1300–1819	*Not covered*	'Early Beginnings • Singapore before 1819'
1819–1942	'The Colonial Period' (including a passing mention of 1300–1819, and covering the arrival of the British, the island's strategic position, importance of free trade and immigrants, character of British rule, Japanese invasion of China, the Japanese Occupation and return of the British in 1945)	'Growth and Development of Modern Singapore as a British Settlement before World War II • Establishment of Singapore as a British trading settlement • Contributions of the immigrants • British rule in Singapore before World War II • Impact of world events before World War II on Singapore: Industrial Revolution; the Opening of the Suez Canal; World War I; Great Depression of 1929'
1942–1945		'The Turbulent Years • World War II and its impact on Singapore • Political and social unrest in the 1950s: Communist-led riots and strikes; Maria Hertog riots. • Struggle for self-government • Merger and separation, 1963–1965'
1945–1955	'Political Awakening' (focusing exclusively on the Maria Hertog riots and 'the communist threat')	
1955–1961	'Communist Threat'	
1961–1963	'Battle for Merger'	
1963–1965	'The Merger Years'	
1965–1971	'From Survival to Progress'	'Nation-building efforts in independent Singapore'
1971–Present		*Not covered.*
The Future	'Future in Our Hands'	*Not covered.*

3. The British exit strategy was disrupted by communist and racial violence and upheaval, but eventually self-government was granted, and Singapore was governed from 1959 by the nationalist PAP government.

4. In an effort to deal with the communist problem, Singapore was accepted into Malaysia as a constituent state, but after a difficult 18 months, Malaysia expelled Singapore in 1965.

5. Since 1965 Singapore has, under the leadership of the PAP, solved the problems of racial discord and social disharmony, and has taken the country 'from the Third world to the First'.

A more reflective and critical interrogation of The Singapore Story follows.

Colonial Period (1819–1945)

In this CD-ROM, as in nearly all accounts of Singapore's history, the arrival of Raffles in 1819 to found a trading outpost for the East India Company marks the foundation of Singapore. The Singapore Story identifies this as the beginning of the 'Colonial Period', and includes only passing references to the pre-colonial period during which Singapore was variously a tenth-century trading city called Temasek, part of the fourteenth-century Majapahit Empire, and part of the Johore-Riau Sultanate immediately before the arrival of the British. The Singapore Story starts Singapore's history proper with the arrival of Raffles. Until he arrived there was 'not much there', but he saw its potential. Through the introduction of free trade, open immigration, and capitalising on its strategic position at the crossroads of the Pacific and Indian oceans, his successors built Singapore into a thriving trading port. Apart from that, nothing much happened until Japan invaded China in 1937, and then occupied Singapore from 1942 to 1945 (which sits rather awkwardly as part of the 'Colonial Period'). After that the CD-ROM becomes rather more graphic, conveying some notion of how the failure of the British defences wiped away local assumptions of the white man's superiority and the British right to rule. It also gives a vivid depiction of the horrors of the Occupation.

Raffles plays a critical role in this version of *Overcoming the Odds*, but this pales against the giant status he has assumed in Singapore's broader mythology since the 1980s, demonstrated by the front cover of the Lower Secondary and Secondary One history textbooks in use from 1984–99, one of which is reproduced in Figure 2.1 near the opening of this chapter. In these representations of the Singapore history, a larger-than-life image of Raffles gazes beneficently over Lee Kuan Yew and his Cabinet colleagues.[9] It was not always thus. In 1969, during the 150th anniversary celebrations of the founding of Singapore, Lee Kuan Yew was at pains to play down the importance of Raffles compared to that of his own government of 10 years.[10] A contemporary editorial in the Chinese newspaper, *Sin Chew Jit Poh*, dismissed the 'discovery' [sic] of Singapore by Raffles as 'a historical accident' that merely 'accelerated the growth of Singapore'.[11] The then Education Minister, Ong Pang Boon, also warned against giving 'too much' emphasis to the personal contribution of Raffles, preferring to 'play up the meritorious services rendered by our pioneering forefathers' and the 'industry of the various races' of Singapore.[12] Most critical of all during the anniversary celebrations were the Malays. The Singapore Malay National Organisation criticised the celebration *in toto* because they 'do not portray the existence of Malays in the Republic'.[13] Here lies the nub of the place of the question of Raffles.

There is, of course, no doubt that Raffles's founding of a trading colony is a significant marker in the city's history, but if it is the beginning of the story, then The Singapore Story starts to look like a Chinese story, because after the first few years, most of the immigrants who flocked to the free port were Chinese. It was precisely because of the Chinese character of this story that Lee Kuan Yew and Ong Pang Boon were at pains to play down the role of Raffles in 1969 – because at that stage they regarded Chinese 'chauvinism' as one of the new country's greatest dangers, and they did not want to encourage the local Chinese population into a smug sense of superiority or an exaggerated sense of their deserts. The government at that stage was in the business of suppressing, not encouraging expressions of communal and ethnic pride.

The perception that The Singapore Story narrates the history of Singapore as an implicitly Chinese story is confirmed by the fact that on the CD-ROM the next tangible event of note after Singapore's establishment was Japan's invasion of China! No mention of Singapore's history as a British colony under Indian administration as it was from 1819 to 1867. No mention of Singapore having been a British colony as one of the Straits Settlements, along with Melaka and Pinang, or that until Britain separated Singapore from Malaya after the Second World War Singapore was a Malayan city, and was considered by all to be an intrinsic part of Malaya.

Despite the Raffles story being so deeply ingrained in The Singapore Story, it is actually not difficult to find an alternative perspective. Carl Trocki did just that in the opening paragraph of his book, *Singapore: Wealth, Power and the Culture of Control*:

> There was more to the foundation of the British colony of Singapore in 1819 than a stroke of brilliance by Thomas Stamford Raffles, who is usually credited with the creation of the city. We are occasionally apt to forget that the city is located in Asia and is largely populated by Asians. At the time, it was also a vital part of the Asian maritime economy and should be seen as the heir of a long line of Asian maritime trading centres located in or near the Straits of Melaka. Singapore's history, properly understood, can be traced back to the Malay *entrepôts* of Srivajaya and Melaka.[14]

The paradigm shift involved in this re-alignment of perspective is indicated on the following page where Trocki described the Riau island of Bentan as 'the eighteenth century predecessor of Singapore', a 'Malay/Bugis centre … located near the present [Indonesian] town of Tanjong Pinang'.[15] From this perspective, the Malays – who were the first to begin flocking to Singapore after 1819 – are not 'immigrants', as they are labelled in all versions of The Singapore Story,[16] but are members of *Nusantara* (the Malay world) relocating from one island to another, following the shifting focus of business.

Another major omission from *Overcoming the Odds* (and from school classrooms until junior college [pre-university]) is the heroic role of the Chinese communists and nationalists in fighting the Japanese during the Occupation.[17] Their contribution is freely acknowledged in other versions of official historiography, so their absence here is odd.[18] The reason is presumably to avoid confusing school children with inconvenient facts. The inconvenience centres on the fact that over the next three chapters the Chinese communists had to be presented as ruthless villains, so it would have been awkward to introduce them in the first instance as heroes. This is also an opportune place to note that in dropping the Chinese communists, the CD-ROM also dropped the mass of Chinese-educated Singaporeans from the narrative, but whereas the communists entered in the next act as villains, the Chinese-educated remain curiously absent from the whole narrative, despite being the single most politically important group that the rival elites sought to win over, and the primary political battle ground of the 1960s and 1970s. This absence appears to cut across the pro-Chinese slant of the presentation as a whole, but in fact it just helps us to take a step in refining our understanding of the ethnic discourse of The Singapore Story. The 'pro-Chinese slant' identified in The Singapore Story to date is not a generic bias, but one that plays up particular aspects of the local Chinese culture and history, as determined by the ruling elite. Enterprise, adaptability, resourcefulness, strength of character, and toughness are admired and make for a good Singapore Chinese (and by implication a good Singaporean), but intransigence and fanatical adherence to either out-of-date or dangerous traditions, values, cultural practices or ideologies make one a Chinese 'chauvinist' or worse, and stand in the way of Singapore's progress. We devote much of this book to interrogating this official perception of a connection between 'Chineseness' and certain desirable traits, and the consequent role that this perception plays in providing a contemporary template for the ideal Singaporean. The authors of *Overcoming the Odds*, however, clearly decided to keep their narrative simple by reducing the old-style Chinese-educated to bit-players, unfortunately writing yet another part of Singapore's history out of The Singapore Story.

Political Awakening (1945–1955)

Overcoming the Odds tells us that the British returned in 1945 to face local discontent, and handed over limited self-government in 1955, but it tells only two other stories of the intervening years. We are asked to believe that nothing of significance happened in these years except for a set of savage religious-cum-racial riots in 1950 (the Maria Hertog riots) and the rise of the communist threat. Each of these stories is central to Singapore's nation-building project because they legitimise the regime's heavy-handed approach to ethnic relations and dissent, but this linear approach to historiography does a great disservice to Singaporeans. The first thing to realise is that although left-wing and anti-colonial radicalism flourished to unprecedented levels during the first half of the 1950s, the Communist Party itself was diminishing as a controlling force in Singapore over the same period. The Party machinery was almost completely smashed by the colonial security forces in 1948, and although the surviving operations – most notably the Anti-British League – were notionally answerable to the party, their members and activists were mostly free radicals, swept up in a surge of anti-colonialism. Many were not communists at all and some were much more militant than the Party. Those who did accept Party discipline spent much of their time trying to restrain their more militant, less strategic followers. The period from 1945 to 1955 was actually a period of vitality and energy at all levels of civil society, and although the communists struggled to maintain control over the radical and militant movements, their control was sporadic and incomplete.[19] Beyond the communists and the racial communalists that are the exclusive focus of The Singapore Story, political movements flourished at all levels of society. Enormous energy was expended on education, the most public of which was the groundswell of grassroots support for building the Chinese Nanyang University. Spontaneous Malay and Chinese arts and cinema flourished, as did business-oriented conservative politics, and cosmopolitan discourses about nationalism, leftist politics and anti-colonialism. Activism among tertiary students and trade unionists found expression in many languages and movements.[20]

Communist Threat (1955–1961)

The identification of the period 1955–1961 solely with the 'Communist Threat' invites all the criticisms levelled at the previous period, with the added concern that it downplays the coming of limited self-government in 1955, of democratic pluralism, and constitutional development. It also rather parsimoniously refrains from giving Chief Ministers David Marshall and Lim Yew Hock most of the credit for winning full self-government in 1959. Despite the characterisation of the 'Communist Threat' as the overriding motif, the narrative actually breaks the period down into sub-sections based on changes of government: 1955–56, David Marshall's Labour Front government; 1956–59, Lim Yew Hock's Labour Front government; and 1959–61, Lee Kuan Yew's PAP government in its left-wing phase. It finishes with a rather abrupt announcement that in 1961 the Prime Minister of Malaya, Tunku Abdul Rahman, unexpectedly announced that he wanted Singapore to join Malaya, Brunei, Sarawak and Sabah in a new state of Malaysia, and that the PAP government thought this was a good idea. The original announcement by the Tunku was certainly unexpected, but this is nothing compared to the abruptness of the announcement in The Singapore Story's narrative. Because the Malaya connection in Singapore's history had been so successfully excluded from the narrative, this sudden talk of merger with Malaya has no historical context. In this section it is given only a political context: the Tunku was concerned about the communist problem in Singapore. Thus the narrative manages to stay strictly within the regime's favoured version of nation building. At no point in the presentation was it conceded that Lee Kuan Yew was even more desperate than the Tunku for merger, so as to see Malaysian authorities bring the Left to heel and it is only in the following section that one realises Lee also wanted merger for economic reasons.

Battle for Merger (1961–1963)

The 'Battle for Merger' section is the most self-serving section in The Singapore Story. The use of 1961 as a divider would be completely appropriate in a history of the PAP, since it marked the split with the Left of the party, which formed the rival Barisan Sosialis (Socialist Front), but in the history of the nation, it was just the third effective change of government (from a leftist PAP to a conservative PAP government) since the introduction of self-government in 1955. The 'Battle for Merger' is the title of a series of radio talks given by Lee Kuan Yew in 1961, in which he set out his case for joining Malaysia on the terms he had negotiated with the Tunku. In *Overcoming the Odds* 'The Battle for Merger' is nothing more than a platform in which the voice of Lee Kuan Yew (as recorded for those broadcasts) presents a justification for what turned out to be a disastrous course of action. Three justifications are presented: that tiny Singapore needed a common market with Malaysia to have a large enough economic base to survive and prosper; that this was the only viable way for Singapore to free itself from colonial rule; and that this was a good way to control the 'pro-communists' and ensure stability. Perhaps the greatest irony of this section is that the series of anonymous voiceovers parodying the case against merger were actually very prescient. They warned that Sukarno would make life difficult for Singapore in Malaysia, that Kuala Lumpur just wanted to control Singapore, that Kuala Lumpur was trying to put a financial squeeze on Singapore, and that Singaporeans would be second-class citizens. It is an oddity of the presentation that the following section, 'The Merger Years', managed to repeat all these complaints on behalf of Lee Kuan Yew and the Singapore government without giving the impression that Lee might have made a mistake, or that the opponents of the government's merger deal might have had a point. Nor is it mentioned that after the referendum but before the next elections, there was a major security swoop called 'Operation Cold Store' in which nearly 150 leftists, including most of the leadership of the opposition Barisan Sosialis, were detained without charge. This action finally broke the remaining strength of the Communist Party, Barisan Sosialis, and the Left in general. This action truly was a turning point in Singapore's nation-building narrative, and should have provided the denouement to the 'Communist Threat' theme that had been running so strongly through The Singapore Story, but this victory – though real – was not claimed, probably because the legitimating theme of the 'Communist Threat' still had a lot of life. Indeed, it continued to be a major theme in government rhetoric for another quarter of a century.

The Merger Years (1963–65)

'The Merger Years' refers to the 18 turbulent months in which Singapore was a state of Malaysia. Its main significance is that it led directly to Singapore's independence, and it came to form the basis of Singaporeans' ongoing and deep-seated practice of juxtaposing Singapore's 'success and efficiency' with Malaysia's bumbling 'failures and inefficiency'. The Singapore Story's account of the Malaysia years begins with Sukarno's campaign of Konfrontasi and the very real threat it posed to Malaysia and Singapore, and then moves on to cover Singapore's 1964 racial riots, which have become an iconic image in Singapore's nation building (along with the religious-cum-racial riots of 1950).

The events of 1963–65, which culminated in Singapore's separation from Malaysia are still contested, but it appears that they were substantially a clash of temperaments and worldviews, with consequent misunderstandings among the key players. This makes it difficult, and perhaps fruitless, to try to pin absolute blame on anyone,[21] but such nuances are wilfully absent from The Singapore Story. At one point the story is presented through a series of anti-Malaysian cartoons taken from the Singapore newspapers of the time. Whereas The Singapore Story presents the failure of Singapore in Malaysia almost completely as a story of Malaysian hostility towards Singapore, Lee's own colleagues tell a story of Lee Kuan Yew in overdrive, aggressively engaging in brinkmanship and pushing the Malaysian experiment to the precipice. As Barr has written elsewhere,

> Lee even found it difficult to exercise self-control in front of a microphone, and he developed a pattern of making outrageous and inflammatory speeches, which Toh Chin Chye later characterised as anti-Malay. When Lim Kim San, a key Cabinet minister during the period, was asked by Melanie Chew whether

he counselled Lee to tone down his speeches, he replied: 'Oh yes! We did! But once he got onto the podium in front of the crowd, paah, everything would come out. Exactly what we told him not to say, he would say!'[22]

Lee at this time was driving himself to the brink of a breakdown, and his judgement was impaired by a regime of prescription drugs designed to help him cope with the stress.[23] He was not at his best, and all his prejudices about Malays and his fears about the future were being given a free rein, just at the time when he needed to keep them under strict guard.[24]

From the point of view of setting the stage for our account of nation building in Singapore, perhaps one of the more significant contributions of *Overcoming the Odds* is the intrusion of a didactic red-writing-against-black-background still-frame that is left on the screen for many seconds in this section. It reads, 'Singapore believed in the equality of opportunity, meritocracy and multiracialism.' This is preceded by a less dramatic still-frame that reads, 'The indigenous Malays in the peninsula enjoyed special privileges while Singapore practised an equal opportunity for all policy.' The ideals of meritocracy and multiracialism are thus presented as central planks in Singapore's nation-building mythology, intrinsically linked as the method by which equality of opportunity is achieved.

The last glaring distortion of the section on the Malaysia years is the omission of the pro-active role of Singapore government ministers in the negotiated 'expulsion' of Singapore from Malaysia. The CD-ROM repeats the unquestioned orthodoxy for 30 years: that the expulsion of Singapore from Malaysia was the Tunku's idea and it was foisted upon Singapore. It was no such thing. Singapore's Minister for Finance, Dr Goh Keng Swee, was the first to raise the issue. He won the second tier Malaysian leadership over to the need for a negotiated separation; then he won over Lee Kuan Yew while the Malaysian leaders consulted with the Tunku.[25] These facts had been public since Goh Keng Swee revealed them in an interview with Melanie Chew, which she published in *Leaders of Singapore* in 1996.[26] They are available to History students in junior college,[27] but in *Overcoming the Odds* and in Lower Secondary school history classes, the old myth is still being perpetuated presumably because it feeds so well the national mythology of Singapore 'Overcoming the Odds'.

Before moving on to the period of independence, it is worth noting that the periodisation covering the years 1942 to 1965 has been consistently monopolised by images of crises, struggles, challenges and confrontations. Such motifs have been placed on the centre-stage of Singapore's nation-building project, with crises and challenges purporting to recur at fairly regular intervals though Singapore's short history as a country. They explain the title of the CD-ROM under study. Barr argues elsewhere that Lee Kuan Yew borrowed from the British historian, Arnold Toynbee, the concept of 'challenge and response' as a tool for driving progress,[28] but for the purposes of this study it is sufficient to note that crises are a routine plot device in The Singapore Story, and are claimed to be intrinsic to Singaporean identity.

From Survival to Progress (1965–present)

With Separation in 1965, Singapore's history as an independent republic began. In The Singapore Story this is presented as the country setting about standing on its own, building infrastructure, industrialising, building a defence force, and building 'this small nation' into a success story. The smallness of the nation is closely linked to its vulnerability and is an essential element in the theme of 'Overcoming the Odds'. The 1994 caning of an American graffitist, Michael Fay, against the diplomatic pressure of the Americans, and the 1995 hanging of Filipina maid Flor Contemplacion, for murder, are both presented through the prism of Singapore 'as a small country' standing up to larger bullies to retain its self-respect. The major nation-building themes are articulated clearly in voiceovers: 'Whatever our origins, we had to come together as one people', and 'As a small country dependent on open trade and commerce, we adopted a pragmatic foreign policy of friendship with as many countries as possible'. The only gross distortion of the piece is the voiceover that says that from 1967 'all male citizens' had to serve a period of National Service, whereas it is now publicly acknowledged that until at least the mid-1970s, Malays were deliberately and completely excluded from National Service because they were not trusted. Yet overall this section is superficially rather than seriously distorted – as we might expect in a presentation designed for school students.

It might still be worthwhile considering some of the more significant omissions in this section of the presentation. It is important to note, for instance, that the late 1960s and the whole of the 1970s was an era dominated by an unspoken, but very real social compact whereby the population, the media, the trade unions, academia and all the ethnic groups sacrificed their sectional interests and freedoms to allow the government to get on with the job of providing jobs, housing, health services, education, and – perhaps most important of all – fair arbitration between the sectional interests, particularly between the ethnic groups.[29] The compact was extremely conservative and 'safe', and was little more than a slight repackaging of the 'developmental state' model that had been proven successful in post-war Japan and South Korea.[30] The economic principles in place were simple and were described succinctly by former Permanent Secretary J.Y. Pillay in 2004:

> On the economic side, the problem was essentially an existential one – employment and growth. It was tackled by attracting enough factors of production, that is, resources of capital, manpower, and technical and managerial know-how. Also land – think of Jurong [the massive industrial estate created on the western end of the island in the 1960s]. … Management and technical know-how, as well as markets, could be acquired through joint-ventures with MNCs [Multi-National Companies].[31]

Ten years earlier Paul Krugman described the methodology more phlegmatically: it was the application of 'perspiration not inspiration', and 'a mobilization of resources that would have done Stalin proud'.[32] It may have been a primitive model of development, but it delivered the goods, which was all that mattered.

The existence of this social compact does not imply that everyone was happy with all decisions or that all decisions were 'fair', but it does mean that the expression of grievances was limited to dimensions that could be kept easily under control by the government. The relatively docile acceptance of PAP rule by the population was an essential element of the social compact. This implied that the PAP was not just another political party, but was to be trusted as the custodian of the Singapore nation and its interests. Indeed at that time – 1960s and 1970s – there was no choice but to trust the PAP because there was no credible alternative leadership offering itself. Those opposition politicians and labour and social activists who refused to play along with the government were detained or otherwise neutralised, but such heavy-handed repression was needed only in exceptional cases. Among the most sensitive disputes were those that involved ethnic and cultural issues (such as Chinese education and language, and discrimination against Malays) and these resulted in some of the heaviest handed examples of repression (such as the clampdown on Chinese newspapers in 1971) but, in the main, the

Chinese majority and the Indian and Malay minorities grudgingly accepted that they were better off accepting half a loaf than seeing the entire eaten up in inter-communal bickering. Workers were generally aware they were being exploited, but most were willing to put up with that in exchange for a job. There were also widespread grievances among former kampong and shanty-town dwellers who had been shifted into impersonal high-rise apartment blocks, often being proletarianised (drafted into the waged and salaried workforce) in the same motion, but their complaints became less pronounced as the new style of work and housing gained acceptance and popularity.

In the late 1970s the social compact began breaking down, though this started becoming obvious only in the early 1980s. This disturbance occurred partly because of the creeping embourgeoisement of Singaporean society, but substantially because the government itself (by now dominated utterly by Lee Kuan Yew following the retirement of the rest of the 'first generation' of leaders) began taking initiatives that broke the spirit of the compact. Some of these shifts are central motifs of this book, notably the government's disturbance of the status quo in language policy, education, and the management of ethnicity.

The Future in Our Hands

The final section of *Overcoming the Odds* is a pure distillation of the nation-building jingoism that has been threading the narrative with varying degrees of subtlety. They remind the viewer of the virtues of the status quo and re-assert the value of self-reliance. A few quotations from the voiceover and still-frames are sufficient to convey the essential message:

> This history of Singapore reminds us to treasure what we have today. There will be new challenges ahead which we may not anticipate. And whether we succeed or fail would continue to depend entirely on us.
>
> One lesson from the past is that we have to count on ourselves. No one owes us our security. No one else can promise us peace. No one can deliver us prosperity.
>
> We will have to govern ourselves, stay as one people and take our place in the world. Only in unity can we meet the challenges head on. Only in unity can we overcome difficulties.
>
> We were a diverse people, but we have managed to come together through turmoil and turbulence, struggle and upheaval to become one people, one nation, one Singapore.

Much of the visual background for this section has a fiery motif, with flames associated alternatively with chaotic cityscapes burning and skies alight with virtual fireworks, presenting starkly the choice for the future.

The other major theme for the section and indeed for the entire CD-ROM is the face and words of Lee Kuan Yew. Indeed, even when you remove the disk from the case you find yourself uncovering a Delphic quotation from Lee. Beyond the CD-ROM version of The Singapore Story, the presence of Lee in the nation-building narrative is even more ubiquitous. Not only has he subsumed the nation's narrative into his own personal story by calling his memoirs *The Singapore Story*, but he has happily generated a small library of hagiographical books in several languages, including several edited versions of his memoirs for school children,[33] books based on his interviews and old speeches,[34] and even a comic book entitled *Growing Up with Lee Kuan Yew*.[35] The personality cult being built around Lee is not only a function of his ego, but is a tool in the nation-building project.

'Making' Singaporeans

The Singapore Story may be seen, of course, as just a children's story. Yet it is a children's story with a difference. Its aim is to contribute to 'making' the new generation of Singapore citizens. Throughout the world, school history textbooks routinely establish and maintain the existence of nations in the personal and public imagination, in order to sustain the political reality of a nation-state.[36] In states in which the regime is intimately linked to the life of the state, such stories are instruments of governmental power. They serve as facilitators of social communication, legitimating the existing political order and providing political direction to the populace (particularly to the young). Yet the concept of 'making' Singaporeans refers to much more than just propagating such a national narrative. Perhaps our use of the concept is best explained by referring to Craig Reynolds's account of the making of a 'new' Thai in the first half of the twentieth century. Reynolds wrote of the curious diversity in the writing *opus* of one of Thailand's leading nationalist writers, Luang Wichit. As well as his overtly political writing he also wrote what Reynolds describes as pop psychology: self-help and 'how to' manuals, and biographies of 'great men'.[37] Reynolds concludes his consideration of Luang Wichit with the observation that most historians tended to separate his political writings from his pop psychology works as if they came from two completely different people. But, says Reynolds, they came from the pen of the same person. The pop psychological works ... belonged to his nationalist project. These were the qualities on a personal level that he saw [as] necessary for the collective Thai people, the *chat thai*, to pursue.[38]

Just as the inner soul of the Thai nation-building project was founded on the efforts to make Thais in a particular mould, we propose that the heart of the nation-building project is found, not primarily in the propaganda found in abundance in The Singapore Story and National Education, but in the social engineering through which generations of young Singaporeans have been passing for decades, making 'new' Singaporeans in a new mould. We see The Singapore Story not just as a piece of jingoism designed to make Singaporeans feel good about their heritage. Its primary purpose is to ensure that young Singaporeans accept the narrative of the official nation-building project. Such acceptance would allow them to make a first step on the path of becoming 'good' Singaporeans and play their part in perpetuating The Singapore Story in its relentless march into the future.

Notes

1   Hong Lysa, 'Making the history of Singapore: S. Rajaratnam and C.V. Devan Nair', in Lam Peng Er and Kevin Y.L. Tan (eds), *Lee's Lieutenants: Singapore's Old Guard*, St Leonards, NSW: Allen & Unwin, 1999, pp. 96–115.

2   Lee Kuan Yew, *The Singapore Story. Memoirs of Lee Kuan Yew*, Singapore: Prentice Hall, 1998, and *From Third World to First. The Singapore Story: 1965–2000. Memoirs of Lee Kuan Yew*, Singapore: Singapore Press Holdings and Times Editions, 2000.

3   Ministry of Information and the Arts, *The Singapore Story: Overcoming the Odds. An Interactive Media*, CD-ROM, a National Education Project by the Ministry of Information and the Arts, 1999. This CD-ROM has been widely distributed to school children as part of a package entitled 'The Singapore Story: A Choice Collection', which also included a collection of facsimile reproductions of historical documents, and the book, National Heritage Board, *Singapore: Journey into Nationhood*, Singapore: National Heritage Board and Landmark Books, 1998.

4   Zlatko Skrbiš, *Long-distance Nationalism: Diasporas, Homelands and Identities*, Ashgate: Aldershot, 1999, p. 97.

5   For an exposition of the natures and guises of such 'special bonds', see Anthony D. Smith, *Chosen Peoples: Sacred Sources of National Identity*, Oxford: University Press, 2003. Also, William Huthinson and Hartmut Lehmann (eds.), *Many Are Chosen: Divine Election and Western Nationalism*, Minneapolis: Fortress Press, 1994.

6   Benedict Anderson, *Imagined Communities*, London: Verso, 1993, Chapter 11.

7 Herbert Butterworth has written of the capacity of historians to bury their interpretations of history in their narrative, though he did not single out periodisation as a tool towards this end. See Herbert Butterworth, *A Whig Interpretation of History*, London: G. Bell & Sons, 1931.

8 The lower secondary syllabus has been chosen for comparison because it is a compulsory unit of study, whereas History is an elective in senior secondary and junior college.

9 Singapore History Project Team, *History of Modern Singapore (Lower Secondary)*, Singapore: Addison Wesley Longman for the Curriculum Development Institute of Singapore, 1984, 1994; and Singapore History Project Team, *History of Modern Singapore (Secondary 1)*, Singapore: Addison Wesley Longman for the Curriculum Development Institute of Singapore, 1984, 1994.

10 'Singapore's achievements and challenges', *Tamil Malar*, 10 August 1969, cited in *Mirror of Opinion: Highlights of Malay, Chinese & Tamil Press*, Ministry of Culture, Singapore, 1969.

11 'Celebrating Singapore's National Day and 150th Anniversary', *Sin Chew Jit Poh*, 9 August 1969, cited in *Mirror of Opinion*.

12 'What one should know when celebrating the anniversary of the founding of Singapore', *Sin Chew Jit Poh*, 8 July 1969, cited in *Mirror of Opinion*.

13 '150th Anniversary celebrations to commemorate the founding of modern Singapore "do not portray the existence of Malays in the Republic – PKM"', *Utusan Melayu*, 28 August 1969, cited in *Mirror of Opinion*.

14 Carl A. Trocki, *Singapore: Wealth, Power and the Culture of Control*, London and New York: Routledge, 2005, p. 8. Also see J.N. Miksic, *Archaeological Research on the Forbidden Hill of Singapore: Excavations at Fort Canning*, Singapore: National Museum, 1985.

15 Trocki, *Singapore*, p. 9.

16 For instance in Lee Kuan Yew's personal version of The Singapore Story, he dismissed the Malays as 'immigrants from … the Dutch East Indies'. Lee Kuan Yew, *From Third World to First*, p. 19.

17 The recommended reading list for the 2006 A-level History syllabus contains books that tell of the communist role during the war. See Ministry of Education website at http://www.moe.gov.sg. Accessed 5 December 2005.

18 The role of the Chinese communists during the war is in fact a major focus of *Riding the Tiger*, a DVD produced by the Ministry of Information and the Arts in 2001.

19 This revisionist account of communist strength is based primarily on C.C. Chin's paper, 'The United Front Strategy of the MCP in Singapore During 1950s and the Early 1960', delivered at the symposium, 'Paths Not Taken: Political Pluralism in Postwar Singapore', 14–15 July, 2005 at the National University of Singapore, hosted by the Asia Research Institute. Revised versions of these papers are available in Michael D. Barr and Carl A. Trocki (eds), *Paths Not Taken: Political Pluralism in Postwar Singapore*, Singapore: National University of Singapore Press, 2008.

20 This overview of the dynamics of political and social movements in the immediate post-war period is based on papers delivered at the Paths Not Taken symposium.

21 For accounts and opinions related to the story of merger and separation, see Michael D. Barr, *Lee Kuan Yew: The Beliefs Behind the Man*, Richmond, UK: Curzon, 2000, pp. 29–31; Michael D. Barr, 'Lee Kuan Yew in Malaysia: A reappraisal of Lee Kuan Yew's role in the separation of Singapore from Malaysia', *Asian Studies Review*, vol. 21, no. 1, 1997, pp. 1–17; Patrick Keith, *Ousted!*, Singapore: Media Masters, 2005, pp. 9–53; and Albert Lau, *A Moment of Anguish: Singapore in Malaysia and the Politics of Disengagement*, Singapore: Times Academic Press, 1998.

22 Barr, *Lee Kuan Yew*, p. 31.

23 Ibid., p. 76.

24 Ibid., pp. 29–31.

25 Ibid., pp. 79, 80.

26 Melanie Chew (ed.), *Leaders of Singapore*, Singapore: Resource Press, 1996, p. 147.

27 *Leaders of Singapore* is on the recommended reading list in the 2006 A-level History syllabus.

28 Barr, *Lee Kuan Yew*, pp. 49–96.

29 Barr's interviews and many informal conversations confirm the popular impression that there was a widespread acceptance in the late 1960s and throughout the 1970s of the need to put aside sectional interests in order to further national interests. The sense of urgency seems to have begun dissipating in the late 1970s as the future of Singapore seemed to be more assured.

30 Chalmers Johnson, *MITI and the Japanese Miracle: The Growth of Industrial Policy, 1925–1975*, Stanford, CA: Stanford University Press, 1982; W.G. Huff, 'What is the Singapore model of economic development?', *Cambridge Journal of Economics*, vol. 19, 1995, pp. 735–759.

31 J.Y. Pillay, 'Reflections of a recycled bureaucrat', *Ethos* (Journal of the Civil Service College), April 2004, p. 10.

32 Cited in W.G. Huff, 'Turning the corner in Singapore's developmental state?', *Asian Survey*, vol. 39, no. 2, 1999, p. 238.

33 For instance, Lee Kuan Yew, *The Singapore Story: Memoirs of Lee Kuan Yew* (abridged student's edition), Singapore: Federal Publications, 2000.

34 For instance, Lee Kuan Yew, *A Selection of Lee Kuan Yew's Speeches Over 40 Years* (Chinese Edition), Singapore: Federal Publications, 1993; Han Fook Kwang, Warren Fernandez and Sumiko Tan (eds), *Lee Kuan Yew: The Man and His Ideas*, Singapore: Singapore Press Holdings and Times Editions, 1998; S.J. Rodriguez (ed.), *Lee Kuan Yew in His Own Words, Book 1 1959 to 1970*, Singapore: Hurricane, 2003; *Lee Kuan Yew at 80: 80 quotes from a life* [in English and Mandarin], Singapore: Lianhe Zaobao, 2003.

35 Koh Choon Teck, *Growing Up with Lee Kuan Yew*, Singapore: Educational Publishing House, 2000, 2001.

36 See R. Haggay, 'The immemorial Iranian nation? School textbooks and historical memory in post-revolutionary Iran', *Nations and Nationalism*, vol. 6, no. 1, 2000, pp. 67–90, and; C. Jelavich, 'Serbian textbooks: toward greater Serbia or Yugoslavia?', in *Slavic Review*, vol. 42, no. 4, 1983, pp. 601–619.

37 Craig J. Reynolds, 'Nation and state in histories of nation-building, with special reference to Thailand', in Wang Gungwu (ed.), *Nation-Building: Five Southeast Asian Histories*, Singapore: Institute of Southeast Asian Studies, 2005, pp. 30–33.

38 Ibid., p. 33.

THREE

Constructing the Nation:
Elitism and Ethnicity

We have made Italy, now we must make the Italians.
  Ferdinando Martino, Italian Minister of Public Instruction, 1896.[1]

Are we Chinese? Yes, three-quarters of Singaporeans are Chinese. But we're Chinese with Singaporean characteristics. We're Western-educated with Singapore characteristics. We are Indians with Singapore characteristics. We are Southeast Asians with Singapore characteristics.
  George Yeo, Singapore Minister for Foreign Affairs, 12 October 2005.[2]

NATION BUILDING CONTAINS two closely intertwined and co-dependent dimensions that are difficult to separate in practice. The first dimension refers to the *building* of physical infrastructure while the second refers to the *construction* of the national community of belonging. All hitherto existing nation-building projects have striven to achieve both. Some attempts associated with 'building' of infrastructure are rather raw and elementary, involving the shovels, picks, wheelbarrows and the sweated bodies of pioneers. The Zionist zeal for the construction of fertile oases in the desert sands of Palestine in the post-1948 period and the construction of 'brotherhood and unity' highways in Titoist Yugoslavia exemplify this kind of 'building'. On the more highbrow end of the spectrum, this process manifests itself in the architecturally unique Petronas Towers in Malaysia and the hi-tech images of micro-chip making in Shanghai. The act of building physical infrastructure and public provisions acts as a tool and sometimes as a surrogate for the act of building the intangibles of a nation – a conflation that is relatively easy because nation building itself is an act of construction and, as Karl W. Deutsch reminds us, it always follows an architectural and mechanical model.[3] The new roads, bridges, factories, airports and housing complexes represent thus more than merely useful utilities. They are, along with monuments built to memorialise the heroic efforts of nation builders, public displays of a successful nation-building project. The new infrastructure is a foundation for national imaginings and visibly articulates youthful enthusiasm, attempts to succeed against the odds and represents the previously inconceivable. In other words, they are the solid, visible manifestations of the spirit of a new national community.

The second dimension of nation building, the efforts to 'construct' the community of belonging, is a much more complex and intricate process which, as Benedict Anderson has postulated, involves the creation of both horizontal (communal) and vertical (institutional) bonds of belonging.[4] The establishment of the national community has been commonly achieved (and accompanied) by deploying devices such as ideology, demagoguery, religion, coercion and combinations of the above, though with different levels of success and durability. The concomitant process of construction of national identity is an open-ended process, never completed and continuously in need of nurturing and pragmatic repositioning as the project unfolds. There are also no guarantees that the nation, once built, will last and survive.

Nation building is a process, not an act. The words of the Italian Minister for Public Instruction at the opening of this chapter illustrate the disjuncture between the state- and nation-building processes.[5] The processes are not even necessarily time-aligned with one another. In the case of the Italian state we clearly have the precedence of statehood over the emergence of a sense of Italianness. The primacy of statehood, however, can hardly be seen as universal. It is probably true for Italians but rather less so for the English.[6] These tensions pervade the ongoing discussions about the dating and emergence of modern nations and nationalism, especially in Singapore where the act of state creation preceded the process of nation building completely. As a product of the decolonisation of the British Empire and an unwanted child of the Malaysian federation, Singapore was literally, and quite suddenly, abandoned into statehood with no established or even embryonic notion of nationhood on which to build. With this limitation in mind, this chapter examines the nation-building project in Singapore through the prisms of two issues that we identify as central. The first relates to the role of elites and the associated ideas of meritocracy. Elitism is an undisputed key building block of the Singaporean nation. Singapore's governmental rhetoric is inherently linked to the Singapore brand of elitism, and we see it as representing a colourful

fusion of romantic, primordialist, and technocratic elements. The second issue relates to ethnicity, specifically to the tension between ethnic/racial and
civic elements of identity engaged in the nation-building process.[7] These two
themes are central elements in any understanding of the dynamics of nation-
building in Singapore, and we consider them each in turn.

Elitism and Meritocracy

In theories of nationalism, elites are the key animators of nationhood. In
Europe, the birthplace of the modern nation-state, the elites have performed
a crucial sensitising role in the process of articulating the sense of nationhood. They have been a mixed bunch, including historians, poets, linguists,
musicians, novelists and composers. Palacký, the Czech historian comes to
mind, as do the German philosophers J.G. Fichte and F.W.J. von Schelling,
the Serbian linguist Karadžić, the Russian writer Chekhov, together with the
critical contributions of musicians such as Chopin among Poles and Wagner
among Germans. Poets have been among the most effective nationalists:
Goethe did for the Germans what Prešeren did for the Slovenes, Yeats for
the Irish, and Mickiewicz for the Poles. The capacity of these individuals
to articulate or express national sentiments and identity placed them in
the pantheons of their respective nations. History charges them with playing a pivotal role in the process of nation building, although some of them
exercised more influence in death (or dying, as in the case of the Philippine
nationalist and novelist José Rizal) than life. The relationship between the
nation and the intellectual and cultural elites mentioned above often extends
into a peculiar sort of national infatuation. The task of elites is to give tone to
national identity and provide direction and inspiration to the nation-building
process. These cultural elites represent a specific type of elite and they played
a particularly important role in the Enlightenment period and nineteenth-
century romanticism. Although acting from 'above', their ultimate impact was
in animating the horizontal bonds of communal belonging. They have mostly
played an indirect role in the political process, primarily through assimilation
of their ideas into the mainstream nationalist political discourse.

It is worth differentiating these cultural elites from political and ideological
ones that are mostly directly linked with political projects, movements, parties or oligarchies. Political elites have generally been even more consciously
elitist than cultural elites. Elitism was an integral part of most 'progressive'

nineteenth-century political thought (not to mention conservative thought) of which the work of John Stuart Mill is representative. Mill entertained a conception of freedom that was consistent with his idea that 'the only freedom which deserves the name is that of pursuing our own good in our own way, so long as we do not attempt to deprive others of theirs, or impede their efforts to obtain it'.[8] This principle was, however, limited by a societal view on the part of Mill and the whole middle class of his time, that regarded the 'lower classes' and 'Orientals' – in short anyone who was not 'just like us' – through the prism of a thoroughly patronising beneficence. They accepted their superiority without a blush or a doubt and considered it their moral and social responsibility to care for those who could not be expected to look after themselves. As an employee of the East India Company, Mill was especially concerned with colonial subjects who, he believed, required a particularly generous dose of enlightened governance. The colonial elite's task was to responsibly govern the masses that he characterised as being like children. In a similar but more phlegmatic vein he identified the English working class as 'the most disorderly, debauched and unruly, and least respectable and trustworthy of any nation whatsoever'[9] and came to the same conclusion: that they were as equally needy of an elitist guidance and control as colonials. The characteristic that distinguished these racist and class-conscious outbursts from many of those uttered by others was that Mill really did see himself as a champion of the interests of both colonial subjects and of the working class, and furthermore he was viewed in this fashion by many of the working class in Britain. (The admiration of his Indian subjects is a bit more problematic.) Mill's impulse towards beneficence was just as strong as his elitism, and indeed was intimately bound up with it.

At around the same time as Mill was writing *On Liberty*, but using very different philosophical premises, Karl Marx was manufacturing a revolutionary social and political movement that operated on this same linkage of beneficence and elitism. In his *Eighteenth Brumaire of Louis Bonaparte* he argued that workers cannot represent themselves but need to be represented.[10] This idea was later applied through a Leninist doctrine in state-socialist countries where the elites were called upon to lead and re-educate the masses and create – what was never to be – post-ethnic, classless nations. While the elites continued to play an important role in nation-building processes throughout the twentieth century, something important happened to the very conception of the elite early in this period. Although the elites persisted and their importance continued to be exerted in various contexts – including nation building – the *perceptions* of elites changed with the rise of democracy as the twentieth century's great idea of political legitimation. Elitism *per se* had to clothe itself with the newfound modesty of democratic discourses and so elites transformed themselves into exponents of popular aspirations. Elitism as a conscious, overt foundational concept of nation building now seemed to have been left behind in the old century. As an overt foundational idea of national leadership, it was seldom evoked, with one notable exception: Singapore.

When Singapore was granted self-government in 1959, the process of de-colonisation produced insecurities that, in the minds of Singapore's political leaders, could only be resolved through absorption into a larger political unit based on Malaya. So when Singapore and Malaysia went their separate ways in 1965, this parting provided opportunities that few envisaged or wanted. The Singaporeans were left to construct a nation on weakened social, political and economic infrastructures and a scarcity of historical and cultural resources. There were no idealised histories to recount, no indigenous heroic figures to mobilise the populace, and no autochthonous literary works that would lend themselves to nation building. Furthermore the only ethno-nationalist impulse offering itself as a basis for nation building – 'Chineseness' – was out of bounds to Lee Kuan Yew and his conservative, English-educated group. Playing the 'Chinese card' would have evoked loyalty to another power and a range of alternative worldviews, none of which had much in common with the world of English-educated Singapore Chinese. In any case it had been established by bitter experience that tapping these resources directly was beyond the capacity of Lee: he had learnt the main languages of the local Chinese – both Mandarin and Hokkien – as an adult, but whatever connection he was able to build with these communities was a house of straw. Any populist orator who came from the streets could undo Lee's supposed 'connection' with the Chinese-educated without serious effort, and they could be defeated only if Lee marshalled the considerable resources of the state, and every shred of his own energy and his political brilliance. He could not even rely upon close allies among the Chinese-educated, because both his most formidable rivals for the heart and soul of these communities were his former allies – Lim Chin Siong, the Mandarin-speaking leftist student and trade union leader, and Ong Eng Guan, the Hokkien-speaking populist politician. Singapore politics and the Chinese communities themselves would have to be re-shaped beyond recognition before Lee could hope to play this game successfully.

In order to compensate for these multiple voids, the government cobbled together an awkward collection of ideological foundations for nation building: an emphasis on modernity and progress, to be built through multiracialism and meritocracy. Yet by themselves these were weak tools for nation building. In the short term the challenges facing the young country were of such severity that the imperatives of the struggle to survive[11] were sufficient to paper over these weaknesses, but it was obvious that 'survivalism', by its nature, could not be relied upon as a long-term resource. Having such a weak substratum on which to build a national identity, there was a dire need for an alternative. In this milieu, elitism emerged quickly and forcefully as the government's central resource.

The utilisation of elitism in the Singapore context was partly a result of Lee Kuan Yew's natural proclivities.[12] Lee's life is a story of elitist upbringing, education, aspirations and practice. As the eldest son born into an elite, English-speaking Chinese family, he was surrounded by considerable comfort throughout his early years and grew up steeped in the idea of patrilineal mission and responsibility.[13] Showing high academic aptitude, he was admitted into elite educational institutions, from Raffles Institution in Singapore to the Cambridge Law School in England. Cambridge was the point at which his personal experience and philosophy of elitism articulated into an ideological position. There he found legitimacy for his elitist ideas in the work of English philosopher of history, Arnold Joseph Toynbee (1889–1975), particularly in his *magnum opus, A Study of History*.[14] In this work Toynbee argued that social progress depends on a 'creative minority', which embodies progressivism and is a repository of positive social initiatives. On the opposite side of the spectrum, the societal majority is largely bereft of creativity and vision and thus reduced to simply following the elite. In this scenario, social progress is a function of the elite, in conjunction with the capacity of the masses to follow their lead. Lee's ideas of elitism turned out to be a close reflection of Toynbee's vision.

Yet elitism would have been a useless tool if it was no more than part of the make-up of Lee Kuan Yew. It was an effective tool of nation building only because it resonated strongly with the indigenous societal vision of the Singaporean Chinese communities, and to a lesser extent with those of the other communities. Barr has argued elsewhere that although the discourses on 'Asian values' and their derivations promoted in the 1990s by Lee Kuan Yew, Dr Mahathir, Suharto and the leadership of the PRC were constructed and manipulated by these elites for utilitarian purposes, the only reason that they were able to be used effectively was that the messages they conveyed resonated with large sections of their respective constituencies, finding voices even among reformist civil society and opposition activists.[15] As a forerunner to these later discourses Lee Kuan Yew, in collaboration with like-minded colleagues in Cabinet, capitalised on resonances between his personal and strategic elitism and many of the cultural impulses and mores held instinctively by much of his constituency. He later characterised this variously as 'Asian values', 'Confucian values', Singapore's 'Shared Values', and 'Chinese values'.[16] Of these labels the latter is by far the most appropriate, though even here it would be more accurate to describe them as 'Singaporean' or perhaps 'Malayan' Chinese values, since the values and culture of the Chinese in the diaspora were necessarily a mixture of many cultural impulses and historical drivers. But such characterisation was still in the future. In the 1960s and throughout most of the 1970s 'Chinese values' were given negative associations in public discourse and they were linked with Chinese communism and Chinese 'chauvinism'. Yet these negative associations did not stop him from capitalising on aspects of these cultural impulses – cherry picking in the orchard of cultural discourse. As early as 1966 Lee was selectively embracing the values of Singapore's ethnic communities as it suited him, and he was particularly enamoured with what he saw as the 'toughness' of the Chinese-educated, who had the 'cultural values which make up a civilisation'.[17]

One of the most important cultural impulses of Singapore's Chinese communities was their propensity to view society as a series of hierarchical relationships. In both classical and peasant Confucianism this manifested itself as the five relationships: emperor and subject; father and son; elder brother and younger brother; husband and wife; and – the only exception to the rule – friendships. The other basic impulse of Malayan Chinese societies was the importance placed on education and the virtual veneration of scholarship, which also had its foundation in Confucianism. None of the other communities of Singapore held such rigid hierarchical views as did the traditional

Chinese, nor did they venerate scholarship like the Chinese; but both the Malays and the Indians did premise their social cognition on relationalism, did accept a hierarchically organised social world, and did hold education in high regard. Lee's conscious understanding of these cultural impulses in the 1960s was rudimentary but he nevertheless knew instinctively that there was strong resonance between his own worldview and that of his constituents on critical points. The two impulses described above – hierarchy/relationalism and education/scholarship – fitted naturally with Lee's instinctive elitism.

Lee's earliest political statements after separation from Malaysia were immersed in the language of elitism and he confessed to being 'constantly preoccupied with what the near-geniuses and the above average are going to do'. It is they 'who ultimately decide the shape of things to come. It is the above-average in any society who sets the pace'.[18] There is a quasi-enlightenment streak running through Lee's conception of elitism. In his view the elite and elitism should be neither ends in themselves nor tools for the abuse of power. Rather, they should be the instruments for a progressive reform of society from above and for unapologetic interventionism in the name of higher goals as defined by benevolent leaders. The elite became one of the most important furnishings of the new Singapore state and its crucial strategic asset in building a nation. Its political neutrality and efficiency were characterised by supposed freedom from self-interest; a sense of common purpose and contribution to the goals of the government; paternalistic concern for the well-being of citizens; refusal to succumb to sectionalism or the whim of the electorate; technical proficiency of government; and the acceptance of smooth continuity from one generation of leaders to the next.

In Lee's mind, the state and its citizens are to join efforts to ensure the plentiful supply of talent. The key mission of the elite, however, was to progressively reform society from above. This was to sound the death knell to second-class leadership and inefficient and sluggish administration, which in Lee's mind and that of many Singaporeans, characterised Singapore's experience in the Malaysian federation. The post-separation vision of Singapore was clearly predicated on the idea of elitism. It was a vision of a select, effective and visionary leadership working in close cooperation with a highly effective administrative apparatus. As Lee put it soon after the separation, the future of Singapore was in the hands of 'you, the admin. machinery; [and] my colleagues and I, the political leadership'.[19]

Lee grounded his attitude of paternalistic beneficence in his elitism, but these ideas were also entwined with his preoccupation with eugenics and the idea that Singapore needed to be able to reproduce 'talent' across generations and in the national interest. He believed that elites are the result of genetic ordering and that talent is unequally distributed within the society. He argued on various occasions from the 1960s onwards – and with a vigour that has very few parallels in modern state politics – that there is a link between genes and talent and a correlation between educational achievements of the parents and the quality of the progeny. His belief in the almost mechanical self-replication and trans-generational transmission of talent led to a concern that there was a shrinking pool of talent from which elite cadres could be recruited. Lee put eugenics on the forefront of his political agenda in the early 1980s and it was central to his 1982 and 1983 National Day Rally speeches.[20] This emphasis was prompted by Lee's reading of the 1980 Census data, which showed that educated women were having fewer children than poorly educated ones. He argued that this trend would lead to a diminution of Singapore's talent pool and thus to national catastrophe. Lee was alarmed not only by the inordinate fervour among the less educated to reproduce, but particularly by the lack of reproductive enthusiasm among the better educated, who supposedly possessed the inherent capacity to produce 'genetically-superior offspring'.[21] This apparent concern with the class-based pattern of reproduction has more sinister, race-related implications. Geraldine Heng and Janadas Devan have produced an insightful analysis of these implications, emphasising that Lee's public argument was stripped of its essential dimension – race. It was the Chinese women who tended to be higher educated and have low fertility rates. By implication, Lee's fertility anxieties were symptomatic of his Sino-centrism and the belief that the weakening of the Chinese core in Singaporean society would lead to major social problems.[22] In Lee's imagination, Singapore's Chinese are naturally inclined to absorb and reproduce 'Confucian values' simply because they are Chinese and they have a disciplined work ethic both because they are Chinese and because they are descended from tough and resourceful immigrant stock.[23] Lee's fixation on fertility issues was more than his private obsession. He saw this issue as one that was capable of undermining the very core of his nation-building project: 'Unless the better-educated and better-equipped stake out a bigger part of the future for their progeny, then the future will be that much poorer for all.'[24]

From the very start of Singapore's independent nationhood, the official pronouncements about its future were predicated on a belief that only the elite is capable of securing national survival. The nation-building project was also an elite-building process. The new nation required both a political elite that was to guide with wisdom, and an effective administrative elite that was to execute this wisdom, but he saw no absolute distinction between them. They were two aspects of the same jewel, which was the elite *per se*.

Lee recognised the potential for divisiveness and political alienation in his emphasis on the top-end of the social pyramid. This meant that only one relatively small segment of society had a sense of link with the government. For this reason, in the earliest days of his premiership, Lee initiated structures that allowed non-credentialed men and a few women to partake in governmental and political processes, though without sharing in real power. The earliest such bodies were government-endorsed trade unions, and the locality-based Citizens' Consultative Committees (CCCs). The unions provided avenues for people of all races to find a sense of purpose in the political structure and boasted healthy Indian and Malay leadership working alongside the Chinese. The early CCCs, however, were comprised almost completely of local ethnic (mainly Chinese) community leaders – owners of businesses, leaders of clan and dialect groups, etc., with the balance comprising nominees of the local MP. These uncredentialled grassroots leaders thus played a vital role in the creation of a new Singapore in which they would have only a minor role. They acted as a circuit breaker in the fractious relationship between an assertive government convinced it knew best about everything and restless constituencies unhappy with a government that seemed to be imposing so many changes upon them, but which were generally willing to give it the benefit of the doubt in the interests of the greater good. The CCCs were notionally providing feedback to the government from the grassroots, but acted mainly as the marshals of the grassroots, sometimes leading them but more often merely neutralising them on behalf of the government. Some of these 'grassroots leaders', as they were called, were utterly submissive to the government, though they did not see it as submission, but as subordinating sectional interests for the greater good. By contrast, many, especially in the trade unions and the Chinese cultural associations, were willing to joust with the government, displaying high levels of brinkmanship and assertiveness. In their minds, commitment to the country and to nation building was not yet the same as commitment to the government, though even at this stage the lines were becoming blurred.

These early generations of non-credentialed grassroots leaders in the 1960s and 1970s turned out to be the last to routinely fill these roles. They were engaged only out of necessity, and by 1980 the dire need had passed as the government's sense of insecurity subsided. The country was becoming increasingly more middle class, and the younger generations were generally better educated than their parents. From this point onwards the government began re-organising the grassroots structures and leadership along elitist lines. Scholars were placed into leadership positions in trade unions as part of a process of 'modernisation'.[25] Moreover in 1980 a new initiative in providing middle-class public housing ensured that each housing block had a number of well-educated, materially successful families as residents, for the specific purpose of ensuring that the grassroots would have competent leadership (*Sunday Times*, 30 November 1980). Much of the role of CCCs was given over to new Residents' Committees, which were dominated by these middle-class residents. This principle of appointing elite and middle-class leaders to represent the interests of grassroots constituencies gradually became the government's preferred technique for managing ethnicity. First there was MENDAKI, the government-endorsed self-help group for Malays and Muslims, formed in 1981. Other self-help groups followed: Singapore Indian Development Association (SINDA), Chinese Development Assistance Council (CDAC) and the tiny Eurasian Association. All these associations were creatures of the government, but in 1990 a new Muslim self-help group, the Association of Muslim Professionals, was established and was allowed a modest degree of independent life. The technique of constructing vertical structures of political and social representation is identifiably corporatist and elitist, and has very effectively brought civil society under the heel of the government.[26]

The purpose of these corporatist initiatives was to narrow the emerging gap between the elite and the rest of the community and also to create a society that was permeated at nearly every level with the influence of a new ruling class. Co-option of a broad spectrum of the population into the imagined community of an elite-governed society created a sense of participatory governance that helped to soften the edges of a hierarchical social organisation. At the same time, however, it also provided tools for managing two of the key potential sources of tension in Singapore society: class tensions and – the second focus of this chapter – ethno-racial vulnerabilities.

Ethnicity and Race

As descriptors of culturally distinct groups of population, the terms 'race' and 'racial group' might be out of vogue in theories of ethnic and race relations, but in the Singapore government's discourse they remain the master category for more broadly accepted terms, such as 'ethnicity' and 'ethnic group'. Indeed, race and ethnicity are often used interchangeably – a practice that we regrettably found difficult to avoid in writing this book. The Singapore Department of Statistics defines ethnicity through racialised categories: 'Ethnic group refers to a person's race as declared by that person.'[27] Racial groups are seen as the central building blocks of Singapore society. According to 2005 data, the Chinese comprise 76.8 per cent of the total population, Malays 13.6 per cent and Indians 8.7 per cent. The remaining 2.1 per cent is subsumed in the umbrella category called 'Other Ethnic Group', which comprises 'all persons other than Chinese, Malays and Indians. They include Eurasians, Europeans, Arabs, Japanese, etc.'[28]

While the Singapore census statistics is currently using ethnicity as a measure of ethno-cultural diversity, in practice it is 'race', 'racial harmony' and 'multiracialism', rather than 'ethnicity', 'ethnic harmony' and 'multiculturalism' that preoccupy the Singapore government. In the government's discourse, the concept of race is bereft of pejorative connotations and is used as convenient shorthand for ethnic and religious identities. The three main racial groups are portrayed as distinct, each playing a discrete part in the ideology of multiracialism, and society at large. In Singapore, racial ascriptions inform every aspect of people's lives. In the highly structured and micromanaged context of Singapore, race is a fundamental instrument of social engineering and the means for the organisation of social complexity.

Although Singaporean multiracialism is an ideology of 'unity in diversity' aimed at horizontally and vertically integrating society, it differs quite radically from multicultural agendas that we find in places like Australia and Canada. These countries manage diversity by emphasising the importance of minority rights and they tend to deploy affirmative policy agendas to redress the imbalance of power. The Singapore case also differs from the multicultural agenda in neighbouring Malaysia, where the overt and public focus of attention and affirmative action programmes is the Malay majority – a process which Cheah Boon Kheng calls 'multiculturalism in reverse'.[29] What distinguishes Singapore's multiracialism is that it extends recognition exclusively through the distinctiveness and fixity of group identities, without official distinction between dominant and marginalised groups. One of the consequences of this approach is that it cements existing imbalances in race relations and impedes the chance of upward mobility for disadvantaged groups. It deploys agendas based notionally on equality of opportunity in such a way that they actually promote inequality in outcomes. Adapting and extending Cheah Boon Kheng's terminology, we may say that Singaporean multiracialism is a form of 'multiculturalism in neutral'. It aims to retain the *status quo* and make a virtue out of it, but at the same time it ignores the inherent inequalities embedded in society.

Singapore's nation-building project may be based on the existence of overarching values and commitments of citizenry, enacted through songs, public campaigns and rallies, but since independence in 1965 it has not attempted to melt or synthesise ethnic differences into a new form of Singaporean ethnic identification.[30] Such attempts have been deployed in other multi-ethnic contexts, such as the former Yugoslavia, where the political elite encouraged the creation of a new universal Yugoslav identity at the expense of specific ethnic ascriptions, such as Serb, Macedonian or Croat.[31] The American melting pot model follows a similar logic, although it rests on very different ideological premises. In Singapore, the Census quadratomy of CMIO[32] (Chinese, Malay, Indian and Others) is sacrosanct and the distinctiveness of these building blocks of the Singapore nation has been set in concrete. These categories are both fixed and invariable[33] and representing, to use an analogy from Giddens, culture containers.[34]

In Singapore, race stands in for ethnicity, multiracialism is the equivalent of multiculturalism and race defines and circumscribes culture. Furthermore, in the Singaporean multiracial framework, individual racial categories are associated with corresponding characteristics, such as culture, language and religion. It is a strictly primordialist conception of society, whereby ethnic characteristics are inborn, unchanging and unchangeable. In the words of Clifford Geertz (writing of primordialist visions of ethnicity more generally), the 'congruities of blood, speech, custom, and so on, are seen to have an ineffable, and at times, overpowering, coerciveness in and of themselves.'[35]

Hence Lai Ah Eng talks about 'one-to-one correspondence'[36] in the official discourses on race in Singapore where, for example, Chinese race is taken to represent a repository of Chinese culture, Mandarin language and Chinese religion, Malay race a repository of Malay culture, Islamic religion and Malay language, and following the same logic, Indian race equals Indian culture, Tamil language and Hinduism. Ethnicity, culture and race thus become self-fulfilling prophecies, always generating outcomes that are somewhat independent of social reality and seen as deeply seeded in each of the ethnic and racial groups concerned.

Such a rigid understanding of ethnicity makes racial categories administratively transparent, visible and manageable, but their fixity also inhibits ethnic boundary porousness and discounts multiple identity crossings that are realities in Singapore: Christian, Sikh and Muslim Indians; Indians whose mother tongue is English or an Indian language other than Tamil; Chinese Christians; Chinese who do not speak Mandarin; etc. Nevertheless, as Geoffrey Benjamin argues, thanks to the fixity of ethno-racial categories, their relative stability across time, and their key role in Singapore nation building, CMIO-based multiracialism has become one of Singapore's founding myths (in the sense of 'charter for social action').[37] The fixity of the CMIO quadratomy facilitates the portrayal of Chinese, Malays and Indians as distinct from each other, each playing an important but different part in the nation-building process. But there is also a downside: the crossing of the boundary between different groups is seen as a transgressive act that is neither desired nor encouraged. It has been portrayed by Lee Kuan Yew as an act of adventure:

> My expectations are that there will always be a small group of the adventurous in all the ethnic groups, perhaps those who are less egotistical, who marry across ethnic lines. But they will probably be in the minority. Therefore the chances are that if you come back to Singapore a century from now, you would find people more or less the same.[38]

The Singapore identity has thus existed primarily through the racial quadratomy, and is routinely expressed through hyphenated labels: Chinese-Singaporean; Indian-Singaporean; etc.[39] This practice of perceiving one's personal identity through that of one's communal or ethnic group appeared to be waning under the later years of Goh Chok Tong's premiership, but it was reasserted by Foreign Minister George Yeo in late 2005 when he described Singaporean Chinese as 'Chinese with Singaporean characteristics'.

(See opening of this chapter for a more complete account of his words.) In this interview Yeo was subordinating national identity to racial identity in the clearest terms – a practice that epitomises the dominant construction of Singaporean identity.

Periodisation of the Management of Ethnicity in Singapore

From what we have written in this chapter thus far, one could be forgiven for thinking that the management of ethnicity in Singapore has been constant and static: an unbroken continuum in which Lee Kuan Yew's ideas about race gradually smothered Singaporean society. It is true that in this chapter we have emphasised the points of continuity, but in fact this book is predicated on the assumption that there has been a decisive shift of policy during that time – specifically at around the beginning of the 1980s. As a prelude to the detailed study of this dramatic policy shift in Chapter 5, let us consider briefly the extant literature on this question of periodisation.

In 1994 David Brown provided a framework for understanding the management of ethnicity in Singapore that we, along with most scholars in the field, have found particularly useful. He distinguished between three periods.[40] The first, from 1959 to 1965, was an 'ethnic mosaic' period characterised by the ambition to downplay ethnicity and promote the unifying capacity of the ideology of multiracialism. The second period from 1966 to 1980 was distinguished by the principles of race-blind meritocracy. Brown's final period of 'inclusionary corporatism' began in the 1980s and is characterised by ethnicity being increasingly managed through the mechanisms of a corporatist state. This periodisation has been broadly accepted by most scholars since then, with the main point of difference centring on the characterisation of the last period.[41] At around the same time as Brown was writing, Raj Vasil characterised this post-1980 period as one of 'Asianisation' (by which he meant that ethnic roots were being highlighted).[42] In 2000, Barr characterised the post-1980 period as one of 'Sinicisation', emphasising the growing hegemony and celebration of 'Chineseness'[43] – a theme we are developing further in this book.

Our discussion acknowledges and utilises all these varied explanatory frameworks. In what follows we will be introducing a further nuance to Barr's characterisation of the post-1980s period, describing it as one of 'incomplete assimilation'.[44] We will return to a detailed consideration of matters of race and ethnicity – including 'Sinicisation' and 'incomplete assimilation' – in Chapter 5, but first we consider the role and nature of the elite, elitism and meritocracy in Chapter 4.

Notes

1 A. Pogden (ed.), *The Idea of Europe: From Antiquity to the European Union*, Cambridge: Cambridge University Press, 2002, p. 183.

2 *ST*, 13 October 2005.

3 Karl W. Deutsch, 'Nation-building and national development: some issues for political research', in Karl W. Deutsch and William J. Foltz (eds), *Nation-Building*, New York Atherton Press, 1963, p. 3.

4 Benedict Anderson, *Imagined Communities*, London: Verso, 1993, p. 7.

5 For classical exposition of problems associated with the conflation of the two terms, see Walker Connor, 'A nation is a nation, is a state, is an ethnic group, is a ...', *Ethnic and Racial Studies*, 1, 1978, pp. 377–400.

6 A. Hastings, *The Construction of Nationhood: Ethnicity, Religion, and Nationalism*, Cambridge: Cambridge University Press, 1997.

7 The distinction between ethnic and civic is far from uncontested, but it provides a useful conceptual prism that helps us understand the shifts in nation-building project over the past 40 years. See E. Kaufmann, and O. Zimmer, '"Dominant ethnicity" and the "ethnic-civic" dichotomy in the work of A.D. Smith', *Nations and Nationalism* vol. 10, nos. 1–2, 2004, pp. 63–78.

8 John Stuart Mill (ed. S. Collini), *On Liberty with The Subjection of Women and Chapters on Socialism*, Cambridge: Cambridge University Press, 1989, p. 16.

9 M. Cranston, *John Stuart Mill*, London: Longmans, Green & Co, 1967, p. 23.

10 Karl Marx, *Eighteenth Brumaire of Louis Bonaparte*, Moscow: Progress Publishers, 1958.

11 David Brown, *Contemporary Nationalism: Civic, Ethnocultural and Multicultural Politics*, London and New York: Routledge, 2000, p. 93.

12 Michael D. Barr, *Lee Kuan Yew: The Beliefs Behind the Man*, Richmond, U.K.: Curzon Press, 2000, p. 127.

13 Ibid., p. 7.

14 Ibid., pp. 112, 113.

15 Michael D. Barr, 'Lee Kuan Yew and the 'Asian Values' Debate', *Asian Studies Review*, 24:3, 2000, pp. 309–34; Michael D. Barr, *Cultural Politics and Asian Values: The Tepid War*, London and New York: Routledge, 2002, 2004.

16 Ibid.

17 Barr, *Lee Kuan Yew*, p. 153.

18 Ibid., p. 97.

19 Ibid., p. 112.

20 Ibid., pp. 122–23.

21 Geraldine Heng and Janadas Devan, 'State fatherhood: the politics of nationalism, sexuality, and race in Singapore', in Andrew Parker *et al.* (eds), *Nationalisms and Sexualities*, London and New York: Routledge, 1992, p. 345.

22 Ibid.

23 Barr, *Lee Kuan Yew*, pp. 196, 197.

24 Ibid., p. 120.

25 Michael D. Barr, 'Trade unions in an elitist society: the Singapore story', *Australian Journal of Politics and History*, vol. 46, no. 4, 2000, pp. 481–498.

26 For a broader account of the development of the Singapore system of elite representation of the grassroots, see Barr, *Lee Kuan Yew*, pp. 115–119.

27 See the Singapore government's statistics website, available at http://www.singstat.gov.sg/. Accessed on 28 October 2005.

28 Ibid. Accessed 4 July 2006.

29 Cheah Boon Kheng, 'Ethnicity in the making of Malaysia', in Wang Gungwu (ed.), *Nation-Building: Five Southeast Asian Histories*, Singapore: Institute of Southeast Asian Studies, 2005, p. 103.

30 As discussed in Chapter 5, between 1959 and 1965 the government did envisage the creation of a Singaporean identity completely free of any ethno-cultural baggage, but this fantasy was abandoned immediately after independence.

31 See D. Sekulic, *et al*, 'Who were the Yugoslavs? Failed sources of a common identity in the former Yugoslavia', *American Sociological Review*, vol. 59, 1994, pp. 83–97.

32 Sharon Siddique, 'The phenomenon of ethnicity: a Singapore case study', in Ong Jin Hue *et al.* (eds), *Understanding Singapore Society*, Singapore: Times Academic Press, 1997, p. 108.

33 Lai Ah Eng, *Meanings of Multiethnicity: A Case Study of Ethnicity and Ethnic Relations in Singapore*, Singapore: Oxford University Press, 1995, p. 183.

34 Anthony Giddens, *The Nation-State and Violence*, Cambridge: Polity Press, 1985.

35 Clifford Geertz, *The Interpretation of Cultures*, London: Fontana, 1973, p. 259.

36 Lai Ah Eng, *Meanings of Multiethnicity*, p. 179.

37 Geoffrey O. Benjamin, 'The cultural logic of Singapore's "multiracialism"', in Ong *et al.*, *Understanding Singapore Society*, p. 68.

38 Siddique, 'The phenomenon of ethnicity', p. 107.

39 Chua Beng Huat, 'Racial-Singaporeans: absence after the hyphen', *Social Scientist* vol. 24, nos. 7–8, 1996, pp. 51–68.

40 David Brown, *The State and Ethnic Politics in Southeast Asia*, London and New York: Routledge, 1994.

41 In his later work on contemporary nationalism, Brown somewhat altered his earlier framework, making it more conceptually relevant to discussions in the field of nationalism, and focusing more specifically on the dichotomy between civic and ethno-national in the context of globalisation. See David Brown, *Contemporary Nationalism: Civic, Ethnocultural and Multicultural Politics*, London and New York: Routledge, 2000. We find the ethnic-civic dichotomy a useful interpretative tool while acknowledging the strong normative undertones and problems that this distinction evokes. For limitations, see E. Kaufman and O. Zimmer, '"Dominant Ethnicity" and the "Ethnic–Civic" dichotomy in the work of A.D. Smith', *Nations and Nationalism*, vol. 10, nos. 1–2, 2004, pp. 63–78. The abolition of the term civic nationalism was advocated by B. Yack, 'The myth of the civic nation', in R. Beiner (ed.), *Theorizing Nationalism*, Albany: State University of New York Press, 1999.

42 Raj Vasil, *Asianising Singapore: The PAP's Management of Ethnicity*, Singapore, Heinemann Asia for the Institute of Southeast Asian Studies, 1995.

43 Barr, *Lee Kuan Yew*, pp. 137–184.

44 The exposition of this characterisation has been foreshadowed in Michael D. Barr and Jevon Low, 'Assimilation as multiracialism: the case of Singapore's Malays', *Asian Ethnicity*, vol. 6, no. 3, 2005, pp. 161–182.

FOUR

The Culture of Elite Governance

We can never afford to be satisfied with the status quo, even if we are still okay, even if our policies are still working. People say, 'If it ain't broke, don't fix it'. I say, if it ain't broke, better maintain it, lubricate it, replace it, upgrade it, try something better and make it work better than before.
Prime Minister Lee Hsien Loong, 22 August 2004[1]

FACED WITH THE DAUNTING TASK of steering the reluctantly independent city-state of Singapore in 1965, Lee Kuan Yew initially threw up his hands in despair. He cried on television, had a physical and emotional breakdown and retreated to the relative isolation of a government chalet at Changi to recuperate.[2] So sick was he with exhaustion, worry and the effect of tranquillisers that he records in his memoirs receiving the British High Commissioner in the middle of the day, flat on his back in bed, too ill to rise and greet him properly.[3] As Chan Heng Chee makes graphically clear in her 1971 book, the next several years were dedicated wholly to securing the survival of the city-state at all costs.[4] All matters of ideology, sectional interest, rights and most matters of principle were discounted and made ready for auction to ensure the economic and political survival of the new republic. Socialism – not central in the thinking of the ruling elite for many years in any case[5] – became completely useless except as a tool for securing some diplomatic and political support from old friends abroad. Trade unions became obstacles in the quest to entice multinationals to invest and help Singapore generate the export income it desperately needed. Malays became a potential fifth column, never again to be fully entrusted as equal citizens because of suspicions about their ethnic and religious ties to the Malaysia that had just ejected Singapore from its federation.

Not all members of the ruling group were as apocalyptic as Lee. Indeed Finance Minister Goh Keng Swee had long since given up on Singapore ever having a future in Malaysia and had played a vital role in seeking and negotiating Singapore's theatrical ejection from Malaysia.[6] Yet even Dr Goh, the most phlegmatic and unflappable of Lee's inner circle was fully aware of the seriousness of this move and the challenges ahead. For Lee, who had been going through emotional turmoil for many months, and to whom the responsibility of providing political leadership fell, the pressure was almost too much.

At times of great stress such as this, a weak or insecure person is likely to abandon himself to self-indulgent consolations of one form or another – emotional, sensual or otherworldly. Lee, however, turned to the most deeply set touchstone by which he understood himself and his own place in the world: his faith in himself as a natural member of his society's elite. This was something he understood without question. He 'knew' he was special – had always known it since he was the spoilt eldest son in a *peranakan* family, and nothing in his brilliant academic, professional or political career had ever prompted him to revise his high opinion of himself.[7] He 'knew' he was exceptional, but he also knew that he was merely one of a class of exceptional men who rose to the top of their respective societies. Insofar as he was a product of Chinese culture – modified as it was through the prism of an English-speaking Straits Chinese family – he naturally saw society in terms of hierarchy. His immersion in class-conscious Cambridge University reinforced such preconceptions and exposed him to a society that, in his considered opinion, had survived and flourished by wilfully cultivating an elite on which society relied to provide leadership.[8] Lee married his instinctive self-perception and societal perception to his experiences of elitism in England and arrived at his solution to the challenge of Singapore's societal and national survival.

Lee's concept of 'the elite' became central to the operation of the Singapore system. It grew in his mind into a self-conscious, self-righteous class of talented and brilliant people with strong character, who are imbued with a collective sense of purpose and a consciously collective understanding of the thinking of the group. Its apex and core lie in the political and administrative leadership, but its outer circles include the talented among all walks of society. In 2005 Prime Minister Lee Hsien Loong described the elite prosaically as 'a core group of people who occupy key positions of power and influence, and set the direction for the whole society and country' (*ST*, 20 March 2005), but Lee Kuan Yew has at times spoken of it much more eloquently. His vision is perhaps best conveyed in a speech he gave in August 1966:

We must have qualities of leadership at the top, and qualities of cohesion on the ground. In our present context, it is essential to rear a generation at the very top of society that has all the qualities needed to lead and give the people the inspiration and the drive to make it succeed. In short, the elite. ...

Every society tries to produce this type. The British have special schools for them: the gifted and talented are sent to Eton and Harrow and a few very exclusive private schools which they call 'public schools'; after that they go to Oxford and Cambridge. And they have legends which say that the Battle of Waterloo was won on the playing fields of Eton.[9]

In this speech Lee also directly linked his elitism and his progressivism:

True, not every boy is equal in his endowments in either physical stamina or mental capacity or character. But all those with the potential to blossom forth must do so. That is the spearhead in the society, on whom depends the pace of our progress.[10]

Lee's elite has many characteristics in common with the English concept of 'class', whereby members of the upper class can speak of someone being 'one of us', but in Singapore this has been mixed shamelessly with the Chinese concept of a scholarly 'mandarinate' to produce a conception that has, in the minds of its members, the best of both worlds.

Meritocracy

Lee Kuan Yew's elite at its most ideal was not to be based on such accidental factors as race, consanguinity or class, but on sheer merit. In conscious juxta-position to the Malay-centred affirmative action programs being implemented across the causeway, Singapore's elite would earn their place at the pinnacle of society through sheer talent and hard work as measured by their grades at school and university; and then by demonstrated management, leadership and problem-solving abilities – a meritocracy. The myth of the meritocracy is even more firmly identified with Lee Kuan Yew's leadership than is mul-tiracialism because it was first articulated by Lee soon after independence (whereas multiracialism was seeded by David Marshall in the mid-1950s). Although there are solid grounds for believing that Lee's elitism and his regard for the importance of innate 'talent' is rooted in his childhood, education and character,[11] he gave full rein to expressing his belief in meritocratic elitism only in the aftermath of separation from Malaysia. Since then he has been obsessive about fine-tuning the Singapore system to ensure that the talented

– by which he means the English-speaking academically talented – are given opportunities to rise. In the words of another government minister speaking in the 1990s, the talented must be given the opportunity to act as the 'yeast' that will 'raise the overall performance of society'.[12] Hence Lee's meticulous attention to education and scholarships, and even to the systems of promotion and review in the civil service (*ST*, 19 April 1982). The meritocracy moved quickly to centre stage in Singapore's nation-building mythology after separation from Malaysia and in so doing sharpened the picture of the ideal Singaporean. This shift towards a meritocratic social system was driven not only by declaratory statements from above, but also by incremental structural shifts in education policy that are explored in Chapters 6–10 and which made meritocracy part of the lived experience of generations of parents and children. By this we mean that the institutions of advancement by examination results were put in place and the population – or at least most of the population – adjusted their plans and expectations accordingly, immersing themselves and their children in the mores of the 'new' Singapore.

Ideally, in the new Singapore there would be no distortions to the mechanistic selection of the next generation of leaders through meritocratic sieves, but of course reality always falls short of ideals and in the process of creating this brave new meritocracy, distortions came to abound. Some distortions were deliberate and were a direct result of the fundamental conflict within Lee's vision of the elite: a conflict that pitted sterile grades-based elite selection with the cultivation of qualities like loyalty, leadership, social discipline and selflessness. Thus we see Extra Curricular (later Co-Curricular) Activities (ECAs and CCAs) being moved into the mainstream of school assessment, elite schools modelling themselves consciously on English public schools, and the civil service measuring in its senior members an 'Emotional Quotient', which is taken as the outward manifestation of leadership capacity. Other distortions appear to have arisen only in the course of pursing greater goals: notably the privileging of ethnic Chinese and the imposition of a glass ceiling for women.

Institutions of Elite Formation

This book is premised on the assumption that there have been three crucial institutions in the process of elite formation: the education system; the Singapore Armed Forces (SAF); and the highest echelons of the civil service, the core of which is found in the elite Administrative Service, though it extends to the elite levels of Government-Linked Companies (GLCs) and Statutory Boards. The centrality of the three institutions in the Singapore nation-building project is reflected directly in the strict, if unofficial hierarchy of ministries recognised within the civil service:

1. Prime Minister's Office (PMO) which is not only the supreme ministry, but also trains and manages the Administrative Service and the civil service;[13]

2. Ministry of Defence (MINDEF) which of course manages the SAF;

3. Ministry of Education (MOE);

4. Ministry of Finance (MOF);

5. Ministry of Trade and Industry (MTI); and

6. Ministry of Home Affairs (MHA).

The first three ministries in this hierarchy manage between them the civil service, the SAF and the education system. The supremacy of the PMO is to be expected, but the high ranking of MINDEF and MOE are surprising and particularly notable considering that MOF and MTI – not MINDEF or MOE – comprise the sharp end that delivers and pays for the Singapore system. It is important to note that in identifying these institutions as being at the heart of elite formation we are accepting Lee Kuan Yew's definition of the 'elite' as 'a ruling and administrative elite'. In the early twenty-first century this effectively represents a select group of ministers, members of the Administrative Service, and senior members of the SAF and the security services who are part of the Alpha Domain: the virtual communications network within the Government Information Infrastructure that is strictly for the use of the country's main decision makers.[14] The operation of this virtual domain is one of the more graphic pieces of operational evidence that attests to the blurring of distinction between the political and administrative elites. The administrative and political elites are not equal or identical but their points of common identity and operation mark them out as a world apart from those on the 'outside'.

There are, of course, other elites in Singapore: communal leadership, and economic, academic and religious elites, just to name four alternative constructions. They have in the past possessed degrees of autonomy from the political and administrative elites, yet we have accepted explicitly the self-perception of the ruling elite as the true pinnacle of society primarily because in Singapore this group has successfully developed state power and consequently its own power to the point where they are synonymous and all pervasive: they have crushed or co-opted the alternative elites, making them subordinate players in a rigidly controlled society. This development is a direct consequence of the government's successful conflation of nation building, state building and elite formation; a conflation that we argue leaves grassroots nation building and alternate elite formation in varying states of atrophication. Be that as it may, it would be pointless to deny the reality that has been created, and which is acknowledged with varying degrees of enthusiasm by almost all Singaporeans.

The civil service, the SAF and the education system are therefore the focus of this book. Each of these institutions is a continually evolving entity, and none of the flow of changes in any of these institutions can be taken in isolation from the others. This makes tracking the history of elite formation in Singapore a complicated and open-ended project. Perhaps it is best to begin with a glimpse at the current state of the product at the time of writing to help readers keep their bearings and to follow our analysis. This seems particularly appropriate since early work on this book coincided with the beginning of Lee Hsien Loong's premiership – surely an auspicious time in the ongoing development of 'the Singapore system'.

Technocracy and Beyond

To say that the culture of governance in Singapore is technocratic is a truism, but it is a very limited one. A technocracy is a system of governance in which rule is based on supposedly impartial, objective criteria derived directly or indirectly from disciplines such as economics, management, law, medicine, and engineering.[15] In the Singapore example, systems engineers have been given a particular place of honour at the upper executive level of this schema, though not to the exclusion of other professionals. A technocracy also presumes that the system is able to rise above subjective considerations of politics, ideology and sectional interests. To borrow the words of sociologist Luigi Pellizoni, in a technocracy 'the elite is suitably "protected" against the rest of society and is able to perform its tasks efficiently'.[16] Not surprisingly, Prime Minister Lee Hsien Loong boasts the achievements of the Singapore system in explicitly technocratic terms: The government has 'shielded civil servants from political interference ... [giving them] the space to work out rational, effective solutions for our problems' so they can 'practise public administration in almost laboratory conditions'.[17]

In the most common Platonic ideal of a technocracy, the key personnel will be found in a faceless bureaucracy, but this does not mean that a technocracy is just another word for bureaucratisation. Hegemonic bureaucracies can take pedestrian, regulatory forms; they can be nothing more than outlets for politics in societies where the formal government has little independent life.[18] The use of the term 'technocracy' in the context of Singapore implies much more than just bureaucratisation. It describes the complete or nearly complete hegemony of 'the modernist project' at the level of the nation-state. By this we mean that the authority of bureaucracy in a technocratic system is regarded as an expression of the power of cold, impartial reason itself – in contrast to the dubious emotive or selfish claims of religion, tradition, kings, sectional groups, or democratic politics. When this intellectual conceit is linked to a conviction by the nation's leadership (both inside and outside the bureaucracy) that the state must engage in a unidirectional drive towards 'development', prosperity and, if it has not already been attained, 'modernity', you have the makings of a technocracy.[19]

This coupling of modernist ideas and bureaucratic power was typically found in communist regimes and developmental states. The communist experiments have provided no surviving examples of such a technocracy at work, and every showcase it offered (such as East Germany) proved to be a mirage generated by propaganda and subsidies. The developmental state did succeed in offering a number of showcases, the most notable of which was Japan during the heyday of the Ministry of International Trade and Industry (MITI) when Japan was, in the words of Ezra Vogel, 'Number One'.[20]

Singapore Ideal

Yet the success story of Japan and MITI was tarnished as the technocracy proved inadequate to meet the challenges of the 1980s, and it is at this point that Singapore put its unique spin on technocracy. Like the classical technocratic ideal, the Singaporean form of governance regards itself as being above sectional interests and ideology, but it goes beyond the classical model by acknowledging and embracing the pivotal role of political leadership. It obviates the tension between the political and the technocratic by absorbing the idea of the technocrat into the broader ideal of 'the elite', and then making membership of the 'elite' a precondition for membership of both. The distinction between political and administrative leadership is blurred without being obliterated. Both political leaders and senior bureaucrats need very high levels of leadership and managerial skills. Neither actor can manage without both components. The ideal specimen in this conception of the 'elite' is not a colourless technocrat at all, but a highly educated, proactive, courageous, politically savvy problem solver who can lead people, whether as a civil servant-cum-'manager' or a politician-cum-'leader'.

That the reality falls well short of the ideal is freely acknowledged at the most senior levels of the civil service,[21] but the ideal is nevertheless regarded as achievable. The Public Service Division of the Prime Minister's Office, which manages the Administrative Service, is constantly focused on the task of perfecting the system: particularly avoiding the dangers of conformity in outlook and timidity in imagination and courage that currently beset the system. Its ultimate task is to identify those who have 'helicopter quality', which is a term coined by Lee Kuan Yew to describe those candidates who have qualities of leadership, imagination, character and motivation to match their high intelligence.[22] In the mind of the current premier, Lee Hsien Loong, it is 'the ability to see the big picture in perspective, and simultaneously zoom in on critical details'.[23]

As well as providing a rationale for a system of technocratic governance, the Singapore vision of the elite is also a brilliantly successful exercise in regime legitimation, and it is this aspect on which we intend to focus in the remainder of this chapter. We are especially interested in the way in which the culture of elite governance disguises the role of personal connections and privilege, and the personal nature of power within the system. The logical place to start this study is at or near its apex and centre and knead our understanding outwards from there.

At the Apex: Talent

Singapore's current Prime Minister, Lee Hsien Loong, has a mantra. In April 2004, while still Deputy Prime Minister, he told students at the Nanyang Technological University that they must not be content to inherit and enjoy the Singapore built by their parents and grandparents. Instead he asked them to 'change it, improve it and build on it' (*ST*, 6 April 2004). Several months later, a few days after becoming prime minister, he delivered a similar message, reproduced at the opening of this chapter, which expresses the same challenge in different words. The capacity to deliver on this promise of continuing improvement is the basis on which Singapore's politicians and the senior civil servants – are judged.

While he was Minister for Health in 1982, the current Senior Minister, Goh Chok Tong, expressed the mantra of perpetual improvement in terms of a quest for efficiency. Having just declared Singapore's health system as being among the 'best in the world', he then foreshadowed a complete overhaul of the system in a quixotic quest for organisational efficiency: 'We should not rest on our laurels, looking down from Mount Everest. In organisational efficiency, in the pursuit of quality and excellence, there can be no highest peak', he declared.[24] In February 2004, the then Acting Minister for Health, Khaw Boon Wan, took the quest for efficiency to imaginative new heights by defining the ultimate in health efficiency as a health-care system that has no patients![25]

Yet despite his successful implementation of health reforms in the mid-1980s, for Goh the mantra of perpetual improvement was an imposition. It was put to Barr by a source close to both men that in the later years of his premiership Goh was overshadowed in matters of day-to-day governance by his Deputy Prime Minister, Lee Hsien Loong, partly because Lee is an indefatigable 'policy wonk': always working, thinking, pushing whereas Goh was not naturally well-disposed or well suited for this style of work.[26] In the lead up to Lee's accession to the premiership, this perception was confirmed in newspaper articles and speeches recounting instance after instance of Lee Hsien Loong taking policy initiatives across the spectrum of portfolios, including telecommunications, power, public health care, transport, media, the integrated introduction of recycled water into the reservoirs, and – as far back as 1997 – education.[27] News reports in this period were littered with glowing references to Lee's seemingly limitless capacity to master briefs and go to the heart of issues.

It was Lee Senior who set the benchmarks by which his son was judged so glowingly, both by his personal example and by his obsessive quest to find others who at least approached his exacting standards. He held a deep-seated conviction in the universal applicability of 'talent' to any situation, which has been transformed into the basis and legitimating rationale of the Singapore political system. Lee Senior is convinced that the secret of good governance lies in the identification of those people with a genetic and almost tangible quality called 'talent'. Finding 'good men' and giving them power is the key to good governance.[28] The mechanism by which a society funnels such people to the top is a secondary consideration. Identify them in school, pump all your resources into nurturing them, exposing their minds to an ever-steeper hierarchy of challenges, and then select the best. You then test these elites. You give them test after test so they can learn from experience and you can identify the upper limits of their ability.[29] In an interview with *The Business Times* in 1978, Lee was prompted to state explicitly that testing rather than training was the essence of the system he had instituted. [30] It was as part of this testing process that Goh Chok Tong found himself launching a major reform of the health system in 1982 and proving that he was, in Lee's words, 'equal to the job'.[31]

Even before they have reached the rarefied heights that bring them under the personal gaze of the prime minister, a potential elite's progress is being monitored through official and unofficial reports. In 1982 Lee wrote some brief reflections on his 15 years of studying Public Service Commission (PSC) scholarship award holders 'and reading confidential reports on their work in the public service and the SAF'.[32] In 1984 he streamlined this process within the civil service by adapting the staff review and promotions system used by the Shell oil company. Lee used to devote himself to combing the civil service and the military for talent to be drafted into the elite, resulting in Cabinet being utterly dominated by people recruited from the public sector. Between 1980 and 1994, only two ministers were recruited from the private sector. Similarly, after the 1998 intake of new blood, only two members of Cabinet had been recruited from the private sector.[33] Of the 18 men in Cabinet as of October 2005 (excluding Lee Kuan Yew), only two (Ng Eng Hen and Yeo Cheow Tong) were recruited from the private sector. Four were recruited from the SAF, four from the Administrative Service, three from GLCs, three from Statutory Boards or government hospitals, and two from university.[34]

The current Prime Minister is ostensibly trying to diversify this base. He seeks to recruit 'in government, in the public sector, in business, in the professions, in community work, in arts and sports' (*ST*, 20 March 2005) though the recent record strongly suggests that there is still a strong reluctance to stray very far from the traditional hunting grounds. In the 2001 General Elections there was a major exercise to inject 'new blood' into the government. Of the seven new MPs appointed to ministries only two (Dr Ng Eng Hen and Dr

Balaji Sadasivan) came from private sector backgrounds (as medical doctors in private practice). The other five came from:

- *the Administrative Service*
  Mr Khaw Boon Wan, formerly of the Ministry of Health
  Mr Tharman Shanmugaratnam, formerly of the Ministry of Education and the Monetary Authority of Singapore,

- *government-linked companies*
  Mr Raymond Lim, formerly of DBS Securities and Temasek Holdings
  Mr Cedric Foo, formerly of Neptune Orient Lines and Singapore Airlines

- *a government instrumentality*
  Dr Vivien Balakrishnan, formerly CEO of Singapore General Hospital.[35]

It is notable that Khaw Boon Wan and Tharman Shanmugaratnam came to run ministries in which they used to be senior civil servants. Far from setting a precedent in diversity, this suggests that there is an element of narrowing as well as broadening, in the recruitment focus. The system of selection of the elite is based notionally on the principles of 'meritocracy': a ruthless winnowing process designed to ensure, in the words of Lee Kuan Yew, 'the best man or woman for the job, especially as leaders in government'.[36]

Legitimating Ideology: Pragmatism

The legitimating myth of the primacy of innovative, problem-solving 'talent', unearthed through 'meritocracy' and the quest for ever-higher levels of organisational efficiency in all aspects of society, business and government operates in tandem with another legitimating myth: that the government operates in a purely rational, scientific, problem-solving manner, free of ideological considerations. The mantra for this plank of legitimation is the purest distillation of technocratic ideology: 'pragmatism'.[37] Talk to Singaporeans and they will assure you that the government is 'pragmatic', that Singaporeans are 'pragmatic', and that even if there are problems and faults in outcomes, the Singapore system of meritocracy and 'pragmatic government' is only 'logical'. This is one of the main features that give Singaporeans a perception of their special place in the world. Singapore is tiny, but while most of the world is bound by 'ideology' and 'politics', Singaporeans punch above their weight because they operate as a 'pragmatic' and inherently logical meritocracy – as if 'pragmatism' is not itself an ideological construct. It is in this context that Prime Minister Lee Hsien Loong boasts that 'many countries envy Singapore's ability to take a longer view, pursue rational policies, put in place the fundamentals which the country needs, and systematically change policies which are outdated or obsolete'.[38] Indeed, the self-image of Singapore as being a model of governance admired by world leaders – especially those of post-Mao China – is of great comfort to members of the Singapore elite, and is a conscious part of the process of regime legitimation.[39] A typical outcome of this conceit is the boast by the current Minister for Health that the Singapore system of health care funding 'is far from perfect, but it is probably the best healthcare financing model in the world today'.[40]

Of course, the argument is specious. Far from being the distillation of impartial rationality, the Singapore system of governance is systemically pervaded with ideological, social, ethnic and class biases.[41] Yet the denial of the operation of ideology, or even politics, in the practice of government has a direct and profound effect on politics. It restricts the space for legitimate social and political discourse, de-legitimising the interrogation of aspects of the Singapore system that lie beyond the restrictive parameters of efficiency and effectiveness. This position was formalised in 1994 when then-Prime Minister Goh Chok Tong, through his Press Secretary, declared politics *per se* to be the exclusive preserve of those with technocratic expertise and a professional commitment to governance: 'How can public consultations ... conceive an HDB upgrading programme, or design a Singapore Telecom Group? A share discount scheme? Or Edusave? Or Medifund?' (*ST*, 4 December 1994).

The guardianship role of the technocratic elite is even written into the constitution. Since 1991 the elected position of President of Singapore has been formally and constitutionally reserved for people who have emerged as successful members of the technocratic elite. Some of the categories of eligibility include having been a minister, chief justice, a permanent secretary, chairman of the Public Service Commission or a chairman or chief executive officer of either an important statutory board or a company with a paid-up capital of at least $100 million.[42] In any case all candidates are vetted by a committee of three, two of whom are the Chairman of the Public Service Commission and the Chairman of the Public Accountants Board. Once elected, the President cannot do much without the approval of another committee comprising politicians and more unelected technocrats.[43]

Yet it goes further than just politics. Even the business of justice was formally declared the exclusive province of judges and lawyers by the abolition of the jury system in 1970, a move that was justified explicitly by the need to exclude amateurs from the court system.[44] Extraordinarily, even the ongoing 'Asian values' discourse in Singapore, with its presumption that Singapore operates under a superior 'Asian' value system to that held by the West, has not dented the hegemonic self-perception of Singapore as 'pragmatic' and beyond ideology. It has passed largely unnoticed that belief in the superiority of a particular value system flatly contradicts assertions of impartial and objective 'pragmatism', but the contradiction has not been fatal to either discourse because each one deters inquiry by claiming to be an obvious and self-referential set of truths. Furthermore, each of them has been generated by the same social milieu, and reflects the world-view peculiar to Singaporeans in general, and Chinese Singaporeans in particular.[45]

It might be thought that one advantage of this system of governance is predictability, and indeed many outcomes from the Singapore system are entirely predictable. Just to take one instance, one major result of this system of 'meritocratic' governance is Prime Minister Lee Hsien Loong. He could be the defining standard of the technocratic elite: someone who can pass any test, solve any problem, is sensitive to politics and who has defined the mantra of 'change it, improve it and build on it'. Furthermore the Cabinet is now – as of the late 2000s – hosting two 'rising stars' who are cut from the same cloth. Mr Khaw Boon Wan and Mr Tharman Shanmugaratnam have been plucked from successful careers in the civil service and tested fiercely in portfolios. Days after taking up the premiership Lee Hsien Loong revealed that he had been closely involved in bringing them into Cabinet while he was still Deputy Prime Minister, and there is every reason to believe that he had been micromanaging their training and testing. Lee Hsien Loong has known and worked with Tharman Shanmugaratnam for 23 years from their time together in the Monetary Authority of Singapore (MAS) and he has known Khaw for at least 16 years.[46]

These three men are the epitome of the Singapore technocrat, but their collective story – and particularly the story of Lee Hsien Loong – demonstrates a central feature of the Singapore system of governance that is not celebrated by the regime. We refer to the highly personalised nature of power, a feature that seriously diminishes the transparency of the system and disrupts its predictability. Patronage or sponsorship is a vitally important element in the rise of anyone in the Singapore political and administrative elite. 'Talent' and paper qualifications are sufficient in themselves to attract the notice of those with influence to disburse, but at some point one needs to plug into a patronage network. The earlier in life one is able to do this, the better. Ideally such links would come through one's family, but networks forged at school, or through corporate, civil or military service can prove nearly as advantageous. A substantial part of the networking and patronage is directed at socialising young candidates into the mindset and skill set of the 'elite' to ensure the perpetuation of the system.

Lubricant: Personal Power

Later chapters explore the processes of the selection and socialisation of candidates into the inner core of the elite, but at this stage we will provide only a bare outline. In essence it is a system that feeds people through a high-pressure, streamed national schools system that is dominated by examinations, private tuition and rote learning from kindergarten to matriculation. This system generates a pervasive culture that is heavily conformist, materialistic and risk-averse. Most of the elite students, however, have strong elements of both service and conceit added to that recipe as they pass through a handful of elite schools. The male students do their 2½ years' (recently reduced to 2 years') National Service (NS) and those with excellent matriculation grades and who are judged to be suited to a military career are herded into a 'scholar's platoon'[47] where they do officer training and are considered for SAF Scholarships.[48] The brightest of each cohort – including the women, who are never called for NS – are offered bonded scholarships by one or another of the arms of government to study at a top foreign university, whereupon they return to Singapore to serve out their bond for their employer. As junior members of the elite they join the clubs of the elite (Alpha Society for Administrative Officers, Temasek Society for senior SAF officers) attend the Civil Service College or the SAF Training Institute, and pass through more courses, tests, and extensive bonding sessions. They are also initiated into an exclusive world of privilege, social esteem and wealth from which it would be difficult to walk away. Since the early 1980s there has also been an extensive amount of crossover from the SAF to the Administrative Service, statutory boards and GLCs under a 'dual career scheme', so a common culture has developed in which the distinction between the SAF officers and the Administrative

Officers is often moot.[49] In 1993 dual-career SAF officers made up 10 per cent of the Administrative Service.[50] The extent of the permeation of SAF officers into the Administrative Service in the 1990s is indicated by the rising prevalence of military terminology (such as 'Standard Operating Procedure', SOP) in the civil service.[51]

There is much more to be said, but that is for later, so let us return our focus to the character of this system. Despite possessing genuinely merito-cratic elements, the oil that lubricates the Singapore system is the exercise of personal power. The personal character of power is demonstrated without much effort in the person of Lee Kuan Yew, who remains in Cabinet 15 years and two prime ministers after his retirement from the premiership, with the creative title of 'Minister Mentor'. He was previously 'Senior Minister' for the duration of Goh Chok Tong's premiership, but now Goh holds that title. His presence in Cabinet must be most uncomfortable for Lee Hsien Loong. Not only does he have to work in the shadow of the founding father of modern Singapore, as did his predecessor, but in his case the man in question is his father. Even if Hsien Loong is really his 'own man', who is going to believe it? Hsien Loong did not even get to announce this Cabinet line-up. It was Lee Senior who announced that he would continue in Cabinet for as long as he was fit and able to serve, and it was Lee Senior who announced the new hierarchy (for protocol purposes) within the Prime Minister's Office, whereby he would be third in line behind Prime Minister Lee Hsien Loong and Senior Minister Goh Chok Tong (*Reuters News Service*, 27 July 2004). An anonymous 'government official' was left to confirm Lee Senior's announce-ment six days later (*Asian Political News Service*, 2 August 2004).

Why does Lee Hsien Loong not simply remove him from Cabinet, as is his constitutional right? Why did not Goh Chok Tong do so when he was Prime Minister? Regardless of the power they notionally possess or pos-sessed by virtue of their institutional positions, they both understand that in or out of Cabinet, Lee Kuan Yew retains his personal networks and his per-sonal power. He needs a seat in Cabinet only so that he can legally have open access to Cabinet and other official papers and legally retain his privileged links to the Internal Security Department. On balance Lee Hsien Loong may not even want to see him gone yet because his own power networks are still underpinned by his father. In the case of Goh Chok Tong, his efforts as Prime Minister to build a personal and independent power base[52] were thwarted by both Lees – father as Senior Minister and son as Deputy Prime Minister. [53] In the end, after being outflanked by father and son during a property scandal involving the Lee family in 1996 (*Straits Times Weekly Edition*, 25 May and 1 June 1996), Goh gave up trying to exercise real power and handed the reins of domestic government over to Deputy Prime Minister Lee Hsien Loong. In any case, Goh's efforts were never going to be very complete because he had no relatives in government. It was probably this characteristic more than any other that made him an ideal stop gap between father and son.

Beyond the special place of the first family, the operation of personal power shares many characteristics with routine networking typical of bureaucracies the world over. According to one Permanent Secretary there were, in 2003, a group of six Permanent Secretaries who were of the same cohort and who knew each other well and trusted each other. With a luncheon discussion or a couple of phone calls between members of this group, problems could be fixed without further ado. He went as far as to say that without networks in government, 'it would be difficult to get things done'.[54] A former Permanent Secretary made a different point that also highlights the personal character of power in the Singapore system. He spoke of the importance of finding oneself as a senior civil servant under a minister with clout, capable of getting things done. If a minister is afraid of being 'shot down' at every step, then all the civil servants working under him will endure years of frustration.[55]

Personal Power at Work

The description given above provides a satisfactory outline of the operation of personal power in the elite, but it fails to convey the extraordinary character that separates it from more commonplace examples of civil service networks. The following anecdote conveys an extreme example of the operation of personal power, demonstrating its peculiarly Singaporean character whereby the person is often much more important than the position he or she holds. In March 1998, Singapore's ruling elite treated observers to an extraordinary and highly edifying spectacle that turned the conventional relationship between political leadership and civil service on its head. The event even began in a peculiar way, with a senior civil servant, rather than a politician, launching a new policy initiative. The Economic Development Board (EDB) was becoming concerned over the casualness with which scholarship holders bonded to the EDB were exercising their contractual right to buy themselves out of their bond to take up more lucrative offers. EDB Chairman Philip Yeo regarded honouring the bond as not just a matter of meeting contractual obligations but as a moral obligation, and proposed a moral dimension to the solution: publicly naming (and humiliating) bond breakers (*ST*, 14 August 1997). In March 1998 the EDB put Yeo's plan into effect and began naming bond breakers publicly (*Sunday Times*, 1 March 1998).

In the public debate that followed it emerged that the previous January a government MP had disagreed with Yeo over this approach in a meeting. In the excitement of the argument Yeo – a civil servant – called for the resignation of the MP and asked for the names of any other MPs who shared his views. When the MP complained in Parliament about this civil servant's conduct, two government MPs leapt to Yeo's defence (*ST*, 10 and 11 March 1998). Deputy Prime Minister Lee Hsien Loong finally settled the matter with a contribution that was just as remarkable as what had gone before. He devoted four sentences (one paragraph) to chastising Yeo for overstepping his brief, and nineteen paragraphs to chastising the MP. Lee began by emphasising the respect due to civil servants and the need for 'mutual respect and appreciation' because 'MPs and civil servants both play crucial but different roles in our body politic'. He then criticised the MP's account of the meeting and his views and humiliated the MP by detailing the extent to which he had already backed away from his original position in the light of Yeo's arguments. Deputy Prime Minister Lee left the MP no room to move:

> It is clear from the file note that Mr Chng [the MP] had argued that it was quite alright to break a scholarship bond, because it was just a matter of a legal contract and liquidated damages, and this is what provoked Mr Yeo.
>
> ... On Monday [in Parliament], Mr Chng Hee Kok, to his credit, no longer maintained that there was nothing wrong. ...
>
> Mr Chng has told me that he had thought the matter over and modified his stand. Had Mr Chng taken this more responsible line in his meeting with Mr Philip Yeo on Jan [*sic*] 19, I do not think he would have provoked the reaction that he did.
>
> The Deputy Prime Minister concluded by pointedly reminding Mr Chng that 'MPs are opinion leaders' and that 'the views they propagate in public speeches set the tone for society' (*Sunday Times*, 15 March 1998).

It must have been a relief for the MP to be told that he had some role, because he had been left in no doubt that his views counted for nought in policy formation. He might also have quite reasonably formed the opinion that his political colleagues and superiors regarded the civil service as a normal means of not only developing and implementing policy but even of announcing it. Furthermore, he knew that he could count on no loyalty from his parliamentary colleagues if he did not accept political leadership offered by a senior civil servant – or at least by this particular civil servant. The events of March 1998 had the appearance of an announcement that at certain senior levels of the civil service the distinction between the political and the administrative elite is blurred. In fact it was merely a spectacular confirmation of this reality, which is actually institutionalised in at least two ways. First, it is part of the formal job description of senior civil servants (Administrative Officers) that they 'are responsible for formulating ... Government policy'.[56] Second, the most senior civil servants share with Cabinet ministers the same hierarchy for the purposes of salary and seniority, and some, such as Phillip Yeo in 1998, have held ranks higher than that of a junior minister, let alone a mere MP.[57] It is this blurring of the political and administrative leadership – which has long since been evident to Singapore-watchers[58] – that is the point of this anecdote.

This is not to say that this incident is typical. Several senior figures have gone to great lengths in interview to emphasise that Philip Yeo is a law unto himself and an exception to the rule. They are undoubtedly correct to point out that Yeo's behaviour on this occasion was extreme and extraordinary, but our point is that it was an extreme and extraordinary example of a systemic phenomenon. Philip Yeo is hardly the only civil servant or retired civil servant with huge reserves of personal power, though he is the only one to flaunt it so publicly.

Personal Power as Currency

Personal power is earned through a combination of personal connections and a record of achievement, but once created it is as tangible as currency, and like currency it can be lent, invested, spent or squandered. It is therefore part of the nature of personal power that it can be delegated and disseminated through personal connections, personal endorsement and more formally institutionalised networks of patronage. This function distorts the workings of all aspects of society, including the application of the rule of law. Yet it is so understood by all parties that perhaps it could be argued that the pattern of inconsistencies is so regular that it restores some predictability to the system. Many of the most public examples of the delegation of personal power take place in the realm of politics. We have chosen to highlight just two. The first was the contrasting applications of political censorship laws in two episodes in 2005. On the one hand, Martin See's documentary film, *Singapore Rebel*, on Singapore Democratic Party leader Chee Soon Juan, fell foul of the Media Development Authority, which banned it as a 'political' film that breached the Films Act. On the other hand, MediaCorp's series of five documentary films, *Up Close*, which showcased four Cabinet Ministers and the Prime Minister, was broadcast with impunity on prime time television (*Today*, 21 October 2005). Why was one film banned and the other five celebrated? When challenged in a letter to the Forum pages of *The Straits Times*, the Director of Corporate Communications in the Ministry of Information, Communications and the Arts, Ms K. Bhavani, argued that *Singapore Rebel* was 'political', but *Up Close* was 'non-partisan' and was 'aired by MediaCorp for the purpose of reporting current affairs'. She also made the extraordinary claim that 'in the series, the ministers discussed with invited guests policy issues pertaining to their portfolios, such as youth, employment, education and health' (*Straits Times Interactive*, 15 October 2005). Prime Minister Lee Hsien Loong's episode did indeed consist of relatively thoughtful, if heavily partisan, discussions with invited guests, but the other four did not even make a gesture towards following this format. Those episodes consisted of promotional clips of the politicians engaged variously in door knocking constituents, Meet-the-People Sessions, kicking a soccer ball, bouncing a basketball, singing karaoke, visiting schools, talking to students, and exercising at a gym. The ministers told the viewers in voiceover about their childhoods, education and how they came to be so devoted to serving the public, and all these episodes were interspersed with clips and voiceovers from chatty interviews in which the ministers promoted their political agendas.[59] The significance of this episode is not just the partisan application of the law by the responsible authorities, but the confidence with which MediaCorp proceeded to flaunt the law, knowing full well that it enjoyed the protection of the four Cabinet ministers, and of Lee Hsien Loong himself.

The second incident, involving Opposition MP Chiam See Tong, tells a similar story. In 2005 the regular PAP candidate for Chiam's electorate, Sitoh

Yih Pin, organised a National Day function in the constituency at which the paid entertainment, a Taiwanese singer, sang his praises (literally) and urged those present to 'support' Sitoh. This episode turned the function into an illegal political rally (being held both outside the official election campaigning period and without a permit) at which a foreigner was interfering in local politics (*ST*, 19 and 29 October 2005). Under normal circumstances this would be sufficient to have the singer deported and the organisers of the function charged, if not detained. Despite raising these breaches of the law in Parliament, Chiam has not been able to secure any prosecutions in this instance, because – as everyone involved in the administration of justice in Singapore knows – Sitoh and his foreign talent enjoy the protection of Lee Hsien Loong and the entire political establishment, and Chiam has no power at all.[60]

The extension of personal power to minions, subordinates and associates of those who hold power is an essential element of the Singapore system, to the point where its exercise is taken to be a normal part of life and it is only on the rare occasion when someone has the courage to point out the duplicity in the standards that it even rises to the forefront of consciousness. The examples given above were chosen because they are on the public record. They could be reasonably construed as nothing more novel than the partisan machinations of an authoritarian state, but it is more accurate to say that these are the public manifestations of a much more complex and interesting phenomenon, which is the exercise of personal power. Behind the closed doors of 'Singapore Inc.' – with its network of statutory boards, GLCs, senior bureaucrats and ministers – lie matrixes of personal power that are equivalent to those that operate publicly in the political arena, but are yet to be uncovered and studied. It is these networks that provide the lubricant that is the essential facilitator of the Singapore systems of governance and government-linked business.[61]

Prime Minister Lee Hsien Loong

Prime Minister Lee Hsien Loong's *curriculum vitae* reads as an exemplary case study of the way that personal power, personal connections and related social advantages lubricate the meritocratic system: it is the public tip of an otherwise hidden iceberg that is the matrix of personal power in Singapore. Lee Hsien Loong was born in 1952 as the eldest son of two brilliant solicitors, one of whom was to become Prime Minister. His economic position was comfortable without being wealthy (at least not in his early life) but more important he had the immense advantage of being born into an English-speaking Chinese household. Even without other considerations, this made him part of a small privileged elite in the Singapore of the 1950s because the Chinese were the dominant ethnic group and English was the language of the colonial elite. After independence in 1965, his father (as prime minister) successfully set out to make English the dominant language of the republic and the prime language of education (*ST*, 25 February 1978). Lee, however, was not content with his children being just monolingual. Even at this early stage Lee Senior had developed a fixation with what he would later call the 'cultural ballast' provided by one's 'mother tongue'.[62] In the mid-1950s he began arranging private tuition in Mandarin for his children from age three and then he sent them to top Chinese-medium schools for their primary and secondary education.[63] Yet despite this immersion in a Chinese-language environment, Hsien Loong was failing his Mandarin; his parents thus arranged for private tuition so he could pass his A-levels (*ST*, 21 January 1999). His basic proficiency in Mandarin was sufficient to put him in good stead since, contrary to all expectations, his father was later going to place bilingual Chinese (English and Mandarin-speaking) at the apex of the political and administrative elite. This is not to suggest that in the mid-1950s Lee Senior had a secret language agenda for the 1980s and beyond. (Lee Kuan Yew also had the young Hsien Loong learn Malay in the original Jawi (Arabic) script and even Russian because he thought they might be useful on either the local or international scene.)[64] We are simply pointing to the importance to Lee Hsien Loong of being the son of the man whose thinking was to shape Singapore's future. The same idiosyncratic set of preconceptions about 'cultural ballast' and 'Chinese culture' that caused Lee Senior to thrust all his children into Chinese-medium schools was later to thrust Mandarin and 'Chinese values' onto centre stage in Lee's Singapore, giving his son an inside run as a Chinese-educated English-speaker from an establishment family.

Then, just as Hsien Loong finished his senior years of school the first of the junior colleges opened to offer elite students a specialist study and tuition environment to prepare for university. It is barely conceivable that this is a coincidence, but it remains a fact that Hsien Loong was in the first intake of the first junior college, National Junior College (NJC) and against all common practice he sat for the Cambridge A-levels in two stages. He matriculated with A1s in pure and applied mathematics and an A2 in physics in the Cambridge Higher School Certificate in 1969 (*Sunday Times*, 31 May 1970; and *ST*, 1 June 1970) and then returned as a part-time student to sit for the full set of examinations and the Cambridge A-levels a year later (*ST*, 15 October 1971). On the strength of his 1969 results alone he was one of eight winners of the prestigious President's Scholarship in 1970, and also won a Public Service Commission scholarship to Cambridge to study mathematics.

After attending NJC, he also voluntarily began his National Service (NS) while waiting to depart for Cambridge, even though, as a scholarship winner, he could have deferred (*ST*, 1 June 1970). His decision to start his NS early served him well. On 5 March 1971, while Hsien Loong was doing his NS, his father initiated an SAF scholarship system for school leavers.[65] Barely two and half months later the MINDEF announced that Lee was in the inaugural group of five winners (out of only 20 applicants) and would study in Cambridge as an SAF Scholar (*ST*, 20 May 1971). Upon his return to Singapore in 1974 the SAF initiated a scholarship and leadership programme for serving officers. Unsurprisingly, Lee Hsien Loong was in the first intake.[66] All in all, Lee made good use of his study opportunities while he was in the SAF. From 1971 to 1974 he studied at Cambridge, where he graduated with Double First Class Honours in Mathematical Statistics and Mathematical Economics and a distinction in a Diploma in Computer Science. After a mere three years working as a regular officer in the SAF, he was posted to Fort Leavenworth, USA, where he studied at the US Army Command and General Staff College from 1978 to 1979. Upon completion of these studies he stayed in the US for another year as a Mason Fellow at the Kennedy School of Government, Harvard University, graduating in 1980 with a Masters in Public Administration. By this stage he had risen to the rank of Major in the SAF, despite having served for only about three years on operational duty. He was made Director, Joint Operations Planning Directorate from 1981 to 1982, and then became Chief of Staff (General Staff) from 1982 to 1984, by this time having risen to the rank of Brigadier-General.[67] The SAF did not get very good value out of their investment, however, for Lee Hsien Loong left the SAF to run for Parliament in 1984.

We have no precise knowledge of the operation of favouritism during his military career, so we can only speculate about the importance of his family name in his rapid rise through the ranks. On his entry into politics, however, there is less need to speculate. Many months before the announcement of his candidature, a team of civil servants in the Housing and Development Board (HDB) were told that their job was to prepare the ground in Ang Mo Kio constituency for an Army officer who was going to retire soon and enter politics at the upcoming election. In this case the business of 'preparing the ground' involved ensuring that the creation of the first Town Council (a municipal body headed by the local MP and charged with the management of the local HDB estates) went smoothly. Zulkifli Baharudin, an officer in the HDB, was put in charge, and apart from the administrative work of setting up a new municipal authority, he oversaw and engaged personally in door knocking, talking to hawkers and shop owners, and making sure everyone was happy. Zulkifli says that this was his first political education and his first 'real contact with the constituency'. He said in interview that even without knowing that it was Lee Hsien Loong who was being parachuted into the electorate, the work was given a high priority because the ruling PAP 'was going to fight the election on the basis that it is best able to manage and lead a new municipal entity'.[68] A few months before the election he was told that the candidate was 'the son of Mr Lee'. After that, the work intensified, and he remembers it as the hardest working period of his life. Lest anyone is left with lingering doubts that the selection of Lee Hsien Loong's constituency for the first Town Council might have been an arbitrary selection, it is worth noting that the next assignment given to Zulkifli was setting up the second Town Council in Prime Minister Lee Kuan Yew's electorate, Tanjong Pagar. It is doubly significant to this study of personal power, patronage and special opportunities that having proved his worth and – it was assumed – political reliability, Zulkifli was later invited to stand for Parliament as a PAP candidate.[69]

The unofficial secondment of a team of civil servants to work for the re-election of the PAP government in an election is not extraordinary in itself. Entire ministries routinely devote their resources to the PAP during General Elections. Two other former civil servants have told in interview how they each took part in election work on behalf of the PAP during the 1991 election. One (in the Ministry of Information and the Arts) was involved in a ministry-wide exercise of monitoring and managing the press on behalf of the PAP. The other (in the Prime Minister's Office) was part of a team of civil servants that attended political rallies and reported on the mood and responses of the crowds. This was a comprehensive exercise that involved overtime, scheduled shift work, taxi vouchers and full use of the civil service infrastructure. Another interviewee who was campaigning for an opposition candidate during the 1996 elections was followed during his waking hours by two people he presumed to be ISD agents (from the Ministry of Home Affairs). The exercise was carried out without any serious effort at subterfuge, so its primary purpose was presumably intimidation rather than surveillance.

The dedication of civil service resources on behalf of the PAP is therefore considered routine within the civil service, but the significant feature of Zulkifli's story is the special treatment accorded 'the son of Mr Lee', even by the standards of PAP candidates. At that stage of his career, Lee Junior's handling of his constituency was so clumsy that he would have been in trouble without this help. He tried to approach his early 'walkabouts' like a military inspection, allocating a set time to each floor in each block and expecting his constituents to fit into his schedule (*Straits Times Interactive*, 12 August 2004). Not that you would have known that from reading the press reports at the time. The press at the time brimmed with adulatory reports about the PAP's new candidate for Ang Mo Kio, beginning with reporting the occasional political speech that he was allowed to make while he was still a serving officer in the Army (*ST*, 3 May 1984).

At this point it is worth noting that there is no reason to question Lee Hsien Loong's intelligence or his dedication to work and study. His path through life was cleared by family connections, but family connections are not sufficient to win a double first from Cambridge University, or to hold down very senior positions in a highly professional army. He did these things and then went on to do more after he was parachuted into Parliament and the Ministry. Lee was given test after test set by his father the prime minister, and he 'aced' them all, riding on his energy, intelligence and problem-solving ability. His first test was to tackle the recession of the mid-1980s as the Chairman of the Economic Review Committee.[70] From there he went from strength to strength. He had a dream run through the sensitive and powerful Trade and Industry and Finance ministries and became a Deputy Prime Minister in 1990. His progression was interrupted only by a cancer scare that set back his succession to the premiership by a few years. Yet without belittling the scale of his achievements, it is important to note that he had an immense advantage over and above his innate 'talent' in that he had much greater freedom to act than any other member of Cabinet apart from his father. Whereas his more experienced and more senior Cabinet colleagues had to take tiny, incremental steps to unwind any of Lee Kuan Yew's initiatives,[71] from the start Lee Hsien Loong was fearless in striking down sacred cows, beginning with the Central Provident Fund (*Straits Times Interactive*, 12 August 2004). He could afford to be. He could live up to the mantra, 'change it, improve it and build on it' with a freedom enjoyed by almost no one else in the country. As prime minister (and even as a disproportionately powerful deputy prime minister) he was also able to invite others into his aura of autonomy, though their autonomy was heavily circumscribed because it was dependent on his patronage. Current beneficiaries of Lee's largess include the 'rising stars' he has been nurturing in Cabinet – especially Tharman Shanmugaratnam and Khaw Boon Wan. Thus Lee's mantra is a circumlocutious cry of self-legitimation that is personified in Lee Hsien Loong himself. Others may share in it only insofar as their education and 'talent' allows, and insofar as they have been socialised into the world of the elite.

Conclusion

The Singapore system of elite governance is truly a remarkable beast. Under the legitimating ideology of meritocratic elitism it delivers an effective and thoroughly modern style of technocratic governance that is nevertheless riddled with distortions and failings that seem to make a mockery of the basic principles of its legitimacy. Some of these distortions – notably the exercise of personal power and the operation of privilege and connections – are actually intrinsic to the operation of the system to the point where the legitimating ideology starts to look like a threadbare cover for the perpetuation of a dynasty. And yet the system works. There is enough talent in the dynasty and enough truth in the myths of meritocracy, elite governance and pragmatism to ensure that the city-state is stable and profitable. If the reality were allowed to stray too far from these ideals the whole system would degenerate into crony politics – and that is not going to be allowed to happen. The imperfections and distortions do indeed make a mockery of a good deal of the regime's legitimating rhetoric, but they are not fatal to the system. The ruling elite clearly believes that they are an acceptable price for peace, prosperity and a smooth, if imperfect system of elite regeneration.

Notes

1   Lee Hsien Loong, 'Prime Minister Lee Hsien Loong's National Day Rally Speech 2004, Sunday 22 August 2004, at the University Cultural Centre, National University of Singapore'. Available on Sprinter [Singapore Government news service] http://www. sprinter.gov.sg/. Accessed on 9 November 2004.

2   Former DPM Toh Chin Chye in Melanie Chew (ed.), *Leaders of Singapore*, Singapore: Resource Press, 1996, pp. 97, 98.

3   Lee Kuan Yew, *From Third World to First: The Singapore Story: 1965–2000: Memoirs of Lee Kuan Yew*, Singapore: Singapore Press Holdings; Times Editions, 2000, p. 25.

4   Chan Heng Chee, *Singapore: The Politics of Survival 1965–1967*, Singapore and Kuala Lumpur: Oxford University Press, 1971.

5   Michael D. Barr, 'Lee Kuan Yew's Fabian phase', *Australian Journal of Politics and History*, vol. 46, no. 1, 2000, pp. 109–124.

6   Former DPM Goh Keng Swee in Melanie Chew, *Leaders of Singapore*, p. 147.

7   Michael D. Barr, *Lee Kuan Yew: The Beliefs Behind the Man*, Richmond, UK: Curzon, 2000, pp. 98–104

8   Lee Kuan Yew, *New Bearings in Our Education System*, Singapore: Ministry of Culture, [1966–67], pp. 9, 10.

9   Ibid.

10 Ibid., p. 12.

11 Barr, *Lee Kuan Yew*, pp. 97–105.

12 Lily Zubaidah Rahim, *The Singapore Dilemma: The Political and Educational Marginality of the Malay Community*, Kuala Lumpur: Oxford University Press, 1998, p. 39. The minister concerned was Wong Kan Seng, who was at the time (1992) Minister for Foreign Affairs. At the time of writing, he is a Deputy Prime Minister.

13 The PMO is generally regarded as being outside and above the hierarchy but at the risk of oversimplification it is listed here as part of the hierarchy.

14 Ross Worthington, *Governance in Singapore*, London and New York: RoutledgeCurzon, 2003, pp. 304, 305, note 120.

15 Langdon Winner, *Autonomous Technology: Technics-out-of-Control as a Theme in Political Thought*, Cambridge, Mass. and London: The MIT Press, 1977, especially pp. 144–165.

16 Luigi Pellizzoni, 'The myth of the best argument: power, deliberation and reason', *British Journal of Sociology*, vol. 52, no. 1, 2001, p. 64.

17 Speech by Prime Minister Lee Hsien Loong at the 2005 Administrative Service Dinner, 24 March 2005. Available on Sprinter [Singapore Government news service] http://www.sprinter.gov.sg/. Accessed 30 March 2005.

18 Junko Kato, *The Problem of Bureaucratic Rationality: Tax Politics in Japan*, Princeton, NJ: Princeton University Press, 1994, pp. 17–21; and B.C. Koh, *Japan's Administrative Elite*, Berkeley; Los Angeles; Oxford: University of California Press, 1989, pp. 1, 2.

19 Junko Kato, *The Problem of Bureaucratic Rationality*, p. 21.

20 Chalmers Johnson, *MITI and the Japanese Miracle: Growth of Industrial Policy, 1925–1975*, Stanford: Stanford University Press, 1982; and Ezra Vogel, *Japan as Number One: Lessons for America*, Cambridge, Mass: Harvard University Press, 1979.

21 See various articles in *Ethos*, the journal of the Civil Service College, which is available online at http://www.ipd.gov.sg/ethos/ethos.html. Accessed 22 March 2005.

22 Eddie Teo, 'Can public servants be leaders?', *Ethos*, September 2003, p. 10; Lee Hsien Loong at the 2005 Administrative Service Dinner.

23 Lee Hsien Loong at the 2005 Administrative Service Dinner.

24 Goh Chok Tong, Singapore Government Press Release. Speech by Mr Goh Chok Tong, Minister for Health and Second Minister for Defence, at the Singapore General Hospital (SGH), Nite 1982, 6 March 1982. Available at National Archives of Singapore, at http://www.museum.org.sg/NAS/nas.shtml/. Accessed 10 May 2004.

25 *The Sunday Times*, 29 February 2004. At the time Khaw was Acting Minister for Health, but he has since been made a full minister.

26 De-identified interview with Barr, Singapore, 2003.

27 *Straits Times Interactive*, 12 August 2004; and Lee Hsien Loong, 'Speech by Prime Minister Lee Hsien Loong at the 2005 Administrative Service Dinner, 24 March 2005', when he told of how 'in 1997, when we needed to strengthen and invigorate the Ministry of Education, I sent [Lim Siong Guan] to MOE. As the Permanent Secretary, he motivated the teachers and principals in all the schools, and was a principal architect of the "Thinking Schools, Learning Nation" programme.'

28 Lee Kuan Yew, *From Third World to First*, p. 735.

29 Diane K. Mauzy and R.S. Milne, *Singapore Politics Under the People's Action Party*, London and New York: Routledge, 2002, p. 115; and Barr, *Lee Kuan Yew*, pp. 97–136.

30 Lee's interview with Roy Mackie and Quek Peck Lim, *Business Times*, 16 September 1978, cited in Barr, *Lee Kuan Yew*, p. 124.

31 Lee Kuan Yew, *From Third World to First*, p. 123.

32 Barr, *Lee Kuan Yew*, p. 122.

33 Worthington, *Governance in Singapore*, p. 145.

34 Singapore Cabinet website, at http://www.cabinet.gov.sg/. Accessed 31 March 2005.

35 See the *curriculum vitae* of these seven men on the Parliament of Singapore website at http://www.parliament.gov.sg/. Accessed 31 March 2005.

36 Lee Kuan Yew, *From Third World to First*, p. 763.

37 Langdon Winner provides a description of the role of 'pragmatism' in classical technological politics in *Autonomous Technology*, p. 259.

38 Speech by Prime Minister Lee Hsien Loong at the 2005 Administrative Service Dinner, 24 March 2005.

39 See, for instance, Lee Kuan Yew, *From Third World to First*, pp. 668, 669, 675–77, 703, 706–709, 714–719.

40 Khaw Boon Wan, Ministry of Health Budget Speech (Part 1), on Wednesday, 17 March 2004 by Mr Khaw Boon Wan, then Acting Minister for Health. Available on the Singapore Government website, http://www.moh.gov.sg/. Accessed on 5 April 2004.

41 For the author's developed thoughts on the ideology and the social, ethnic and class biases inherent in the Singapore system, see Michael D. Barr, 'Perpetual revisionism in Singapore: the limits of change', *The Pacific Review*, vol. 6, no. 1, 2003, pp. 77–97; and Michael D. Barr, 'Singapore', Chapter 7 in Robin Gauld (ed.), *Comparative Health Policy in the Asia-Pacific*, Maidenhead, UK: Open University Press, 2004, pp. 146–173.

42 Kevin Y.L. Tan, 'The presidency in Singapore: constitutional developments', in Kevin Y.L. Tan and Lam Peng Er (eds), *Managing Political Change in Singapore*, London and New York: Routledge, 1997, p. 63.

43 Ibid., pp. 58, 59.

44 Alex Josey, *Lee Kuan Yew: The Crucial Years*, Singapore; Kuala Lumpur: Times Books International, 1980, p. 520.

45 A description of this Chinese Singaporean world-view begins in Chapter 5 and continues throughout the book.

46 Khaw joined the Prime Minister's Office as Principal Private Secretary to Goh Chok Tong in 1992 while Lee was Deputy Prime Minister. Khaw then became Permanent Secretary at the Ministry of Trade and Industry (1995–2001), in which role he worked closely with Lee Hsien Loong as Minister for Finance and Deputy Prime Minister. (See Khaw's curriculum vitae on the Singapore Cabinet website.)

47 Barr's interview with Zulkifli Baharudin, Singapore, 26 March 2003. Zulkifli Baharudin was briefly a member of the 'scholar's platoon' for his cohort.

48 Interview with Barr, Singapore, 28 March 2003. The interviewee was a member of a 'scholar's platoon', was nurtured by a group of officers and 'invited' to apply for an SAF Scholarship while on NS in 1992.

49 Barr's interview with a Bilahari Kausikan, Singapore, 15 April 2003; Tim Huxley, *Defending the Lion City: The Armed Forces of Singapore*, St Leonards, NSW: Allen & Unwin, 2000, p. 232; and Worthington, *Governance in Singapore*, pp. 23, 24.

50 Huxley, *Defending the Lion City*, p. 232.

51 Conversations with retired and serving civil servants.

52 Ross Worthington has made a valiant but not completely reliable effort to unearth the intricacies of Goh's efforts to build a power base. See Worthington, *Governance in Singapore*.

53 This assessment is based on the interview referred to in note 26 (above), and the authors' assessment of the evidence that immediately follows the account of this interview in the text.

54 Barr's interview with a Permanent Secretary, Singapore, 8 May 2003.

55 Barr's interview with a former Permanent Secretary, Singapore, 24 April 2003.

56 Worthington, *Governance in Singapore*, p. 322, note 52.

57 Ibid.

58 See, for instance, Raj Vasil, *Governing Singapore*, first revised edition, Singapore: Mandarin, 1992, p. 145.

59 *Up Close with Vivien Balakrishnan*, aired on Channel NewsAsia, 7 April, 2005; *Up Close with Tharman Shanmugaratnam*, aired on Channel NewsAsia, 14 April, 2005; *Up Close with Ng Eng Hen*, aired on Channel NewsAsia, 21 April 2005; *Up Close with Khaw Boon Wan*, aired on Channel NewsAsia, 28 April 2005; and *Up Close with Lee Hsien Loong*, aired on Channel NewsAsia, 5 May 2005.

60 The *Up Close* and the Sitoh Yih Pin episodes are very contemporary examples of the phenomenon of the transferability of personal power, but even the most superficial surveys of Singapore's modern history demonstrate that this is not a new phenomena. See, for instance, Garry Rodan, *Transparency and Authoritarian Rule in Southeast Asia: Singapore and Malaysia*, London and New York: Routledge, 2005, p. 103; and Michael D. Barr, 'J.B. Jeyaretnam: thirty years as Lee Kuan Yew's *bête noir*', *Journal of Contemporary Asia*, 33:3, 2003, p. 310.

61 Worthington has contributed a valuable starting point for uncovering the networks of connections that lubricate Singapore Inc. See Worthington, *Governance in Singapore*.

62 Barr, *Lee Kuan Yew*, pp. 150–157.

63 Lee Kuan Yew, *From Third World to First*, p. 749; and Lee Kuan Yew (ed. by Chua Chee Lay), *Keeping My Mandarin Alive*, Singapore: Global Publishing and World Scientific, 2005, p. 47.

64 Lee Kuan Yew, Press Conference with Malay Journalists at Studio of TV Singapura (Translation), 11 August 1965, Lee Kuan Yew, *Prime Minister's Speeches, Press Conferences, Interviews, Statements, etc.*, Singapore: Prime Minister's Office, 1965; Lee Kuan Yew, *From Third World to First*, p. 490.

65 'DPM Lee Hsien Loong's speech at the SAF Overseas Scholarship 30th Anniversary Dinner, 15 April 2001', Ministry of Trade and Industry website, available at http://www.mti.gov.sg. Accessed 27 September 2005.

66 Worthington, *Governance in Singapore*, p. 260, note 136.

67 The chronology of Lee Hsien Loong's military service is pieced together from his entry in Low Kar Tiang and Peter K.G. Dunlop (eds), *Who's Who in Singapore*, Singapore: Who's Who Publishing, 2000, pp. 128, 129; his entry *curriculum vitae* published on the Singapore Government website, http://www.cabinet.gov.sg/p_pmlee.htm (accessed 21 March 2005); *STI*, 12 August 2004; *ST*, 3 May 1984; and *ST*, 1 September 1984. Lee's promotion to Brigadier-General came some time between 3 May and 1 September, just before his departure from the army.

68 Barr's interview with Zulkifli Baharudin, Singapore, 26 March 2003.

69 Ibid. Zulkifli declined the invitation to stand for parliament as a PAP candidate, but later accepted a government invitation to become a semi-independent Nominated MP.

70 Lee Kuan Yew, *From Third World to First*, p. 752.

71 See Barr, 'Perpetual revisionism in Singapore'.

FIVE

Incomplete Assimilation: From Civic Nationalism to Ethno-Nationalism

In looking back over the last 30 years, I believe we were fortunate that 77% of our people had strong Chinese traditional values which put emphasis on the strength of the family, the bringing up of children to be modest, hardworking, thrifty, filial, loyal and law abiding. Their behaviour had an influence on non-Chinese Singaporeans.

Lee Kuan Yew, 25 August 1992[1]

THE MYTHS OF THE MERITOCRACY and multiracialism enjoy a truly symbiotic relationship in Singapore's nation-building project, between them emphasising both the 'fairness' of the Singapore system and purporting to guarantee the minorities that they enjoy full status as members of the nation-building project.[2] As Prime Minister Lee Hsien Loong put it in May 2005, 'We are a multiracial society. We must have tolerance, harmony. ... And you must have meritocracy ... so everybody feels it is fair'.[3] The previous chapter began probing the Singapore system of meritocracy for weaknesses and distortions and found evidence of distortions based on personal connections. This chapter presents the argument that the Singapore system of multiracialism is also seriously flawed: that it is no longer concerned primarily with inter-communal tolerance, as it was until the end of the 1970s, but has become an aggressive programme of assimilation of the racial minorities into a Chinese-dominated society. We chose to use the case of the Malays (particularly in the final section of this chapter and in Chapter 7) as an extreme, rather than a typical example of the workings of Singapore multiracialism to demonstrate the government's assimilationist agenda at its clearest. They are also a special case because as a group they sit at the bottom of Singapore's socio-economic and educational scales, and have done so since independence. This is true whether one chooses to measure average or highest incomes, income per household or per individual, highest or average educational achievement, or the 'status' or type of employment.[4] They are also by the far the most cohesive of all of Singapore's ethnic groups because of their almost universal adherence to Islam. This makes them easily identifiable, reduces their intermarriage with other ethnic groups, and in the world of post-September 11 fears, makes them particularly vulnerable to stereotyping. The Malay community is also of major significance in its own right because it is Singapore's largest racial minority, its members comprising two-thirds of the non-Chinese population (with most of the rest being Indians).

Evolution of Singapore's Multiracialism

Singapore's version of multiracialism has changed several times over the decades. These changes were outlined in the closing pages of Chapter 3,[5] but we wish to begin this stage of our examination with a focus on the point of continuity that links the current version and the original version introduced by Singapore's first Chief Minister, David Marshall in 1956. The point of articulation lies in the fact that this and all subsequent versions of multiracialism were based on a presumption that Singapore's future lay with assimilating its various ethnic cultures into a dominant hegemonic culture. To understand the significance of this simple statement in the Singapore context it should be understood that colonial Singapore was a Furnivallian plural society, where

> there was a racial division of labour. All the various people met in the economic sphere, the market place; but they lived apart and continually tended to fall apart unless held together by the British Government.[6]

Colonial ideology ranked the myriad of races under its jurisdiction according to stereotypes of racial attributes. Racial groups were distinguished one from the other and included in colonial society in distinctive ways that minimised inter-communal interaction.[7] The role of the coloniser was seen to be one of an umpire, arbitrating the relationships and conflicts between the various communities. The division of colonial society into ethnic silos facilitated the generation of stereotypes that persist to today.

The Malays were viewed by both the Chinese and the colonial administration as being 'endowed with traits of complacency, indolence, apathy, infused with a love of leisure and an absence of motivation and discipline'[8] while

Indians were stereotyped as being dirty, argumentative and troublesome. Chinese viewed themselves as hard-working, thrifty and materialistic. These stereotypes were reproduced in mainstream post-colonial Chinese social cognition, as is demonstrated in the following quotations, recorded as part of a sociological survey of Chinese Nanyang University students in 1969:

> [Malays] are lazy but lavish spenders. They are comparatively uncultured and untrustworthy.
>
> [A]lmost all Malays are Muslims and their intelligence on the average is lower than among the Chinese.
>
> Malays are not diligent, have very dark skins and the majority of them attain a very low level of education.
>
> [Malays, Indonesians and Filipinos] are selfish, lazy, and dirty.
>
> Malays are lazy and indulge too much in impractical things, while Indians are dirty, talkative and lack a sense of mutual understanding.
>
> The Indians are greedy, who would sacrifice anything for a small profit, short-sighted, and they make the worst coloured 'large nation' in Asia.[9]

The relative economic success of the Chinese was thus attributed to their thrift and hard work, whilst Malay poverty was a result of their laziness and refusal to take advantage of economic opportunities under colonial rule.

The evolution of colonial Singapore's Furnivallian pluralism into what we now call multiracialism began with Chief Minister David Marshall's attempted political settlement of what he described as the Chinese education 'situation' in 1956.[10] As Singapore's first Chief Minister, Marshall was trying to construct an inclusive society built on Singapore citizenship, multilingualism and mutual respect between communities.[11] Faced with an alliance of Chinese-educated school students and trade unionists in which concern for the future of Chinese education and culture was being channelled into insurrectionary violence, Marshall set out to neutralise what he viewed as legitimate concern about the future of Chinese education in the hope that this would facilitate rational discourse by segregating highly sensitive issues from each other. He established the All-Party Committee on Chinese Education to investigate the issues. The Committee's solution was the creation of a quad-lingual educational system, whereby each of the main languages of Singapore – English, Mandarin, Malay and Tamil – would be treated equally in the education system, and parents could choose any of these options for their children. The intention of this move was to dissipate communal tensions and facilitate nation building, and it seems from the reaction of the Chinese and Tamil press that the moves were welcomed on both counts in those quarters, though the Malay press was much slower to accept the good intentions of the government.[12] This move provided the long-term basis for reinforcing and perpetuating the sense of communal separateness that had been long established, but another recommendation balanced this impulse somewhat by taking Singapore a step down the path of assimilation. The Committee recommended the revision of all textbooks used in all language streams to ensure their content encouraged a locally focused Malayan consciousness (as opposed to consciousness of a distant 'homeland').[13] The Malay language (Bahasa Melayu) was also encouraged for use as Singapore's *lingua franca*. The initiatives of the All-Party Committee did not end the violence or re-solve the Chinese school 'situation', but together with Marshall's successful advocacy of multilingualism in general, it did place Singapore on the path that we now recognise as 'multiracialism', complete with its ongoing tensions between communal separateness and assimilation.

Civic Nationalism under the PAP

When the PAP assumed power in late-colonial Singapore in 1959 it continued to pursue a policy of tolerant assimilation but, in an effort to seduce Malaya into forming an economic and political union with Singapore, Malay culture and language were given fresh emphasis. This Malaya-centrism seemed to bear fruit when Singapore and Malaya (with Sarawak and Sabah) joined to become Malaysia in 1963, but it came to an abrupt end with the acrimonious separation of Singapore from Malaysia in August 1965.

After the separation from Malaysia, the Singapore government had no use for a Malaya-centred assimilation, but had little confidence that a merely Singapore-centred focus could subdue ethnic pride and separatism (or even worse, a primordial loyalty to the ethnic 'homelands': China, India and Indonesia/Malaysia). In a supreme effort of nation building, assimilation-ism after 1965 became overt and forceful, but it was not Chinese-dominated in any but a demographic and political sense. In fact in the drive to build a 'modern' society, the Chinese communities of this period were allowed very little public space in which to express and effect their cultural and educational aspirations.

The programme of assimilation in these first decades of PAP rule was not being driven by Lee Kuan Yew in particular but was the result of the collective decision making of a Cabinet comprised of men who regarded Lee as merely a first among equals. They had diverse views about Singapore's future and on the nature of multiracialism, ranging from the sentimental devotion to the idea of Malaysia held by Toh Chin Chye and S. Rajaratnam, to the well-disguised Chinese suprematism of Lee Kuan Yew.[14] The resultant compromises focused on a vision of a highly rational, implicitly contractual multiracialism, whereby stability was assured by guaranteeing respect for the mores of the ethnic communities, but only within the limits imposed by the government's modern, capitalist nation-building programme. Allegiance to the putative Singaporean nation became the overriding motif of political and social discourse to the point that it overrode not only the Malay-centrism of the pre-unification period but mitigated against any tendency to overtly ethnicise the nation-building effort. At this stage the symbolism of the official nation-building project was racially inclusive and Singapore's success was routinely attributed to the 'industry of the various races' – to use Minister Ong Pang Boon's words of 1969.[15]

Until the late 1970s a major element of the government's nation work was devoted to suppressing racial prejudices and downplaying cultural expressions of race and ethnicity in favour of building a nearly race-blind nation, with then-Prime Minister Lee Kuan Yew as perhaps the most enthusiastic advocate of the civic-nationalist model in public. This work was premised substantially on what the PAP's first generation of leaders (leaving aside the Chinese-educated) knew of their own class of English-educated Asians (including Indians, Eurasians and Malays). Such people had grown up generally regarding themselves as 'Malayans' (reflecting their loyalty to British Malaya) in substantial disregard for their race,[16] and Lee's inner group in the PAP was drawn almost exclusively from this class. It seems undeniable that from the earliest days of Lee's adult life his social cognition must have been viewed through prisms of race and ethnic culture, but until the late 1970s he nearly successfully expelled such notions from public discourse and from his own rhetoric.[17] The rare occasions on which he breached his own embargo were overlooked by a compliant media, the best documented instance being his 1967 speech to students at the University of Singapore when he told the parable of the three women admitted to Singapore General Hospital, recounted in the 'Elitism and Ethnicity' section of Chapter 1. This situation was not without its tensions and blemishes, but it is nevertheless remembered with nostalgia by members of the minority races as a little golden age of tolerance and respect. In this period it was the Chinese-educated who most routinely suffered at the hands of the government, as it set out to quash what it derisively called 'Chinese chauvinism'.

Towards Ethno-Nationalism under the PAP

The situation for minorities started to deteriorate towards the end of the 1970s, when signs of a shift away from civic- and towards ethnic-centredness began to emerge.[18] It was not known to the public at the time, but as early as 1978 Lee Kuan Yew had begun referring to Singapore as a 'Confucian society' in his dealings with foreign dignitaries.[19] This proved to be the beginning of a shift from communally neutral assimilation towards a society dominated by overt manifestations of 'Chineseness'; a shift that coincided with the systematic retirement of all the 'Old Guard' leaders, except for Lee himself. This generational change produced a Cabinet that was, for the first time, utterly dominated by Lee. Until then, Cabinet had acted as a genuine collective leadership with the entire 'Old Guard' serving as co-rulers in the full sense of that expression. It was not the case that the men who replaced the 'Old Guard' leaders in the late 1970s and early 1980s were necessarily lacking in talent or courage, but such was Lee's personal power as the last remaining member of the 'Old Guard' and as Singapore's 'founding father' that it was only in the face of extreme policy failures that they could even tinker at the edges of policies initiated by the prime minister.[20] Lee treated his new-found power as an opportunity to indulge his private prejudices and whims, the most notable of which was his beliefs about the superiority of 'Chinese culture', 'Chinese values' and Chinese people.[21]

The early outward signs of the consequent Sinicisation programme were the privileging of Chinese education, Chinese language and selectively chosen 'Chinese values' in an overt and successful effort to create a Mandarin-and-English-speaking elite that would dominate public life. Two of the most important planks of this campaign were launched in 1979: the decision to promote an annual 'Speak Mandarin Campaign' (which comes with a myriad of associated mechanisms of promotion that each year overwhelms the island with a celebration of Chineseness) and the decision to preserve and foster a collection of elite Chinese-medium schools (Special Assistance Plan or SAP schools).[22]

In this book we concern ourselves particularly with the SAP schools, which, according to Raj Vasil were explicitly designed 'to have an essentially Chinese ambience, in both linguistic and cultural terms',[23] right down to Chinese gardens, windows shaped like plum blossoms, Chinese orchestra and drama, and exchange programmes with the PRC and Taiwan (*ST*, 14 October 1995). The children in SAP schools were given multiple advantages over those in ordinary schools: a pre-primary-cum-preparatory year programme before Primary 1 and special consideration for Pre-University scholarships.[24] At this time there was a serious shortage of graduate English teachers in schools, but MOE ensured there were enough allocated to SAP schools 'to help improve standards of English among the Chinese-medium students, in the hope that they will be able to make it to university' (*ST*, 14 March 1982) – a target brought closer by the granting in 1981 of two O-level bonus points exclusively to SAP school students when they applied to enter junior college (*ST*, 7 February 1983).[25]

By contrast, neither Indians nor Malays received any special help or schools of their own to address their special needs. They were not only left to fend for themselves, but were sometimes subjected to wanton neglect. On 18 March 1982, *The Straits Times* carried a report of a debate in Parliament the previous day when a PAP backbencher, Mr Lawrence Sia, alluded to the fact that some Indian students had not been even allocated a classroom, desks or chairs for their Tamil lessons (*ST*, 18 March 1982). Tellingly, the response of Minister of State (Education) Dr Tay Eng Soon did not include an acknowledgement that this was a problem nor a commitment to fix it. Yet in the same parliamentary debate, Parliamentary Secretary for Education Ho Kah Leong congratulated the SAP schools on their outstanding O-level results, mentioning incidentally that they were not only given the 'best teachers' but also 'annual grants and interest-free loans' to enable them to upgrade their facilities, which, it later emerged, took the form of 'good libraries, modern language labs and more experienced graduate teachers' (*ST*, 18 March 1982 and 15 August 1983). No one – either in Parliament or in the media – drew attention to the juxtaposition of the treatment of the two communities.

We have no record of whether the Indian children were eventually given desks and chairs, but we do know that the privileging of SAP school children continued to escalate. In 1985 MOE revealed that at secondary school level, SAP schools had a 22.8 per cent advantage over ordinary schools in their student-teacher ratio and that per capita government funding of SAP secondary students was 56.45 per cent higher than that of other secondary school students (*ST*, 16 May 1985). Some SAP schools benefited not only from privileges based on being in the SAP system, but also by being part of the Gifted Education Programme. The GEP was introduced in 1983 to give the best 0.25 per cent of students (later to be expanded to 0.5 per cent and eventually 1 per cent – approximately 500 students per cohort in the 2000s) in designated schools an enriched and stimulating learning environment, specially trained Gifted Education teachers, even lower student–teacher ratios and an extended curriculum (*ST*, 17 September 1983). As of 1994 each GEP student was attracting a government subsidy – over and above ordinary funding levels – of $4,300 per annum for primary students and $6,100 per annum for secondary students (*ST*, 6 November 1994). When GEP was first introduced it operated in only one primary SAP school (Nanyang Girls' Primary) and no SAP secondary schools (*ST*, 25 November 1988), but even at that stage it was, according to Education Minister Lee Yock Suan, already taking in a disproportionate number of Chinese students (*ST*, 6 November 1994). Far from taking efforts to correct this imbalance, in 1998 two more SAP schools (Tao Nan Primary and Dunman High) were added to the GEP programme (*ST*, 8 April 1995). As of 2005, four of the nine GEP primary schools and two of the six GEP secondary schools were also SAP schools, while a third secondary school, Hwa Chong Institution, was a de facto part of the SAP system.[26] Given these institutional advantages it would have be an indictment on the Chinese community if they did not come to overshadow the other communities in educational outcomes.

Parallel with these changes, the broader nation-building project gradually became considerably less inclusive. Instead of ministers attributing Singapore's success to the 'industry of the various races', then-Prime Minister Lee Kuan Yew began attributing it to the presence of Chinese values within society; values such as 'a desire to be educated, to acquire knowledge, to be useful'.[27] On the other hand, other aspects of the local Chinese culture that Lee considered contrary to the state's nation-building project – speaking Chinese 'dialects', Chinese business networking, clan associations, affection for the 'homeland', etc. – were discouraged or ground into subservience to the state.[28] Much of this agenda was concerned with bringing Chinese education into the mainstream nation-building project – hence the government's hostility and mistrust of independent Chinese schools and the Chinese-medium Nanyang University, which was eventually absorbed into the National University of Singapore in 1980.

Many aspects of the programme of Sinicisation during the 1980s – expressed in part as a campaign to teach and promote Confucianism – were aimed explicitly at making Singapore's Chinese community more self-consciously 'Chinese'[29] but, granted the ubiquitous nature of these measures and Lee's faith in his ability to mould and 'improve' cultures,[30] it was natural that the minority races would feel pressured, and almost inevitable that they would be targeted in some fashion. Seminal signs of a secondary agenda promoting 'Chinese virtues' to the minority races came early in the 1980s when stories promoting the commercial and social advantages of 'Confucianism' began appearing in the English-language press and on television (*ST*, 14 October 1980, 24 July 1982, 19 August 1982). In 1982 Chinese-American professors of Chinese Studies were brought into the country to announce that Confucianism is suitable for non-Chinese and for followers of 'other religions': 'Confucianism can be practiced by all, regardless of their colour or creed. It may have natural appeal to the Chinese, but it is meant to be universal as it just teaches a person how to be a human, how to live' (*ST*, 5 September 1982). Confucianism is at work in Singapore's anti-littering drive, they said (*ST*, 5 September 1982). The secretary of the Hindu Centre gave the assurance that Hindus can take classes in Confucian Ethics with a clear conscience (*ST*, 20 November 1988). Chinese values – or at least the government's narrow, sectarian version of Chinese values – were promoted to the whole population through the thin disguise of the 'Asian values' rhetoric and enshrined in the national ideology through the *White Paper on Shared Values* in 1988. In the same year Singaporeans witnessed the spectacle of an Indian Minister, S. Jayakumar, recommending the explicitly Confucian virtue of filial piety (*ST*, 20 November 1988).

Practical manifestations of the all-pervasive promotion of 'Chinese virtues' could be found across housing policy with the promotion of three-generation families modelled on the Chinese patriarchal extended family (*ST*, 24 January and 8 February 1982; and *Sunday Times*, 23 May 1982) and the introduction of ethnic quotas that ensured that all housing blocks have an overwhelming Chinese majority.[31] It impinged upon social policy (with the institutionalisation of a crude monetary version of filial piety, whereby aged parents can lay claim to money in their adult children's Central Provident Fund accounts), and education policy and civil service management (with the intensification of the examination and scholarship system; a thinly disguised version of the Confucian examination and scholar system). In 1990 Lee Kuan Yew actually criticised an opposition politician of Indian extraction for being 'unChinese' and contrasted his performance with that of opposition politicians of Chinese extraction, who were 'at least on the same side of the river' as himself.[32] In May 1991 Lee declared his satisfaction that the physical interspersion of the Malays throughout Chinese-dominated housing estates had 'helped increase competitiveness in the Malay community by example and interaction' (*Straits Times Interactive*, 4 March 2001). As the quotation at the opening of this chapter shows, by 1992 Lee was comfortable arguing publicly that not only was Chinese culture good for the development of Singapore, it also had a positive influence on the other races. Lee's sense of achievement in having influenced the non-Chinese to behave more like 'the Chinese' reveals less about the reality of Singaporean society than it does about the motivation and mind-set of Singapore's ruling elite. The Malays and Indians had not started speaking Mandarin or become Daoists, but clearly in Lee's mind they had begun to adopt social mores and habits that he identified as 'Chinese'. It was not a chance choice of words that Lee Kuan Yew once described a Malay who was doing well in business as 'acting just like a Chinese. You know, he's bouncing, running around, to-ing and fro-ing'.[33]

Lee has listed hard work and thrift among the Chinese virtues, but the essence of this perception of 'Chineseness' is extremely nebulous. The following chapters explore the character of this vision through a study of the praxis of the Singapore education system, but at this point it is sufficient to say that Lee is speaking about a peculiarly Singaporean type of 'Chineseness' that is materialistic, concerned with education as measured by grades and certificates, obsessively concerned with social mobility, worldly success, and above all, is *kiasu*. '*Kiasu*', a Hokkien word meaning 'afraid to fail', has come to refer, in Singapore parlance, to a manic fear of losing out on something or to someone. Being *kiasu* is considered to be a distinctively Singaporean – and particularly a Chinese Singaporean – characteristic and the label is worn with a mixture of pride and embarrassment. On the one hand it is condemned because it generates anti-social and foolish behaviour – pushing to the front of queues, grabbing seats on public transport, or travelling across the island rather than risking to miss out on the latest fad (e.g. a 'Hello Kitty' doll). It is caricatured mercilessly on television shows such as *Kiasu Man*, which is based on a (Chinese) character who takes this obsessive behaviour to humorous extremes. On the other hand, *kiasu* parents are proud of how they spare no expense or effort to push their children to excellence, *kiasu* workers boast about how they leave no stone unturned to meet the deadline, get the sale, impress the boss or win the promotion, and *kiasu* students crow about how they learned all the possible answers to the exam by heart to get the scholarship. A publicly documented instance of *kiasu* behaviour was uncovered by the Ministry of Community Development and Sports in 2004, when it discovered that couples were deferring conception for fear they would miss out on an anticipated new baby bonus, yet to be announced.[34]

Minority Races and Incomplete Assimilation

What place do minority races occupy in a society so overwhelmingly defined through a notion of 'Chineseness'? Given that Singapore is a society that exists through racial silos, it should come as little surprise that minorities are expected to keep a certain sense of separateness expressed by external markers such as diet, dress, religion and language. In fact it is demanded that they retain their 'mother tongues' and throughout Singapore's post-independence history they have, with rare exceptions, been excluded from learning Mandarin in school. Since the 1980s, this has been tantamount to being prevented from assimilating into the dominant cultural norm, since Mandarin has become a major vehicle of communication and its lack is an obstacle to participating in the social and economic life of the country (*ST*, 13 December 1970; *Straits Times Interactive*, 29 June and 7 July 2004).[35] It is in an effort to compensate for this deprivation that there has been a recent trend by non-Chinese adults to learn Mandarin, as is evidenced by the heavy Malay patronage of Mandarin classes offered at mosques (*Berita Harian*, 27 June 2005) and the provision of adult Mandarin classes for Indians and Malays by the Singapore Chinese Chamber of Commerce and the Singapore Federation of Chinese Clan Associations (*ST*, 17 March, 2006).

Yet while minority races are expected to retain various external markers of their ethnic cultures, they must also be prepared to jettison aspects of their culture that conflict with the national agenda. For instance, the proximity of the toilet to the kitchen in HDB flats (a practice inherited from the common design of colonial Chinese shop houses) presents serious difficulties for Hindus trying to follow traditional customs and rituals of purity and cleanliness, but the HDB makes no allowances for such needs, so they must make do.[36] Under this nation-building imperative Singapore has also become possibly the only country in the world where the end of Ramadan is determined by the calendar rather than by imams sighting the new moon – because a thriving capitalist society needs more predictability in its schedule of public holidays than can be given by the vagaries of cloud cover. It should also be noted, however, that the minorities are not alone in making such compromises, since many traditional Chinese practices, such as setting off fireworks at Chinese New Year, have also been curtailed. From 1981 to 1991 the government was even interfering with how Chinese children spelt their own names, insisting that they be recorded using Hanyu Pinyin (the modern system of Romanising Chinese characters) – a process that destroyed the integrity of most 'dialect' names beyond recognition (*ST*, 20 November 1980 and 14 December 1991).

Nor were such impositions a feature only of the period that we identify with 'Sinicisation' and 'incomplete assimilation'. From the earliest days of PAP rule, the nation-building project has always taken precedence over the traditional practices of any ethnic community. The difference now is that having established its ideal vision of a Chinese Singaporean, the government has, since the early 1980s, been using this as the template and the standard of its ideal Singaporean. Thus if members of a minority race want to go further than merely meeting the minimum requirements of acceptance and actually prosper in this society, then they need to internalise 'Chinese virtues' and become 'like the Chinese' in subtle but important ways, even as they are excluded from full participation in this ethno-national project in vital ways. This is what we mean by the term, 'incomplete assimilation' – a balancing act between the imperative that minority members need to strive to act 'like Chinese' in order to succeed and the insistence that at the end of this process they will continue to be relegated to a minority status. 'Incomplete assimilation' is a programme whose goal is perpetually suspended between these seemingly contradictory impulses.

It is difficult to compare this program of assimilation with the ones known historically in countries with high immigration intakes. In such societies complete assimilation is often promoted openly, but with inbuilt mechanisms that allow the process to be accomplished over several generations. The first generation is typically expected to adopt many overt and public mores of the dominant majority (particularly language) but thoroughgoing assimilation is achieved only in the second or third generation as education, intermarriage and social mobility have their natural effects. Of course, this assumes that assimilation has a point of completion, which is a problematic supposition given that vestiges and symbols of ethnic identity and culture continue to linger around for generations, but we use it to make a point.[37] Singapore is of course a different case altogether, but it is worthwhile considering what a Singaporean programme of complete assimilation might look like, simply so that we can demonstrate more clearly what we mean by 'incomplete assimila-tion'. A Singaporean programme of complete assimilation would certainly involve learning the language(s) of the majority (English and Mandarin in Singapore), probably accepting the dress standards of the dominant majority (ironically in Singapore this would be Western dress), and would very likely involve relegating religious and dietary requirements strictly to the private sphere, if not compromising them seriously.

Under a programme of incomplete assimilation minorities would be expected to retain much of their cultural distinctiveness, and would in fact be actively excluded from fully assimilating in critical ways that would be advan-tageous, but would nevertheless be expected to mimic generic aspects of the dominant group from the margins of society. Their cultural distinctiveness would then become a basis of separation from the mainstream, reducing their chances of worldly success and their opportunities to influence society. In the case of Singapore the most overt form of exclusion is in restricting the oppor-tunities for non-Chinese to learn Mandarin while simultaneously promoting it as a mainstream *lingua franca*, but others that are explored in later chapters of this book include systemic exclusion from the best educational and career opportunities. Less significant and less systemic forms of exclusion also oper-ate at more informal levels of society. For instance Western dress is the norm and even though wearing traditional dress is generally accepted among the Indians and Malays, it can inhibit employment and professional advancement (as we shall see later in this chapter). There is notional consideration for the religious and dietary requirements of the minorities, but this is honoured more often in the breach, commonly leaving Muslims (in particular) sitting at work-related luncheons and dinners pretending to eat. The inclusive aspects of Singapore's programme of incomplete assimilation are in the imposition of those nebulous 'Chinese values' on which Lee Kuan Yew is so keen. The essential elements of the inclusionary parts of Singapore's programme of 'incomplete assimilation' are a good education and a *kiasu* approach to work, study and life.

The acquisition of these attributes is generally sufficient to facilitate a modest level of social mobility and a moderately fruitful career, but it seems that even this is insufficient for those with aspirations to high office. It is striking how many prominent non-Chinese figures have been learning Mandarin. President S.R. Nathan is one case in point. According to his Mandarin teacher, he has been learning Mandarin 'to better communicate with his Chinese countrymen' (*CNA*, 16 August 2005). Another prominent example is Finance Minister Tharman Shanmugaratnam, who is learning Chinese calligraphy and has learnt to give karaoke performances in Mandarin. He demonstrated his Mandarin karaoke skills on 9 April 2005 at an 'Appreciation Nite' organised by the Jurong Community Consultative Committee (in his constituency).[38] In fact Tharman Shanmugaratnam has gone one step further than just learning Chinese himself. Clearly wanting the best for his children, he has ensured that they are part of that tiny number of non-Chinese children who can attend a SAP school and study Mandarin as their 'mother tongue' (*Lianhe Wanbao*, 8 June 2004).

These indicators, and others that are documented elsewhere in this book, suggest that, even as we write, the 'incompleteness' of Singapore's programme of assimilation may be diminishing, leaving it looking more and more like a fuller, more aggressive form of assimilation such as that described in Chapter 1 as operating in Thailand. We are also reminded of the words of the Secretary General of the Lao People's Revolutionary Party in 1981, when he explained at length that the Lao must be the dominant ethnic group in revolutionary Laos because not only are they the largest group but also they have the highest level of cultural development.[39] Yet there still remains a critical difference between the Singapore version of assimilation and that practiced in either Thailand or Laos. Whereas in Thailand and Laos the language of the dominant group has been imposed upon the minorities, in Singapore the minorities face severe restrictions in learning one of the two main languages of the majority. The barriers to learning Mandarin at school are undiminished for the vast majority of ordinary Malays and Indians and continue to operate as a device of exclusion from the mainstream of society.

Sinicisation and Multiracialism

Lee Kuan Yew was the prime generator of this programme of Sinicisation and assimilation, but the reason for the eruption of his love for all things Chinese in the late 1970s remains something of a mystery. Barr has argued elsewhere that the *volte face* finds its origins in his exploration of his own 'Chineseness' over the previous decade or more, and his concomitant repulsion at aspects of the bourgeois society that he had created, attributing them to Western-inspired decadence.[40] There can also be no doubt that the prospective opening up of China to investment and trade with the rise of Deng Xiaoping was a contributing factor in accelerating the programme of Sinicisation once it had started. The full story is undoubtedly more complicated than these accounts suggest but, regardless of the reasons, at the beginning of the 1980s the state began sponsoring an ethnocentric concept of nation in which the Chinese were expected to share, and which the minorities were expected to mimic. This primordial and ethnic streak in nation building encroached on the space of multiracialism, but did not evict it. The two continue to live together, with multiracialism jammed uncomfortably into a spare room while Chinese ethno-nationalism unthinkingly dominates the main living area. Significantly, however, ethno-nationalism seems to be unaware of the discomfort it is causing for its silent, defensive housemate. Depending upon the context, government leaders are just as comfortable upholding the supreme place of Chinese culture and virtues[41] as they are in insisting on the importance of multiracialism to social harmony (*CNA*, 6 November 2000) because the basis of promoting each is completely different. Multiracialism equals peace. Chinese values equal prosperity. This bifurcated thinking is the fundamental dynamic in the new multiracialism.

The obverse side of Sinicisation was the renewed emphasis on racial identifiers. Students in primary schools had been expected to learn English and a racially determined 'mother tongue' since 1968, but the 'mother tongue' was not taken very seriously until 1973, when the second language was given double weighting at the Primary School Leaving Examination (PSLE). The emphasis increased again at the end of the 1970s, when success in the 'mother tongue' was made a major factor in secondary school streaming and a pre-requisite for entry into junior college and university (*ST*, 17 January 1980). Cross-racial learning of languages was discouraged by the government,[42] leading to the entirely predictable result that today racial consciousness is routinely heightened by the school experience.[43] Ethnic identifiers are by their nature a form of stereotyping, and strong ethnic identification is a form of self-stereotyping that is reinforced by clear delineation from 'the Other', so it was probably inevitable that this new emphasis on ethnic identification generated a resurgence of racial stereotyping. In Singapore this phenomenon has affected the image (including the self-image) of all the minority races adversely, but it is the Malays who have borne the brunt. The popular image of the Malays in Singapore as rural and backward has fed the commonly held stereotype that Malays are lazy, and at home only in kampongs, amongst the fruit trees.[44] In a more contemporary context, this equates to lazing around the void decks of public housing estates, strumming guitars and smoking cannabis all day long. These prejudices have been regurgitated by members of the PAP government, such as when Minister George Yeo claimed that Malays remained marginalised due to the effects of their relocation from a rural to an urban setting. This is despite the lack of evidence that Malays are more accustomed to rural settings than other races.[45]

The ascension of Goh Chok Tong to the premiership at the end of 1990 made very little impact on the evolution of the government's policies of multiracialism and assimilation. His distinctive contribution to the development of Singaporean multiracialism is the concept of 'common ground' or 'common space', whereby it is proposed that Singapore develop and continually expand an overlapping area of common ground between the ethnic groups, whereby they increase their elements of interaction, co-operation and sense of national identity. Eugene Tan has identified this phase with a 1999 speech by PM Goh:

> Each circle represents one community. The four circles overlap each other … What we can do is to maximise the overlapping area. This is where all Singaporeans, whatever their race, work and play together. It is an open level playing field with English as the common language, and equal opportunities for all.[46]

Goh's approach represented only a slight shift of the version of multiracialism left by his predecessor but it was notable for its attempt to deflate the emphasis that Lee Kuan Yew had placed on essentialist visions of racial and communal cultural bonds. A practical result of this shift was his open encouragement of race-based educational and social self-help groups to reach beyond their own communities; a move that slightly weakened the ethnic silos bequeathed by Lee, and went some way towards transforming social services and educational self-help into new areas of 'common space'.[47]

Assimilation as Multiracialism

With Goh's retirement from the premiership, it is unlikely that his modest reforms will have any long-term effect. Far from the assimilationist pressure on the Malays easing, there are clear signs that it is intensifying as a reaction to the rise of militant Islam as a threat in the region. A major indicator of this shift emerged in dialogue between Lee Kuan Yew and union leaders in 2003. *The Straits Times Interactive* of 25 July 2003 reported:

> [Lee] noted that Malay women who put on the Muslim *tudung*, the headscarf [as in adjacent image], were finding it especially hard to find jobs. He said: 'They complain that when the employer asks them: "Do you wear a *tudung*?", when they say "yes", the employer says: "I'm looking for a Chinese".'

Figure 5.1: Tudungs, Singapore style.

> While conceding the issue was indeed 'a problem', he also said it was a real-
> ity of living in a multiracial society.
>
> [...] The long-term answer to help unemployed Malays to get jobs is
> though better education, especially for women.

Note the dismissive denial in Lee's response. Malay women were facing open discrimination based on the clothes they wear, and Lee told them that their problem was a lack of education. In the face of discrimination in employment against minority Malays by majority Chinese, he said this was 'a reality of living in a multicultural society' and that the Malays would have to live with it. He exhibited no inclination to engage in one of his famous social engineering efforts to ameliorate these discriminatory practices. Coming from the mouth of Lee Kuan Yew, this was tantamount to a government endorsement of discrimination against *tudung*-wearing women in matters of employment. This passage is extremely significant because it indicates that the programme of incomplete assimilation referred to earlier can and does extend beyond encouraging the minority races to mimic 'Chinese values', and includes neutralising aspects of external cultural markers that are seen to be negative or dangerous – and since September 2001, the *tudung* has been seen as dangerous.

From the perspective of the Chinese employers, this is a simple case of conformity to a (Chinese) standard, but for the victim it is much more complex. It translates into a demoralising cycle which has been described poignantly by one of the victims of this form of discrimination in *The Straits Times*, 29 September 2002:

> Miss Siti Shafrida Sulaiman, 21, an electronics engineering graduate from
> Nanyang Polytechnic, said she was asked to remove her headscarf by more
> than 10 potential employers who interviewed her. They said that they wanted
> work attire to be standardised. 'It's demoralising because the *tudung* has noth-
> ing to do with work performance or my ability.'[48]

Since removing the *tudung* at work is a physical and practical option (unlike changing one's race or sex) such women find themselves under pressure to conform to this imposition: to jettison this aspect of their cultural identity in order to move ahead (or even just to work) in this society.

This relatively sophisticated mode of discrimination operates over and above baser modes of Chinese-generated discrimination based on race, often using the predominance of Mandarin in the community as an excuse. In 1999 then-Deputy Prime Minister Lee Hsien Loong acknowledged the presence of such discriminatory practices, but dismissed them as 'something that will work itself out over time', requiring no particular action by the government (*Business Times*, 1 February 1999). He was vague about how much time was needed for this to 'work itself out', but certainly six years later the problem was still destroying livelihoods and sowing bitterness. This became obvious in 2005 when Channel NewsAsia aired its *Up Close* series on rising stars in the government, during which it displayed viewers' text messages as screen crawlers. In doing so it unintentionally unleashed an avalanche of anger and frustration from non-Chinese viewers about the discrimination they faced in Singapore, and in particular the difficulties they face in the workforce because of racial discrimination by Chinese employers. Nine text messages on this subject were directed at Minister for Manpower Ng Eng Hen, and a record 17 at Prime Minister Lee Hsien Loong.[49] A sample of these text messages is reproduced below:

1.　　i m a 18 yr old malay gal who has v gd result but end up wkg on a job tat pays $4/h while my fren which did not do well is nt gd in talking got a job tat pay $1000/per month cos she's Chinese.

2.　　y r there many job ads alwys asking 4chinese speaking applicants Stop this practice. Other races r capable of doin the job as well ...

3.　　all employer I have call they first ask can u speak mandarin or r u chinese when I say i'm not Chinese they say sorry we want chinese. why

4.　　open the classified ads any day, 70% of them require chinese speakers for no apparent reason

5.　　Wats e diff between malay n Chinese in e working industry Why require mandarin speaking only

6.　　I want Singapore to be an english speaking country. But why are most employers still employing mandarin speaking employees not giving a chance to oth[50]

Anonymous text messages need to be treated with considerable caution as a guide to public sentiment and social reality, but these messages resonated so strongly with the talk in the coffee shops and letters to the newspapers (e.g. *Straits Times Interactive*, 26 October 2005) that three months later Lim Boon

Heng, trade union leader and Special Minister of State in the Prime Minister's Office, condemned racist employers in terms almost identical to that used in the *Up Close* screen crawlers: employers asking for Mandarin speakers for no good reason, and if a non-Chinese happens to be able to speak Mandarin, say they need someone who can write it (*CNA*, 8 August 2005). Soon after that Prime Minister Lee himself condemned such discriminatory practices, a move that opens a small point of differentiation with his father (*ST* and *CNA*, 15 November 2005; *CyBerita, Tamil Murasu, Lianhe Zaobao*, 16 November 2005). Since Lee's statement Deputy Prime Minister Wong Kan Seng has reinforced the message in a speech to the Singapore Federation of Chinese Clan Associations, describing the practice as 'building a time-bomb of disaffection among a group pushed to the margin by a lack of employment opportunities' (*CNA*, 9 December 2005). These calls from the political leadership drew forth public admissions from leading Chinese associations that this form of discrimination was commonplace, together with public calls for Chinese employers to end such practices (*CNA*, 7 March, 2006). The character of this form of discrimination underlines the particularly insidious nature of what we have called 'incomplete assimilation': make Mandarin a vital commercial and social language but exclude segments of the population from learning it, forcing them into economic ghettos generated by their commercially useless 'mother tongues'. The worst effects of incomplete assimilation are thankfully ameliorated by the place of English as an even more vital commercial and social language than Mandarin and may be dampened still further if Chinese employers respond to the recent calls to end discrimination, but even with these caveats the 'mother tongue' and other race-based educational policies will ensure that the marginalisation of the minorities will continue into the foreseeable future.

Chinese Singaporeans are generally unconscious of the operation of these forms of discrimination and the sense of marginalisation they create, but members of minority races – Malays, Indians and Eurasians – have consistently confirmed in interview that members of the minority races are highly conscious, not only of the discrimination, but of the pressure to conform. Some Malay parents encourage their children to mix with Chinese children explicitly so they will pick up their habits. Muslim women abandon traditional garb at work because they believe it will remove an obstacle to acceptance and promotion.

How much accommodation do the Malays have to make to be accepted into the mainstream of society? One might have thought that employment in private enterprise is a place where Goh Chok Tong's 'level playing field' should operate with the least compromise. Or do Malays have to jettison public manifestations of their culture and religion before they are allowed into the 'common space'?

The only way to understand Lee's statement on the *tudung* at work as anything other than cynical duplicity is to accept that contemporary multiracialism in Singapore is at heart a Chinese construction and that the minority communities are not being asked to accommodate themselves to an ethnically neutral hegemony, but a Chinese-generated and Chinese-dominated hegemony. This phenomenon has certainly been intensified in recent times in reaction to anti-Muslim stereotypes generated by September 11 and the emergence of Jemaah Islamiyah,[51] but the Chinese-centric assimilationist impulse pre-dates these developments by two decades. At one level this is to be expected. Minority groups usually accommodate themselves to dominant majorities, and often suffer discrimination as a consequence of living in an ethnic niche rather than in the mainstream. The problem for the Malays, however, is that the dominant majority refuse to admit that it is dominant, or that the Malays' economic and social marginalisation is caused at least partly by discrimination. The Chinese communities, with 77 per cent of the population, dominate the country economically, politically and socially, but they are treated as just one of the country's ethnic groups – 'multiculturalism in neutral', to use the expression we coined in Chapter 3. This practice has its origins in the 1956 All-Party Committee on Chinese Education when it was used as a device for quelling ethnic tension by promising to treat the four main languages of Singapore equally. The elevation of the English language to a place of communally neutral supremacy after independence reinforced the 'ethnic' status of the Chinese communities by making Mandarin just another ethnic language. The perpetuation of the fiction that the Chinese are not the dominant ethnic group allows the Chinese community (or, to be more precise, those dominant elements within it that are linked to the national elite) to meet challenges to its dominance of public life from the high ground of neutral umpire.[52]

Yet despite the blind spot that enables the government to base its policy and actions on the fantasy that the playing field in the 'common space' is neutral, in another part of the regime's collective mind there is a frank ac-knowledgement that the hegemonic culture is Chinese-generated. On occa-sions the minority races have even been asked to welcome the privileging and promotion of Chinese hegemony because, in the words of Lee Kuan Yew in 2001, it helps 'increase competitiveness' in the other communities 'by exam-ple and integration' (*ST*, 4 March 2001).

Conclusion

This chapter sets the broad parameters of one of the central arguments of this book – that since the early 1980s the Singapore principle of multiracialism has not been applied as a tool to protect minority races, as it had been in the 1960s and 1970s, but as an instrument of ethnic assimilation into a peculiarly Singaporean Chinese-dominated society. Much of the remainder of this book is devoted to providing detailed evidence of how this *volte face* has operated in and through the education system and broader processes of elite forma-tion and elite selection. In so doing, we shall also seek to demonstrate how the noble principles of meritocracy have been subverted into becoming yet another tool of assimilation.

Notes

1   Michael D. Barr, *Lee Kuan Yew: The Beliefs Behind the Man*, Richmond, UK: Curzon, 2000, p. 161.

2   See Lily Zubaidah Rahim, *The Singapore Dilemma: The Political and Educational Marginality of the Malay Community*, Kuala Lumpur: Oxford University Press, 1998; and R. Quinn Moore, 'Multiracialism and Meritocracy: Singapore's Approach to Race and Inequality' *Review of Social Economy* 58:3, 2000, pp. 339–360.

3   *Up Close with Lee Hsien Loong*, aired on Channel NewsAsia, 5 May 2005.

4   See, for instance, tables of statistics in Sukmawati bte Haji Sirat, 'Trends in Malay political leadership: the People's Action Party's Malay political leaders and the integration of the Singapore Malays', PhD thesis, Department of Government and International Studies, University of South Carolina, 1995, and in Rahim, *The Singapore Dilemma*.

5   Also see Eugene Tan, '"We, the citizens of Singapore…": multiethnicity, its evolution and its aberrations' in Lai Ah Eng (ed.), *Beyond Rituals and Riots: Ethnic Pluralism and Social Cohesion in Singapore*, Singapore: Eastern Universities Press by Marshall Cavendish for the Institute of Policy Studies, 2004; Raj Vasil, *Asianising Singapore: The PAP's Management of Ethnicity*, Singapore: Heinemann Asia, 1995; Barr, *Lee Kuan Yew*, pp. 137–185.

6   J.S. Furnivall, *Colonial Policy and Practice: A Comparative Study of Burma and Netherlands India*, Cambridge: Cambridge University Press, 1948, p. 123.

7   The main exception to this rule, apart from the market place, was in English-medium schools. But this was not so much an exercise in inter-communal interaction, as assimilation of individual 'Asiatics' into the dominant, British-generated culture. Lee Kuan Yew proved to be a prime example of this phenomenon.

8   Rahim, *The Singapore Dilemma*, p. 49.

9   Andrew W. Lind, *Nanyang Perspectives: Chinese Students in Multiracial Singapore*, Honolulu, University Press of Hawaii, 1974, pp. 192, 207. The survey was conducted four months after the May 13 racial riots in Kuala Lumpur.

10 John Drysdale, *Singapore: Struggle for Success*, Singapore; Kuala Lumpur: Times Editions, 1984, p. 116.

11 See Marshall's speeches during his term of office, held in The David Marshall Papers in the Institute of Southeast Asian Studies, Singapore, e.g. his 1955 speeches at the openning of a new building for Chong Hock Girls' School and Ai Tong School by the Singapore Hokkien community and Raffles Institution's Founders' Day, and his speech over Radio Malaya on 1 December 1955 outlining the multilingualism that he was advocating in his constitutional negotiations with the Secretary of State for the Colonies.

12 See, for instance, the editorials in the *Nanfang Evening Post*, 8 February 1956; *Nanyang Siang Pau*, 9 February 1956; *Chung Shing Jit Pao*, 9 February 1956; *Sin Chew Jit Poh*, 11 February 1956; *Tamil Murasu*, 5 February 1956; *Utusan Melayu*, 6 February 1956, all cited in *The Weekly Digest of Non-English Press*, Singapore: Singapore Public Relations, 1956. For more details, see Michael D. Barr and Carl A Trocki (eds), *Index of Political Headlines of Singapore's and Malaya's Vernacular Press: December 1953–September 1961*, Brisbane: Centre for Social Change Research, Queensland University of Technology, 2002, available online at http://www.pathsnottaken.qut.edu.au/.

13 Drysdale, *Singapore: Struggle for Success*, pp. 122, 123.

14 See the account of Lee's speech to university students in 1967 in Chapter 1. Also see Barr, *Lee Kuan Yew*, Chapters 5 and 6.

15 *Sin Chew Jit Poh*, 8 July 1969, cited in *Mirror of Opinion: Highlights of Malay, Chinese & Tamil Press*, Singapore: Ministry of Culture, 1969.

16 For background on this group, see Chua Ai Lin, 'Negotiating national identity: the English-speaking domiciled communities in Singapore, 1930–1941', MA thesis, Department of History, National University of Singapore, 2001.

17 Barr has explored the place of race in Lee's thinking in Barr, *Lee Kuan Yew*, pp. 185–210.

18 As acknowledged in the previous chapters, the notions of civic and ethnic nationalism are highly contested but they nevertheless serve as useful heuristic tools to demonstrate the shift in ideological, policy and factual changes in the history of Singapore nation building project.

19 Lee Kuan Yew, *From Third World to First: The Singapore Story: 1965–2000: Memoirs of Lee Kuan Yew*, Singapore: Singapore Press Holdings and Times Editions, 2000, p. 542.

20 Michael D. Barr, 'Perpetual Revisionism in Singapore: The Limits of Change', *The Pacific Review*, vol. 16, no. 1, 2003, pp. 77–97.

21 A case could be made that the post-1978 escalation of Singapore's programmes of systemic elitism (streaming, elite schools, etc.) was another manifestation of Lee's new-found freedom after the departure of the rest of the 'Old Guard'. We have, however, provisionally rejected that argument, primarily on the grounds that there are such strong lines of continuity in the development of Singapore's programmatic elitism (as detailed in Chapter 4) that it seems unlikely that the rest of the 'Old Guard' was ever seriously opposed to Lee's views on elitism, though it is reasonable to hypothesise that they may not have been as extreme or dogmatic as Lee.

22 Rahim, *The Singapore Dilemma*, pp. 128–131.

23 Vasil, *Asianising Singapore*, p. 73.

24 Lai Ah Eng, *Meanings of Multiethnicity: A Case-study of Ethnicity and Ethnic Relations in Singapore*, Singapore: Oxford University Press, 1995, p. 153, note 13.

25 Similar concessions were eventually introduced for those studying Malay and Tamil, but not until 1989.

26 Ministry of Education website, available at http://www.moe.gov.sg/gifted/GEP_Schools.htm/. Accessed 14 November 2005.

27 Barr, *Lee Kuan Yew*, p. 161.

28 For an exploration of some of these elements, see Sikko Visscher, *The Business of Politics and Ethnicity: A History of the Singapore Chinese Chamber of Commerce and Industry:*, Singapore: National University of Singapore Press, 2007.

29 Chua Beng Huat goes as far as to argue that it *only* targeted the Chinese communities. See Chua Beng Huat, 'Culture, multiracialism, and national identity in Singapore', in Kuan-Hsing Chen *et al* (eds), *Trajectories: Inter-Asia Cultural Studies*, London and New York: Routledge, 1998, p. 191.

30 Barr, *Lee Kuan Yew*, pp. 139–141.

31 It is an unintended consequence of the ethnic quota system in housing that it routinely stops members of minority races from living near their family members, leaving the Chinese as the main beneficiaries of the promotion of extended families.

32 Barr, *Lee Kuan Yew*, p. 158.

33 Lee in Han Fook Kwang, Warren Fernandez and Sumiko Tan, *Lee Kuan Yew: The Man and His Ideas*, Singapore: Singapore Press Holdings and Times Editions, 1998, p. 184.

34 Tan Yew Soon, 'Practising public consultation', *Ethos*, July 2004, p. 16.

35 See Rita Elaine Silver 'The discourse of linguistic capital: language and economic policy planning in Singapore', *Language Policy*, vol. 4, 2005, pp. 47–66.

36 This and other examples of housing-related compromises by both minorities and Chinese are given in Chua Beng Huat, *Political Legitimacy and Housing: Stakeholding in Singapore*, London and New York: Routledge, 1997.

37 A classical exposition of this argument is located in Herbert Gans, 'Symbolic ethnicity: the future of ethnic groups and cultures in America', *Ethnic and Racial Studies*, vol. 2, no. 1, 1979, pp. 1–20; and Herbert Gans, 'Symbolic ethnicity and symbolic religiosity: towards a comparison of ethnic and religious acculturation', *Ethnic and Racial Studies*, vol. 17, no. 4, 1994, pp. 577–592.

38 *Up Close with Tharman Shanmugaratnam*, aired on Channel NewsAsia, 14 April, 2005.

39 Grant Evans, 'Laos: minorities', in Colin Mackerras (ed.), *Ethnicity in Asia*, London and New York: RoutledgeCurzon, 2003, pp. 212, 213.

40 Michael D. Barr, *Cultural Politics and Asian Values: The Tepid War*, London and New York: Routledge, 2002, pp. 33–39.

41 Barr, *Lee Kuan Yew*, pp. 185, 186.

42 Chua, 'Culture, multiracialism, and national identity in Singapore', p. 190.

43 Lana Khong, Joy Chew and Jonathan Goh, 'How now NE? An exploratory study of ethnic relations in three Singapore schools' in Lai, *Beyond Rituals and Riots*, p 186.

44 Tania Li, *Malays in Singapore: Culture, Economy, and Ideology*, Singapore: Oxford University Press, 1989, pp. 166, 167.

45 Rahim, *The Singapore Dilemma*, p. 54.

46 Tan, '"We, the citizens of Singapore …"', p. 73.

47 Michael D. Barr, 'Perpetual revisionism in Singapore: the limits of change', *The Pacific Review*, vol. 16, no. 1, 2003, p. 82.

48 Cited in Kamaludeen bin Mohamed Nasir, 'Disciplining Islam: a Foucauldian analysis of Islam in Singapore', Honours Thesis, Department of Sociology, National University of Singapore, 2004.

49 *Up Close with Ng Eng Hen*, Channel NewsAsia, aired in Singapore 21 April 2005; *Up Close with Lee Hsien Loong*, Channel NewsAsia, aired in Singapore 5 May 2005.

50 Ibid.

51 The government's sensitivity on public expressions of the Muslim faith post-dates 11 September 2001. Until then, even the prospect of Muslim girls wearing the tudung to school did not disturb the government. See Tan, '"We, the citizens of Singapore …"', p. 88.

52 It is not just Malays and other racial minorities that are marginalised by the designation of the Chinese as just another ethnic community. Chinese Singaporeans who fail to conform to the hegemonic paradigm (by not being English-speaking well-educated moderns) are also subordinated. For an interrogation of some of the implications of the ethnicisation of the Chinese communities, see Chua Beng Huat, 'Multiculturalism in Singapore: an instrument of social control', *Race and Class*, vol. 44, no. 3, 2003, pp. 58–77.

SIX

Building the 'New' Singaporean and New Elite

Singaporean children are over-conscientious, the Minister for Education Dr Tony Tan said yesterday.

And Singaporean thinking is such that unless a second language is a pre-requisite for further education, schoolchildren will not put in the necessary effort to learn this second language.

'Rationale for the second language', *The Straits Times*, 7 June 1980

IN THE HISTORY of both nation building and elite formation in Singapore, no institution has had as much impact on the lives and outlook of ordinary Singaporeans as the education system. National Service (NS) (taken broadly to include service in the SAF Reserves) might make a rival claim, but it fails to permeate ordinary life and outlook to the same extent as education – if only because it only indirectly impacts on the female half of the population. In contrast, most generations of Singaporeans living today have passed through the education system of independent Singapore; this has been their primary point of socialisation into Singapore society. The education system, however, has not been a static entity and its impact has not been consistent across generations, classes or ethnic groups. For instance, no adult Singaporean has been socialised into 'the Singapore system' by attending a kindergarten in which examinations, mugging, work sheets, or private tuition had much, if any place. Soon, however, there will be a generation of school leavers for whom this is their reality. The generation that is currently rising to pre-eminence in the military and the civil service is the first to have passed through an education system that bears a strong resemblance to that in place in the mid-2000s. Even so, this generation is still a step or two away from being in positions of full leadership in either of these institutions. In politics the lead time is even longer. There are no candidates for political leadership in the next couple of decades who were educated in anything resembling the current Singapore education system and it will be half a lifetime before any product of National Education steps up to be prime minister. But at some stage they will take their turn, and they will arrive armed with a reality that was formed in the current Singapore education system. Then the country will reap what it has sown, for better or for worse.

With these temporal parameters in mind, we devote chapters 7–10 to a study of the function of the education system in both nation building and elite formation. Before we launch ourselves into this study, however, we wish to set out a brief account of what we believe to be the three central phenomena that have driven the shape of the current education system: the introduction of streaming in 1979; the concomitant emergence of bilingualism as the decisive feature of Singaporean education; and the unashamed privileging of elite education, beginning in the mid-1980s. Not that we regard any of these as being primary drivers. They were all tools in the kit of Lee Kuan Yew and his closest confidants – notably education ministers Goh Keng Swee and Tony Tan – as they set out to build the 'new' Singaporean and the new elite. The remote drivers have been outlined in Chapter 3, but in the rest of this chapter

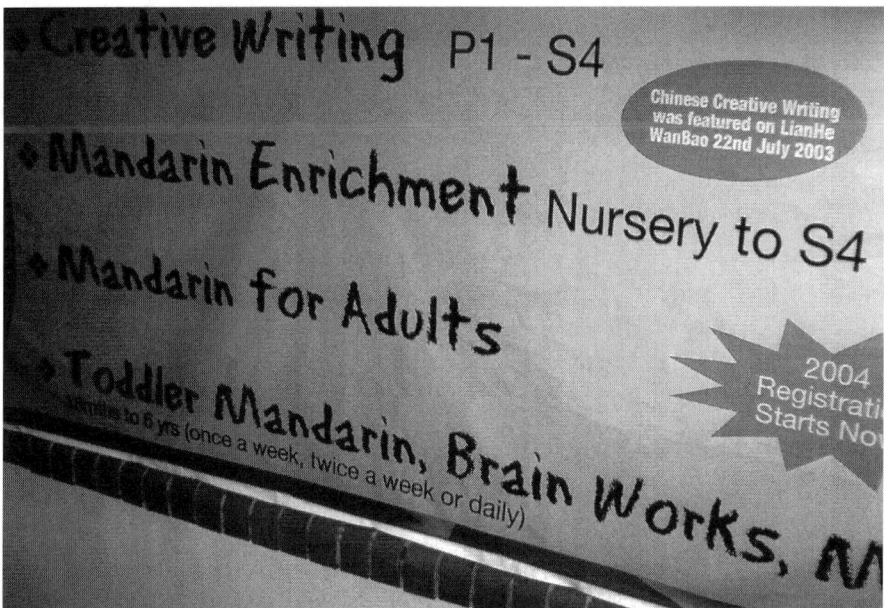

Figure 6.1: Advertising billboard in Singapore, April 2004.

we shall stay with the immediate causes, which are important in their own right, not least because some of their effects appear to have been unintended. The result, towards which this narrative is moving, is the creation of a *kiasu* education system characterised by stratification based on race, grades and wealth; conformist thinking; an obsession with measures of performance; and a culture that regards private tuition as a normal and necessary part of education.

Streaming

School life in Singapore has been affected by many things, but none of them have struck more profoundly than the document known as *The Goh Report*, being the 1979 report by Dr Goh Keng Swee and 'the Education Study Team' on the education system.[1] This report heralded the introduction of the 'New Education System' and is directly though not solely responsible for the creation of the current Singapore school system's pressure-cooker emphasis on grades and examinations. The express purpose of *The Goh Report* was to eliminate 'education wastage' in the Singapore school system, referring specifically to four phenomena: 'failure to achieve the expected standards, premature school leaving, repetition of grades, and unemployable school leavers'.[2] The particular problem that was causing this attrition was the government's language policy, whereby students were expected to learn both English and their 'mother tongue', and its implications were being made painfully obvious by the failure of 40 per cent of students to 'graduate' into secondary school at the PSLE.[3] It should not be surprising to find that some students did not cope well with learning two languages, but *The Goh Report* was especially concerned that many Chinese students were coping particularly poorly because their designated 'mother tongue' was not the language of their mother or anyone in their family. Most Chinese spoke a Chinese language other than Mandarin (pejoratively referred to as 'dialects' in official Singapore parlance) and were, according to the analogy used in *The Goh Report*, in a position akin to English students receiving their schooling in Mandarin and Russian.[4] This had become a practical problem affecting the defence of the nation, since it was discovered that there were entire platoons in the SAF, known as 'Hokkien platoons', who could not understand orders given in any of the official languages of the country, only in one or other Chinese 'dialect'.[5] The simplistic solution, devised by the team of system engineers that Goh brought over from

MINDEF where he was minister, was that such students should be identified early and given a less extensive and less expensive education than their peers. An innocuous form of streaming already existed in secondary schools,[6] but Dr Goh's New Education System brought streaming forward to the end of Primary 3 (for children aged nine) and forced it through a rigid prism of Lee Kuan Yew's creation, whereby it was deemed that 'talent' was an indivisible whole, and a person was either good at practically everything, or was good for very little. At Primary 3 those who failed to make the 'Normal' stream would be channelled into either the 'Extended' stream (whereby they would take an extra two years to complete primary school because they were slow learners) or the 'Monolingual' stream (whereby they would not even be eligible to apply for secondary school). Primary 3 streaming was implemented in 1979 and only loosened up in 1992, when, among other reforms, streaming was put back to Primary 4 (age ten) and all students were made eligible to apply for a place in secondary school.

The mechanistic, output-oriented character of the streaming 'solution' to the problem of 'wastage' reflected the absence of professional educationalists on the Education Study Team and the domination of the process by a profession – systems engineering – that thinks purely in terms of inputs and outputs. The fact that these professionals had recently engaged in a review of MINDEF and even based themselves in MINDEF while reviewing the education system[7] seems to have exaggerated these tendencies, since MINDEF was a recipient of the products of the school system – the 'Hokkien platoons' – and so they already considered themselves to be experts on the outputs before they even investigated the school system itself.[8]

The intent and the unintended effects of streaming in Primary 3 are highlighted in an interview given many years later by the then Director of Education, Mr Chan Kai Yau to the Oral History Centre (OHC) in 1995. Chan revealed that the results of streaming were much less significant than had been forecast or targeted. Goh and the systems engineers had assumed that when streaming was introduced everyone would accept it with complete passivity and most people would meekly allow the children in their charge to be streamed downwards, or even out of secondary school. Goh was furious to discover that the introduction of streaming had driven principals, teachers, students and parents to increase the academic standard of the cohort, thus thwarting the objective of the streaming exercise. He put the Director of Education 'on the carpet' and demanded the dismissal of school principals who raised the standard of their school results.[9]

In some societies the introduction of streaming at such an early age might have been of minor consequence, but Singaporeans – especially but not exclusively Chinese Singaporeans – are acutely sensitive to changes in the educational landscape that affect the economic and social opportunities of their children. In fact for most parents it was a much more personal matter than even career prospects. Former teachers remember the angst of parents in the early 1980s who agonised over the humiliation and stigma of their children being labelled as 'failures'.[10] Many such parents successfully appealed against

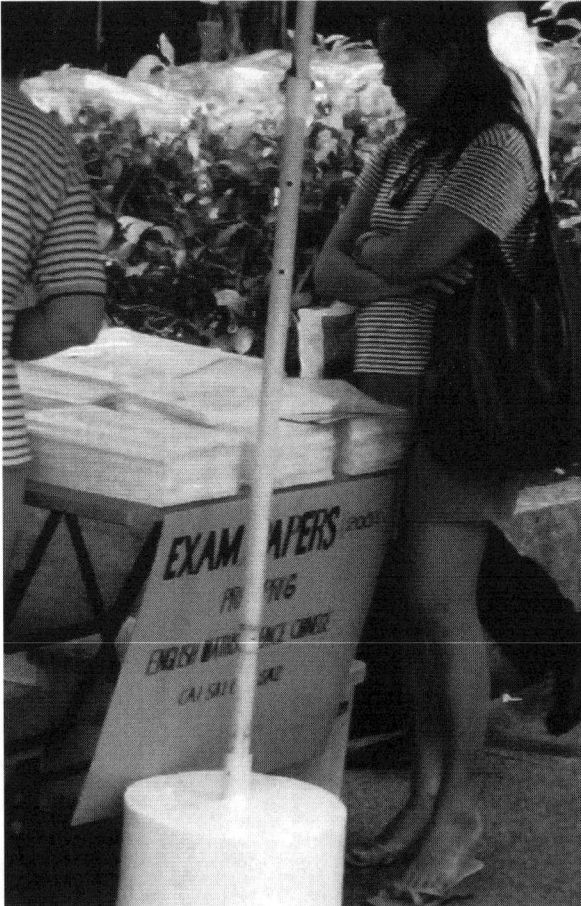

Figure 6.2: Examination papers for sale, Bedok, March 2004.

streaming decisions and had their children moved up one stream, but then the parents had to take responsibility (at least moral responsibility) for their children's future grades, and ensure that they justified the move upwards.[11] The response of parents in general should have been predictable: a drastic increase in recourse to private tutors, and Japanese-style pressure on children to cram and get perfect results throughout every step of their school careers. The *kiasu* (afraid to fail) parent became the norm and many Singaporean children lost their childhood. One of the anecdotal stories that started circulating in Singapore schools in the aftermath of streaming was conveyed by Mr Rudy Mosbergen, a former principal of Raffles Junior College in a 1994 interview with the OHC: 'The story was told that teachers in some schools would tell the students, "Okay, if you don't understand what I was teaching you during this lesson, you go home and ask your private tutor to explain it to you."'[12]

The prevalence of private tutors alongside the official Singapore education system is now ubiquitous and it is unusual to find university students who have not had private tutoring. By the early 1990s, an underground market had developed in examination papers stolen from 'top schools' and sold with correct answers so that parents could help their children to cram even without a private tutor (*ST*, 4 July 1996). Today such examination papers are still sold from fly-by-night stalls in hawker centres and shopping centres (see Figure 6.2.) Alternatively parents could have phoned an anonymous trader on a pre-paid and therefore unidentifiable mobile phone and the papers would have been delivered to their doors, no questions asked. In 2003 the going rate was $10 for a set of three examinations (English, Maths and Chinese from one school) or $75 for a bundle of examinations. The black market examinations covered all years, down to Primary 1.[13] Parents who balk at trading in stolen goods can buy packets of 'Monthly Achievement Tests' from mainstream bookshops.[14]

The Goh Report was the immediate cause of the development of the cramming/tutoring culture of the 1980s and after, but it can also be seen as part of a longer term historical development. Going back to the mid-1960s most students were still being educated in non-English medium schools as a consequence of the plural education system introduced in the late 1950s. It was part of the colonial legacy that education was loosely controlled by the government and in the main was directed to addressing communal concerns about culture, language and, in the case of the Malays, religion. Few children learnt English as a main language and so the limited opportunities in the civil service and English business houses were monopolised by the small group of graduates from the elite English-medium schools. Before independence the PAP government had also been reluctant to be seen to promote English education because it was trying to present itself as a good citizen of Malaya-cum-Malaysia, and hence was encouraging the study of Malay. As a consequence the small cadre of graduates from the elite English-medium schools knew that they simply had to pass their Cambridge Examinations to be guaranteed a position in the higher echelons of society; many of them took pride in doing this, but no more.[15] By the 1970s this cosy world was already being threatened because the government had made a conscious decision in the late 1960s to expand English-medium education. Competition increased and schooling became more rigorous. This was not sufficient in itself to transform schools into the pressure cookers of the 1990s and 2000s. Time and time again, people who were school students during the 1970s and went on to civil-service, professional or academic careers, dismissed in interview any suggestion that education was intense or stressful in those days, even in Raffles Institution, which has always regarded itself as the premier school on the island. Yet even so, by the late 1970s this new competition had already edged private tuition into the mainstream,[16] and in a single stroke the introduction of early streaming in 1979 turned it into an obsession.

Bilingualism

Early streaming also intensified – and was intended to intensify – Singapore's language policy, which in retrospect should be seen as the most significant driver for the evolution of the *kiasu* education system. After separation from Malaysia, Singapore adopted a policy of emphasising English as the language of Singapore for various reasons, the most significant being its commercial and international utility. English was to be the language of government, justice, international business and technical education. English language was to be the key to worldly success, so the opportunities for an English language education were expanded greatly. By the end of the 1970s, the unofficial but overt encouragement of English-language education had already pushed Tamil- and Malay-stream schools to the brink of extinction, and Chinese-medium schools were facing difficulties in getting enrolments, teachers and good-quality teaching and reading resources.[17] And even in the non-English-medium government schools, Maths and Science were taught in English.[18] This policy caused a measurable drop in Maths and Science standards among those outside the English-language schools, thus making a full English education even more desirable (*ST*, 7 June 1980).[19] This emphasis on the English language was, however, balanced somewhat by a lesser emphasis on one's 'mother tongue', which was made a compulsory subject for the PSLE in 1968.[20] Lee Kuan Yew believed that learning the ancestral language would enable children to imbibe the 'cultural ballast' of one's racial ethnic group, one advantage of which was to build resistance to Western fads.[21] To this end, from 1968 onwards, Chinese primary students in English-medium government schools were segregated and taught Civics in Mandarin[22] as a prelude to all children being taught Civics in their 'mother tongue'. Government ministers routinely highlighted the importance of 'mother tongue' education for moral education.[23] This device for replenishing 'cultural ballast' was intended to be a central feature of both elite formation and nation building for the embryonic society, yet as of the late 1970s it was substantially a failure and was regarded as such in the Ministry of Education.[24] Hence *The Goh Report* listed 'non-attainment of effective bilingualism' as a 'main shortcoming' in the education system and devoted a lot of attention to concerns about the second language. *The Goh Report* makes it clear that by the late 1970s the government was disappointed that English-plus-'mother tongue' bilingualism had failed to emerge as a basic standard for students in the Singapore school system: that standards of fluency and literacy in both English and 'mother tongue' were low.

Part of the reason for this failure became manifest in Barr's interviews and conversations with people who were school students during the 1970s. They consistently report that the emphasis on the 'mother tongue' was not intense while they were at school. It was taught with the same vigour with which English schools might teach French or Australian schools Japanese. There was none of the nation-building urgency that is evident in *The Goh Report* or a myriad of speeches by Lee Kuan Yew or various government ministers over the previous decade. The government began addressing this shortcoming in 1980 and 1981 with a tightening up of the second-language requirements needed to gain entry into junior college and university (*ST*, 17 January 1980). Other initiatives targeted specifically at the Chinese community also served to underline the new importance being attached to the 'mother tongue': specifically the initiatives mentioned in the previous chapter, being the launch of the first annual 'Speak Mandarin Campaign' and the Chinese-medium SAP schools. From the consistent pattern of stories told in interview by Chinese Singaporeans who were children in the early 1980s, it seems that very many 'dialect'-speaking parents heeded the pressure to switch to Mandarin at home in order to give their son or daughter the best educational chance in life. Many also enrolled their child in an English-medium school in a deliberate effort to maximise economic opportunity in the new Singapore (*ST*, 8 April and 5 May 1978).

The government's initiatives also had implications beyond language and education policy, since they marked the beginning of government sponsorship and privileging of a tame, government-controlled Chinese cultural resurgence: a *bonsai* version of the wild and energetic Chinese cultural life that the government had successfully razed to the ground over the previous fifteen years. The main point of interest for the current chapter, however, is to note that these initiatives heralded a new era in language policy, where English-plus-'mother tongue' bilingualism was the new basic standard for educational achievement. Whether or not it was intended, the combination of upgraded streaming and bilingualism requirements spurred parents and teachers into a new paroxysm of grades-obsession, a point that was reluctantly but explicitly acknowledged by new Education Minister Tony Tan at the time (*ST*, 22 November 1980). Good grades were needed, even in Primary 3 to merely survive in the education system, so every effort was made in school hours and outside them to achieve good grades.

Stratification and Diversification

The final cog in the machine that would turn the education system into a factory for the manufacture of 'new Singaporeans' was the stratification of schools and the commensurate re-introduction of a modest amount of diversity into the education system. This process began in 1984 when a small number of 'elite' schools were selected to host a Gifted Education Programme (which would act as a de facto highest stream for the top 0.5% of students in primary and secondary school),[25] but it became overt only in the mid-1980s when the government began encouraging 'elite' schools to go 'Independent' or 'Autonomous' – effectively and openly introducing a new class of privileged schools that would mould the future elite. This initiative is usually considered by participants and academic commentators to be a development separate from the introduction of streaming, sometimes going as far as regarding it as the beginning of a completely new 'ability-driven' phase in the education policy.[26] We believe that Jason Tan is closer to the mark when he identified the beginnings of the diversification programme as a process beginning in 1982 when the then Director of Schools announced plans to decentralise educational management away from MOE.[27] Yet even if diversification is taken in isolation, Tan's estimate still ignores the introduction in 1981 of rival series of textbooks into schools, leaving individual principals to decide which series to use (*ST*, 7 October 1981). This decision must have been taken in 1980 at the latest, making the beginning of the diversification programme almost commensurate with the introduction of streaming. With the two developments – the stratification programme and the diversification programme – beginning almost simultaneously it does not seem sensible to continue to regard them as unrelated phenomena. It is more reasonable to regard the diversification programme as an aspect of the stratification programme introduced with *The Goh Report*.

Streaming students within schools according to performance in examinations, and the policy of English-plus-'mother tongue' bilingualism – especially the creation of SAP schools – separated them according to a combination of ethnicity, general academic excellence, and excellence in language skills, usually against the will of their parents who nearly universally resisted and resented such stratification.[28] In retrospect the introduction and privileging of SAP schools, combined with the introduction of streaming, was the beginning of a long process of stratification of children and schools that has still not finished in the late 2000s. The key steps in the process were those associated with:

- the 1979 *Goh Report* (streaming and intensified bilingualism)
- the 1987 *Excellence in Schools* report (stratification of secondary schools paralleling streaming within schools),[29] and
- the 2002 *Report of the Junior College/Upper Secondary Review Committee* (the intensification and extension of stratification).[30]

The Independent and Autonomous schools that resulted from the 1987 report took streaming to the next logical step, physically separating the best students from the rest, so that even more special advantages and resources could be visited upon them. A major impact of these moves was to intensify all the effects of streaming outlined above, but it had ramifications far beyond this. With the future elite herded together into a handful of schools, it became possible to take them in hand and cultivate in them the 'virtues' and characteristics that the government regarded as desirable. This was no less than a programme to turn the education system into a refined system of elite selection and elite formation. Elite regeneration, so the thinking went, would thus be reduced to a controlled, bureaucratic exercise, with measurable inputs and outputs. The elite end of the English-stream education system – basically Raffles Institution, Anglo-Chinese School and St Joseph's Institution – had possessed elements of this purpose for many decades, but now it was being systematised and professionalized to remove the element of chance. The elite stratum in the new hierarchy comprises the Raffles, Anglo-Chinese, and Hwa Chong families of schools, and the new NUS High School for Mathematics and Science.

The most recent set of changes ushered in by the 2002 *Report of the Junior College/Upper Secondary Review Committee* completed the stratification process, placing the top strata of schools under completely different rules to the rest of the education establishment. Beginning in 2004, these schools began plucking about half their students directly from primary school under their own private and variable rules, bypassing the PSLE. They are free to favour students from their feeder schools if they have them, and to take into account 'personal statements' by students (which most do). In the case of 'Integrated Programme' schools they can admit their whole cohort using such discretionary criteria.[31] They have relatively high fees (which is sometimes compounded by an expectation that students will board for a semester to imbibe the atmosphere more fully), privileged funding from the government, and their students can skip their O-levels, proceeding straight to matriculation.[32] These developments subvert the level playing field of PSLE and O-levels and introduce an element of opaqueness to an otherwise transparent (if flawed) system of meritocracy. It seems likely that these recent changes will come to be regarded as the turning point at which the ambiguities in the Singapore system of meritocracy were settled, leaving no doubt that the Singapore meritocracy operates within a broader context of social and economic privilege, allowing socially marginalised children (whether because of socio-economic status, race or some other factor) to rise only under sufferance and in exceptional circumstances. It is a central argument of this book and of some other scholarly works that this has been the case to a considerable extent for decades anyway,[33] but to date criticism has had to acknowledge that there seems to have been a steady supply of poor children who have risen through the meritocracy. Our concern is that even this modest phase of relative beneficence may have run its course, and that meritocratic stratification may have finally been overwhelmed by stratification based on socio-economic class.

A Study in 'Waves'

The cumulative result of these three imperatives – streaming, bilingualism and stratification-cum-diversification – has been a climacteric shift that has spurred the transformation of the education system into a factory for produc-ing 'new' Singaporeans and a new elite. Today the production of both starts in pre-school, and this is where we pick up the story in the next chapter. A study of the impact of the school system on both nation building and elite formation is a study of waves of change and perpetual, continuing innovation. This feature is in part due to the nature of modern social phenomena *per se,* which despises stasis; but whereas in many societies the pace of change is sufficiently slow to enable it to hide in the shadows of study, in Singapore the pace of change is so fast and so tightly directed from above that the phenom-enon of change must remain a prime parameter of any study. The following chapters are a study of the changing role of the pre-adult education system in the related but distinct processes of nation building, elite selection and elite formation. Their structure mirrors that of a Singaporean child's school life, with consecutive chapters on pre-school and primary school, and one chap-ter covering secondary school and junior college. The generational 'waves of change', referred to above, are studied in sweeps within the narrative confines of these compartments, with a disproportionate amount of attention being paid to pre-school and primary school, these being the crucial years in char-acter formation.

Notes

1   Goh Keng Swee and The Education Study Team, *Report on the Ministry of Education 1978*, Singapore: [Singapore National Printers], 1979.

2   Ibid., Chapter 3, p. 1.

3   Ingrid Glad, *An Identity Dilemma: A comparative study of primary education for ethnic Chinese in the context of national identity and nation-building in Malaysia and Singapore*, Oslo: Scandinavian University Press, 1998, pp. 88, 89. Only half of the 40 per cent who failed were diverted from secondary school permanently, since the other half passed their PSLE at a second or subsequent attempt.

4   Goh Keng Swee, *Report on the Ministry of Education 1978*, Chapter 1, p. 1.

5   Interview with Mr Rudy Mosbergen, given to the Oral History Centre, National Archives of Singapore, 1994, p. 401 of the official transcript.

6   R. Quinn Moore, 'Multiracialism and meritocracy: Singapore's approach to race and inequality', *Review of Social Economy* vol. 58, no. 3, 2000, p. 353.

7   Mosbergen, Oral History Centre interview, p. 411.

8   The Goh Report states in part: 'The fate of those who fall by the wayside is not generally known. Army Commanders who have to train them and turn them to be effective soldiers are well-informed on this. These school dropouts, especially those who could not pass the PSLE constitute the majority of problem soldiers, those who wind up as court martial cases, summary trials, for disciplinary offences, drug addicts and attempted suicide cases. Case histories of these soldiers have been published recently by a former MINDEF officer. It should be made compulsory reading for senior officials in the Ministry of Education.' Goh Keng Swee, *Report on the Ministry of Education 1978*, Chapter 1, p. 3.

9   Interview with Mr Chan Kai Yau given to the Oral History Centre, National Archives of Singapore, 1995, p. 339 of the official transcript. Also see *ST*, 29 August 1980, for confirmation that the 'systems engineers' who designed the streaming seriously misjudged the results of the exercise.

10 Interview with Mr Eugene Wijeysingha given to the Oral History Centre, National Archives of Singapore, 1995, p. 402 of the official transcript; and interview with Mrs Anna Tham given to the Oral History Centre, National Archives of Singapore, 1994, p. 216 of the official transcript.

11 Ibid.

12 Mosbergen, OHC interview, p. 389.

13 Barr bought two sets of Primary 1 examinations at Clementi Town Centre in 2003 and saw one mother buying three sets of the $75 bundles of papers.

14 See, for instance, Hoe Hock Hing and See Saw Hong, *Primary 3 Science Monthly Achievement Tests*, Singapore: All-Star Publishing, 2004, purchased by Michael Barr in Popular Books, Boon Lay, July 2005. Also see the publisher's website at http://www.ASTARpub.com.

15 Michael Barr's interview with Bilahari Kausikan, Singapore, 15 April 2003. Bilahari Kausikan entered Raffles Institution in 1966.

16 Mosbergen, OHC interview, p. 389. Mr Mosbergen was a teacher in the first half of the 1970s, then became Assistant Director of Curriculum at MOE.

17 Chan Kai Yau, OHC interview, pp. 316, 317.

18 Richard Juve, 'Education as an integrating force in Singapore, a multi-cultural society', dissertation for Doctor of Education, Graduate School of Education, Rutgers University, 1975, p. 79.

19 Lim Soon Tae and S. Gopinathan, '25 years of curriculum planning', in John Yip Soon Kwong and Sim Wong Kooi (eds), *Evolution of Educational Excellence: 25 Years of Education in the Republic of Singapore*, Singapore: Longman, 1990, p. 69. Official concern about the skewing of academic results against 'vernacular' stream students can be seen in *ST*, 20 March 1978. Official concern about the poor standard of English-language skills was reported regularly by the end of the 1970s. See, for instance, *ST*, 7 March and 18 April 1978.

20 Juve, 'Education as an integrating force', p. 79.

21 Michael D. Barr, *Lee Kuan Yew: The Beliefs Behind the Man*, Richmond, UK: Curzon Press, 2000, pp. 150–57. Also see Lee Kuan Yew's covering letter in Goh Keng Swee *et al.*, *Report on the Ministry of Education 1978*, p. v.

22 Juve, 'Education as an integrating force', p. 79.

23 See, for instance, Education Minister Lim Kim San's speech at the presentation of prizes at the All Singapore Chinese Essay Competition, where he praised Chinese education for trying 'to inculcate good moral character' and teach 'courtesy, integrity, kindness, civic-mindedness and justice' (*ST*, 25 May 1971).

24 Wijeysingha, OHC interview, p. 371.

25 See Chapter 8 for more details on the Gifted Education Programme.

26 Barr's interview with Eugene Wijeysingha, Singapore, 11 April 2003; Anne Pakir, 'Singapore', in Ho Wah Kam and Ruth Y.L. Wong (eds), *Language Policies and Language Education: The Impact in Asian Countries in the Next Decade*, Singapore: Eastern Universities Press by Marshall Cavendish, 2004, p. 286; Charlene Tan, 'Driven by pragmatism: issues and challenges in an ability-driven education', in Jason Tan and Ng Pak Tee, *Shaping Singapore's Future: Thinking Schools, Learning Nation*, Singapore: Pearson Education, 2005, p. 5.

27 Jason Tan, 'The marketization of education in Singapore: what does this mean for Thinking Schools, Learning Nation?', in Jason Tan and Ng Pak Tee, *Shaping Singapore's Future: Thinking Schools, Learning Nation*, Singapore: Pearson Education, 2005, p. 96.

28 The early history of SAP schools and streaming was one of overcoming and placating parental resistance to the introduction of the programmes, including the Special Assistance Plan. See, for instance, *ST*, 29 January and 14 March 1982, and 17 March 1983.

29 Goh Chi Lan and the principals of the Study Team, *Towards Excellence in Schools: A Report to the Minister for Education February 1987*, Singapore: Ministry of Education, 1987.

30 Tharman Shanmugaratnam and the Junior College/Upper Secondary Education Review Committee, *Report of the Junior College/Upper Secondary Education Review Committee*, Singapore: Ministry of Education, 2002.

31 Ministry of Education website, http://www.moe.gov.sg. Accessed 6 October 2005.

32 Trivina Kang, 'Diversification of Singapore's Upper Secondary Landscape: Introduction of Integrated Programmes, Specialised Independent Schools and Privately-Funded Schools', in Tan and Ng, *Shaping Singapore's Future*, pp. 52–67.

33 See Jason Tan, 'Independent schools in Singapore: implications for social and educational inequalities', *International Journal of Educational Development*, vol. 13, no. 3, 1993, pp. 239–251.

SEVEN

Catching Them Young: Afraid to Fail in Kindergarten

THE WORLD OF THE SINGAPORE student in the first decade of the twenty-first century is one of stratification and hierarchy based on 'meritocratic', examination-based measures of 'talent' and on race. It is one of high levels of racial consciousness, and a *kiasu* approach both to serious achievement and to the minutia of life. It might be assumed that the making of this 'new' Singaporean would start at the beginning of schooling. Primary 1 is, after all, the earliest opportunity for the state to start dominating the lives of Singaporean children directly. It would be a reasonable assumption, but it would be wrong. The process of immersing children into the *kiasu* world of examinations, mugging

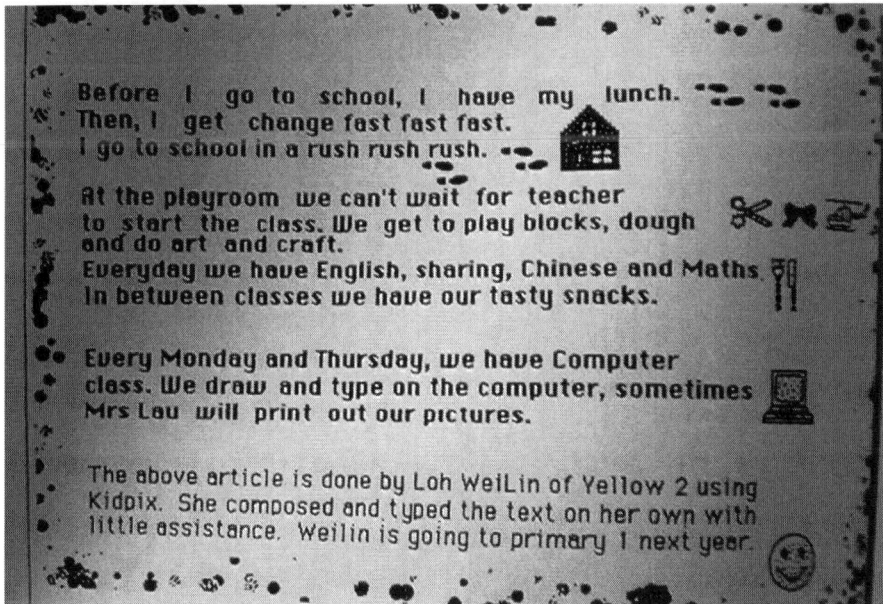

Before I go to school, I have my lunch.
Then, I get change fast fast fast.
I go to school in a rush rush rush.

At the playroom we can't wait for teacher to start the class. We get to play blocks, dough and do art and craft.
Everyday we have English, sharing, Chinese and Maths In between classes we have our tasty snacks.

Every Monday and Thursday, we have Computer class. We draw and type on the computer, sometimes Mrs Lau will print out our pictures.

The above article is done by Loh WeiLin of Yellow 2 using Kidpix. She composed and typed the text on her own with little assistance. Weilin is going to primary 1 next year.

Figure 7.1: Life of a pre-schooler, 1992.[1]

and tuition begins in pre-school. Today, Singapore's nurseries and kindergartens are places where examinations, textbooks, study and even private tuition are the norm. Despite making some official noises about the importance of not pressuring pre-school children with study,[2] the government seems to be content to see kindergartens continue as microcosms of Singapore's *kiasu* society as children study their maths, English and 'mother tongue' as a matter of deliberate policy. Yet this obsession with grades and examinations in pre-school is a relatively new phenomenon. It has developed since the 1970s under the direction of one of Singapore's most powerful ministers, Dr Tony Tan. Today it has reached the stage where the process has usually begun even before a child begins nursery.

This chapter explores the forced and deliberate government-driven evolution of Singapore's informal pre-school education system from circa-1980 onwards into what has become a key tool for making 'new' Singaporeans. We pay particular attention in the second half of the chapter to how PAP Community Foundation (PCF) kindergartens and the new Kindergarten Financial Assistance Scheme (KiFAS) are being used as aggressive tools for assimilating children into Singapore's hegemonic culture, permeated as it is by the elite's version of 'Chinese values'. We demonstrate this by focusing once again on the ethnic minority that has been most resistant to assimilation – the Malays – simply because their case demonstrates most clearly the seriousness of the government's assimilationist intent and the thoroughness of its methodology. For minorities this intent leads to incomplete assimilation, but it is important to note that this assimilation programme applies even more fully to the majority Chinese who, it seems, still need to be proactively shaped to fit the government's preferred mould of an ideal Singaporean.

Background

Private and government kindergartens had been a feature of life in Singapore since colonial days, but in those more easy going times they reached only a very small proportion of the pre-school-aged population.[3] In the years before the PAP's split with Barisan Sosialis in 1961, the PAP was one of the more significant suppliers of pre-school services in Singapore, almost exclusively servicing its Chinese grassroots base. When Barisan walked off with most of the party's kindergartens the PAP government developed the old colonial kindergartens – then run by the People's Association (PA)[4], which operated out of the Prime Minister's Office – as a rival to the Barisan network until the party was in a position to start rebuilding kindergartens through its branch structure. Yet the kindergartens of the 1950s and 1960s were a far cry from those of today. Even the kindergartens of the 1970s are unrecognisable as precursors of the current system. Interviewees who were in PAP kindergartens in the 1970s remember no sense of pressure, no examinations and no textbooks, despite the fact they were more academically oriented than an outsider might expect – reflecting their origins as a system of Chinese kindergartens. Their official brief was to 'prepare [children] in reading, counting and writing skills',[5] but they did not pursue this goal to the point of obsession.

The first signs of a move away from this innocent approach to pre-school were a series of government initiatives in 1978 that had the immediate objectives of professionalising pre-primary teaching. In that year the Institute of Education (IE) introduced the country's first formal, centralised and academic training course for pre-school teachers (replacing the more basic training offered by the Adult Education Board),[6] and MOE announced that all present and future kindergarten teachers had to undertake and pass this course (*ST*, 10 June and 1 November 1978). In the same year the PA announced that it was consciously trying to increase the standards in its kindergartens. At the same time the then Senior Minister of State for Education, Dr Chai Chong Yii, tried to lower the starting age of school by introducing a one-year Pre-Primary Programme in all primary schools (*ST*, 1 November 1978) – though in the end the programme did not proceed beyond 68 Chinese-medium schools chosen ostensibly as a 'pilot scheme'.[7] At the same time the IE prepared itself to meet the anticipated demand generated by this expansion by adding pre-school teaching to its O-level teacher training curriculum, and advertising in British newspapers for 20 lecturers in pre-school education (*ST*, 9 June, 14 September and 1 November 1978).

As significant as these initiatives were, however, they paled against the long term impact of *The Goh Report* in 1979. Once there was a risk that a child could be streamed away from university – and even, *in extremis*, away from secondary school – at the end of Primary 3, the pressure on pre-schoolers and the pressure on parents to send their children to pre-school increased inexorably. Thus one person reported in interview that as early as 1982 and 1983 her PAP kindergarten classes involved 'really studying', complete with 'all the exams and tests'. In another interview a retired junior primary teacher noted that whereas in 1970 hardly anyone went to kindergarten, by the early 1980s the majority of children in the ordinary government school in which she taught had been to kindergarten.[8] Just as significant was her observation that by 1985 the majority of children whom she taught arrived in Primary 1 able to read and write because 'streaming was pushing the parents to push the children, and to start earlier'.[9]

PCF to the Fore

Yet despite these short-term results, the government was still not satisfied. At some time in the mid-1980s a decision was taken (though never formally announced) by the then Education Minister, Dr Tony Tan, to push forward with the government's pre-school ambitions using the PAP kindergarten network as his vehicle of choice. He began in 1986 with a half-million-dollar-a-year programme to upgrade the PAP kindergarten network (*ST*, 15 November 1990), which by 1987 was already 120-strong and teaching 46,000 children a year (*ST*, 7 August 1987).[10] Granted that Dr Tan still harboured ongoing ambitions to universalise pre-school education (*ST*, 3 February, 18 March and 12 July 1986; 17 November 1990), this was almost certainly an act of frustration over Dr Chai's failed efforts to introduce universal pre-school. Dr Tan had clearly decided that pushing forward with a less-than-ideal kindergarten system over which he could exercise direct control was preferable to waiting for an ideal pre-school scheme that might never arrive. The kindergarten 'upgrade' programme covered all the essentials of kindergarten service delivery: physical premises and facilities, curriculum and teacher training.[11]

This decision to develop pre-school through a party instrument has never been properly explained or justified, but the fiction that it was a private initiative was not allowed to deter it from receiving official backing. The kindergarten network was removed to (barely) an arm's length distance from the party in 1987 when the PAP created the PAP Community Foundation (PCF) to manage the PAP kindergarten network (*ST*, 7 August 1987), after which the largesse and co-operation from government ministries and instrumentalities flowed freely. The IE immediately began increasing its throughput of pre-school teachers (*ST*, 15 November 1990) to accommodate the anticipated expansion of PCF kindergartens and the PA assisted the new PCF to revamp its kindergarten curriculum (*ST*, 14 July 1986; 7 August 1987). In 1988 PCF kindergartens were already educating two-thirds of Singapore's kindergarten pupils,[12] and the normal regime was one of uniforms, examination and textbooks (*ST*, 18 August 1986). Then, as if on cue, Pre-Primary Programme classes were closed in 1989 except in the SAP Schools (which were allowed to keep them under the guise of the 'Preparatory Year programme' that is discussed in the next paragraph) and the PCF kindergartens (by then 191 strong) took up the slack and expanded again (to 201 by May 1990) (*ST*, 21 March and 13 June 1989; 29 May 1990; 12 and 28 May 1991). By this stage the transformation of the kindergarten culture into a pressurised, grades-oriented system had already reached ridiculous proportions, with parents camping out overnight to enrol their children in 'good' kindergartens (*ST*, 15 March 1990).

The next critical turning point came at the end of 1990 with the organisa-tion of a joint PCF-, PA- and IE-sponsored national conference on kindergar-ten education, which foreshadowed the climacteric shake-up of Singapore's pre-school education system (*ST*, 29 May 1990). The conference and political agenda of 1990 re-ran the complete agenda of the 1978 and 1986 pre-school education initiatives – upgrading facilities, curricula and teacher training; universalising pre-school (now to be called a 'Preparatory Year'); and bring-ing the starting age for kindergarten back to three (*ST*, 30 October, and 15, 17 and 18 November 1990). This time, however, they were determined to get it right. Tony Tan ensured that the conference had a top-level profile by opening it with a provocative and ground-breaking speech in which he began the now-routine practice of comparing the educational achievements of chil-dren through the prism of race – a comparison that was most unflattering to the Malays and Indians (*ST*, 16 November 1990). The $90,000 conference was not held at a tertiary campus, but at the Raffles Convention Centre in the middle of the city, and was accompanied by a free public exhibition of 'the latest audio-visual equipment, books, children's physical development programmes, and educational toys' that was expected to attract 5,000 visit-ors (*ST*, 30 October 1990). In his opening speech at the conference Dr Tan left no one in doubt about the purpose of the conference or kindergarten education *per se*: it was to 'prepare a child for a successful and fulfilling career in school', through facilitating the teaching of English, mathematics and the 'mother tongue'.[13] In fact Tan was using this speech to flag a renewed focus on these three areas throughout the education system, which resulted directly in an intensification of Chinese-language education (through the introduction of more demanding textbooks) in primary and secondary school in 1992.[14]

No one should have been surprised when, immediately following the conference, the transformation and expansion of pre-school in general and PCF kindergartens in particular reached a qualitatively higher level of seriousness. By the beginning of 1991 there were already 210 PCF kindergartens, yet the PCF system was to share in 12,000 new pre-school places being funded by the government (with the balance going to SAP schools for their 'Preparatory Year programme') (*ST*, 15 April 1990; 12 May 1991). The same year saw the launching of a PCF kindergarten upgrade programme sponsored by MOE without any pretence of giving equal treatment to other kindergarten systems in the first instance (though the project was to be opened up to other non-profit kindergartens in 1993) (*ST*, 13 February 1991 and 1 January 1992). This 'Project Preschool' had three stated aims:

1. reviewing and revising the curriculum, modelled on the new Preparatory Year programme for SAP Schools;

2. building and upgrading of PCF kindergartens; and

3. improving the training and development of PCF teachers.[15]

The curriculum review was facilitated by the secondment of three MOE staff to the PCF to develop syllabus and teaching materials (*ST*, 27 May 1991). Upgrading the physical facilities, including the introduction of computers, was assisted by direct grants of millions of dollars from the government, the first instalment of which was $4.2 million (*ST*, 27 May 1991). Teacher training was undertaken by the IE, which was formally thanked by the PCF for its support.[16] Daily classroom hours were increased (from three to four) as part of this exercise (*ST*, 28 May 1991) and by the end of 1992 the number of PAP kindergartens had increased again to 230 (teaching 55,000 children) with plans for another 60 by 1994 (*ST*, 1 February 1992).[17]

Between the expansion of the PCF network and its gifted leadership role in curriculum development, the PCF cemented its hegemonic role in pre-school education, which it had been working hard to establish since the mid-1980s. Until then the main driver of pre-school curriculum development had been MOE through the Pre-Primary Programme. The growing hegemony of the PCF from the mid-1980s to the mid-1990s saw a new intensification in the inflation of pre-school expectations, but it would be wrong to attribute the trend just to the PCF. Rather it was part of a broader pattern of escalating pre-school expectations driven by the government. Hence the Pre-Primary

Programme curricula from 1979 to 1987 also reveal a gradual, though less dramatic escalation of expectations. The curriculum originally introduced with the Pre-Primary Programme was a simple one of games, songs, drawing and observation that matches intuitive expectations of a curriculum for five-year-olds. It explicitly rejected the desirability of trying to teach five-year-olds to write and of using 'paper and pencil' exercises to test numeracy.[18] Its worksheets for the first two semesters contained only 44 words.[19] Despite the claim that it was bilingual,[20] the 1979 curriculum was geared almost completely towards encouraging Chinese children to become familiar with the English language: the *Curriculum Guidelines* were printed in English and the nursery rhymes and singing games recommended as teaching devices were English: 'Twinkle Twinkle Little Star', 'Humpty Dumpty', 'Jack and Jill', 'Five Little Sparrows', 'We All Clap Together'.[21] The 1979 curriculum was a set of guidelines that left much to the discretion of the teacher. Only a year later, however, this curriculum was superseded by a much more sophisticated version that came with 30 centrally-issued worksheets (for Term I alone) covering 'Language Skills' and another 20 for 'Beginnings of Mathematical Concepts'. Teachers were asked to plan their own activities for the other two terms using these as a model. Its content had also been extended considerably and now included some oral Chinese language content (songs and rhymes related to Chinese New Year), the beginnings of literacy in English (tracing shapes of letters and words, reading nursery rhymes, home-made books and other materials) and the beginnings of numeracy (tracing numbers, counting up to five, pretend shopping, counting money, identifying the missing number, making numbers with play dough).[22]

The Singapore pre-schooler had begun edging towards *kiasu* education, but its full flowering was still more than a decade away. The number of Term I worksheets in the Pre-Primary Programme was again increased in 1987 (from 30 to 48 for Pre-Reading and Pre-Writing and from 20 to 32 for Numeracy) but this was the only significant change.[23] Then in 1987 the PCF announced that it was developing a common syllabus for all PAP kindergartens, ostensibly to deal with those PAP kindergartens that were resisting the national trend towards formal teaching in pre-school education (*ST*, 18 August 1987). In retrospect it seems that this was the point at which the driver for pre-school curriculum upgrades shifted from MOE to the PCF, with the IE and sometimes the PA playing supporting and subordinate roles.

Escalating Expectations

The ground-breaking role of the PCF in setting new standards is indicated in its 'showcase' publications from the early 1990s. The PCF's *Project Pre-School 1991–1994* put on display essays written by kindergarten children in English, Chinese, Tamil and Malay. One Chinese essay had 44 characters, and an English essay revealed a startling level of complexity:

> This years [sic] National Day parade was in the night. I saw the fireworks. They were bright and colourful. The parachutists jumped from the helicopter. I hope I can watch it at the National Stadium next year.[24]

Nothing, however, could surpass the 1992 yearbook of the Tampines West PCF Education Centre. Following the essay by Loh Weilin (See Figure 7.1 at the opening of this chapter) there followed another 11 handwritten essays in English by the centre's remarkable kindergarten children, most of which are of a similar length and nearly the same standard.[25] Pity the children in the Tampines East PCF Education Centre whose 1990 yearbook merely has a photograph of them in line while the teacher marks their 'Language' workbooks. At least the caption assures their parents that they are learning 'English language, number concepts and a second language (Mandarin/Malay) during … formal lessons'.[26]

In 1995 the hegemony of the PCF over pre-schooling was confirmed both formally and informally. The informal recognition came when Oxford University Press published a series of kindergarten and nursery textbooks for the Singapore market that assured parents that they were 'based on the syllabus set by the PAP Community Foundation for its kindergartens'. This series of 21 books was 'designed according to the guidelines in the PCF Curriculum (Revised, 1994)' and covered Nursery, Kindergarten 1 and Kindergarten 2 English, Kindergarten 1 and Kindergarten 2 Chinese and Kindergarten 1 and Kindergarten 2 Mathematics.[27] The Nursery Activity Book in Oxford's PCF Kindergarten series, designed for four-year-olds, was more advanced than the Pre-Primary Programme curriculum of 1979, containing exercises in tracing letters, counting, and – for those who could manage it – simple reading.[28] The Kindergarten books were also much more demanding than anything in the 1987 Pre-Primary Programme, let alone the 1979 version, including writing missing words in sentences, reading entire sentences, and independent counting.[29]

The formal recognition of the PCF's hegemony was announced in 1995 by the then Deputy Prime Minister, Tony Tan, when he opened the PCF Early Childhood Institute: a centre for teacher training and curriculum development for PCF teachers, built with a $5 million government grant, and which planned to offer the only Certificate in Early Childhood Studies available in the country (*ST*, 29 May 1995).[30] Dr Tan urged the PCF's new institute to make its courses, curriculum and teaching materials available to all kindergartens in Singapore, and not just the PAP kindergartens, which by now had grown to 280 in number: 'In this way the PCF can play a national role to inculcate good habits and attitudes in young Singaporeans so that they will be better prepared and can benefit more when they commence their formal schooling in Primary 1' (*ST*, 30 July 1996).

Once the PCF was driving the pace of curriculum development, the inflation of standards became endemic. In about 2000 a local Christian publishing house issued its own kindergarten textbook that was clearly aspiring to match the standards set by the PCF a few years earlier. This very substantial textbook had young children reading sentences, writing words, starting simple English grammar, counting, subtracting and adding.[31] Judging by kindergarten textbooks purchased in one of the mainstream bookshops (Popular Books) in an HDB estate (Bedok Town Centre) in 2004, the standards have continued to climb since them. In fact one of these textbooks asked children to choose between 'standard' and 'level' as the missing word in 'I select the ———— of difficulty' and between 'instructions' and 'manual' for 'I read the ———— on the screen'.[32] Even more disturbing is the parallel evolution of the Nursery textbooks. The Chinese Language and Numbers textbooks for Nursery are admittedly much more basic than the Kindergarten 1 equivalents, but they are remarkable primarily because there is a market for them at all.[33] The Educational Publishing House is now selling a range of Pre-Nursery books covering the writing of numbers, English letters and Chinese characters.[34] No wonder there is a demand for courses such as 'Mandarin Enrichment' for Nursery children and 'Toddler Mandarin'. (See also Figure 6.1.) In 2005 President S.R. Nathan actually declared 'zero tolerance' for those parents who insist on waiting until primary school before beginning their children's formal education, endorsing the SINDA scheme of 'picking up children as young as six months' and imposing 'a family mentor scheme making sure the parents understand the importance of going to childcare and then to kindergarten'

(*CNA*, 14 August 2005). Those who can afford it pay serious money – in some cases more than a quarter of average household income[35] – to place their children in elite kindergartens. The pressure on parents and children has grown to a point that would have been unrecognisable to an earlier generation. In interview a mother confessed that, against all her instincts and with a protestation that she is 'not one of those *kiasu* mothers', she had arranged private tutoring for her son in kindergarten because she was worried he would be behind on his first day in primary school:

> We are talking about tuition in kindergarten now! [My child] has to know his alphabet, times tables, spelling, everything. He is very far behind – in kindergarten! He will turn 5 in October. He is in Kindergarten 1 now and already they must know some phrases like 'I taste with my tongue, I see with my eyes', learn to recognise the word and which phrases to join together. He must do everything, so his kindergarten teacher came in twice a week to give him tuition because he is so far behind and in Nursery [which he missed out on] they have done a lot of things. And also for Chinese. ... He has to have tuition to help him to catch up to Kindergarten 1 standard. Now he's only doing Nursery Chinese. If he doesn't make it by Kindergarten 2 he will have a problem when he turns seven and joins Primary 1. So I hate to do this but he has tuition for one-and-a-half hours. His teacher actually says two but I put my foot down and say, one-and-a-half hours each session, times two sessions in a week. So my child is feeling a bit stressed.

This mother may or may not be *kiasu*, but the threat to her son's future when he faces Primary 1 is real. Since the 1990s many schools have begun unofficial streaming at the end of Primary 1, making the stakes of academic failure in kindergarten even higher (*ST*, 7 November 1996).

The reality today is that although the Singaporean education system officially starts in Primary 1 at age seven, it effectively starts in Nursery at age three or four. Children on the first day of Primary 1 are expected to already have a basic level of English, mathematics and their mother tongue. Kindergartens and Nurseries therefore teach these subjects, set examinations and give grades. Any doubts can be removed by a perusal of the MOE website which reveals an official MOE document entitled *Nurturing Early Learners: A Framework for a Kindergarten Curriculum in Singapore*, which comes complete with a personal message from the then Minister of State for Education, Tharman Shanmugaratnam, declaring on page 7 that kindergarten is 'integral to our broader efforts in education.'[36] Elsewhere the website announces, 'Kindergartens are "schools" that provide a structured 3-year pre-school education programme for children aged 3 to 6.' These statements confirm the impression given earlier that the starting age for de facto entry into the education system has been pushed back even further to the beginning of Nursery (age three/four) just as Dr Chai Chong Yii and Dr Tony Tan wanted in the 1970s and 1980s. But the curious feature of this arrangement is that, despite MOE's official declaration of the kindergartens' 'integral' role in education, they are run privately. This was a deliberate decision taken by the government in 1991 following its 1989 decision to end the Pre-Primary Programme experiment because it was not cost-effective (*ST*, 23 January and 21 March 1989; 13 February 1991). This stance was reaffirmed as recently as 1999, when the then Senior Minister of State for Education, Aline Wong, rejected a call for the government to 'enter the pre-school market' (*ST*, 18 September 1999).

Kindergarten as a Tool of Assimilation: The Case of Malays

This history of pre-schooling demonstrates beyond all doubt that the pre-school system has been deliberately used as a tool to socialise young children into the world of study, grades and examinations. It has, in fact, imbued children with the values of the 'new' Singaporean, and become a critical instrument in generating instinctive reactions and cognitive responses that will most commonly stay with them for life. These are Singaporean 'virtues', but more particularly they are virtues that are thought to characterise the ideal 'Chinese Singaporean' in the mind of Lee Kuan Yew. It should not, therefore, be a complete surprise that the only two attempts to institute a pre-school year as part of the school system (Pre-Primary Programme and the Preparatory Year) were offered exclusively in Chinese-medium and SAP schools. The Chinese were given priority in this programme. The rest could be attended to later, if ever.

Having established this as background, we are now ready to support the contention made at the opening of this chapter, that the programme is one of conscious and aggressive ethnic as well as social assimilation. The critical point to understand at this turn of our argument is that unlike the 'neighbourhood' school system, which is government funded and almost free to parents, kindergartens are private and fee-charging. Recent MOE figures on children entering Primary 1 who are 'not ready for school' suggest that around 14 per cent of children are missing out on most or all of kindergarten (*CNA*, 15 January 2006), while the Ministry confirms that about 5 per cent miss out on kindergarten altogether.[37] Various mechanisms are in place to help the children of low income earners to attend kindergarten, but some of the most important of these are designed explicitly to ensure that the PCF kindergartens are the most affordable and accessible options. In the sections below we shall survey some of the mechanisms by which the privileging of PCF kindergartens has been effected, and consider the practical effect that such measures have had on the community that has been most resistant to assimilation and – possibly not a coincidence – the lowest users of kindergarten services. We refer, of course, to Malays.

As of January 2004, there were 501 registered kindergartens in Singapore, of which 308 were run by the PCF.[38] Most of the PCF kindergartens offered all three mother tongues[39] and another 155 non-PAP kindergartens offered Chinese; 9 offered Tamil; and 33 offered Malay.[40] There appears to be no shortage of suitable kindergartens for anyone, and yet there is evidence emerging (but not yet reliably quantified) from official and semi-official sources that many Malays and Indians are missing out on their pre-school education. An indication of the plight of the Indian children is President Nathan's condemnation of Indian parents who fail to send their children to kindergarten (*CNA*, 14 August 2005). It seems, however, that this 'problem' affects the Malay community much more severely. One Malay teacher writing in *Berita Harian* said in 2004 that in his experience about one in seven Malay pupils enter Primary 1 without being able to read or write because they have missed out on kindergarten (*Berita Harian*, 3 March 2004), suggesting that they make up the majority of the 14 per cent of students who are 'not ready for school'. A more official indicator of this problem was the statement by Parliamentary Secretary for Education Hawazi Daipi in August 2002 that Malay children are disproportionately represented among those missing out on pre-schooling: hence the government's endorsement of the new Singapore Malay-Muslim Education Trust Fund (*ST*, 22 August 2002). Another piece of evidence is the much-publicised move by MENDAKI in November 2003 to launch a two-month 'crash course' for six-year-old Malays to be taught some 'basic skills such as how to write their names' before school starts (*ST*, 19 November 2003). This programme was officially launched by Yaacob Ibrahim, the PAP's then-Minister for Community Development and Sport

(MCDS) and Minister-in-Charge of Muslim Affairs, which gives our analysis added credence. Furthermore, Syed Haroon Aljunied, Secretary of MUIS (Majlis Ugama Islam Singapura, or Islamic Religious Council of Singapore) also claims that Malay children are routinely missing out on kindergarten, and starting Primary 1 at a serious disadvantage:

> A lot of [Malays] opted out because they can't afford it. For one thing pre-school is more expensive than primary school. Pre-school is very expensive, but the way the primary school operates is that they assume that you would have some education already in pre-school. So that when you come to Primary 1, they don't teach you all the basics. They assume that you are able to read and if you don't go into pre-school, there is a problem.[41]

There does not seem to be much room for doubt about the reality of Malay under-representation in kindergarten, but the underlying reasons for it are not so clear. Despite Syed Haroon Aljunied's stated view, it seems unlikely that the question of cost fully accounts for the phenomenon. Malay children are entitled to attend a low-cost PAP kindergarten along with Chinese and Indian children, and if cost were the only consideration, then surely kindergarten entry for low-income Malay children would be nearly as commonplace as it is among low-income Chinese, even allowing for the Malays' tendency to have larger families. The need to adhere to Muslim dietary requirements should not be an impediment either, since the PAP kindergartens all offer *halal* meals.[42]

With these factors eliminated, it is difficult to escape the conclusion that the failure of some Malay parents to send their children to kindergarten is a matter of choice, not necessity. In the absence of empirical studies that reveal the thinking of Malay parents, we are left to speculate on the deeper reasons for this phenomenon. It seems to us that the unspoken assumption behind Syed Haroon Aljunied's account of Malay concerns about cost is the Malays' desire to immerse their children in an environment that will teach Muslim and Malay values, if not the Muslim faith. But Muslim kindergartens registered with the MOE are much more expensive than the PCF kindergartens for various reasons that will be discussed below. While some Muslim parents are clearly willing to send their children to PCF kindergartens, it seems likely that many would prefer to send them to a Muslim kindergarten but cannot afford it. If our survey of Malay-teaching kindergartens registered with MOE is restricted to just those that are properly Muslim, affirmed by either their association with a mosque or their endorsement by MUIS,[43] then the number comes down to between 24 and 31 inclusive.[44] This represents between 4.8 and 6.2 per cent of the total number of kindergartens in Singapore, to cater for around 15 per cent of the kindergarten-age population.[45]

It should not be surprising that many Malay parents are uncomfortable sending their children to PCF kindergartens. *The Straits Times* of 18 September 1999 carried a story of a Chinese mother who put her son into a PCF kindergarten, and her daughter into a YWCA kindergarten. According to the newspaper report,

> She could not help but be struck by the difference. She noted that her [daughter] learnt to be sociable and confident, and knew her numbers and letters too. [Her son] was good academically, but he would hide from strangers and was poor in social skills. So [the mother] moved him to the YWCA centre and he … improved.

This testimony confirms the apocryphal evidence about the nature of socialisation in PCF kindergartens conveyed in several interviews. PCF kindergartens socialise children into an academic and examination-oriented education system at the expense of social skills. It may be a stereotype to assert that Malays value family, motherhood, social skills, inter-personal relations and personal virtues like generosity, but there is no escaping that these virtues are given a position of pre-eminence in this community, and that Malay mothers strive to instil such virtues in their children. Malays are capable of adapting to Singapore's materialistic examination-oriented culture and they have no intrinsic problems with engaging in capitalist pursuit of profit, but it seems that they are reluctant to enter wholeheartedly into the milieu of the Singaporean education system at the expense of these virtues. Hence, Malay reservations about the sterile anti-humanistic culture of the PCF kindergartens, coming on top of issues of cost and a lack of Muslim kindergartens have combined to generate a situation of under-representation of Malay children in kindergartens.

Regardless of the ultimate reason for Malay under-representation in kindergarten, the disadvantage generated by the phenomenon has exaggerated the usual array of socio-economic disadvantages that beset poor, marginalised minorities.[46] In the case of the Malays, the lack of English-language conversation in the home environment adds to the usual list of suspects. (Judging by the small number of young Malay academic achievers surveyed in interview, television (particularly *Sesame Street*) seems to be the most important circuit breaker in this cycle of English-language inadequacy.)

The Malays' neglect of kindergarten has an immediate flow-on in school since, after missing kindergarten, Malay children form a natural ghetto of those who are 'behind', and when they are streamed at Primary 4 (Primary 3 until 1992) this status is institutionalised. Early educational underachievement generally becomes a self-fulfilling prophecy of future failure; just as early educational achievement has the opposite effect. Interviews with a number of young Malays – both 'underachievers' and academic success stories – make it clear that this dominant group creates a Malay sub-culture in school that spurns study and academic achievement. One young Malay actually expressed pity in interview for his high-achieving uncle who is 'a genius', but who never seems to stop working. For them the game of the meritocracy is over before it has begun. Scholarships are beyond comprehension, and 'N' and 'O' levels are usually their highest aspiration in school.

On the other hand, if Malay parents are willing to see their children assimilated into the mainstream to the extent of sending them to a PAP kindergarten, then their children will be able to start Primary 1 on an equal footing with Chinese children from poor families. The systemic advantages of the PAP kindergarten system, and the concomitant pressure to accept assimilation

Figure 7.2: A PCF kindergarten at Clementi, April 2003.

into it, are overwhelming. First, the PAP kindergartens are the most popular because they are almost universally situated on the ground floor of public housing estates, which makes them both highly visible and very convenient (see Figure 7.2). Second, they are cheap because of subsidies, favouritism, and economies of scale. The full extent of subsidies and favouritism for PAP kindergartens is unknown, but we have already documented gifts of millions of dollars from the government to facilitate their expansion and upgrade programmes and we document two more forms of favouritism in the following section. We also note that it seems unlikely they pay full commercial rent for their prime-frontage on the ground floors of public housing estates.

Up to this point in our analysis of the under-representation of Malays in kindergarten it should be acknowledged that there is only incidental evidence that the Singapore system's price for Malay assimilation into the mainstream is the surrender of Malay cultural distinctiveness. It is true that there are some institutional pressures to join their futures to the dominant hegemony, and that multiracialism and meritocracy operate as tools of assimilation, but this is not unique or insidious in itself, even if it does not accord very well with the official rhetoric. What nation-state does not have a dominant hegemony with which minorities must come to an accommodation? The question to be asked at this point is not, 'Is there an ethnic agenda behind the Singapore programme of assimilation?', but 'To what extent is the assimilationist agenda respectful of the plural cultures in Singapore?' and 'To what extent do minorities have to surrender their essential identities in order to be assimilated?' A pluralist, tolerant form of assimilation would minimise the compromises and sacrifices that members of minority groups need to make in order to assimilate, for instance retaining and utilising traditional institutions as vehicles for delivering social goods, rather than forcing minorities to choose between the national project and their traditional loyalties and affections. A monopolistic, intolerant form of assimilation would make few concessions to the mores of minorities, insisting that they surrender many aspects of their traditional identities in order to be accepted as equals, or near-equals.

KiFAS

Judging by the most recent developments in the kindergarten system, it seems that the government must be judged to have a severely monopolistic and ethnic intent – and one that seems to be hardening. We refer to the new direct government subsidy gifted through the Kindergarten Financial Assistance Scheme (KiFAS), run by the Ministry of Community Development, Youth and Sport (MCYS, successor of the MCDS). This is a subsidy scheme for kindergarten fees launched in September 2003 whereby government subsidies are paid directly to private kindergartens under eligibility rules that were originally crafted for the purposes of funding a programme launched by MOE in 2001 to upgrade the professional qualifications of kindergarten teachers.[47] Both the teacher training scheme and the KiFAS scheme exclude all kindergartens not run by the PAP. The eligibility criteria to benefit from KiFAS state that a kindergarten must:

1. be registered with the Ministry of Education and be non-profit;

2. have no religious affiliation or relation to racial groups;

3. have a good track record and offer programmes approved by the Ministry of Education;

4. meet the Ministry of Education's requirements for trained teachers and principals; and

5. have a minimum paid-up capital of $5 million.[48]

According to the MCYS website in 2003 and 2005, the PAP kindergartens are the only ones eligible, though MCYS has taken some clumsy measures to hide this fact. When the KiFAS scheme was first launched in September 2003, the website of MCDS (as it was then) provided the list of eligible kindergartens by providing a link to the PCF kindergarten website, making the correlation between KiFAS-eligible kindergartens and PCF kindergartens transparent. Upon checking the MCYS website on 29 March 2005 we found that the link had been removed. The list published in its place takes the extraordinary step of publishing the addresses and contact details, but not the names of the eligible kindergartens, thus deliberately hiding the fact that all the kindergartens on the list are PCF kindergartens – and incidentally making it more difficult for parents who need information on KiFAS. In fact the new MCYS list of 289 KiFAS-eligible kindergartens was identical to the list of 289 kindergartens listed separately on the PCF website. The MCYS website even grouped KiFAS-eligible kindergartens according to the pattern used by the PCF website, which is to say that it grouped them by PAP Branch rather than list them in, say, alphabetical order.[49] A check of the MCYS website in April 2008 revealed that MCYS has now removed the list of KiFAS-eligible kindergartens completely. Parents are now merely told through a Media Release of March 2008 that KiFAS is available only if their child is enrolled in 'an eligible non-profit kindergarten', but for more information they must 'either approach the kindergarten where KiFAS is available, or [their] nearest Community Development Council (CDC)'.[50] These clumsy attempts to hide the exclusive link between KiFAS and the PCF demonstrate that MCYS is aware of the link and that it wants to hide it.

Yet the KiFAS-PCF link is only the public face in this exercise. The logic behind the particular elements of the rules that create this outcome is revealing in its own right. For instance, considering that the Malay-Muslim community is the largest target group for this initiative, the exclusion of groups with religious affiliations or a relationship with a racial group is staggering. Why exclude kindergartens run by mosques (or churches for that matter)? It is not as if they are unregulated *madrasahs*. They are already registered with MOE and follow the national curriculum guidelines. In a multiracial system where race permeates every aspect of life and race-based groups are the government's preferred delivery vehicle of social services, why exclude kindergartens run by these same groups? If the main purpose of the KiFAS scheme was simply to improve educational access for the poor, it would seem logical to target the vehicles with which the poor are most comfortable – those that are already operating on the principles of self-help that the government holds so dear in other contexts. Instead it is trying to drive poor Malays into sending their children to kindergartens with which they are clearly uncomfortable. It also begs the question of what possible rationale the government used when it decided to privilege kindergartens affiliated to a political party while excluding religious and racial groups, especially since the Muslim community expanded its network of mosque-based kindergartens in direct response to Tony Tan's suggestion in 1991 that religious groups were one of the government's preferred vehicles for providing pre-school education (*ST*, 13 February and 16 August 1991). Why exclude any kindergarten – or at least any non-profit kindergarten – that is properly registered with MOE? The rationale may escape the imagination, but it does demonstrate how the government is using communally neutral institutions to achieve communally biased ends. Having forced society into operating through race-based and communally-oriented institutions, the government then excludes those institutions from selected aspects of public life, leaving institutions that are not explicitly communal, but which reflect its Chinese-generated ethos and values, in positions of privilege.

This is a major institutional manifestation of the dark underside of the expansion of 'common space' about which government ministers speak so freely these days. It seems likely that in the future we will see this technique being used in fields other than kindergarten funding. The KiFAS eligibility rules are a classic example of the aggressive ethnic assimilationist programme that lurks within Singapore's system of 'meritocracy' and multiracialism. The success of the programme at the elite level is demonstrated by the fact that the minister who implemented KiFAS, Dr Yaacob Ibrahim, is himself a Malay-Muslim who undoubtedly believes that he is acting in the best interests of his community and Singapore as a whole. MUIS's Syed Haroon Aljunied also spoke approvingly of the KiFAS initiative in interview, despite the fact that every kindergarten recommended by his organisation is excluded from the scheme. The end result, however, is that most poor Malay parents who want their children to prosper in the Singapore meritocratic system can only do so by socialising their children away from their communities and away from their own values. It is too early to say how enthusiastically the KiFAS/PCF package is being accepted by Malays, but the indications in the Malay press suggest that it is having some effect in attracting more Malay children to PCF kindergartens (*Berita Harian*, 1 July 2005). There is therefore every reason to think that KiFAS, together with other initiatives that privilege PCF kindergartens,[51] will eventually wear down any reluctance that may be holding back the Malay community from engaging fully with the pre-school education sector.

Assimilation through Meritocracy

Taken in the context of the government's agenda over three-decades of privileging Chinese 'values', language, and education, the KiFAS scheme is merely the latest, but one of the more overt tools of incomplete assimilation. Given a clear choice between levelling the playing field for Malays (and Indians for that matter) by addressing the problem of under-representation in kindergarten, or furthering its programme of assimilation, it has chosen the latter. Given the long term impact of socialisation at pre-school age, this development has the potential to be one of the more significant and successful initiatives in this direction.

Notes

1   PAP Community Foundation, *Book of Memories*, Singapore: PAP Community Foundation, Tampines West Education Centre, 1992, p. 24.

2   See, for instance, Speech by Dr Aline Wong, Senior Minister of State for Education at the PCF Education Centres Graduation Ceremony, 13 November 1999; Speech by Tharman Shanmugaratnam in Parliament, 21 May 2002; and Speech by Mr Tharman Shanmugaratnam, Senior Minister of State for Education and Trade and Industry, at the opening ceremony of the 'Nurture the Genius in your Pre-Schooler Seminar', 28 May 2002. All available on MOE website, http://www.moe.gov.sg/. Accessed 23 February 2006.

3   Speech by Senior Minister of State for Foreign Affairs, Encik A. Rahim Ishak, at the Siglap Community Centre Kindergarten, 5 November 1977, Singapore Government Press Release, located at http://www.sprinter.gov.sg/. Accessed 24 May 2005. Speech by Mr Teo Chong Tee, Parliamentary Secretary (Social Affairs), and MP for Changi, at the Kindergarten Graduation Ceremony/Variety Show for Parents at the Education Centre of PAP Changi Branch, 8 November 1981, Singapore Government Press Release, located at http://www.sprinter.gov.sg. Accessed 24 May 2005.

4   Speech by A. Rahim Ishak at the Siglap Community Centre Kindergarten, 5 November 1977.

5   Speech by Mr A. Rahim Ishak, Senior Minister of State for Foreign Affairs and MP for Siglap Constituency, at the PAP Siglap Branch Kindergarten Presentation of Certificates, 18 November 1977, Singapore Government Press Release, located at http://www.sprinter.gov.sg/. Accessed 24 May 2005.

6   Speech by A. Rahim Ishak at the Siglap Community Centre Kindergarten, 5 November 1977.

7   The Chinese schools were ostensibly chosen as a pilot scheme, but it has since been revealed that these schools were selected to provide help for Chinese children learning English and to stop the free-fall in Chinese stream enrolments (*ST*, 16 February 1982 and 29 January 1989).

8   Interview with a retired junior primary school teacher, Singapore, 31 March 2004.

9   Ibid. Another interviewee told of his experience as a P1 student in 1981. On the first day of P1 his class was divided into those who could read and those who could not, with the former forming a majority.

10 Speech by Goh Chok Tong at the PCF Education Centre, Tampines Branch, 6 August 1987, Singapore Government Press Release. Available at http://sprinter.gov.sg/. Accessed 24 May 2005.

11 Ibid.

12 Ibid.

13 Speech by Dr Tony Tan, Minister for Education, at the opening of the First National Conference and Exhibition on Kindergarten Education, 15 November 1990, Singapore Government Press Release, available at http://sprinter.gov.sg/. Accessed 24 May 2005.

14 Janet Shepherd, *Striking a Balance: The Management of Language in Singapore*, Frankfurt, Peter Lang, 2005, p. 136.

15 'Message' from Tony Tan, Chairman of the PCF Council of Management, in PAP Community Foundation, *Project Pre-School 1991–1994*, Singapore: PAP Community Foundation Pre-School Development Unit, 1994.

16 Tony Tan, 'Message' in *Project Pre-School*. Tony Tan's 'Message' is indicative of the level of official involvement in supporting the PCF's supposedly private project. As well as the NIE, Tan also thanked the following government bodies for their support: MOE, People's Association, Housing and Development Board, Urban and Redevelopment Authority, Public Utilities Board, and several Town Councils.

17 In fact the PCF did not meet its expansionary targets, having opened 'only' a further 50 kindergartens by 1995, instead of 60 by 1994 (*ST*, 30 July 1996).

18 MOE, *Curriculum Guidelines for the Pre-Primary Programme: Development of Skills (Semester I and II)*, Singapore: Educational Publications Bureau, 1979, pp. 1, 2.

19 Ibid., p. 14.

20 Ibid., 'Objectives of the Pre-Primary Curriculum', before first numbered pages.

21 MOE, *Curriculum Guidelines for the Pre-Primary Programme (Semester I & II)*, Singapore: Ministry of Education, 1979.

22 MOE, *Ministry of Education Pre-Primary Programme: Suggestions for Planning Activities*, Singapore: Educational Publications Bureau, 1980.

23 MOE, *Ministry of Education Pre-Primary Programme (Revised Edition): Suggestions for Planning Activities*, Singapore: Educational Publications Bureau, 1987.

24 *Project Pre-School*.

25 *Book of Memories*, pp. 24–29.

26 PAP Community Foundation, *PAP Tampines East Education Centre Year Book '90*, Singapore: PAP Community Foundation Tampines East Education Centres, 1990.

27 See Joyce Goh, *English Kindergarten 1 Term 3*, Singapore: Oxford University Press, 1995, Contents page.

28 Y.B. Liow, *Nursery Activity Book Term 2*, Singapore: Oxford University Press, 1995.

29 Joyce Goh, *English Kindergarten 1 Term 3*.

30 The source of the $5 million is not known to the authors, but it is known that the PCF intended to seek financial assistance from the MOE (*ST*, 18 September 1994).

31 Leong Yf and Zenda Leu, *From Kindergarten to P1*, [Singapore]: Teacher-Pupil Connections, [c. 2000].

32 Lydia Lau, *Pre-School, Covering Primary 1 Syllabus, Vocabulary, Book 3*, Singapore: Casco Publications, [c. 2004], p. 70.

33 Tang Qing, *Nursery, Recognising Words, B*, [Singapore]: Educational Publishing, [c.2004]; Cheryl Goh, *Learning Skills for Early Years, Numbers, Nursery*, [Singapore]: Educational Publishing, [c. 2004]; *Chinese Enrichment for Nursery*, Singapore: Success Publications, 2002; *Child Development Programme, Nursery Book 4*, Singapore: System Publishing House, 2001 (revised 2002, reprinted 2003, 2004).

34 Educational Publishing House website, http://www.eph.com.sg/. Accessed on 8 June 2005.

35 Household income figure derived from Lee Bee Geok, *Census of Population 2000: Household and Housing*, Singapore: Department of Statistics, 2001, p. 11. The observation about the high cost of elite kindergartens is made from anecdotal evidence gained in interviews.

36 MOE website, http://www.moe.gov.sg/. Accessed 6 November 2003.

37 Tharman Shanmugaratnam, Keynote address by Mr Tharman Shanmugaratnam, Minister for Education, at PAP Community Foundation's 20th Anniversary Celebration Dinner, 19 May 2006. Available on the MOE website.

38 MCDS website at http://www.mcds.gov.sg. Accessed 6 November 2003. PCF website, at http://www.pcf.org.sg/. Accessed 6 November 2003.

39 Barr's phone calls to PCF Education Centres, January 2004.

40 This adds up to more than 155 because many kindergartens offer more than one mother tongue.

41 Barr's interview with Syed Haroon Aljunied, Singapore, 29 April 2003.

42 Barr's phone calls to PCF Education Centres, January 2004.

43 See MUIS website, at http://www.muis.gov.sg/. Accessed 6 November 2003.

44 We cannot be very precise because the MUIS list did not distinguish between Muslim childcare centres and kindergartens. It also appeared to endorse some unregistered kindergartens, but it failed to list some registered kindergartens associated with mosques. We are confident, however, that there were at least 24 registered Muslim kindergartens, but no more than 31.

45 According to the official *Singapore Infomap* at www.sg, 14.9 per cent of the population is Muslim (mainly Malay-Muslims and a small number of Indian Muslims). Since Malays are the most fecund community in Singapore it follows that they must have an even larger share of the kindergarten-age population.

46 Quinn R. Moore, 'Multiracialism and meritocracy: Singapore's approach to race and inequality', *Review of Social Economy*, vol. 58, no. 3, 2000, pp. 339–360.

47 'Pre-school recurrent grants to help kindergartens get better qualified kindergarten teachers and financial assistance', press release on the MOE website, 8 October 2001, at www.moe.gov.sg/. Accessed 21 February 2006.

48 MCYS website at http://www.mcys.gov.sg/. Accessed 29 March 2005.

49 See http://www.mcds.gov.sg/, accessed December 2003; MCYS website at http://www.mcys.gov.sg/, accessed on 29 March 2005; and the PCF website at http://www.pcf.org.sg/index.htm/, accessed on 29 March 2005.

50 MCYS website at http://www.mcys.gov.sg,accessed 14 April, 2008, particularly MCYS Media Release No: 15/2008, issued 5 March 2008, available at http://www.mcys.gov.sg/MCDSFiles/Press/Articles/15-2008.pdf. This Media Release also announced increases

in KiFAS funding and personal eligibility levels without any mention of the matter of institutional eligibility. It also foreshadowed an extension of the KiFAS scheme to the Nursery Programme through a new Centre-Based Financial Assistance Scheme for Childcare (CFAC) – also without any explanation of the basis on which nursery schools are judged to be eligible.

51 See, for instance, Tharman Shanmugaratnam's speech to the PCF's 20th Anniversary Celebration Dinner, 19 May 2006.

EIGHT

Grades, Kiasuism and Race: Primary School and Beyond

IN TODAY'S PRIMARY SCHOOL, the construction of the 'new' Singaporean is a continuation of the modest beginnings made in kindergarten, but until the early 1980s it was, for most children, the true beginning of their government-directed socialisation. This chapter investigates the history of the primary school experience (mostly since the late 1970s) and examines how it has been crafted into a tool for constructing 'new' Singaporeans and new elites. It investigates this experience through two prisms: the escalation of academic expectations of primary school pupils and the consequent creation of a *kiasu*, examination-driven and tuition-fed school system; and the treatment of race, ethnicity and language in primary schools, producing a racially conscious society driven by often ignorant racial stereotypes.

Background

In the early years after independence, standards in government schools were generally low. As the government strove to expand a small and inadequately resourced school system inherited mainly from the disparate efforts of the colonial administration and communal organisations, it was almost inevitable that the quest for quantity would impede the pursuit of quality. The exceptions to this were a few well-established elite schools provided variously by the government, Christian missions, and Chinese associations. For the most part, however, children attended what came to be called 'neighbourhood schools' – free government schools that catered indiscriminately for any child in a given locality. Teachers in those schools were generally poorly trained, yet the government was nevertheless struggling to meet the growing demand – especially the demand for English-speaking teachers that it was deliberately, though quietly generating through its promotion of English-medium education. During this period the traditional Chinese emphasis on rote learning

150

became a convenient way to cover many inadequacies and insecurities on the part of teachers and curriculum designers. On top of these impediments, the language environment of the island *per se* presented yet another obstacle to the pursuit of quality. Most children did not come from English-speaking families but spoke any one of the three other official languages of the new republic – Mandarin, Tamil, Malay – or, more likely, one of half a dozen or so 'unofficial' Chinese and Indian languages that could be commonly heard in the markets and housing estates. With this in mind, from the late 1960s to the late 1970s a special effort was put into teaching English to children who came from non-English-speaking homes without much regard to their race. From the late 1970s to the early 1990s, however, the 'special effort' was restricted to Chinese children in the form of the Pre-Primary Programme,

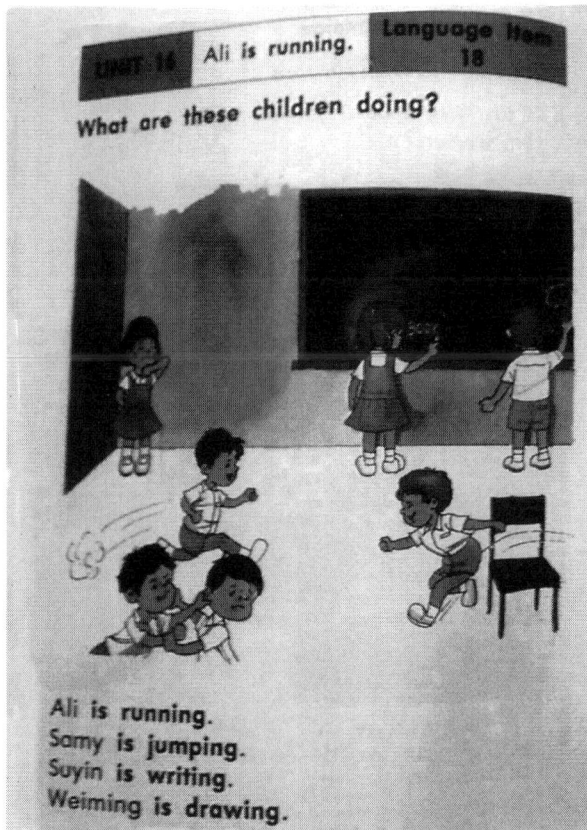

Figure 8.1: Racial stereotyping in a Primary 1 textbook, 1981.[1]

the Preparatory Year programme, and the provision of dedicated Chinese schools (*ST*, 29 January 1989 and 27 June 1990; *Business Times*, 21 March 1989; see also Chapters 5, 6, 7). Malays and Indians, by contrast, have had to fend for themselves without special help.[2] After two decades of ambivalence about the place of Asian languages in schooling, English was finally made the official First Language of all school children in 1987, and since the early 1990s there has been a working assumption in the curriculum that all children already possess a working and social knowledge of English and the task has been to increase the standard of English as a first language. It is implicitly acknowledged that large sections of the school-age population do not fit this description, even today, but the curriculum has been set on the presumption that this is true.

Beginning Primary School

For most parents today, there is no choice about their children's primary school enrolment because cost prohibits them from sending their children anywhere other than the local neighbourhood school. They provide notionally the same standard of education as elite schools but everyone knows this is a well-intended fiction and those who can manage it opt for a school with a 'name' and a reputation (*ST*, 23 May 1984). Yet, even for the wealthy, entry into a 'name' school is not usually a straightforward matter of writing a cheque, though this is clearly a good start. It involves a labyrinth of bureaucratic criteria, some of which involve interviews with parents and the prospective students, and which can involve a study of a child's kindergarten results. When streaming was first introduced parents started going to extraordinary lengths in an effort to enrol their children in good schools – even risking jail by signing false declarations (*ST*, 18, 20 and 23 December 1980). A major criterion for acceptance is living in close proximity to the school in question, prompting the practice of shifting house to get one's children into a good school. By the early 1990s this had become a common practice among those who could afford it, but of course it was an option available only to wealthy and upper-middle-class parents (*ST*, 13 March 1992; 9 July 1995). In 1984 Lee Kuan Yew gave mothers with tertiary qualifications priority in enrolling their children in these 'good' schools, though this particular exercise in eugenics was so unpopular and ineffectual that it was brought to an abrupt end in 1985.[3] The obsession with enrolling one's children in a 'name' school pre-dates *The Goh Report* of 1979 and was almost an inevitable result of the government's rapid expansion of the school system in the 1960s, but it was given a new impetus by the early streaming, introduced in 1979, and by the mid-1990s a minor private industry had developed to cater for parents desperate to understand the entry procedures and requirements of schools, and keen to absorb information to help them choose a suitable primary school for their children (*ST*, 12 December 1996). As of 2005 the dominance of 'name' schools was such that in the PSLE of that year, only one of the top six students came from an ordinary 'neighbourhood school' (*CNA*, 24 November 2005).

Standards in Primary School

After our outline of the inflation of academic expectations in kindergartens it should come as no surprise to learn that primary schools followed a similar path. Whether in English, Maths or 'Mother Tongue', there is a consistent pattern of soaring curriculum targets. For the first decade or so, this can be explained by the fact that the education system was launching itself from such a low base, but in this chapter we concern ourselves mainly with the period since the end of the 1970s, when most of the early challenges were receding. The immediate drivers for this second round of inflation can be identified with precision, and they seem to apply as readily to secondary school as they do to primary: the escalating stakes involved in streaming; escalating requirements in the curricula; the introduction of rewards for anticipated excellence; and escalating expectations of parents. Though listed separately, none of these drivers has acted independently of the others. They feed off each other and between them have generated Singapore's *kiasu* education system.

ࢠ *Escalating stakes involved in streaming*

Without the introduction of high, life-affecting stakes into the process of streaming, Singaporean society would have a very different character – more relaxed, less *kiasu*, more humanistic. From today's perspective, it seems strange to think that until 1976 even passage through primary school was an automatic process, with the first external examinations applying only in Primary 6.[4] The decision to make passage beyond Primary 2 conditional upon passing examinations was not directly connected with the introduction of streaming four years later, but in retrospect it was the beginning of a process of stratification of students according to academic performance that was going to dominate the character of Singaporean society into the twenty-first century.

Streaming proper was introduced into Singapore schools at Primary 3 in 1979. From then until 1992, the top students were streamed at the end of Primary 3 into the Normal Stream for the remainder of their primary schooling. The alternatives were to go into the Extended Stream (with an extra two years of primary school but still being eligible to sit for the PSLE at the end of Primary 8) or the Monolingual Stream (which would lead into vocational training rather than secondary school, after Primary 8).[5] This system was modified in 1992 so that streaming was moved back to the end of Primary 4 and the existing streams were replaced by EM1, EM2 and EM3. The first two assume English-language proficiency and separate students by their levels of proficiency in 'Mother Tongue'. EM3 teaches only a basic 'Foundation' level of both English and 'Mother Tongue' and is the social equivalent of the old Monolingual Stream.[6] In 2004, EM1 and EM2 were suddenly and without warning collapsed into one stream, while EM3 students were given permission to take some higher level subjects for which they had displayed particular aptitude (*ST*, 29 October 2004). It is not at all clear what prompted these changes, although the universal acclamation given to the reforms by parents and teachers suggests that it might be more appropriate to ask why they were delayed for so long. Regardless of the motivation, these changes have left the basic structure of streaming unscathed, at least for the moment, but if they are ever taken to their logical conclusions they will lead to a breakdown of streaming and create a severe rift with Lee Kuan Yew's practice of viewing 'talent' as an organic, indivisible whole.

In 1979, PSLE also became a streaming examination, determining whether a child was streamed into the Special, Express or Normal stream in secondary school, with further divisions of Special and Express into the prestigious Science and the less prestigious Arts streams. In 1994 the Normal stream was further divided into Normal (Academic) and Normal (Technical). In 2005, 2.2 per cent of PSLE candidates were streamed away from secondary school, and a further 35.6 per cent were streamed into Normal (Academic) or Normal (Technical) streams, leaving 62.2 per cent eligible for Special or Express streams (*CNA*, 24 November 2005).

Such is the pressure in the PSLE that today 50 to 60 per cent of upper primary students are taking tuition in subjects in which they already excel, for fear of missing out on the stream or the school that they want.[7] Note the special place that streaming has given languages. With streaming it has become necessary to have proficiency in both English and one's 'Mother Tongue' at all stages from ages 9 or 10 onwards just to avoid being streamed to the bottom of the educational, economic and social ladder. In fact between 1973 and 1985 the languages had a double weighting in the PSLE, which would be enough to drive any parent to distraction.

❧ Escalating requirements in the curricula

The second element in the inflation of expectations was an increase in the demands of the various subject curricula. In this survey we restrict ourselves to English, Maths and Chinese Language. In both English and Maths the steady, unrelenting increases in standards have been reflected in the radical changes introduced to the streaming examinations over the decades. A comprehensive study of the content of PSLE papers has yet to be undertaken, but we have found no shortage of evidence suggesting that it underwent qualitative increases in difficulty.

In 2004 a retired Primary 6 teacher who had been teaching almost continually from 1968 to 1991, and had returned to relief teaching in 1997, spoke of her experiences in interview. From the 1970s to the 1980s she noticed a distinct escalation of difficulty of the PSLE papers in both Maths and English. The Maths papers came to include two or three particularly difficult questions to sort out the exceptional students from the average, while the English paper became 'tougher' in terms of vocabulary, comprehension, and the expectations that good grammar would be used in the open-ended questions. Yet these changes paled against those that came in between her retirement in 1991 and her return to teaching in 1997. The English papers were basically unchanged, but the Maths paper was unrecognisable. It was filled with complex 'problem sums' that involved a careful reading of English prose to understand the questions, and usually a series of calculations, each dependent on getting the correct answer in the previous calculation. She observed that these questions required skills that the students would not need again for years in secondary school.[8] The predominance of 'problem sums' meant that those who were already struggling in English were also placed at a disadvantage in Maths, regardless of how good their Maths might otherwise be (placing all children from non-English-speaking home environments at an exaggerated disadvantage) while even good

Maths students could be expected to struggle with some of the questions. She complained that the government seemed to be creating an unnecessarily high hurdle just for the sake of raising the bar. She also insisted that her perception of this matter was shared widely by Primary 6 and Secondary Maths teachers,[9] an observation that is supported by press reports that take it for granted that this is the popular perception among parents (see, for instance, *CNA*, 11 October 2005; *Straits Times Interactive*, 17 October 2005). One parent with undergraduate, masters and PhD degrees in maths-related disciplines complained that even he could not readily solve some of the questions on the 2005 PSLE Maths Paper. He said that 'some questions are utterly unreasonable as they require unique, tedious and often one-of-its-kind model approach ... [that will] only create a legacy of fear ... ' (*Straits Times Interactive*, 26 October 2005).

Impressions of examinations by parents and teachers are only an indirect means of judging curricula, but a study of the syllabi directly leads to the same conclusions.

English: A simple comparison of the English syllabi of 1981 and 1990 reveal escalating expectations of Primary 3 children. In 1981 the complete list of a Primary 3 child's ideal writing skill set was to write 'guided compositions of about 50 words', 'simple narratives of about 30 words based on pictures', and 'simple sentences based on familiar situations'.[10] In 1990 six of the thirteen writing objectives for Primary 3 children were:

- 'writing creatively and imaginatively for self-expression',
- 'writing creatively and imaginatively on a given topic',
- 'writing after gathering ideas from brainstorming etc.',
- 'writing clearly and intelligibly, using correct grammar and syntax, good diction and appropriate register',
- 'editing, revising and re-drafting in discussion with other children and/or teacher', and
- 'writing to reconstruct information given'.[11]

A comparison of 1981 and 1990 Primary 3 requirements for speaking, listening and reading skills provides a similarly stark contrast.

Another easily managed guide to the development of English curricula as it was really applied in the classroom is found in the primary textbooks and teachers' manuals from 1970 to 2000. Here the difference is startling.

The 1970 *English This Way 1* textbook states clearly that it assumes 'zero' knowledge, and begins with spoken phrases like 'Good morning teacher' and the most basic vocabulary ('a book', 'a bag').[12] The *PEP* series of the 1980s starts at a similar level, while its rival, the *NESPE* series, starts with the children learning spoken dialogue correctly by rote and teaching common sentences 'as formula'.[13] By 2000 things had changed drastically. The *Celebrate English 1A Teacher's Edition* assumed that most children could already read and provided reminders to teachers to read material aloud for the benefit of those pupils who 'are not yet able to read or are unable to read proficiently, yet'.[14] They moved almost straight away into expanding reading vocabulary to include parts of the face, forms of plurals, and their oral vocabulary to include words such as 'suspect' and 'connect'.[15] The rival *Treks* textbook took Primary 1 children almost immediately into identifying nouns, pronouns and verbs and constructing simple sentences using flashcards with words written on them.[16]

Maths: Without going into a detailed examination of all the Maths syllabi issued since independence, a comparison between that of 1980 and 1999 confirms the reality of an escalation of expectations over these years. Table 8.1 compares the declared expectations of Primary 1 children in each of these syllabi. Going into slightly more detail we also note that the 1980 syllabus required Primary 1 children to solve 'one step word problems using one function', whereas in 1999 they were required to solve 'one step word problems using four functions and two step word problems using two functions'. In 1980 they were taught to 'interpret pictograms (scale) and column graphs', whereas in 1999 they were taught to 'make picture graphs to scale, read and interpret picture graphs with scales, and solve word problems using data presented in picture graphs'.

Significantly the 1999 syllabus expected Primary 1 children to perform some functions that in 1980 were not learnt until much later. For instance in 1999 a Primary 1 child was expected to learn how to construct, read and interpret picture graphs, whereas in 1980 a child was not expected to read or interpret column graphs until Primary 3, and even then they were not expected to construct them. In 1999 Primary 1 children were expected to solve word problems using addition, subtraction and money, which meant that a child who could not read upon entering Primary 1 not only began school by failing English, but also struggling with Maths.[19] In 1980 the equivalent word

Table 8.1: A comparison of the stated objectives of the Primary 1 Maths syllabi, 1980 and 1999

1980[17]	1999[18]
• Count from 1 to 100 and to develop the notion of magnitude in numbers;	• Develop understanding of mathematical concepts: numerical, geometrical, statistical;
• Read and write numerals from 1 to 100;	• Perform operations with whole numbers;
• Add and subtract numbers up to 20;	• Recognise spatial relationships in two and three dimensions;
• Develop the concepts of multiplication and division;	• Use mathematical language, symbols and diagrams to represent and communicate mathematical ideas;
• Identify and name familiar shapes;	
• Arrange objects and make patterns according to given attributes;	• Present and interpret information in written, graphical, diagrammatic and tabular forms;
• Estimate and measure length and weight with non-standard units;	• Recognise patterns and structures in mathematics;
• Construct and read pictograms.	• Develop and perform mental calculations;
	• Use mathematical concepts learnt to solve problems;
	• Develop an inquiring mind through investigative activities;
	• Enjoy learning mathematics through a variety of activities.

problems were introduced only in Primary 2. If this is the level of escalation in junior primary, it is not at all hard to imagine the escalation of standards in the PSLE described earlier by the retired Primary 6 teacher.

Chinese Language: It appears that the story of standards in Chinese Language is not as straightforward as it is for English and Maths, though it must be acknowledged that language barriers mean that we are heavily reliant upon secondary and indirect sources in making our assessment. The most startling difference between the story of Chinese language and that of the other subjects is that Chinese language standards have dropped, rather than increased, since independence. These days English language is commonly used in Chinese Language classes (*ST*, 4 February 2004), Hanyu Pinyin is now in standard usage, Chinese characters have been simplified in line with those used in the PRC, and dictionaries can be taken into examinations. A round of pedagogical reforms announced at the end of 2004 and implemented in 2007 were designed to lighten the burden of learning Chinese Language even further – with comparable changes following for Malay and Tamil languages in 2008 (*CyBerita*, 9 March 2006) – but at the time of writing the impact of the changes on student load and the demand for tuition is still uncertain.[20] From this cursory picture it is apparent that far from being subjected to an escalation in expectations, Chinese Language education has been struggling for four decades to regain some semblance of the glory days of the old Chinese schools in the face of seemingly insurmountable odds. In the 1970s the particular problems were poorly trained and grossly overworked Chinese Language teachers, and children for whom Mandarin was almost a foreign language because they came from 'dialect-speaking' backgrounds. By the 1980s the standards of training and the workloads had improved, but teachers were dealing with a new generation for whom Mandarin was virtually a foreign language because they had grown up with English and possibly a 'dialect'. At all times the competing demands of learning English, Maths, Science, etc. made learning Chinese Language a major imposition for most children.[21] The net result has been that the demands of Chinese Language studies have been the main single driver of the demand for private tuition among students, accounting for nearly half the 13 hours or so a week that students were spending in private tuition in 1998.[22] Yet it seems that the curriculum *per se* is not the culprit. Standards were increased between 1992 and 2000,[23] but this is not a story of escalating standards as such. Rather, generations of students have been driven to extraordinary lengths in Chinese Language because of the stakes involved in streaming and university admissions requirements (which are considered elsewhere).

❧ *Rewards for anticipated excellence*

Rewarding excellence before it has been achieved is one of the most peculiar characteristics of the Singapore system of 'meritocracy' and one of the most direct drivers of *kiasu*ism. At face value one might assume that a meritocracy is like a foot race where everyone runs on the same track and those who finish first are the 'winners', and then receive the rewards. The Singapore system, however, is more like a poker game where each incremental win or loss places you at an advantage or a disadvantage in the next hand. Being dealt winning hands early in life (for instance by attending a good kindergarten and primary school, receiving tuition when it is needed, and then doing exceptionally well in Primary 3 or Primary 4 streaming) means that you can attend smaller classes taught by better teachers, using the most stimulating syllabi and textbooks, and have the most opportunities for Co-Curricular Activities. The unspoken spirit of this culture was institutionalised in 1983 with the introduction of the Gifted Education Programme (GEP) in selected elite primary and secondary schools. The programme, modelled initially on the Israeli gifted education programme (*ST*, 10 January 1982) was explicitly designed to give a competitive edge throughout their schooling to children who excel in special selection tests in Primary 3 or Primary 6 (*ST*, 4 September 1983).[24] The GEP gives such an advantage that one teacher from Raffles Girls' School observed in mid-2004 that, even with the introduction of the Integrated Programme in 2004 (whereby entire schools have come to act as the replacement of the GEP in post-primary schools),[25] those students who had gone through the GEP in primary school were still being taught in separate classes because

> gifted students already have had a certain momentum in the type of learning environment that we've created. They're used to divergent situations; they're used to inquiry process; they're used to independent thinking. So we want to keep to that momentum. (*CNA*, 3 June 2004)

Other teachers were quoted in the same report as saying GEP students 'go through the syllabus faster than their peers, allowing them to have more enrichment activities in class'.

If, however, you were dealt a poor hand or failed to focus and achieve academic success in lower primary school for whatever reason, you found yourself, according to an Institute of Education report from the 1980s, being taught an 'unstimulating learning menu' in large classes by teachers who did not want to be there, and who lacked adequate training.[26] The training and professionalism of the teachers has improved drastically since the 1980s, but EM3 students still struggle with large class sizes (typically of 40 children), few resources and such a basic curriculum that even the most conscientious teachers struggle to bring out the best in students (*ST*, 30 November 1999 and 26 February 2001). On top of these disadvantages the students know that even if they overcome the odds and are streamed into Normal (Academic) or Express Streams for secondary school, the very basic curriculum they studied in primary school put them behind their classmates and they will have to work hard just to catch up (*The New Paper*, 27 January 2005). It should not take much imagination to realise that such a system is going to transpose the pressures to strive and excel usually associated with matriculation examinations to the earliest years of primary school (and even earlier).

❧ Parental expectations

Parental expectations are significant inputs into the creation of the *kiasu* education system, so that the outcome might be said to be, to some extent, a result of a dialogue between *kiasu* government and *kiasu* parents, whereby each party feeds the other's expectations and fears. Parental expectations cannot be measured reliably and we do not intend to try, though the legend of the *kiasu* mother should leave little doubt that it is powerful. Beyond legend, however, *kiasu* parents leave tangible evidence of the pressure they bring to bear. Some indicators can be listed easily:

- The ubiquitous presence of private tuition. This was already a $52-million industry in 1981, and by 1992 a $260-million 'shadow education system' had developed, servicing half of all primary students and one-third of all secondary students (*ST*, 29 June 1981 and 4 April 1992). This presence is continuing to grow, with the number of 'tuition schools' registered with MOE increasing by 86 per cent between 1999 and 2004;[27]
- The problem of teachers facing harassment from angry parents over their children's grades (*ST*, 17 December 1980);
- The sale of illegal copies of examinations from 'good schools' that can be purchased at fly-by-night hawker stalls in any housing estate;
- The thriving market in monthly practice tests, workbooks, model answers and primers that occupy a full quarter of the shelf and floor space of most bookshops on the island.

Yet even as we point to these factors we must acknowledge that they are not so much indicators of escalating parental expectations *per se*. It would be more accurate to describe them as indicators of parents' responses to the inadequacies and pressures of a school system that cannot stand on its own. Without resort to private tuition, primers, practice examinations and the pressure of *kiasu* parents, the Singapore education system would collapse. What is a concerned parent to do under these circumstances? They are driven to be *kiasu* as a logical response to the logic of the school system and the unforgiving nature of the streaming system so that, although we can reasonably point to escalating parental pressure as a factor in escalating standards, we acknowledge that this is just the last step in a process that is managed from on high by MOE.

There is another point to be noted from the primers – as there is from many of the official textbooks and workbooks. This refers to the predominance of test questions across all subjects that require a child to fill in the blanks. This includes English and Chinese language. Even English composition is learnt by drill! This observation accords with the observations of recent students who recalled in interview that filling in the blanks and regurgitating textbooks word for word were standard methods of teaching and testing, even in junior college. The preponderance of such pedagogical methodology was probably to be expected in the 1960s and 1970s when well-trained teachers were a rarity, but its perpetuation in the early years of the twenty-first century, when Singapore is striving for the status of a global city with a knowledge-based economy, risks exposing the country to ridicule.

This observation also places a serious caveat on this chapter's discourse on increasing expectations and standards in schools. The students are certainly better than their predecessors at taking examinations and meeting the demanding requirements of 'filling in the blanks', and they undoubtedly excel in narrow bands of technical proficiency that make them good engineers and technocrats, but it is doubtful if they have really been taught to think any better than their predecessors. Rather, what comes more readily to mind is the common complaint that Singaporean students have been drilled in unthinking conformity – perhaps the epitome of a 'new' Singaporean?

Race in the Classroom

We move now to a study of race in the Singapore education system. In Chapters 5 and 7 we considered the role of the race of the child as an input in educational access, particularly the special privileges granted to SAP schools and the neglect of the minority races. Now we explore the projection of race in the actual process of teaching and in the school setting *per se*, especially through the use of English textbooks. The first thing to acknowledge is that the 1970s English primary school textbooks and classroom environments contained very little stereotyping according to race and only incidental consciousness of race *per se*.[28] In the early 1980s, however, while the government was taking a number of initiatives that exacerbated consciousness of 'race' in broader society, it was taking complementary initiatives in the classroom. One aspect of this programme of racialisation of the classroom and society was Lee Kuan Yew's 1980 decision to identify Malays collectively as underachievers in national examinations (while exonerating the government of any responsibility, of course) (*ST*, 19 November 1980).[29] Ten years later, the then Minister for Education Tony Tan took this initiative to its logical conclusion when he began the now-routine practice of issuing statistics on educational achievement and examination results broken down by race, a step that took the racialisation of education out of the classroom and put it on the front page.[30]

Another racialising initiative was the new emphasis on learning one's 'mother tongue', which inadvertently served to herd children through school according to their racial classification. Because of this particular innovation, many children have spent and continue to spend much of their school life in almost mono-racial classrooms. This is most obviously the case in SAP schools, which are almost completely all-Chinese environments, but *de facto* racial segregation has been much more extensive than this suggests. One Indian man told in interview how he came to study in an almost completely Indian environment in secondary school in the 1990s. He wanted to study Tamil during school hours (as opposed to attending after-school classes) so he had a very limited number of schools from which to choose. This resulted in him moving to a school with a disproportionately high number of Indians. Then these Indian children found that their teachers had put them into the same classes to make it easier to timetable their Tamil lessons. This was language-based segregation that served as *de facto* racial segregation and it was standard practice throughout the 1980s and 1990s (*ST*, 1 January 1987). Ooi Giok Ling has referred to this practice as 'bunching' children according to their racial classification.[31] In the case of Malays this 'bunching' effect was compounded by their generally poor academic performance in Primary 3 and Primary 4 streaming, which left most of them nearly monopolising the lowest streams of school. Chinese children seem to have been unaware of this effect, however, because they accept the predominance of Chinese as normal.

Even without compounding this situation with forms of structural discrimination, the Singaporean classroom was loaded with opportunities for unthinking episodes that highlighted race and community. Some instances of such behaviour have been documented by Trivina Kang in her sociological study of a girl's secondary school: Chinese teachers and Chinese classmates lapsing unthinkingly into Mandarin in the classroom; Chinese teachers speaking Mandarin to Malay children in class; and Chinese children choosing to speak Mandarin as a conscious expression of social power.[32] Lily Rahim has exposed another aspect: condescension towards Malays for being 'burdened' with a culture that supposedly promotes laziness, thus encouraging them to think of themselves as failures.[33]

Compounding racialising factors such as these was a major shift in pedagogical methodology at the beginning of the 1980s, whereby primary textbooks – particularly English textbooks – were revised to give them a 'local' setting.[34] Educationists were commissioned to produce English textbooks with which Singaporean children could easily identify because of the familiarity of the society and places being portrayed in stories and pictures. With this initiative the presence of race in the classroom became ubiquitous overnight because the peculiarly Singaporean worldview that sees society through the prism of race – and primarily from a Chinese perspective – was given free rein. To help the children relate to the world being depicted in their new textbooks, they were even presented with little picture and reading lessons that were obviously designed to help children learn to identify people by race: 'The Malay girl [pictured with dark skin and wavy hair] is Minah. She

Figure 8.2: Miss Li, from the *PEP* textbooks.

has [i.e. is the one holding] a doll. The Chinese girl [pictured with fair skin and straight hair] is Sufen. She has [i.e. is the one holding] a kitten.'[35]

It was also a direct but probably unintended consequence of this initiative that the primary school English textbooks of the 1980s became vehicles for transmitting and reinforcing racial stereotypes. The *New Course English* textbooks went to considerable lengths to portray the life and work of Mohammed the Malay hotel porter, Cik Alimah the Malay domestic worker, Ahmad the Malay street sweeper, Encik Samad, another Malay street sweeper, and – by contrast – Mrs Li and Miss Li the Chinese school teachers.[36]

The *Primary Education Programme (PEP)* series was filled with stories about Singaporean children and adults with names like Ali, Sumei and Ravi, accompanied by drawings of identifiably Malay, Chinese and Indian characters playing games and living life. It also taught children to expect that Malays and Indians would work predominately in relatively menial jobs. Thus we see the Sikh policeman (Mr Singh),[37] the Indian hawker stall holder,[38] and the Indian and the Malay zookeepers (Muthu, Maniam and Hassan).[39] On the other hand we see rather more uplifting images of Chinese characters, such as the civic-minded Chinese leader in the housing estate (Mr Lin)[40] and the Chinese doctor.[41]

A particularly strong and consistent stereotype was the depiction of teachers as Chinese (with names such as Miss Li, Mrs Li, Mrs Chan, Miss Chen, Mr Chen, Mr Shih, and Miss Wu, Mrs Wu and Mr Wu).[42] The principal is a Mr Chen and in this series even the scout master is Chinese (Mr Ying).[43] In the minds of Singaporean primary school children – and junior primary school children in particular – the teacher was and is a god-like being: a fount of authority and a dispenser of wisdom and knowledge. The ordinary tendency of little children to be in awe of teachers was and is exaggerated by the traditional Chinese veneration of teachers. The characterisation of teachers as Chinese in these textbooks, therefore, must have been one of the most powerful positive images that Chinese could have monopolised, subliminally telling both Chinese children and non-Chinese children that Chinese have a natural place of authority and leadership in society.

Children using the rival *New English Series for Primary Education (NESPE)* series of English textbooks faced similar stereotyping, with a plethora of Chinese teacher-characters: Mrs Huang, Miss Huang, Mrs Li, Miss Li, Miss Lin, Mr Lin, Mrs Fu, Mr Chen, Mr Han and – the most frequently recurring

Figure 8.3: Miss Chen, from the *NESPE* textbooks.

character in the whole series – Miss Chen (see Figure 8.3).[44] Miss Chen even appears as a teacher in the class progress tests.[45] We also see the Chinese school principal (Mr Li at one point; and an unnamed Chinese woman at another),[46] Chinese doctors (such as Dr Chen and Dr Li) and Chinese nurses.[47] The only 'businessman' found in the whole sample is a Mr Chen: 'Mr Chen is a busy businessman. He has no time to do some things himself. Look at the pictures and say what he does not do himself. (Answers: Type letters, make coffee, iron clothes, wash his car … .)[48] Barr's survey of 1980s textbooks uncovered only three definite mentions of non-Chinese teacher-characters: a Mr Singh and a Mrs Devan (one-off text- and-illustration-based characters) and a Mrs Rama (a one-off text-only character).[49] The near-omission of Indian teachers is particularly striking as Indians have always been well represented in the teaching profession in Singapore, confirming that the world being depicted in these textbooks is not so much a reflection of the social reality as it is of Chinese prejudices.

The other side of these prejudices – negative stereotyping of the other races in menial roles – is also obvious in the textbooks. See the emphasis with which the stereotype is depicted in Figure 8.4, which could be mistaken for being a deliberate juxtaposition with the ubiquitous Miss Chen.[50] This particular dialogue was intended to be acted out in class, with picture cards. The teacher was supposed to 'talk about the pictures' that go with the dialogue and explain them.[51] Malays and Indians might be nearly excluded from teacher roles, but they comprise a disproportionately high number of the police-characters: 'Mr Bala is a policeman. His brother is a policeman too.' (Mr Ali is also a policeman, but Dr Chen is a doctor.)[52] The night watchman (Mr Singh) is a Sikh.[53] In one story about lorry drivers they all work for two rival Chinese companies (Wen Limited and Chang Brothers).[54] Meanwhile Ramu the Indian Secondary 4 student has a burning ambition to become a zookeeper.[55]

It is difficult to believe that this consistent stereotyping across three sets of textbooks written by three sets of authors was not deliberate, but bearing in mind that the three writing committees contained no Malays and only two Indians between them, it is just possible that this was an unconscious, rather than a deliberate reproduction of stereotypes.[56] In the case of the *NESPE*

Figure 8.4: Mr Ahmad in *not* a teacher. From *NESPE* textbooks.

committee, it is known that at least in their early years it was short-staffed and its members worked in extremely primitive conditions, without even recourse to reference books or a decent dictionary (*ST*, 4 April 1982). It is very easy to imagine that in this case at least the racial biases were driven by unconscious and unchecked prejudices rather than anything more sinister. Yet the consistency of these patterns across many series of textbooks makes such considerations a moot point. Whether deliberate or unconscious, these textbooks persistently presented uplifting role models and self-images for the Chinese children – particularly the hegemonic image of the Chinese school teacher – and deprived Malay and Indian children of such models, telling them that they should aspire to less lofty places in society. Beyond the depiction of adults in racially stereotypical occupations, there were also racial lessons to be drawn from the depiction of the children themselves in these textbooks. For instance, Indian boys doing Primary 4 Extended using the *PEP* textbooks saw themselves depicted not once, but twice as being precocious, just as the stereotypical Singaporean Indian should be.[57] In one lesson from 1981 (see Figure 8.1 at the opening of this chapter), Primary 1 children using the *NESPE* series were taught that Chinese children (personified by Suyin and Wieming) are studious while Malays and Indians (personified by Ali and Samy) engage in horseplay.[58]

The cumulative effect of this and the other racialising initiatives of the 1980s help to explain why so many people over the age of 40 identified the 1980s in interview as a period of heightened racial consciousness. One Indian interviewee had been overseas for the middle of the 1980s and upon his return in 1988 was shocked by the high level of racial consciousness displayed by his ten-year-old niece. Not only did the niece give a racial identification to each of her school friends as she spoke of them, but every one of her friends was a fellow-Indian. There was no reason for her to even mention race because he had not referred to it at all. This informant had never known such a level of racial consciousness when he grew through childhood in the same family during the 1960s. This anecdote is at odds with the official mythology of Singapore's multiracialism, but it accords with the common experience of living in today's Singapore, where it is often difficult to avoid thinking in terms of racial identifiers.

Stereotyping in textbooks has become weaker as they became less parochial in the 1990s and 2000s – balancing stories about racially identifiable

Singaporean children with racially neutral characters and stories and myths about places, people and animals around the world.[59] Although the *NESPE* textbooks from the 1980s were still in use until at least 1994, by that stage the *PEP* series had been replaced by a new one called *Primary English Thematic Series (PETS)*. The racialisation of characters in this series was still overt (using skin colour, clothes, etc.) but there were very few situational illustrations and stories that lent themselves to perpetuating prejudice, and in those few that were present there seems to have been some effort to provide characters who contradicted the prevailing stereotypes. One pair of pages of a Primary 1 text even depicted a Malay or Indian teacher alongside a Chinese gardener and a Chinese street sweeper, something that would have been unimaginable a few years earlier, while a 1996 6B textbook clearly depicted a female Malay teacher, complete with *tudung*, followed a few pages over by a picture of an Indian teacher.[60]

Since the final demise of the *NESPE* series some time in the mid-1990s, Singapore's primary English textbooks have been free of overt racial stereotyping, but the racialisation of the characters in these textbooks has remained strong. In the *PETS* series of the 1990s, and the *In Step, Celebrate English* and the *Treks* series of the first half of the 2000s the racialisation of the drawings and characters was highly sophisticated, training children in the nuances of skin colouring, and the implications of ethnic markers like names, dress, hair styles (more curly for Indians; straighter for Chinese) and religious markers (e.g. a *bindhi* for Indian girls).[61] While the overtly offensive stereotyping of the non-Chinese has been discontinued completely, some of the series retain subtle biases that favour Chinese and deprive Malays in particular of the chance to see themselves portrayed positively. Kwa Kok Beng has done a count of the mention of racial/ethnic characters in the Primary 1 *In Step* English textbooks in the 2000s, finding that Malays were portrayed pictorially at half the rate suggested by their prevalence in the national population, while both Chinese and Indians were portrayed at rates higher than their national representation suggests as 'fair'.[62] She also found that the Chinese characters in this series were consistently portrayed in dominant, proactive postures, addressing the reader or the other characters in a friendly, smiling fashion, but the Indian and Malay characters were drawn in passive, non-speaking roles, looking away from the reader and more rarely smiling in a friendly fashion.[63] She identified one page in which Malay and Chinese children are portrayed as happy while the clearly identifiable Indian is angry (with steam coming out of her ears).[64] Furthermore the focus groups that Kwa conducted with pupils using the series revealed that illustrated characters without overt racial markers were commonly assumed to be Chinese, which both exaggerated the Chinese ethnic hegemony in the series and confirms Chinese ethnic hegemony in Singapore society as a whole.[65]

While the racialisation of the textbooks shows no signs of waning, it is at least fortunate that MOE seems to have made a qualitative breakthrough in banishing the worst of the racial stereotyping. Both the *Treks* textbooks and the more recent *My Pals are Here!* series have successfully avoided stereotyping completely. The secret of their technique is simplicity itself: unlike all the other series considered to date, neither of these series was written by a Chinese-dominated committee. The *Treks* series was written by a truly multiracial panel headed by Duriya Azeez (who must be either a Muslim Indian or a Malay) and the *My Pals are Here!* series is sole authored by this same Duriya Azeez.[66]

Let us not, however, dismiss the continuing racialisation of characters lightly. Even the best of these books are socialising children at the most impressionable age to see the world through the prism of race, and training them to racially categorise people by physiological characteristics such as skin colour and hair texture, and secondary ethnic and religious markers such as names and clothing. This practice lends itself to perpetuating racial stereotypes, and indeed recent sociological research suggests that this has been the result. In about 2002 Angeline Khoo and Lim Kam Ming questioned 348 trainee teachers (who would almost all have studied English using the *New Course English*, the *PEP* or the *NESPE* textbooks as children) and found evidence of strong racial stereotyping. To take just one aspect of their results, the Chinese trainee teachers viewed other Chinese as 'industrious, practical, ambitious and superstitious', but they thought of Malays as being 'happy-go-lucky, lazy and kind'. Indians were regarded as being 'loud, argumentative and talkative'.[67] With teachers carrying such stereotypes into the classroom, it is insufficient to merely avoid reproducing them in the textbooks; they need to be actively counteracted.

Turning to the children themselves, another study has revealed that the overwhelming majority (up to 80 per cent in some samples) of Singaporean school children socialised exclusively with members of their own race.[68] The same study also found that skin colour was a major racial identifier, with dark skin being a particularly strong and negative racial indicator. Being dark skinned in a Singapore playground is to invite derisive nicknames like 'Black Coffee' and 'Blackie', together with racist remarks about the alleged personal characteristics of Indians or Malays as the case may be.[69] The odd thing about this being a major identifier is that the difference between the skin colours is not a very reliable indicator of race because there are so many tanned Chinese, fair-skinned Indians, and Malays who look Chinese or Indian. Yet it is the racial characteristic that is most prominently portrayed in primary school textbooks. Of course there should be nothing surprising in the tendency of these children to identify and socialise racially. Not only have they been taught about race in their textbooks, but they have been socialised throughout their schooling to mix with 'their own kind' as a result of 'bunching' children along racial lines, mentioned earlier. This practice was put in place only to facilitate the timetabling demands of 'mother tongue' language classes, but it created a situation where it would have been extraordinary if a large proportion of students failed to find their closest friends among their own race.

SAP Schools

At this point it is worth recalling that from 1979 onwards a substantial group of the best Chinese students could have suffered no temptation to bully Indian and Malay children because they were in all-Chinese environments at school. We refer to the children in SAP schools that were created specifically to promote and perpetuate 'Chinese values', 'Chinese culture' and high standards of Chinese language. These children did not have the chance, however slim, to have stereotypes learnt in textbooks overturned by interracial friendships formed in the classroom or the playground. As Lee Hsien Loong said of SAP schools in one of his understatements, 'It is not the same learning about other cultures vicariously as it is having a class of mixed students' (*ST*, 12 March 1999). Though students are taught to be proficient in both English and Mandarin, the SAP schools were explicitly designed 'to have an essentially Chinese ambience, in both linguistic and cultural terms'.[70] Since these schools are almost exclusively Chinese and their pupils are encouraged even more than usual to speak Mandarin socially, the children attending them rely to an even greater degree on textbooks and teachers for their mental images of the other communities. Furthermore, not only do they learn their stereotyping from their English textbooks but also their teachers actively teach them to take pride in their 'Chineseness'. Ingrid Glad tells of her experience as an observer in an SAP primary school in the mid-1990s:

> The Chinese characters are by themselves cultural manifestations, and listening to Chinese children reciting Chinese characters in chorus seems like assisting in a very Chinese ritual, a ritual which undoubtedly reinforces their ethnic community feelings. One of the teachers ... said to her students:
>
> ### 我們是華人9。華文是我們的母語。 我們應該把它寫好 。
>
> 'We are ethnic Chinese.
> Chinese is our mother tongue.
> We must write it correctly.'
>
> She wanted the children to show her how to draw the character for ethnic Chinese, 华 (simplified system). All the children would raise their arms and paint the imaginary strokes in the air while reciting [the names of the strokes] in chorus.[71]

Glad also conducted surveys of teacher attitudes, comparing the attitudes of 18 SAP school teachers with those of 19 Chinese Language teachers in non-SAP schools, and found significantly different levels of ethnic-cum-racial consciousness and insularity, with SAP school teachers being more likely than other Chinese teachers to identify their personal historical roots as being in China (16.7 per cent against zero).[72] Unsurprisingly they also had a significantly lower level of belief in a common Singaporean identity (61 against 84 per cent).[73] The Chinese teachers in SAP schools even socialised separately from the (ethnic Chinese) English teachers in their own school.[74] One can imagine the outrage if Malay or Indian teachers displayed similar levels of ethnic pride and isolationism.

Conclusion

Neither the racialisation of Singaporean primary schools in the 1980s, nor the escalation of academic expectations was a 'natural' or undirected process. Even if many of the individual steps involved – such as generating racial stereotypes, or assuming competency in English on the first day of Primary 1 – were enacted unconsciously by the individual teachers or textbook designers, they were merely following a template laid out by Lee Kuan Yew and some of his colleagues – a pattern of social cognition that has been superimposed onto the whole society, not just the education system. By this stage of our inquiry, we are well on our way to understanding how the education system has been used as a primary tool of nation building since the 1980s, producing a new type of Singaporean, radically different to that inhabiting Singapore in the 1940s to 1960s. The society of the old post-war Singapore, with its thriving, dynamic polyglot culture, bursting with energy, friction and fun – along with poverty, ignorance and filth – was gone forever, and so was the relevance of the Singaporeans who inhabited it. The 'new' Singapore needed 'new' Singaporeans and the education system produced them *en masse*. It purported to be a thoroughly modern Singapore, ruled by a coldly rational, analytical, technocratic elite, eschewing prejudice and archaic, pre-modern world views and loyalties. Such is the foolishness of human wisdom.

Notes

1   *New English Series for Primary Education [NESPE] Course Book 1B* (1981), Singapore: Pan Pacific Book Distributors and the Curriculum Development Institute of Singapore, 1981, p. 36.

2   The systemic neglect of Malays' educational disadvantages and needs is a central aspect of Lily Zubaidah Rahim, *The Singapore Dilemma: The Political and Educational Marginality of the Malay Community*, Kuala Lumpur: Oxford University Press, 1998.

3   Michael D. Barr, 'Perpetual Revisionism in Singapore: The Limits of Change', *Pacific Review*, vol. 16, no.1, 2003, pp. 77–97. For race implications of the privileging of tertiary educated women, see Geraldine Heng, and Janadas Devan, 'State Fatherhood: The Politics of Nationalism, Sexuality, and Race in Singapore', in Andrew Parker *et al.* (eds), *Nationalisms and Sexualities*, London and New York: Routledge, 1992, pp. 343–364.

4   Ingrid Glad, *An Identity Dilemma: A Comparative Study of Primary Education for Ethnic Chinese in the Context of National Identity and Nation-Building in Malaysia and Singapore*, Oslo: Scandinavian University Press, 1998, pp. 88, 89.

5   Department of Employment, Education and Training (Australia), – DEET, *Country Education Profiles: Singapore, A Comparative Study*, Canberra: Australian Government Publishing Service, 1991, p. 19.

6   MOE, *Nurturing Every Child: Flexibility and Diversity in Singapore's Schools*, Singapore: Ministry of Education, 2004, p. 6. Available on MOE website, http://www.moe.gov.sg/. Accessed 23 February 2006.

7   Charlene Tan, 'Driven by pragmatism: issues and challenges in an ability-driven education', in Jason Tan and Ng Pak Tee (eds), *Shaping Singapore's Future: Thinking Schools, Learning Nation*, Singapore: Pearson Education, 2005, p. 7.

8   A Malay interviewee complained that the prevalence of complicated 'problem sums' in this period was the single biggest obstacle to his Malay classmates in Maths, and caused most of them to do poorly in PSLE.

9 Interview with a retired Primary 6 teacher, Singapore, 31 March 2004.

10 *English Syllabus for the New English System. Primary 1 to 6 (Normal Course), Primary 4 to 8 (Extended Course), Primary 4 to 8 (Monolingual Course)*, Singapore: Ministry of Education, 1981, p. 7.

11 *English Language Syllabus for Lower Primary Classes (Primary 1, 2 and 3)*, Singapore: Ministry of Education, 1990, pp. 51, 52.

12 *English This Way 1* (1970), before the beginning of the text and pp. 1, 3.

13 *PEP 1A* (1981); *NESPE 1A Teacher's Edition* (1981), p. 28.

14 *Celebrate English 1A Unit 1 Teacher's Guide*, p. 8.

15 Ibid., pp. 10, 12, 14.

16 *Treks 1A Teacher's Edition 1A* (2000), pp. 24, 25.

17 *Mathematics Syllabus for the New Education System. Part A Primary 1to 3 (Common Course)*, Singapore: Ministry of Education, 1980.

18 *Syllabus for Implementation from January 1999. Mathematics Primary EM1, EM2 and EM3 Streams*, Singapore: Ministry of Education, 1998.

19 Barr has interviewed a parent whose daughter was good with figures but was barely passing Primary 1 Maths in the late 1990s precisely because she had not learnt to read properly in kindergarten. Her Primary 1 examination papers contained a large proportion of word problems that she could not even attempt, despite having no difficulties with the rest of the paper. Her teachers were unaware of or indifferent to the fact that she could not read.

20 'Government Accepts Recommendation for a More Flexible and Customised Chinese Language Curriculum', MOE Press Release, 15 November 2004. Available on the MOE website, www.moe.gov.sg/. Accessed 23 February 2006. The new Chinese language curriculum is a two-track programme reminiscent of streaming, with one track for high performers who follow an enhanced curriculum leading to new educational and post-secondary opportunities and the other track offering a simplified curriculum that is much less challenging than the pre-2007 syllabus. See MOE website (accessed 14 April 2008) as well as media reports such as 'SAP schools still play key role in prompting Chinese', *ST*, 20 August 2007; 'Dunman High to be 5th Chinese Language Elective Programme Centre', *CNA*, 4 September 2007; 'SAP schools starting new programmes to stay unique', *ST*, 12 February, 2008 and 'More zip for SAP schools: Changes include poly tied-ups, non-exam courses', *Today*, 12 February 2008.

21 For a good overview of the historical stages of Chinese Language teaching in Singapore, see Ang Beng Choo, 'The teaching of the Chinese language in Singapore', in S. Gopinathan, Anne Pakir, Ho Wah Kam and Vaithamani Saravanan (eds), *Language, Society and Education in Singapore: Issues and Trends*, Second Edition, Singapore: Times Academic Press, 1998, pp. 335–352.

22 Janet Shepherd, *Striking a Balance: The Management of Language in Singapore*, Frankfurt, Peter Lang, 2005, p. 137.

23 Ibid., pp. 135–139.

24 Note that selection into the primary school GEP is still conducted in Primary 3, even though the streaming examination was moved back to Primary 4 in 1992, thus exaggerating even further the importance of pre-school and early primary education. See MOE website at http://www.moe.gov.sg. Accessed 20 January 2006.

25 Since 2007, allocation to the GEP in primary schools has been done on a subject-by-subject basis and from 2008 the GEP in secondary schools has been completely replaced by the Integrated Programme. MOE has attributed the latter decision to the popularity of the Integrated Programme, which it said had made the GEP redundant and inefficient in post-primary education. The break-up of GEP cohorts in primary schools was justified by the need to encourage GEP students to mix more freely with their non-GEP peers. See *Today*, 21 September 2006 and *CNA*, 28 September 2006.

26 Eng Soo Peck *et al.*, *Principals' and Teachers' Views on Teaching Monolingual Classes*, Singapore: Institute of Education, 1982. See also *ST*, 18 January 1982.

27 Tan, 'Driven by Pragmatism', p. 7.

28 Evidence to support these general observations about the 1970s may be found in Michael D. Barr, 'Racialised education in Singapore', *Educational Research for Policy and Practice*, 5:1, 2006, pp. 15–31, which is a fuller version of the section on 'Race in the classroom'.

29 Lee Kuan Yew, *From Third World to First: The Singapore Story: 1965–2000: Memoirs of Lee Kuan Yew*, Singapore: Singapore Press Holdings; Times Editions, 2000, pp. 238, 239.

30 Dr Tony Tan, Minister for Education, speech at the opening of the First National Conference and Exhibition on Kindergarten Education, 15 November 1990, Singapore Government Press Release, available at http://sprinter.gov.sg/, accessed 24 May 2005; and *ST*, 16 November 1990.

31 Ooi Giok Ling, 'The role of the development state and interethnic relations in Singapore', *Asian Ethnicity*, vol. 6, no. 2, 2005, p. 117.

32 Trivina Kang, 'Schools and post-secondary aspirations among female Chinese, Malay and Indian Normal Stream students', in Lai Ah Eng, *Beyond Rituals and Riots: Ethnic Pluralism and Social Cohesion in Singapore*, Singapore: Eastern Universities Press by Marshall Cavendish, 2004, pp. 155, 159, 160.

33 Lily Zubaidah Rahim, *The Singapore Dilemma: The Political and Educational Marginality of the Malay Community*, Kuala Lumpur: Oxford University Press, 1998.

34 Interview with Catherine Lim, Singapore, 24 March 2004. Dr Lim was the co-ordinator of the Primary English Programme in the early 1980s.

35 *NESPECourse Book 1B* (1981), p. 19.

36 *New Course English 6A/B* (for use in 1982, 1983), Singapore: Educational Publishing Bureau for Curriculum Development Institute of Singapore (October 1981, second imprint November 1982, pp. 19–28, 30, 31, 63, 64, 127–31; *New English Course 6D/C* (for use in 1982, 1983; published December 1981, second imprint November 1982, pp. 63, 64.

37 *Primary English Programme [PEP] Textbook 6B Extended* (1984), Singapore: Longman and Curriculum Development Institute of Singapore, 1984, pp. 48, 49,

38 *PEP Textbook 4A Extended* (1982), pp. 1–5; *PEP Textbook 6B Extended* (1984), p. 32.

39 *PEP Textbook 6B Extended* (1984), p. 68.

40 *PEP Textbook 4A Extended* (1982), pp. 8–11.

41 Ibid., p. 78.

42 *PEP Textbook 1A* (1982), pp. 1–8, 19, 22, 29, 60, 62; *PEP Textbook 4B Extended* (1982), pp. 36, 49, 55, 70; *PEP Textbook 4A* (1983), pp. 17, 37, 68; *PEP Textbook 4B* (1983), pp. 7, 31; 52, 56, 75, 87; *PEP Textbook 6A Extended* (1984), pp. 9, 54; *PEP Textbook 6B Extended* (1984), pp. 10, 32, 44, 52, 53, 67, 79; *PEP 6A Textbook* (1985), p. 11. Figure 8.2 from *PEP Textbook 6A Extended* (1984), p. 9.

43 *PEP Textbook 4B* (1983), p. 87; *PEP Textbook 4A* (1983), p. 68.

44 *NESPE Course Book 1A* (1981), pp. 2–5, 16, 48; *NESPE Course Book 1B* (1981), pp. 3, 6, 56; *NESPE Course Book 4B Extended* (1981), pp. 7, 10, 21, 43; *NESPE Course Book 4A* (1982), pp. 12, 33; *NESPE Work Book 4A Extended* (c.1982), pp. 13, 26, cited in *NESPE Teacher's Edition 4A Extended* (1982), pp. 109, 122; *NESPE Course Book 4B* (1983), pp. 4, 21, 66; *NESPE Course Book 4B* (1983), p. 45; NESPE Course Book 6A Extended (1983), pp. 1–3; *NESPE Course Book 6A* (1983), p. 34; *NESPE Course Book 6A* (1985–94), p. 49; *NESPE Course Book 6B* (1985–94), p. 37. Figure 9 from *NESPE Course Book 1A* (1981), p. 2.

45 Class Progress Test 2, *NESPE Teacher's Edition 4A Extended* (1982), p. 13.

46 *NESPE Course Book 1A* (1981), p. 51.

47 *NESPE Course Book 1A* (1981), pp. 14–16; *NESPE Course Book 1B* (1981), p. 3; *NESPE Course Book 4B Extended* (1981), p. 18; *NESPE Course Book 4A* (1982), p. 6; *NESPE Course Book 4B* (1983), p. 5; *NESPE Course Book 6A* (1984–94), p. 48. Indians fair moderately well in this series' depiction of the medical profession. This survey of 1980s primary textbooks uncovered: one instance of an illustration of an Indian doctor-character (standing with a Chinese doctor-character); one instance of a text-and-illustration-based Indian vet-character; two instances of text-based Indian doctor-characters. See *NESPE Course Book 1B* (1981), p. 5; *NESPE Course Book 6A Extended* (1983), p. 14; *NESPE Course Book 6B Extended* (1983), pp. 19, 30.

48 *NESPE Course Book 4A* (1982), p. 27.

49 *NESPE Course Book 4B* (1983), p. 26; *PEP Course Book* 4B, 1983, p. 87; *NESPE Course Book 6B* (1985–94), p. 48.

50 Figure 10 from *NESPE Course Book 1A* (1981), p. 14.

51 *NESPE Teacher's Edition 1A* (1981), p. 41.

52 *NESPE Course Book 1B* (1981), pp. 2, 17; *NESPE Course Book 4B Extended.* (1981), p. 18; *NESPE Course Book 4A* (1982), p. 6.

53 *NESPE Course Book 4B Extended* (1981), pp. 25, 26; *NESPE Course Book 4A* (1982), pp. 9–11.

54 *NESPE Course Book 6B* (1985–94), pp. 35, 36.

55 *NESPE Course Book 6A* (1984–94), pp. 52–54.

56 The *New Course English* books were written by three Chinese. The *PEP* books were written by four Chinese, an Indian and someone with a European surname (Ridge). The *NESPE* books were written by four Chinese, an Indian and someone with a European-sounding surname (Baruch).

57 *PEP Textbook 4A Extended* (1982), pp. 74–77; *PEP Textbook 4B Extended* (1982), pp. 13–16.

58 *NESPE Course Book 1B* (1981), p. 36.

59 See, for instance, *New English Thematic Series Course Book 1A* (1991), Singapore: EPB Publishers and Curriculum Development Institute of Singapore, 1991; *In Step: A Course in English for Primary Schools 2B* (2001), Singapore: Pan Pacific Publications and approved by the Ministry of Education, 2001.

60 *Primary English Thematic Series [PETS] 1A* (1991), Singapore: EPB Publishers and Curriculum Development Institute of Singapore, 1991, pp. 32, 33; *PETS 6B EM3* (1996), pp. 28, 35.

61 See *In Step: A Course in English for Primary Schools* [various classes], Singapore: Pan Pacific Publications, beginning in 2001; *Celebrate English* [various classes], Singapore: Pearson Education, beginning 2000; and *Treks. Setting Off: Interactive English for Primary Levels* [various classes], Singapore: SNP Education, beginning 2000.

62 Kwa Kok Beng, 'Multiculturalism or multiracialism? A critical analysis of the portrayal of race in Primary One English textbooks in Singapore', Honours thesis in English Language, National Institute of Education, Singapore, 2004, pp. 34, 128.

63 Ibid., pp. 36, 37, 41, 42.

64 Ibid., p. 77.

65 Ibid., pp. 50, 51.

66 *Treks Coursebook 1A* (2000), before page 1; and *My Pals are Here! English 6A*, Singapore: Times Media Private, 2005, before page 1.

67 Angeline Khoo and Lim Kam Ming, 'Trainee teachers' stereotypes of ethnic groups in Singapore', in Lai Ah Eng (ed.), *Beyond Rituals and Riots: Ethnic Pluralism and Social Cohesion in Singapore*, Singapore: Eastern Universities Press by Marshall Cavendish for Institute of Policy Studies, 2004, pp. 201, 207, 208. For a more complete picture of the Khoo and Lim's results, see their chapter, pp. 197–227.

68 Christine Lee, Mary Cherian, Rahil Ismail, Maureen Ng, Jasmine Sim and Chee Min Fui, 'Children's experiences of multiracial relationships in informal primary school settings', in Lai, *Beyond Rituals and Riots*, pp. 114–145.

69 Ibid., pp. 128–130.

70 Raj Vasil, *Asianising Singapore: The PAP's Management of Ethnicity*, Singapore, Heinemann Asia for the Institute of Southeast Asian Studies, 1995, p. 73.

71 Glad, *An Identity Dilemma*, p. 149.

72 Ibid., p. 196.

73 Ibid., p. 203.

74 Ibid., p. 183.

NINE

Sorting the 'Scholars' from the 'Commoners': Secondary School and Junior College

The government at the moment ... is running on the ability, drive and dedication of ... a very thin crust of leadership. Therefore it has to be enlarged, quickly but systematically. After that comes the middle strata of good executives ... to carry out his ideas, thinking and planning. Finally comes the broad base.

Social organisation is analogous to military organisation. One battalion comprises of over 60 to 70 officers, 100 to 200 corporals, and about 500 privates. This hierarchy must be.

Lee Kuan Yew, 29 August 1966[1]

THE CHAPTER TITLE'S REFERENCE to 'scholars' and 'commoners' is derived from the common parlance of the civil service. In the SAF they have slightly different terminology: 'scholars and farmers'.[2] Both refer to the same phenomenon and each is derived from the traditional social ranking found in classical Confucianism. At the top of society is the scholar, followed by the farmer, then the worker, and at the bottom of the pile is the merchant. A scholar is self-consciously and proudly at the top of both the civil and military services. Those who are not scholars are referred to only slightly facetiously as 'commoners' or 'farmers'. Although this terminology is intended to reflect the Chinese-cum-Confucian culture on which Singapore society is supposedly built, the use of the term 'scholar' in this context is profoundly misleading. In Confucian terminology a scholar was a *junzi*, a 'cultured gentleman' who eschewed practical knowledge for enlightened humanistic thought that would provide the basis of fearless advice to the emperor. In the rest of the world a scholar is someone who pursues scholarly activity: an academic, a student, or an amateur pursuing study. In Singapore, however, a 'scholar' is someone who has won a government scholarship awarded by the Public Service Commission, a statutory board, a

GLC or the SAF, usually to study a utilitarian discipline such as engineering, and has been bonded to government or government-linked service. It is entirely possible for a particular 'commoner' to have better qualifications than a particular 'scholar' and to actually be more of a scholar in the conventional sense.

We have placed this chapter in the context of scholars and commoners because we want to shift the focus of the reader's mind away from the journey of Singaporean children through school, to the destination of a small number of them as members of Singapore's administrative and political elite. This is a deliberate shift of emphasis intended to ensure that the focus on elite formation is not overshadowed by our efforts to explore the nation-building project. It is ultimately not possible to separate either of these components of the Singapore project completely, but there are times when one needs more attention than the other. In the following pages, therefore, we will explore the developments in secondary school and junior college education, but in a less detailed fashion than we did for kindergarten and primary school, focusing more on outcomes than processes. In the process of shifting our focus from nation building generally to elite formation in particular we have consciously allowed the polytechnics to slip under our radar, since members of the elite rarely emerge from this path. We have also collapsed our consideration of four or five years of secondary school and two years of junior college (pre-university education) into one study, since there are only a few degrees of distinction between their lived environments and cultures – at least for the 25 per cent of students[3] who follow this path to the end, and who are increasingly the focus of this study.

We begin by extending the previous chapters' study of the factors that have produced generations of *kiasu* students, and heightening our focus on the role of economic and social privilege in the process of elite selection. We are also including a study of the moral and civic education programmes of the 1980s onwards, since in recent years they appear to have become significant components of both nation building and elite formation. Yet in a break from the most recent chapters, we give ethnicity only passing consideration – with the promise of re-engaging it fully in Chapter 10.

Streaming and Ranking

We have already seen that the reach of *The Goh Report* did not stop at Primary 3. The New Education System intruded into secondary school with a force comparable to that projected into kindergarten and primary school, generating a *kiasu* environment. The most immediate and obvious input was the institutionalisation of what had up till then been an informal practice: streaming at the end of Primary 6 (age 12) through the PSLE. The PLSE had always been one of the important criteria that determined whether a child would be accepted into one of the better secondary schools, but after 1979 it also determined one's precise place in a school hierarchy that typically consisted of eight or more unofficial sub-levels within three official streams. The best students in the New Education System win places in the Special Stream, which requires not only top grades, but also excellence in both English and 'Mother Tongue'. The next tier down is the Express Stream. These students are generally just as good as the Special Stream students in everything except their 'Mother Tongue'. Since 1984 many of these Special/Express students have also been inducted into the GEP, which runs alongside the streams without being a stream itself. Such students have specially trained teachers and enrichment programmes designed to bring forth their best academic performance.

The New Education System's lower status alternative to the Special/Express Stream and the GEP options is the Normal Stream, which since 1992 has been divided into Normal (Academic) Stream and Normal (Technical) Stream, each of which takes five years instead of the standard four.[4] Normal (Technical) students have a curriculum that 'is all woodwork, metalwork and vocational stuff' according to a former student in interview. Normal (Technical) students are on an educational path that will probably lead to the Institute of Technical Education (ITE) where they will learn a trade, and Normal (Academic) are likely candidates for a place in a polytechnic. Only 1.5 per cent of Normal (Academic) students enter junior college, which is the usual path into university (*ST*, 28 January 2002). Although it is technically possible to move up a stream during the life of one's secondary schooling, the shift is rarely successful because the Normal (Academic) and Normal (Technical) curricula are so basic and the deprivation of essential learning experiences (such as using laboratory equipment for experiments) is so extensive that they can almost never catch up.[5] On the rare occasions when a Normal (Technical) student succeeds in gaining entry to a local university it is a matter worthy of celebration in the communal press (see, for instance, *Berita Harian*, 27 June 2005). For Normal Stream students school is not only dull, it is also demeaning as they put up with the not very suppressed contempt from Express and Special Stream students and sometimes – despite the presence of dedicated teachers and principals throughout the system – even from their own teachers.[6] A case in point was documented in a 1984 letter to *The Straits Times* from Lim Kwee Hong, a Normal Stream student who complained that some teachers referred to them openly as 'sub-normal', reduced their teaching to monologue lectures and dismissed their requests for explanations with a 'rebuke ... for not being attentive enough' (*ST*, 3 December 1984). 'If you are in the Normal Stream then something is wrong – that is the general opinion – but when we went on and did our O-levels some of us actually did better than some of the people in the Express Stream', said one former Normal Stream (Academic) student in interview.[7] In 2006, MOE introduced new options designed to give 'selected' Normal Stream students more opportunities to extend themselves academically, but it remains to be seen whether this has any significant effect on stream mobility.[8] Access to university for Normal Stream students has also been increased since the early 2000s, though it remains an extraordinarily difficult path to follow, going from Normal Stream to either a polytechnic or the 'Centralised Institute' and then perhaps to university. By contrast Express Stream and Special Stream students can be fairly confident that they will be admitted to at least a local university, and GEP students routinely win top government scholarships to attend overseas universities (*ST*, 12 July 1998).

The pre-eminence of the Science Stream is worth special attention at this point. Several interviewees reported the higher status of Science streams, even before the reforms of 1979. Science has been pre-eminent in the Singapore education system from the earliest days of PAP rule, and was the direct consequence of the modernising, outward-looking character of the Singapore nation-building project. One person who was a student in the 1960s said in interview that in her school the 'brightest girls were put into the Science classes, then there was the Arts class and then the rest'. In fact by the 1990s some of the top schools, such as Victoria School, offered only the Science Stream. A Science Stream education was the ticket to a career, so anything else was second best. This privileging of Science meant that even students who disliked science and maths and whose natural inclination is towards the humanities were pressured by teachers, parents and peers not to 'downgrade'. Interviewees who had gone through school during the 1970s, 1980s and 1990s spoke of having to fight pressures – particularly parental pressure – when they wanted to abandon the Science stream for Arts.[9] This imbalance has recently been recognised as a defect in the system and was subjected to a very slight correction in 2006, when it became mandatory for A-level candidates to take at least one subject from the Humanities and Arts group.[10]

By the early 1990s the pressure to conform to a *kiasu* ethos in school was already overwhelming, but it was given new impetus in 1992 when an official 'ranking' system of secondary schools was introduced to heighten competition between schools and to 'help' parents choose the best school for their children (*ST*, 14 March 1992). Although watered down in 2004, it continues as a multifaceted reporting scheme that seems likely to perpetuate the central problem associated with the old system: fostering a 'factory' mentality to academic performance.[11] This feature of school life was a constant source of complaint among younger people who were interviewed for this book.[12] Under the old system, schools were ranked publicly according to grades, which gave stakeholders (principals, teachers, school boards) yet another reason for pushing students to cram and do well in examinations – for the sake of the school. One interviewee was accepted into Victoria Junior College in the first year that it overtook Raffles Institution as #1, and reported that the pressure on the students to perform for the sake of the school was pervasive in school assemblies and in the classroom. Another recent student from a top school explained that she felt 'like a robot working in overdrive, trying to achieve "A" grades so that she would not pull the school ranking down'. She got the impression that the school was more concerned with its reputation and ranking rather than the consequences that an individual would face if she failed. Students were already feeling under pressure for the sake of their own futures, but with ranking they had to think about the school's reputation as well. Apart from putting pressure on schools, ranking also put immense pressure on teachers and principals. In 2004 a teacher in an elite junior college said in interview that he had gone to some trouble to supplement the official curriculum with a series of external speakers.[13] Such 'enrichment programmes' were being officially encouraged by the MOE at this time. Alas this initiative had nevertheless been wound down because the school authorities were concerned that it was distracting attention from the core work, which was judged to be maximising the number of 'A' grades achieved per year – and this was despite the discontinuation of school ranking.

This manic scramble for 'A' grades is the real driver for *kiasu*ism at the secondary level. Until recently, matriculation examinations have been set at arm's length by Cambridge University, so there has been no reason to think that the curricula played a primary role in driving up expectations as happened in primary school.[14] Yet there has been a persistent and undeniable perception that expectations had been inflated over the decades. In 1969 Lee Hsien Loong won the President's Scholarship and a Public Service Commission scholarship to Cambridge University with two A1s and an A2 in the Cambridge Higher School Certificate (*Sunday Times*, 31 May 1970). When SAF scholarships were introduced two years later, the minimum standard for elligibility was only three distinctions in the Higher School Certificate (*ST*, 20 May 1971). By 1982 grade inflation had already driven MOE to take measures to help the Public Service Commission sort through the 'increase in the number of students obtaining good grades in their A-levels' when it was awarding scholarships (*ST*, 18 January 1982), but by the 2000s, the standard was unrecognisable. In 2001, for instance, 1,364 students (12 per cent of the cohort) scored four 'A's in the Cambridge A-level examinations, and another 2,442 scored three 'A's (*ST*, 7 March 2002). The pinnacle of this group of perfect scores were those like Yeo Wenshen, who scored not only four 'A's, but also two A1s, and three distinctions (*ST*, 7 March 2002). But are these thousands of students all brilliant, or are they just good at taking examinations? According to Leo Tan, a former Director of the National Institute of Education, it is more likely to be the latter. In 1996 he warned that the best students were entering examinations with memorised answers that they just poured forth, which he did not regard as a true measure of intelligence or ability (*ST*, 6 July 1996). Indeed a departmental head in a successful elite school proudly boasted in 1997 that her school's successful A-level results stemmed from 'months of repeated mock examination practice.'[15] Reaching the elite level these days would be nearly impossible without frantic effort, private tuition and all the advantages that an elitist education system is capable of offering. One needs to secure a place in one of the best streams in one of the top schools with the best teachers and resources, and win a place in the GEP. As we have seen in earlier chapters, the lead-up route to such success is considerable and includes a good start in kindergarten, nursery and even pre-nursery to ensure a good start in primary school.

Mother Tongue

One of the other main drivers for *kiasu*ism in education is the continuing emphasis on 'Mother Tongue', and in secondary school and junior college the reason for the emphasis is even more pressing and apparent than it was in primary school. We speak of the language requirements for locally recognised matriculation requirements (which also form the prerequisites for scholarship eligibility). Draconian matriculation requirements based on English language and the 'Mother Tongue' were introduced for the specific purpose of driving parents and children to 'put in the necessary effort to learn [the] second language' (*ST*, 7 June 1980) – all in the belief that this would imbue children with Confucian or 'Asian' values. No threat could have spurred on *kiasu* students or their parents more, yet anguish and tuition was still not enough for many. In the early 1980s the Vice-Chancellor of NUS, Prof. Lim Pin, began instigating reviews of the unintended consequences of the bilingualism policy. His initial report focused on the accidental skewing of university admissions against boys, since language skills persisted in being a predominantly female trait. To correct this 'imbalance' the then Education Minister, Dr Tony Tan, announced that candidates who did not meet language requirements at matriculation would be admitted to university anyway, but before they could graduate they would have to catch up by passing a special language examination (*Sunday Times*, 30 October 1983). The practical effect of this was to ease the pressure on secondary and pre-university students somewhat, but to intensify the pressure for many university students. The group most seriously affected by the 'Mother Tongue' requirements was once again the Chinese, though no group was spared completely. One young Indian described in interview how he too struggled through school with a 'Mother Tongue' that he did not use at home.

Towards the end of the 1990s the pressure to perform well in 'Mother Tongue' kept increasing, with new incentives coming online, such as bonus points for entry into some junior colleges and the local universities.[16] In the end the pressure on 'Mother Tongue' eased in a serious way only in 2004, when MOE removed all but the most basic 'Mother Tongue' requirements as a criterion for entry to local universities, removing compulsory consideration of one's grades, and for Chinese, only requiring a pass in Chinese Language B or a D7 in Chinese Language (*Sunday Times*, 29 February 2004). Oddly enough, this decision came without any public discussion, and no evidence of studies or discussion papers within MOE, but it coincided roughly with Lee Kuan Yew's public revelations that his grandchildren were struggling with their Chinese Language studies.[17] Over many decades he has developed a substantial public record of judging the impact of policies and potential policy changes by the reactions of his own children,[18] and perhaps he has passed this 'burden' onto his grandchildren. Their impending A-levels may have even been the driver that prompted him to focus on the issue at that time.

Learning Conformity

We now have a picture of an education system emphasising grades in the sciences, mathematics and languages. It may not have been deliberate but these subjects are all disciplines that emphasise memory and functionalism at the expense of social imagination and critical thought. Interviews with young Singaporeans confirm a picture of mechanistic, grades-driven rote learning throughout primary and secondary school and even in junior college.[19] Even humanities subjects like History are taught by rote learning. Passages of textbooks and classroom notes (copiously copied at the speed of speech if possible) are routinely served to the examiner at the end of the year.

It seems that in the early days of independence this conformist pedagogy was a conscious aspect of nation building. In late 2003, Lee Kuan Yew admitted that he used to overemphasise conformity in education in his struggle to build a 'cohesive' and disciplined workforce and that he underestimated the value of independent thought for economic development[20] (let alone for the more general good of society). Oddly enough, however, the regime is continuing to pursue conformity as an overt goal in the latest manifestation of its moral and civic education programmes: National Education (NE).

The move to introduce NE came as a slightly panicked reaction to a realisation that the systematic neglect of history and the ineffectiveness of the civics education in schools to date meant that the younger generation was ignorant of the national past.[21] The spark for this realisation was then Senior Minister Lee Kuan Yew's idiosyncratic suggestion in 1996 that Singapore and Malaysia re-merge. This sparked outrage in Malaysia, but little more than a yawn in Singapore. A survey by *The New Paper* uncovered the reason: many Singaporeans lacked even a rudimentary knowledge of circumstances of Singapore's birth.[22] The new NE programme was announced by Prime Minister Goh Chok Tong shortly afterwards, though it took another couple of years before it was ready to start. Its effectiveness is yet to be judged properly, but from discussions with university lecturers, tutors and teacher trainers (who teach tertiary students who were recently subjected to the NE programme in secondary school and junior college) and from the new emerging literature on the attitudes of undergraduates[23] it appears that the Singapore government has found a winning formula for imbuing at least the outward expression of conformity, producing students who faithfully echo the official line in essays and examinations.

Interviews with young adults lend support to the impression given by the conversations with their post-secondary teachers: an extraordinarily uniform degree of unconscious acceptance of the National Education programme and values. At primary level the themes of NE are mostly focused on racial and religious harmony and understanding and good behaviour (politeness, consideration, filial piety, etc.). At secondary and junior college level the messages centre around Singapore's insecurity in the past and the present, and the ongoing programme of nation building. The current Secondary 1 and 2 History syllabi drive these messages home again and again. Unit 4 is about 'threats to [the] existence [of civilisations] and responses to threats'. Unit 6 is entitled 'Our [Singapore's] vulnerability'. Unit 7 covers the 'struggles against the communists in the post-war period' and the 'Maria Hertog [religious/racial] riots' of 1950. In Unit 8 the PAP saves the day and takes the country on 'Our Road to Independence' and Unit 9 is about 'Building our Nation', with three sub-themes: 'Building the economy', 'Housing the people' and 'Defending the nation'. The concepts and values to be imparted are spelled out in black and white, including meritocracy, survival, economic competition, resourcefulness, industry, patriotism, endurance, courage, thrift and racial and religious harmony.[24] Likewise, the Secondary Civics and Moral Education Syllabus has been designed to teach children the essentials of being a Singaporean: including 'how Singapore can stay ahead of competition in a fast changing world', and units that explore concepts such as globalisation, entrepreneurial spirit and networking.[25] At junior college level the message of NE is crystallised into 'S-Cube': 'Survival, Security and Success'. Seminars and the Civics Course emphasise the centrality of this triple concept, which at this point is linked to the junior college student's future leadership role in ensuring its achievement.[26]

It is difficult to know precisely why the NE programme has been more successful than earlier efforts. It could be the fact that it is not just taught formally in the classroom, but is infused into academic subjects and special high profile events (such as the 'Singapore Story Exhibition' in 1998, and the annual Racial Harmony Day and National Day spectaculars) or it could be the omnipresence of the programme through most aspects of public life. Perhaps the explanation lies in the emphasis on 'Success' in S-cube. In materialistic Singapore, 'success' and 'money' are magic words, and perhaps this has provided an effective 'hook' for National Education. Regardless, it is clearly making a significant impression on a new generation of Singaporeans.

Yet, even as we recognise the government's success in nurturing conformity, we find that we need to qualify the terms of its achievement severely. Although it seems to be true that the current crop of students and recent graduates typically have difficulty in thinking outside the parameters of the official 'Singapore Story' in a systematic way, conversations with young Singaporeans reveal a pattern where outward conformity often seems to co-habit with high levels of scepticism and cynicism. The official 'Singapore Story', inculcated through all the arms of propaganda and social control at the government's disposal including National Education, has successfully created a hegemonic discourse whereby even cynics and opponents have trouble thinking outside the parameters of imagination set by the ruling elite, but it seems that it has generally failed to implant passion and conviction. It has oppressed the imagination without uplifting the spirit, leaving the regime in a position that is outwardly secure, but is relying upon emotional roots that are shallow and brittle. We shall return to this theme in Chapter 12.

Diversification for Excellence

The competition for grades and the emphasis on maths, science and languages became the unifying features of the New Education System in the 1980s, joined more recently by NE in the late 1990s. Beyond these markers, however, the system houses very diverse educational experiences based as we have already noted on streaming and race-cum-'Mother Tongue' among other things. The presence of this diversity is not accidental, and it goes beyond these simplistic indicators. For the most part it serves a very simple purpose, which is to separate the student cohort into groups that reflect the social hierarchy that Lee Kuan Yew described in 1966 and which is reproduced at the opening of this chapter. Once the best students had been separated from the mass of average and merely 'good' students, they were given extra resources and special treatment – even special schools with cultures that tried to imbue them with qualities that were perceived to be of value to the ruling elite. Not that Lee was in any position to pursue such an ambitious programme in 1966. First his government had to build schools and train as many teachers as quickly as possible simply so that most children would receive at least a reasonable education, a challenge that persisted well into the 1970s (*ST*, 27 June 1974). In the 1960s and 1970s the priority was not diversity but uniformity. Students had to be driven to learn English, and curricula and examinations had to be standardised. Cambridge N-levels, O-levels and A-levels were settled upon as the uniform standard for curricula and examinations only in 1974, ending the earlier grab-bag of qualifications that were offered according to language stream and sometimes according to the individual school (*ST*, 10 June and 2 August 1974). There were also severe political problems associated with language and race to be tackled.[27] These agendas occupied Lee Kuan Yew and his colleagues until the end of the 1970s, only after which could he start the formidable task of extracting extra value from the elite.

The relative state of inaction at the upper levels of the social pyramid came to an abrupt end with *The Goh Report*'s introduction of streaming and the creation of SAP schools, which were the first steps in separating the 'scholars' from the 'commoners'. This was the beginning of the programme of diversification that reached a high point in the 1980s and 1990s and is continuing even today with the spread of programmes of self-assessment and self-management at school and district level.[28] Streaming is, after all, nothing more than a form of enforced diversification based on examination results. The SAP schools are another mechanism for diversification, this time based upon race and ability in Chinese Language. Yet diversification went much further than this and, under the ministerial leadership of Dr Tony Tan in the 1980s, Singapore's education system began moving through a massive inflation of options available to those who were able to flourish in the system, and which only came to maturity in the 2000s. Yet the earliest signs of this move were seen in primary school in the very early 1980s when it was decided to allow schools to choose between rival series of textbooks.[29] The first definitive indicator of a shift in the wind, however, was a 1985 speech by then First Deputy Prime Minister Goh Chok Tong in which he bemoaned the bland conformity of Singapore's schools and invited the island's premier schools to go 'Independent'.[30] Goh's initiative was picked up by his Education Minister, and so at this point we find ourselves once again pondering the critical role of

Dr Tan. He was a forceful and decisive minister with clear ideas of where he wanted to take the education system. We have already examined his transformation of pre-schools, but he also created a diversified educational 'market' at the secondary and pre-university levels – a process that Ka-ho Mok identifies as 'decentralisation and marketisation of education'[31] – whereby bright, *kiasu* students could be given the advantages they deserved. The elite schools sought to nurture individual 'ability' to the fullest by freeing the brightest students from the constraints of the pack. Significantly though, even while this was the outcome that Dr Tan achieved, he was just as concerned with the values and ethos being imparted to the budding elites as he was with their academic training.

❧ Character building

According to Eugene Wijeysingha, a former Deputy Director of Education who was posted as principal of Raffles Institution in 1986 to turn the school 'Independent' (*ST*, 9 October 1986), Dr Tan took for granted that the best students would excel academically in Singapore schools, but he wanted schools that would build their character and turn them into 'gentlemen.'[32] To this end he engaged in what was effectively a programme of the gentrification of elite education to parallel the privileging of elite education *per se*. Dr Tan's first step was taken in 1986 when he commissioned a group of 12 secondary school principals including Wijeysingha to tour a collection of elite schools in the UK and the USA, apparently to find the best way to implement the privatisation initiatives urged by Goh Chok Tong in 1985. The result was a 76-page report titled *Towards Excellence in Schools*,[33] which was substantially implemented over the next few years. The principals recommended that selected schools be effectively privatised and given both considerable autonomy and extra resources to enable them to offer a better study environment and school experience. In the full spirit of this 'privatisation', the Independent schools were given government grants of $1 million each to launch their endowment funds (*ST*, 1 September 1987) and began charging fees that have progressively moved from being nominal in the 1980s to very substantial in the 2000s (*Business Times*, 3 November 1989; *ST*, 11 August 1990 and 29 November 2005). At the top of the hierarchy of favoured schools came Raffles Institution, which was Lee Kuan Yew's *alma mater* and by folklore the premier school in the country. It was not in the first batch of schools to be privatised, but this did not stop it collecting $1 million from the government along with the first batch of Independent schools (*ST*, 1 September 1987). Furthermore it was the only one to be shifted into premises originally designed for a junior college, giving its students a truly luxurious study environment.

It also appears that the efforts to build 'character' in young people fed an escalation of the importance of Extra-Curricular Activities (ECAs) later to be called Co-Curricular Activities (CCAs). These 'character building' activities – joining the National Cadet Corp or scouts, playing in a school band or the rugby team, cultural activities, etc. – had always played an important role in Chinese education in Singapore[34] and this prominence had flowed through without fuss into the national schools. In 1965 ECAs became a school subject for the purposes of assessing entry into Pre-University courses, and in 1968 MOE set up an ECA Centre to co-ordinate and stimulate ECAs. Interviews reveal that by the late 1990s the CCAs had assumed a central place in education. One interviewee was able to draw on his impressive record of CCAs to win an SAF scholarship with, as he candidly admitted, indifferent A-level results. With so much riding on CCAs it is not surprising that there are now unofficial hierarchies of CCAs, and winning a championship in a sport or a promotion in a uniformed group could be the factor that gets you into university or wins you a scholarship (*ST*, 11 May 1989).

Towards Excellence in Schools placed great emphasis on ECAs, though this should be seen as a symptom rather than a cause of this development. Of course, the creeping incorporation of ECAs/CCAs into assessment has ensured that no aspect of school life – including the 'fun bits' – is free of pressure or *kiasu*ism (*ST*, 4 August 1980) but beyond that it has also accentuated existing distortions in the 'meritocracy', creating new advantages for children who come from well-to-do families. Not only has the capacity to pay for kindergarten, private tuition and so forth created an imbalance, but the range and quality of CCAs offered by a school, and the financial capacity of parents to send their children on approved activities have also become factors in determining success in the Singapore education system.

Yet sociological studies by Lai Ah Eng *et al.* reveal an important upside to the CCA experience based on the fact that CCAs have little or no regard for either race or academic performance. They force youths to mix with members of other races and other streams; they give youths who are not gifted academically an opportunity to shine and even outrank their academic superiors, and give members of minority races a rare chance to exercise leadership.[35] Such 'glimmers of hope' (to borrow the words of Lai Ah Eng)[36] are welcome as a counterbalance to the dominant picture, but are woefully insufficient to counteract the overall thrust of the education system.

❧ *Meritocracy and class*

Meanwhile the growing diversity in education has accelerated the process of rewarding anticipated excellence, setting pre-conditions that would foster the development of what one-time Education Minister Teo Chee Hean has identified as an 'ability-driven education system', aimed at developing each individual's potential to the fullest.[37] With a collection of six elite Independent schools in place by the end of the 1980s, the base had been laid for a broader collection of 'privatised' elite schools to be built. Two more Independent schools were created in 1993, followed soon after by thirteen lower-cost and lower prestige 'Autonomous' schools. These Independent and Autonomous schools were relatively free of the constraints of MOE micromanagement, and set out to become incubators of excellence.

It is an article of faith in the Singapore meritocracy that children are selected for these elite schools on strictly meritocratic grounds, but the operation of class and privilege was clearly identified by Jason Tan as long ago as 1993. His research on three independent schools revealed that from 66 to 69 per cent of the fathers of children in these independent schools worked in professional/technical or administrative/managerial occupations (as opposed to the national average of 26.2 per cent). 40.4 per cent of the adult male population were production workers at that time, but their children occupied from 4.9 to 11.1 per cent of places in those schools. 64.1 per cent of the adult male population at that time did not have a secondary school education, but their children occupied from 2.7 to 9.0 per cent of the places in the three schools surveyed. Unsurprisingly, fathers with university degrees were overrepresented (against the national average) by from 335 to 633 per cent. Furthermore from 25.5 to 59.4 per cent of the children in these schools lived in a condominium, a private flat or in landed property (as opposed to 10.6 per cent for the national average).[38] 40.4 per cent of Singaporeans lived in 1-, 2- or 3-room HDB flats at that time, but they represented from 6.0 to 26.4 per cent of children in those schools. It seems clear that from the start the elite schools have been 'elite' not only in the sense that they have exceptionally high academic and teaching standards, but also in that they cater almost exclusively for children from socially and financially privileged families – this despite the provision of some well-intended scholarships designed to pay the school fees of the few needy students who excel against the odds.

The government itself provides accidental confirmation of the continuing role of economic privilege in the meritocracy by its self-serving celebration of any child from a poor background who wins a place in an elite school. A case in point is that of a Malay student from a poor background and a neighbour-hood school who did so well in her 2005 PSLE that she won a scholarship to study at Raffles Girls' School (*CNA*, 12 December 2005; *Today*, 12 December 2005; *CyBerita*, 13 December 2005). According to the testimony of former students of the elite schools themselves, such students are extremely rare (*Straits Times Interactive*, 14 December 2005), probably because they need to succeed without the luxury of paying thousands of dollars on tuition, private assessment books, and CCAs in primary school, and then be will-ing to continually beg for help meeting the even higher costs of studying in an upper-middle-class environment in secondary school and junior college. A 2002 survey revealed that the typical annual cost of educational extras in Singapore ranged from around $1,500 for a pre-primary pupil to around $12,000 for a university student (*ST*, 5 October 2002). In the case of the celebrated Malay student mentioned above, Malay organisations promised to help her meet these costs (*CyBerita*, 13 December 2005). The irony is that the Malay community is the poorest community in Singapore, so we witness a twisting of the Western welfare state: redistribution of resources amongst the poor, rather than the redistribution of wealth from the rich to the poor.[39]

If anything, the operation of economic and social privilege is even stronger and better documented in the GEP. Both official and unofficial sources confirm that most GEP students begin with the advantage of having middle-class parents with professional occupations (*ST*, 6 November 1994; *Straits Times Interactive*, 14 December 2005). Furthermore the programme is designed with the assumption that parents are able to ferry their child(ren) about by car (*Today*, 21 November 2005) – a possession that in Singapore is the preserve of the upper middle class – and provides for a high level of co-curricular activities, many of which are expensive. Turning the coin over for a moment, we also note that MOE's own research shows that most children identified in Primary 1 as being 'weak' in English and/or Maths and who are regarded as having started school despite being 'not ready' – presumably because they missed out on kindergarten – are from low-income families (*CNA*, 15 January 2006). It appears that this class factor explains the prevalence of 'giftedness' running in families much better than the commonly accepted reference to genetic make-up.

❧ Non-elite schools

The pursuit of excellence was not, however, confined to elite schools. In 1997, then-Prime Minister Goh Chok Tong announced and his Deputy Prime Minister Lee Hsien Loong managed the introduction of a significant revamp of the whole educational sector called 'Thinking Schools, Learning Nation', which lifted the bar for all schools (including primary).[40] Schools were given more resources to create a generation of computer-literate students; the curriculum was revised to reduce content in favour of less-directed exploratory pedagogy through projects; independent, creative and entrepreneurial thinking was encouraged.[41] This initiative drifted seamlessly into the creation in the year 2000 of a 'Schools Excellence Model' in which ordinary schools, not just Independent and Autonomous schools, were to exercise considerable autonomy and initiative in 'self-assessment and analysis', identifying their weaknesses and strengths. These initiatives embraced diversity in approaches to the common goal of achieving excellence, giving schools increased autonomy to build for themselves niche areas.[42]

While there is no reason to doubt that the government was and is serious in its pursuit of excellence for children in government schools, the cutting edge of the programmes in diversity has always been found in the elite schools, and in the decades since about 1985 the privileging of these schools and the privileged backgrounds of the children who win places in them has escalated exponentially. Hence, the rewards for excelling in the Primary 4 streaming examinations and the Primary 3 GEP selection tests – and even of winning a place at a good school after kindergarten – are now immeasurable. The 2004 introduction of Integrated Programmes in selected schools – known colloquially as the 'through train' – is the logical result. Under the 'through train', students in Integrated Programme schools may pay fees at up to 1,500 per cent of the standard rate,[43] but they benefit from more material resources and better educational opportunities. Furthermore they can proceed to pre-university education without the inconvenience of sitting for O-levels.[44] It is planned that under this scheme around 10 per cent of each cohort will be put on a 'through train' to their A-levels so they do not have to waste their time swotting needlessly.[45] In fact since 2005 they have not even had to face the inconvenience of waiting for their PSLE results, since most schools offering Integrated Programmes fill most of their Secondary 1 vacancies through their own private and opaque selection procedures (*ST*, 12 October 2005).[46] As a result of this practice, known as 'Direct School Admission' (DSA), a quarter of all the 2005 cohort of Nanyang Primary School Primary 6 students were offered places in either the Hwa Chong or the Raffles families of schools before they had even sat for their PSLE (*CNA*, 19 October 2005). Having by-passed PSLE for entry purposes, these students are then able to skip their O levels in Secondary 4, saving the trouble of competing for a place in junior college!

It may be an unintended consequence, but the 'through train' is also serving to intensify some of the racially based elements of discrimination within the education system. Indian students have always had to put up with a lack of kindergartens teaching Tamil and a shortage of Tamil teachers because MOE has always refused to recruit overseas Tamil language teachers (in contrast to their routine recruitment of overseas Chinese teachers),[47] thus driving many Indian students to take their 'Mother Tongue' lessons outside the school and outside school hours. On top of this, Indian students can face extra obstacles to entering Integrated Programme schools. The story was told by a distraught Indian parent in a letter to *The Straits Times Interactive*, saying that, whereas Chinese children have a wide choice of Integrated Programme schools offering Mandarin as second language, the only Integrated Programme school that her daughter could attend was Raffles Girls School (RGS), since this is the only one to offer Tamil as a second language. The problem is that RGS has the most stringent entry requirements of any school in Singapore. She concluded: 'A Chinese student with a score of less than 260 points can gain admission to a secondary school which offers the Integrated Programme. My daughter who would have done comparatively well or even better than her Chinese peers is denied an opportunity' (*Straits Times Interactive*, 19 October 2005). Significantly, *The Straits Times* chose to run the letter in the online edition of the paper only and so MOE has not found it necessary to respond.[48]

An MOE media release lamely promises that the IP 'should not reduce access to our top institutions for deserving students', but of course the message of the structure speaks louder than a press release.[49] Since it opened in 2005, the apogee of rewards for excelling in a top primary school – and a privileged background – has been admission to the National University of Singapore High School of Mathematics and Science, which is set to outshine even Raffles Institution for standards and resources. In its first intake this school reserved only 10 of its 150 Secondary 1 places for PSLE entry, the rest being filled by direct application to the school, under its in-house, opaque rules. In the same year – which was also the first year of the operation of DSA across the country – Raffles Institution admitted 209 students through DSA, and 36.8 per cent of these subsequently failed to meet RI's entry requirements in the PSLE, but did not have their admission revoked. In Anglo-Chinese (Independent) the corresponding figure was 38.1% (*ST*, 22 May, 2006). Looking more broadly, about half of the 2005 entry places in the country's 11 Integrated Programme schools were taken before students received their PSLE results (*ST*, 10 September, 12 October and 19 October 2005). This situation will worsen if the Integrated Programme schools begin exercising their right to take up to 100 per cent of their intake through DSA.[50]

Networking for Success

Yet even these tangible advantages of winning a place in a top school fail to convey the rewards at stake. The networking, inside knowledge and the culture of self-conscious privilege available to students in elite schools underline the appropriateness of our decision to describe Dr Tan's reforms at the elite level as a process of 'gentrification'. At the elite schools, the inspiration for the environment of advantage is reminiscent of the British upper class, and we do not refer just to the advantages of ordinary networking. Anglo-Chinese School has always been at the heart of a thoroughly upper middle-class old boys' network that helps professionals and entrepreneurs lubricate business transactions. Similarly, Raffles Institution and RGS have traditionally played an important role in supplying the civil service with dedicated and competent officers, while at the same time providing career paths for the sons and daughters of Singaporeans who were not particularly wealthy. From the 1950s to the 1980s this process lent itself to a considerable amount of networking, but the situation was nonetheless unexceptional and relatively transparent.

The circumstances today are somewhat different and were described in interview by a serving Army officer.[51] This officer was a product of a SAP school and was an SAF scholar who had studied overseas. He described himself as being 'close to the first tier of the scholars' in the SAF and his career at the time of the interview was proceeding as he hoped, so he had no cause for complaint at a personal level. Yet he expressed his amazement when it dawned on him in his early thirties just how much of an advantage was enjoyed by the students from the really top schools and junior colleges. He spoke of top students from these schools being

> pre-identified [before starting National Service] and then they are selected into the 'Delta Company' [in the Army] and during their stay in the Army, they have a lot of opportunities to meet the top ranks in the Army or in the MINDEF as a whole. They are selected based on their results, their A-level results ... [and] are the ones targeted for overseas scholarships and typically they go to UK or US.
>
> I first came in touch with the Delta Company ... when I was tasked to organise an event for them. ... I was one of the organising officers. So I mingled with them and realised that even though they are only 17, 18 years old they really talk like young adults who are quite well aware of what's going on around them in the whole world, not only in Singapore. And they are quite well aware of what's expected of them and what are the opportunities that they have within the SAF and within the country as a whole. Once in National Service, the SAF gives them opportunities to meet the top ranks. The generals come down and speak to them over a barbecue. Ministers too ... .
>
> The first tier of the scholars are drawn from this group, from Raffles JC, Hwa Chong JC ... .

This situation was drastically different in his school, despite it being a good SAP school:

> There wasn't much information on scholarships. Even up to the day I signed up with the Army there wasn't much information on scholarships. Looking back I realised that some of my friends that had come from some other schools, they knew that there were scholarships around that you can choose from and so on and so forth.

This interviewee is not describing anything underhanded or corrupt, but it shows clearly the stakes that are involved in getting into the 'right' school. Winners are ushered into a world where not only minds are trained and opened, but institutional doors and pathways are opened and futures mapped out. Students in such schools routinely have opportunities to undertake a research project supervised by an academic from the National University of Singapore[52] or even take university subjects that will be credited towards their future degree (*ST*, 30 July 2003). By contrast, students in ordinary 'neighbourhood' schools are more likely to be offered courses tied in with a local polytechnic, as does Admiralty Secondary through an arrangement with Temasek Polytechnic (*CNA*, 25 September 2005). In 2005 there was even talk of systematising such arrangements with the creation of a 'through train' to polytechnic (skipping O-levels) to parallel the elite schools' 'through train' to university (*CNA*, 25 September 2005). Barr's interviewee had not attended a neighbourhood school, but even having come through the SAP school system he was still missing out on the optimal advice and networking available in the elite school systems.

From Elite Selection to Elite Formation

Of course there is more to elite formation than networking. There are several processes simultaneously at work here. First, the future elite are herded together into a small group of elite schools. Second, they are given a top education in these schools. Third, they are socialised into the group-think of a dedicated, self-conscious elite. Only then are the doors of privilege opened properly. The educational standards and the culture of service inculcated in these schools – especially in the Raffles family of schools – is the stuff of legend, and of course these schools excel in producing students who get lots of 'A' grades in their A-levels. Beyond this crude measure, however, it has proven difficult for an outsider to get far beyond the legend.

The renowned culture of service inculcated in these schools is indicated by the high numbers of these students who go into government service, especially from the Raffles group, which is a traditional supplier of senior civil servants. The extraordinarily high salary levels of Administrative Officers and SAF officers, however, make it difficult to separate service from self-interest.[53] In 2006 the government informed us that the base salary of a 'typical' Administrative Officer (just entering the Superscale salary band) was $371,900, while Permanent Secretaries started at $2.2 million (a figure recently increased to $2.6 million).[54] In any case it must be much more difficult to pass on the idealism of service today because of the conflicting messages in today's nation-building programme. The 'culture of service' does not fit comfortably with some of Singapore's rival cultural drivers, notably *kiasu-*

ism, materialism and pragmatism. Hence we saw in Chapter 4 the emergence in 1998 of a pattern of scholars buying themselves out of their government bonds to take up better offers. At the very least this suggests that the ethic of 'service' is struggling to win the hearts and minds of young Singaporeans.

In contrast to our cautious assessment about the elite students' sense of 'service', there is no question about the sense of being part of a self-conscious elite, of being 'special'. Chua Mui Hoong, a former RGS girl and a senior *Straits Times* journalist gave a very clear depiction of the image and the self-image of RGS girls in a letter to *The Straits Times* in late 2003. She recounted the virtues of a 1980s RGS education:

> My friends at RGS turned out to be wholesome, productive citizens. We didn't job-hop. Many work in the public sector ...
>
> [RGS] taught me there were no limits to what I could achieve, if only I tried hard and had talent. ... Many of us have a deep-seated urge to achieve, whether in school or at work or in our personal life. We're competitive by nature. Almost unconsciously, we tend to judge a person by her intelligence.
>
> ... Rafflesian girls are assertive ... . (*ST*, 16 November 2003)

It is perhaps even more indicative that, when a group of 10 ex-RGS girls took issue with aspects of her letter, not only did they not dispute these descriptors, but they described themselves as a group of 'Oxbridge graduates, active philanthropists, community volunteers, career women at the top of their fields, as well as wives and mothers' (*ST*, 21 November 2003). A negative expression of the sense of 'specialness' could be seen in early 2004, when it was revealed in a blog that an RGS girl was dating a neighbourhood school boy. The perceived absurdity of an RGS girl dating a boy of such a different 'status' prompted a record 1,000 postings in a short time and the thread had to be closed to new listings. A new thread attracted 140 entries in a week. One listing, reported in *The Straits Times*, depicts the Rafflesian sense of 'specialness' at its most ugly: 'Really don't think that neighbourhood guys stand a chance with a top schooler now or 10 years later ... . You are a product of a sub-standard school' (*ST*, 14 March 2004). Even more recently a student at Raffles Junior College (and the daughter of a PAP MP) made a spectacle of herself by posting a blog in which she scolded a man in his 40s who had complained that life in Singapore is a struggle. She made it clear that she had no time for losers, and that she thought that he should (among other things) 'get out of my elite uncaring face' (*Straits Times*, 24 October 2006). The scandal was compounded when her father defended her publicly. The sense of election, 'specialness' and superiority seems to be even stronger among GEP students, who are cocooned within another layer of insulation in which they mix almost exclusively with fellow-'GEPers' and regard 'mainstreamers' as 'immature' (*Today*, 21 November 2005), a situation that former Education Minister Tharman Shanmugaratnam acknowledged as 'the downside' of the GEP (*Today*, 29 December 2005). According to the testimony of some of their teachers, parents and themselves (both during the programme and after they have left the cocoon to join the workforce) GEPers often have poor social skills and find it difficult to make small talk or to relate to the world of 'mainstreamers' (*Today*, 21 and 29 November 2005). According to one former GEP student born in 1980, upon entering the programme he was even given 'a booklet spelling out how different we [were] from other people and how the programme would meet our needs' (*Today*, 29 November 2005). Teachers sometimes counsel parents of GEPers to expect their child to become more 'impatient, demanding, argumentative, competitive and lacking in social skills', because this is the typical behaviour of a GEPer (*Today*, 21 November 2005).

Conformity in Diversity

Our overview of the elite schools and the elite students – as cursory as it is – and even more so our picture of the stratification of education since the mid-1980s raise a significant dilemma when placed against the general picture of the Singaporean student. Elite students are given stimulating educational environments and are encouraged to be inquiring, open-minded and questioning. Independent and Autonomous schools are encouraged to carve out unique characters and niches for themselves. Under the Schools Excellence Model even neighbourhood schools are expected to show a spark of independence. So how is it that Singaporean students are famous for their conformity and risk aversion? If a hundred flowers are blooming, why do they mostly display slavish, if superficial fidelity to the National Education agenda in post-secondary education? Several explanations suggest themselves.

One partial explanation might be that the elite students are indeed different to the rest: that regardless of the conformity in the masses, the cream have benefited from the stimulating GEP programmes and all their other advantages. But no, according to one very senior civil servant interviewed in 2003, the 'problem' of conformity, intellectual timidity and lack of imagination is also endemic among the younger Administrative Officers. Among the newer scholar-officers, straightforward technocratic and professional skills abound, but he opined that the capacity to transform academic brilliance into brilliant independent thought is restricted to less than 1 in 20. More than 80 per cent of them in a particular sample, with which he had been in professional contact, displayed no capacity for independent thought at all. Bear in mind that the sample group being considered here is already less than the top 1 per cent of an entire age cohort from the school system. A perusal of contributions by junior and middle-ranking Administrative Officers to *Ethos*, the journal of the Civil Service College, seems to confirm this impression. None stray beyond the limits set by their superiors and none are very challenging or interesting – and these are presumably the most enterprising and daring of their cohorts.[55]

If this is the situation among the best of the best, what must be the level of intellectual aridity among the rest of the school and post-school population? There is no doubt that there are independent thinkers among young Singaporean graduates, some of them in Barr's acquaintance, but they are disproportionately from minorities, often from non-elite schools, always bridling at Singapore's culture of conformity, and never candidates for high office in the establishment. This situation stands in stark contrast to that in the early 1980s when it was possible, albeit with difficulty, to combine independent and rebellious thinking with entry into the elite ranks of the civil service. Tharman Shanmugaratnam comes to mind as representative of the broader pattern operating at this time. Though hardly a radical himself he was questioned by the Internal Security Department and almost detained in 1987 for his history of associating with radicals (*ST*, 14 December 2001). Yet he has survived and thrived since then, reaching the heights of the Cabinet, the Monetary Authority of Singapore, the Ministry of Education and the Ministry of Finance. His generation, however, was the last to combine a background of independent thinking and rebelliousness with a successful career in the administrative and political elite.

The Singapore government seems now to have perfected, against its stated intent, a system of cultivating conformity in diversity.[56] Although we cannot be definitive, the explanation might lie in the continuing unidirectional, collectivist character of the Singapore state and society, of which the education system is a central manifestation. In Chapter 4 we placed Singapore's culture of elite governance in a context of developmentalism and technocracy. We posited that Singapore's ruling elite seems to believe that it has perfected both by absorbing the idea of the technocrat into the broader ideal of 'the elite', and then making membership of the 'elite' a precondition of membership of either. We argued that this was a conceit, but one which was likely to prove a satisfactory basis for the perpetuation of the regime. The ruling elite is not so sanguine about the education system, but seems to think that it is at least well on the way to perfecting this system as well, so that it will perform a multiplicity of conflicting services for the neo-developmental state.

At the elite level the education system is expected to provide a flow of top quality, independently minded, but – in apparent contradiction – utterly loyal candidates to regenerate the administrative and political elite. They must be virtuous and principled, but at the same time pragmatic and materialistic. At the middle level the education system is expected to produce cohorts of highly educated, creative, entrepreneurial and independently minded graduates to inhabit the medium and lower echelons of the civil service, and to flourish as entrepreneurs in a modern knowledge-based economy. At all levels it needs to produce citizens who are not only deeply loyal and grateful to the regime but who see themselves as part of a collective entity that is progressing as one entity.

Achieving all aspects of this mix was always going to be problematic, especially given the emphasis on grades and the continuing dialogue between *kiasu* government and *kiasu* parents, which gravitate away from independent thinking and creativity. Something had to 'give', and the most likely candidates were always independent thinking and creativity. Yet the central contradiction lies not in the education system itself, but in the society that it serves. This society retains the intrinsic collectivism and unidirectional focus of old-style developmentalism, along with its strong, authoritarian state. It is truly ironic that no one in government has noticed the contradiction in students working feverishly to foster independent thought and creativity because the government told them to do so. They might very well be able to manage to think independently about all sorts of worthwhile things, but the pathos of the situation comes to the fore when students or newly minted scholars in the Administrative Service are asked to think independently about the government.

Notes

1   Lee Kuan Yew, *New Bearings in Our Education System*, Singapore: Ministry of Culture, [1966–67], p. 12.

2   Barr has heard the civil service terminology in conversations with civil servants. The SAF terminology is found in Tim Huxley, *Defending the Lion City: The Armed Forces of Singapore*, St Leonards, NSW: Allen & Unwin, 2000, pp. 111, 241, 242.

3   Tharman Shanmugaratnam and the Junior College/Upper Secondary Education Review Committee, *Report of the Junior College/Upper Secondary Education Review Committee*, Singapore: Ministry of Education, 2002, p. ii.

4   DEET, *Country Education Profiles, Second Edition 1996*, p. 6. The secondary school Normal Streams (bottom of the secondary schools hierarchy), should not be confused with the Normal Stream in primary school (top of the primary school hierarchy under the pre-1992 system).

5   Trivina Kang, 'Schools and post-secondary aspirations among female Chinese, Malay and Indian Normal Stream students', in Lai Ah Eng (ed.), *Beyond Rituals and Riots: Ethnic Pluralism and Social Cohesion in Singapore*, Singapore: Eastern Universities Press by Marshall Cavendish for Institute of Policy Studies, 2004, pp. 151–153; Joyce James, 'Linguistic realities and pedagogical practices in Singapore: Another Perspective', S. Gopinathan, Anne Pakir, Ho Wah Kam and Vaithamani Saravanan (eds), *Language, Society and Education in Singapore: Issues and Trends*, Second Edition, Singapore: Times Academic Press, 1998, pp. 112, 114.

6   Kang, 'Schools and post-secondary aspirations', pp. 152–155.

7   At the time of the interview with Barr (2002), this student was doing well in an Australian university after having failed to gain admission to a local university.

8   Ministry of Education, *Nurturing Every Child: Flexibility and Diversity in Singapore Schools*, Singapore: Ministry of Education, 2004, pp. 20–23. Available at the MOE website, http://www.moe.edu.sg. Accessed 29 September 2005. Also see, 'Changes Affecting Normal Course', on the MOE website, accessed 14 April 2008.

9   Various interviews with Barr, conducted in Singapore in 2003.

10   MOE, *Nurturing Every Child*, pp. 26–29.

11   'A more broad-based school ranking system', MOE Press Release, 17 March 2004, MOE website, http://www.moe.gov.sg. Accessed 19 September 2005.

12   Various interviews conducted by Barr in Brisbane in 2002 and in Singapore in 2003.

13   Interview with Barr, Singapore, 16 April 2004.

14   Since the mid-2000s the so-called 'Cambridge' examinations have been set locally (*ST*, 31 August 2002.

15   Jason Tan, 'The marketization of education in Singapore', in Jason Tan and Ng Pak Tee, *Shaping Singapore's Future: Thinking Schools, Learning Nation*, Singapore: Pearson Education, 2005, p. 106.

16   Janet Shepherd, *Striking a Balance: The Management of Language in Singapore*, Frankfurt, Peter Lang, 2005, p. 136.

17   Lee Kuan Yew (ed. Chua Chee Lay), *Keeping My Mandarin Alive: Lee Kuan Yew's Language Learning Experience*, Singapore: World Scientific and Global Publishing, 2005, p. 98.

18 Note Lee's discussion of Lee Hsien Loong's hairstyle in his National Day Rally Speech in 1978, and that he based his decision to allow young Singaporeans to visit the PRC on his daughter's reactions to her visit in 1976. See Lee Kuan Yew, *From Third World to First: The Singapore Story: 1965–2000: Memoirs of Lee Kuan Yew*, Singapore: Singapore Press Holdings; Times Editions, 2000, pp. 654–656.

19 See also a letter from two Junior College students in *Straits Times Interactive*, 17 April 2006.

20 'Mavericks a must for nation's growth', MITA (Ministry of Information and the Arts), News email service, 29 November–5 December 2003.

21 Singaporeans who went to school in the 1970s, 1980s and early 1990s consistently reported in interview that their once-weekly civics and moral education class was taken seriously by neither the teachers nor the students because the subject was not assessed. When they were taught, students were subjected to heavy-handed and ineffectual didacticism, but more often classes were dispensed with in favour of catching up on work in 'proper' subjects, or even just to perform routine administrative functions, such as taking the roll. The only notable exception to this rule was the Religious Knowledge classes, which were taught in upper secondary in the 1980s. Students who attended these remember them as less didactic and more interesting. For more on the Religious Knowledge courses, see Joseph B. Tamney, *The Struggle Over Singapore's Soul: Western Modernization and Asian Culture*, Berlin; New York: Walter De Gruyter, 1996.

22 Shamira Bhanu Abdul Azeez, *The Singapore–Malaysia 'Remerger' Debate of 1996*, [Hull]: Centre for South-East Asian Studies and Institute of Pacific Asia Studies, The University of Hull, 1998, pp. 74, 75.

23 See, for instance, Chee Keng John Wang, Angeline Khoo, Chor Boon Goh, Steven Tan and S. Gopinathan, 'Patriotism and National Education: Perceptions of Trainee Teachers in Singapore', *Asia Pacific Journal of Education*, vol. 26 no. 1 (2006), pp. 51–64.

24 *History Syllabus: Secondary 1 to 2 (Special/Express Course), Secondary 1 to 2 (Normal Academic Course)*, Singapore: Ministry of Education, 2000.

25 *Secondary Civics and Moral Education Syllabus: Secondary*, Singapore: Ministry of Education, 2000.

26 *Singapore's Survival, Security and Success*, prepared for a seminar for junior college students, circa 1998, vetted by Ms Ong Chong Lian, Head National Education Office; MAJ Chin Kok Keng, Head Curriculum Branch. Compiled by Mr Alden Teo, Curriculum Staff Officer.

27 Lee refers explicitly to the political problems associated with language and race in Goh Keng Swee and The Education Study Team, *Report on the Ministry of Education 1978*, Singapore: [Singapore National Printers], 1979, pp. iii, iv.

28 This refers to the Schools Excellence Model, which is considered later in this chapter.

29 Ang Wai Hoong and Yeoh Oon Chye, '25 years of curriculum development', in John Yip Soon Kwong and Sim Wong Kooi (eds), *Evolution of Educational Excellence: 25 Years of Education in the Republic of Singapore*, Singapore: Longman, 1990, p. 101.

30 Lim Soon Tae and S. Gopinathan, '25 years of curriculum planning', in Yip and Sim (eds), *Evolution of Educational Excellence*, p. 76.

31 Ka-ho Mok, 'Decentralization and marketization of education in Singapore: a case study of the school excellence model', *Journal of Educational Administration*, vol. 41, no. 4, 2003, pp. 348–366.

32 Barr's interview with Eugene Wijeysingha, Singapore, 11 April 2003.

33 Goh Chi Lan and the principals of the Study Team, *Towards Excellence in Schools: A Report to the Minister for Education February 1987*, Singapore: Ministry of Education, 1987.

34 See, for instance, 'Encourage extra-curricular activities', *Nanyang Siang Pau*, 18 August 1966. Cited in *Mirror of Opinion: Highlights of Malay, Chinese & Tamil Press*, Singapore: Ministry of Culture, 1966.

35 Christine Lee, Mary Cherian, Rahil Ismail, Maureen Ng, Jasmine Sim and Chee Min Fui, 'Children's experiences of multiracial relationships in informal primary school settings'; Kang, 'Schools and post-secondary aspirations'; Lana Khong, Joy Chew and Jonathan Goh, 'How now, NE? An exploratory study of ethnic relations in three Singapore schools', in Lai, *Beyond Rituals and Riots*, pp. 114–145; 146–171; and 172–196 respectively.

36 Lai Ah Eng, 'Introduction: beyond rituals and riots', in Lai, *Beyond Rituals and Riots*, p. 20.

37 Ng Pak Tee, 'Students' perception of change in the Singapore education system', *Educational Research for Policy and Practice*, vol. 3, 2004, p. 79.

38 Jason Tan, 'Independent schools in Singapore: implications for social and educational inequalities', *International Journal of Educational Development*, vol. 13, no. 3, 1993, pp. 245, 246.

39 This twist on welfare-ism is a common thread running through Singapore's social system, and is intrinsic to the application of the 'self-help' philosophy in a context that privileges communal bonds but disregards class divisions. Fortunately the rhetoric about 'self-help' is stronger than the reality, and there are many instances of welfare provisions that involve direct government subsidies to the poor. In education this takes the form of scholarships and small-scale financial assistance schemes. Barr has explored this phenomena in relation to the health system in 'Medical savings accounts in Singapore: a critical inquiry', *Journal of Health Politics, Policy and Law*, vol. 26, no. 3, 2001, pp. 707–724.

40 Ng Pak Tee, 'Students' perception of change in the Singapore education system', p. 78; Speech by Prime Minister Lee Hsien Loong at the 2005 Administrative Service Dinner, 24 March 2005. Cited on Sprinter [Singapore Government news service] http://www.sprinter.gov.sg/. Accessed 30 March 2005.

41 Ng Pak Tee, 'Students' Perception of Change in the Singapore Education System', p. 78.

42 Ka-ho Mok, 'Decentralization and Marketization of Education in Singapore', pp. 357, 358.

43 Trivina Kang, 'Diversification of Singapore's upper secondary landscape: introduction of integrated programmes, specialised independent schools and privately-funded schools',

Constructing Singapore

in Jason Tan and Ng Pak Tee (eds), *Shaping Singapore's Future: Thinking Schools, Learning Nation*, Singapore, Pearson Educational, 2005, pp. 53, 54.

44 'MOE approves the introduction of integrated programmes in four schools', Ministry of Education Press Release, 30 December 2002, available at MOE website: http://www.moe.gov.sg. Cited 13 September 2005.

45 Barr's interview with Eugene Wijeysingha, Singapore, 11 April 2003.

46 Kang, 'Diversification of Singapore's upper secondary landscape', pp. 60, 61.

47 'Foreign Chinese language teachers chosen with due care to supplement our local pool', Forum Letter Replies, 25 October 2005, MOE website, at http://www.moe.gov.sg/forum/2005/. Accessed 7 November 2005.

48 See 'Forum letter replies', MOE website, at http://www.moe.gov.sg/forum/2005/index.htm. Accessed 7 November 2005.

49 'MOE approves the introduction of Integrated Programmes in four schools', MOE Press Release, 30 December 2002, available on MOE website, http://www.moe.gov.sg. Accessed 7 November 2005.

50 Ministry of Education website, http://www.moe.gov.sg. Accessed 6 October 2005. It is worth noting that the introduction of DSA was not restricted to the elite schools. Since 2005 many non-elite schools have also enjoyed considerable freedom to by-pass PSLE in their intake. In the first year (2005), 1,600 students across the country were admitted to secondary schools via DSA and about half of these subsequently failed to achieve the appropriate cut-off score in their PSLE (ST, 22 May 2006). In 2007, the number entering secondary school through DSA jumped to 1,960 students, accounting for 4 per cent of the entire cohort (*CNA*, 20 December 2007).

51 Barr's interview with an Army officer, Singapore, 3 April 2003.

52 Barr met and gave academic advice to two RJC students engaged in such a research project in 2003.

53 Base starting salaries for Administrative Officers are not extraordinarily high, but bonuses, benefits and fast tracked promotions mean that they very quickly become high income earners. In 2005 the basic starting salary for a newly graduated Administrative Officer was $51,000 to $63,000. See the Administrative Service website, at http://www.adminservice.gov.sg/great.htm. By their mid-30s an Administrative Officer on an ascending career path can expect to be on Superscale G salary package. In 1998 this represented a salary of $100,000 to $150,000 p.a. According to Cherian George, in 2000 the income of high performing Administrative Officers in their early 30s was in the 'hundreds of thousands'. At the top of the scale, the highest ranking Permanent Secretaries were paid packages valued at up to $1.2 million in 1998 – the equivalent of a Deputy Prime Minister. See Cherian George, *Singapore: The Air-Conditioned Nation. Essays of the Politics of Comfort and Control 1990–2000* (Singapore: Landmark, 2000), p. 76. 1998 salary values are found in Worthington, *Governance in Singapore*, p. 143.

206

54 Teo Chee Hean, Ministerial Statement by Teo Chee Hean, Minister-in-Charge of the Civil Service, on Civil Service Salary Revisions, 9 April 2007, Singapore Government Press Release, located at http://www.sprinter.gov.sg/.

55 *Ethos* is available on line at http://www.cscollege.gov.sg/main.html.

56 The cultivation of independent thinking has supposedly been a high priority of the Singapore education system since the 1990s. See Tharman Shanmugaratnam's speech, 'Innovation and enterprise in our schools', 16 February, 2004. Cited on Sprinter [Singapore Government news service] http://www.sprinter.gov.sg/. Accessed on 27 September 2005.

TEN

Winners and Losers:
Gender, Race and Class in Elite Selection

Lim Siong Guan was an outstanding student at Anglo-Chinese School. Even then, when he was bagging prize after prize, he never dreamed that he would be awarded the Colombo Plan scholarship in 1965 to study mechanical engineering at the University of Adelaide in Australia.

Nor that he would be selected as one of the six Yang di-Pertuan Agong scholars which the President's scholarship was then known as.

Married and a father of three, Mr Lim, 33, is today principal private secretary to the Prime Minister, a post he was appointed to in 1978. Before that, he was an engineer in the Public Works Department and then he joined the Defence Ministry.

Mr Lim's success story is typical of more than 70 President's scholars since 1966.

'Where have all the President's Scholars gone?',
The Straits Times, 12 July 1980

In a meritocratic society, earning power corresponds to ability. If you are good enough to get into and to stay in the Admin Service, you'll make it.

Prime Minister Lee Hsien Loong, 25 October 1994[1]

THE PATH FROM YOUTHFUL OBSCURITY to the heights of power in Singapore's administrative elite is a well worn one, even though there have been a few changes to the map since Lim Siong Guan's entry into the scholarship system in 1965. Today the process is more sophisticated and tightly directed, and it includes a sojourn through NS for any male candidate. It also encompasses more divergent paths through scholarships offered by the SAF, statutory boards and GLCs. Yet despite many startling changes, the continuities are much stronger than the discontinuities, and Lim Siong Guan's trajectory is mirrored in the lives of many other men and women. Yet not many reach the heights attained by Lim Siong Guan, who went on to become head of the civil service, and one of the most powerful men in government. Most are eased out of the race to the top in their 30s or 40s, leaving only a few stayers in each cohort. Others are diverted into the political elite, sometimes acting as the political master of ministries in which they used to serve. Of the stayers, only a small number reach the heights of real power, while most are satisfied to have served their country in lesser positions that are still very senior, responsible and lucrative.

Since 1965 the system of government scholarships has moved from the periphery of Singaporean society to centre stage as part of the ongoing refinement of the system of elite selection. Even before independence a makeshift system of government and Colombo Plan scholarships sent a few outstanding scholars like Lim Siong Guan and Goh Chok Tong abroad to study, before putting them into government service. Yet as late as 1975 this system had contributed only two out of the 14 members of Cabinet. Even by 1985 only four out of 12 Cabinet ministers were former government scholars. By 1994 the situation had been altered beyond recognition, with eight out of 14 Cabinet ministers being ex-scholars including Prime Minister Goh (*ST*, 13 August 1994). By 2005 there were 12 ex-scholars in a Cabinet of 19; of these, five had been SAF scholars (including Prime Minister Lee).[2] A perusal of the upper echelons of the ruling elite taken more broadly tells a similar story. In 1994 12 of the 17 permanent secretaries were scholars, as were 137 of the 210 Administrative Officers (*ST*, 13 August 1994). Today it would be remarkable if all the permanent secretaries and all the Administrative Officers, except perhaps for a few mid-career entrants and wealthy self-funded 'scholars', did not enter government service through a scholarship.

The government scholarship system claims to act as a meritocratic sieve – the just reward for young adults with talent and academic dedication. In earlier chapters we have investigated ways in which the 'meritocratic' process of elite selection has been distorted, paying particular attention to issues of race and class. In this chapter we shall consider the results of these processes, taking a slightly broader perspective. Here we go some way towards answering the question, 'What are the biases in elite selection processes?'

Gender

The first point to note is that when we talk about the Singapore elite, we are talking overwhelmingly about men. One important factor contributing to this outcome is the fact that the military's SAF Overseas Scholarship (SAFOS) is open only to male candidates (since it is tied to the performance of National Service).[3] Following its inception in 1971, SAFOS winners have come to dominate the SAF hierarchy completely, but since the 1990s they have also come to occupy about 10 per cent of the positions in the Administrative Service, thanks to the now-routine practices of accepting retired SAF officers and seconding serving SAF officers into the Administrative Service.[4] Yet the male domination of the Administrative Service goes beyond this. As of May 2004, there were only 2 females among 20 Permanent Secretaries, though at the level of deputy secretary the figures are more even (11 out of 26) (*ST*, 8 May 2004). Women fare even worse in the SAF, which is almost exclusively a man's world, and in Cabinet, which has yet to admit a woman. A good indication of female representation at the higher levels of the administrative elite (taken more broadly than just the Administrative Service and the SAF) are the tables of elite personnel compiled by Ross Worthington in his 2003 book, *Governance in Singapore*. A close study of these tables reveals that:

- Of the top 30 GLCs, only 2 (6.7 per cent) were chaired by women in 1991.
- Of the top 38 people who were represented on the most GLC boards in 1998, only 2 (5.3 per cent) were women.
- Of the 78 'core people' on statutory boards and GLCs in 1998, only 3 (3.8 per cent) were women.[5]

These figures suggest a bias much deeper than that created by SAF scholarships, and point to deeper prejudices and systemic discrimination. It is beyond the scope of our inquiry to attempt to provide a comprehensive analysis of the causes of this situation, but we can suggest some significant contributing factors.

The imbalance in the early years is easily explained by the prevalence of social attitudes that placed less stress on female education and worldly achievement than that for males. Some remnant of this attitude might still be in operation today, but, as with the role of SAF scholarships, this seems to be only part of the story.

In Singapore the highest level of schooling achievement has always been to win a President's Scholarship. When we study the outcomes at this level we find that from 1966 to 2007 there have been 228 President's Scholarships awarded, of which 70 (30.7 per cent) went to female candidates. The full figures are given in Table 10.1.

Table 10.1: President's Scholars by gender, 1966 to 2007[6]

Year	Male	Female	Year	Male	Female
1966	10	0	1987	3	3
1967	7	0	1988	3	2
1968	5	1	1989	3	3
1969	4	0	1990	2	3
1970	6	2	1991	2	2
1971	7	2	1992	2	2
1972	9	2	1993	1	2
1973	8	3	1994	2	2
1974	7	1	1995	2	1
1975	6	1	1996	2	1
1976	6	3	1997	1	2
1977	4	1	1998	2	0
1978	5	2	1999	1	0
1979	5	2	2000	2	1
1980	5	1	2001	2	1
1981	6	3	2002	2	2
1982	4	2	2003	4	1
1983	3	1	2004	2	0
1984	3	1	2005	1	2
1985	2	3	2006	2	2
1986	4	4	2007	1	3
			Total	158	70

The period of greatest imbalance was that before 1981, when there were 114 President's Scholarships awarded, of which only 20 (17.5 per cent) went to female candidates. 1985 was a turning point at which the gender imbalance suddenly disappeared for 10 years, only to reappear just as suddenly (though in a milder fashion) in 1995. From 1985 to 1994 female candidates won 26 (52 per cent) of the 50 Scholarships, but from 1995 to 2007, female candidates won 16 (40 per cent) of the 40 Scholarships awarded.

The question is why is there a discrepancy in outcomes between male and female candidates and why did the pattern change so dramatically in the mid-1980s and mid-1990s? The apparent removal of gender barriers for girls in the mid-1980s might be explained by the effects of improvements in girls' access to education and perhaps a softening of Asian parents' traditional bias towards boys' education as Singaporean society became less traditional. But what of the reversal in the mid-1990s?

We can suggest three plausible explanations that between them go a long way towards explaining this phenomenon.

The Gifted Education Programme. The introduction of the GEP in 1984 appears to be a causal input in the return of gender as an educational factor, because the GEP has become the normal path to a scholarship (*ST*, 12 July 1998) and boys have been generally overrepresented in the GEP by about 2:1. The GEP took its first intake into selected primary and secondary schools in 1984, giving these students extra resources, better trained teachers, extended curricula etc. The programme began in Primary 4, so it took 8 years for the first cohort to reach matriculation, which places its full impact on the President's Scholarship in the early-to-mid-1990s. The first intake comprised 136 boys and 64 girls, an imbalance of more than 2:1 (*ST*, 6 November 1994). In 1986 the Singapore education system offered a total of 20 GEP classes to boys in secondary school (all in Raffles Institution) but only 2 for girls (both in Raffles Girls' School), suggesting the imbalance may have become even worse (*ST*, 23 December 1986). In 1994 Education Minister Lee Yock Suan admitted with complete equanimity that boys outnumbered girls in the GEP by 'at least two boys to one girl' (*ST*, 6 November 1994). We do not have such precise figures for the 2000s, but we can still see enough of the picture to be sure that it has not changed very much. In 2005 the GEP was offered in eight secondary schools and Integrated Programme schools.[7] We should remove NUS High School from our consideration because it began operating only in 2005, leaving us with one co-ed school, two girls' schools and four boys' schools. A count of schools thus confirms (albeit imprecisely) a strong gender imbalance in favour of boys – probably in the range of 2:1, just as it was in the middle of the 1990s. Considering the GEP is the main recruitment ground for elite scholarships and that there have been twice as many boys as girls enrolled in the GEP over the years, it is hardly surprising that boys have outnumbered girls among the President's Scholars since the mid-1990s.

Subjective criteria. Scholarships are not just based on grades, but also on CCAs, 'character' and performance in an interview. This makes the selection process much more subjective than it appears at first glance, and allows for the possibility that conservative and patriarchal attitudes underpin the selection process. Granted the importance of patriarchal attitudes in Singapore society in general – and in Lee Kuan Yew's thinking in particular[8] – this possibility seems to be more rather than less likely. The interviewing committee is also making a commercial judgement in which it is assessing the value of investing in each candidate, and the likelihood of getting a healthy return. We know as a fact that women have faced some official institutional barriers based on this perception, the best known of which has been the restrictive cap on the number of female candidates allowed into the local medical school. This cap was imposed in 1979 and was lifted only at the end of 2002 (*Business Times*, 6 December 2002). It was justified by the assumption that women would withdraw from their profession either partially or completely after marriage and starting a family.[9] If the sceptical attitude towards the value of investing in women is extended beyond the medical school, it could provide the main key to understanding the under-representation of women.

Aptitude. The bias towards science and maths as school subjects, and towards engineering, science and maths as preferred tertiary courses may also be advantaging boys as a group over girls as a group (which is not to deny that many girls excel in these subjects). Certainly as of the early 1980s the bias of female students towards language, social science and humanities and away from engineering, sciences and other 'hard' disciplines was well established,[10] and this was resulting in better PSLE scores for boys than for girls (*ST*, 6 June 1982). Until 1998 girls were also not given the option to study Design and Technology through secondary school, being steered instead towards Home Economics (with options to take Technical Studies as an elective subject or as an ECA). The bias in the higher level of scholarships towards engineering may have then left girls at a disadvantage in their scholarship applications.[11] The gender bias on the languages/maths continuum became particularly significant after the introduction of a special set of exams in 1983 by which candidates for the GEP were chosen, because these tests were in First Language and Maths (*Sunday Times*, 14 August 1987). The girls' advantage in languages was minimised by not testing Second Language, but the boys' advantage in Maths was considered to the full.

It is worth noting that the education system's only systemic bias towards girls is the importance placed on languages, which is a field in which females generally excel, but in 1983 MOE introduced measures specifically designed to minimise the impact of this bias at matriculation level (*Sunday Times*, 30 October 1983). No such balancing measures have ever been introduced to assist talented female candidates.

Race and Ethnicity

The other bias in the scholarship system (and hence in the administrative and political elite) is the predictable racial bias towards Chinese. Once again Worthington's lists of scholars tell some of the story:

- Of the top 30 GLCs, only 2 (6.7 per cent) were chaired by non-Chinese in 1991 (and neither was a Malay).

- Of the 38 people who were represented on the most GLC boards in 1998, only 2 (5.3 per cent) were non-Chinese (and neither was a Malay).

- Of the 78 'core people' on statutory boards and GLCs in 1998, 7 (9.0 per cent) were non-Chinese (1 of whom was a Malay).[12]

The bias seems to extend into the education system, just as it did for women. In Table 10.2, the scholars' race has been determined by using the recipients' names as the identifying marker. While there is room for error in this methodology, we are confident that the figures are sufficiently accurate to allow us to make a substantiated point.

Of the 228 President's Scholars from 1966 to 2007, only 14 (6.1 per cent) were not Chinese, but this was not a consistent proportion throughout the period. If we take 1980 as a convenient divider, we find that there were 10 non-Chinese President's Scholars out of 114 from 1966 to 1980 (8.8 per cent). However in the period from 1981 to 2007 these figures dropped by more than half, to four out of 114 (3.5 per cent). Perhaps the most revealing statistics are the fact that:

- There was only one non-Chinese President's Scholar in the 23 years from 1983 to 2004.

- Since independence, the President's Scholarship has been awarded to only one Malay (in 1968).

Table 10.2: President's Scholars by race

Year	Chinese	Non-Chinese	Year	Chinese	Non-Chinese
1966	8	1	1987	6	1
1967	6	1	1988	5	0
1968	4	2	1989	6	0
1969	4	0	1990	5	0
1970	8	0	1991	4	0
1971	8	1	1992	4	0
1972	10	1	1993	3	0
1973	10	1	1994	4	0
1974	8	0	1995	3	0
1975	7	0	1996	3	0
1976	8	1	1997	4	0
1977	5	0	1998	2	0
1978	6	1	1999	1	0
1979	7	0	2000	3	0
1980	5	1	2001	3	0
1981	8	1	2002	4	0
1982	5	1	2003	5	0
1983	4	0	2004	2	0
1984	4	0	2005	2	1
1985	5	0	2006	4	0
1986	7	0	2007	4	0
			Total	214	14

Furthermore, if we shift our focus to encompass broader constructions of ethnicity, we find that since independence, the President's Scholarship has been won by only two Muslims (1968 and 2005). We might also add that Mikail Kalimuddin, the 2005 non-Chinese President's Scholar and the only non-Chinese President's Scholar in the 18 years to 2005, is claimed by Singapore Indian Development Association as an Indian success story, but he is actually half Chinese (on his mother's side). He studied in SAP schools (Chinese High School and Hwa Chong JC) and took Higher Chinese as his Mother Tongue (*CyBerita*, 14 October 2005).[13] He undoubtedly deserves all the honours that have been and will be heaped upon him, but his example must leave a lot of non-Chinese wondering about their chances of ever entering the elite. Furthermore, at least four of the five post-1979 President's Scholars that we have identified as 'non-Chinese' in fact have Chinese ancestry, raising the question of whether a formal but unannounced racial, or perhaps a language barrier, was instituted at that time in the selection criteria for President's Scholars.

The position of the non-Chinese in the educational stakes has clearly deteriorated since the beginning of the 1980s. This should not come as a surprise, since it is the logical outcome of the racial biases built into the education system and Singapore society more generally at that time. Lee Kuan Yew's efforts to build Chinese hegemony had quiet beginnings in 1978, and reached full strength around 1980. 1982 was the last year in which non-Chinese students more or less routinely won President's Scholarships and 1983 began a 25-year drought that was broken only twice; in 1987 and 2005. It would be fascinating to read the transcripts of interviews and the deliberations of the interview panels that made these selections to discover how consciously they were reflecting the wishes of Lee Kuan Yew, but perhaps after the first few years there was not even much need for overt discrimination at this level because the job had already been done in school. Chapters 6 to 8 have documented how from the late 1970s the Chinese as a group began enjoying systemic advantages presented to them from pre-primary onwards and how they have been empowered psychologically to present themselves with supreme confidence. These chapters have also shown that the non-Chinese have received no special assistance from the education system, and for a 15-year period from 1980 onwards had been educated by their textbooks to think of themselves as subordinate to the Chinese and to expect less of themselves and for themselves. This is even before we consider the disadvantages presented to minorities (particularly Malays) associated with being a disadvantaged socio-economic group, and being less able to buy educational advantages.

If we consider the pivotal SAFOS scholarship, the overall story is comparable. The Ministry of Defence did not respond to Barr's request for a list of recipients of SAF scholarships, but using newspaper accounts and information provided by the Raffles Junior College Homepage, PSC Scholarship Centre and MINDEF websites, we were able to identify 181 (69.3 per cent) of the 261 SAFOS scholarship winners up to 2007.[14] These have been set

Table 10.3: SAFOS scholarship winners by race

Year	Chinese	Non-Chinese	Total
1971	5	0	5
1972	5 or more	1 or more	15
1973	8 or more	Unknown	9
1974	4 or more	Unknown	Unknown
1975	4	0	4
1976	4 or more	Unknown	Unknown
1978	2 or more	Unknown	Unknown
1980	1 or more	Unknown	Unknown
1981	4	0	4
1982	6 or more	Unknown	Unknown
1983	5 or more	Unknown	Unknown
1984	4 or more	Unknown	Unknown
1985	3 or more	Unknown	Unknown
1986	2 or more	Unknown	Unknown
1987	2 or more	Unknown	Unknown
1988	3 or more	Unknown	Unknown
1989	4	0	4
1990	4	0	4
1991	6	0	6
1992	4	Unknown	Unknown
1993	6	0	6
1994	5	0	5
1995	4 or more	Unknown	Unknown
1996	6 or more	Unknown	7
1997	6	0	6
1998	8 or more	1 or more	10
1999	9	0	9
2000	12	0	12
2001	7	1	8
2002	6	0	6
2003	5	0	5
2004	7	0	7
2005	5	1	6
2006	5	0	0
2007	6	0	0
Total identified	177	4	181

out in Table 10.3, and identified by race, using the recipients' names as the identifying marker.

Although only indicative, this table clearly suggests the Chinese dominance in SAFOS stakes; 97.8 per cent of SAFOS scholarship winners in our sample were Chinese, and 2.2 per cent were non-Chinese (counting Mikail Kalimuddin in 2005 as non-Chinese). Furthermore we found not a single Malay recipient and only one Muslim winner (Mikail Kalimuddin) (*CyBerita*, 14 October 2005). A similar picture emerges in the lower-status SAF Merit Scholarship winners, where we were able to identify 99 (32.5 per cent) of the 305 scholars as of mid-2008; here, there were 97 (98.0 per cent) Chinese winners to only two non-Chinese – though in this case we can identify a Malay recipient in 2004 and Tim Huxley has made an unreferenced claim that there are others.[15] We do not have sufficient information to judge whether the situation in the SAFOS scholarships deteriorated after 1980, but Huxley suggests that at the peak level the SAF has become more exclusively Chinese since the end of the 1980s, as the Chinese SAFOS scholars have come to dominate. Whereas he says there were Indian and Eurasian senior officers (Colonel and above) and even a Malay before 1980, when he did a count in 1999 he found only one non-Chinese in these senior ranks.[16]

The absence of Malays from the SAFOS scholarships and their near-absence from the SAF Merit Scholarships deserves special mention because over and above suffering discrimination in the education system, throughout the late 1960s and early 1970s they were completely excluded from National Service, and during most of the 1980s they were almost completely excluded. Even today promising Malay recruits are routinely kept out of the SAF officer corps or even out of the SAF completely by the mechanism of being funnelled into the Police, or *in extremis*, into the Civil Defence Force to serve their NS.[17] Four Malay men discussed their NS in interview and each independently spoke of similar experiences:

- One (Zulkifli Baharudin, later a Nominated MP) was removed from officer training but allowed to stay in the Army.
- One was transferred out of the Army into the Police, and then out of the Police into the Civil Defence Force.
- Two were placed in the Police to do their National Service.

Significantly three of these four had A-levels and went on to higher study, and the sole example who was allowed to stay in the Army ended up winning the award for the Best Soldier of the Year. One of the other interviews ran like this:

Barr: After your A levels, you did National Service ... You went into the Army?
Interviewee: Of course not.
Barr: The Police?
Interviewee: Ya. (Laughs.)
Barr: Did you pick that?
Interviewee: Pick? We didn't have a choice. We were channelled there. If you are channelled into the Police, you cannot go higher than sergeant's rank. Then they will choose officers from the Army. The officers were all selected from the Army. Those who go to the Army first, do their 9 months officer training, most will stay in the Army, some will go to Civil Defence. Some to the Police. I went to the Police Academy. In every single squad in every company, the majority of them were Malays. And the officers were sent to us from the Army.

Many Malays are allowed to stay in the Army, but generally only as the cooks and drivers. Very few are welcomed as officers. This general impression was confirmed again and again by Chinese and Indian men who had done their National Service and commented – sometimes spontaneously – on the preponderance of Malays among the cooks and drivers in the Army.

Lee Kuan Yew defends such discrimination by questioning the loyalty of Malays: 'In deciding which outfit to post an NSman to, we have to consider the sensitivity of the posts and the racial and religious mix of the units' (*ST*, 4 March 2001). This discrimination hits Malay men hard first because it deprives many of promising careers in the Army, and second – and more pertinent for our study of the production of a class of SAF scholars – it all but completely excludes would-be high-flying Malays of a chance of entering the scholar class through the SAF. A Chinese woman has a much better chance of winning an SAF scholarship than a Malay man. The discrimination against Malays is not a subject that is trumpeted but nor is it a secret. It has been discussed in Parliament and the media and is justified on the premise that Malays, being Muslim and having a racial and ethnic affinity with the Malays in Malaysia and Indonesia, cannot be trusted in sensitive positions. Lee Hsien Loong has historically been a vocal defender of this policy.[18] The discrimination against the Malays undoubtedly peaks in the SAF, where it is public and relatively open, but it seems to permeate much further than just this. It is perhaps indicative that, when *The Sunday Times* (7 March 2004) ran a special promotional supplement on MINDEF scholars in 2004, the Ministry could not supply even one Malay scholar to be photographed or interviewed. This particular supplement featured 10 Chinese scholars and one Indian.

We do not have figures for the myriad of other scholarships in the market, but another 2004 promotional supplement advertising the whole range of

Table 10.4: President's Scholars by Secondary School or Junior College, 1970, 1972, 1975, 1981 and 1982

Year	School/Junior College
1970 (*ST*, 31 May 1970)[20]	2 x Catholic High School 2 x St Patrick's School 2 x Anglican High School 1 x Tanglin Integrated Technical School 1 x River Valley Government Chinese School 1 x Raffles Girls' School
1972 (*ST*, 30 June 1972)[21]	4 x National JC 2 x St Joseph's Institution 1 x St Andrew's School 1 x Anglo-Chinese School 1 x Catholic High School 1 x Raffles Institution
1975 (*ST*, 1 July 1971)	3 x National JC 2 x Anglo-Chinese School 1 x Catholic High School 1 x Raffles Institution
1981 (*ST*, 5 June 1981)	4 x Raffles Institution 2 x Hwa Chong JC 1 x Temasek JC 1 x National JC 1 x Catholic JC
1982 (*ST*, 27 June 1982)	3 x Hwa Chong JC 2 x Raffles Institution 1 x Temasek JC 1 x Anglo-Chinese JC

government scholarships was probably indicative of the current situation (*ST*, 5 March 2004). The promotional articles accompanying the paid advertisements featured one non-Chinese scholar (a Malay on a lowly National Council of Social Service local scholarship) amongst 28 Chinese. Just as revealing were the paid advertisements placed by government ministries, statutory boards and GLCs.[19] Many of these advertisements featured photographs of one or more young persons who represented the attractive and inspirational image of scholars. Of the 30 who were both prominent and could be racially identified by their photographs or names without any doubt as to accuracy, all were Chinese.

Table 10.5: President's Scholars by Secondary School and Junior College, 2001–2007[22]

Year	Secondary Schools	Junior Colleges
2001	1 x Raffles Institution 1 x Raffles Girls' School 1 x Chinese High School [part of the Hwa Chong family]	1 x Raffles JC 2 x Hwa Chong JC
2002	2 x Raffles Institution 2 x Raffles Girls' School	3 x Raffles JC 1 x Hwa Chong JC
2003	3 x Raffles Institution 1 x Raffles Girls' School 1 x Anglo-Chinese School	3 x Raffles JC 1 x Hwa Chong JC 1 x Anglo-Chinese JC
2004	1 x Dunman High School 1 x River Valley High School [both SAP schools, now with Integrated Programmes]	1 x Raffles JC 1 x Hwa Chong JC
2005	2 x Raffles Girls' School 1 x Chinese High School	2 x Raffles JC 1 x Hwa Chong JC
2006	2 x Raffles Institution 1 x Raffles Girls' School 1 x Methodist Girls' School	2 x Raffles JC 2 x Anglo-Chinese JC
2007	1 x Raffles Institution 2 x Raffles Girls' School 1 x Singapore Chinese Girls' School	3 x Raffles JC 1 x Hwa Chong Institution

Elite Students in Elite Schools

The final point to be made about systemic absences from the scholar class is the stranglehold that a handful of schools have on the top scholarships – schools that today are nearly monopolised by the sons and daughters of upper-middle-class parents (see Chapter 9 under 'Meritocracy and Class'). Yet this monopoly is of fairly recent vintage. As Table 10.4 shows, in the early days of the republic, scholars came from schools all over the island.

By 1981, Raffles Institution and Hwa Chong Junior College had already overtaken the Mission schools at the top of the tables. Table 10.5 shows that by the 2000s the dominance of the Raffles and Hwa Chong families and the SAP schools was absolute.

There were 16–17 junior colleges and more than 160 secondary schools in Singapore over the years 2001–2007,[23] but of the 25 President's Scholars in these years only three did not hail from either the Raffles JC or Hwa Chong JC and only five did their secondary schooling outside what are now the Raffles and Hwa Chong families of schools – and two of these were from SAP schools

Table 10.6: SAFOS winners by Secondary School and Junior College, 2004–2007

Year	Secondary School	Junior College
2004	3 x Raffles Institution 1 x Anderson Secondary School 1 x Dunman High School 1 x River Valley High School 1x Anglo-Chinese School	3 x Raffles JC 3 x National JC 1 x Hwa Chong JC
2005	2 x Raffles Institution 2 x Chinese High School 1 x Anglo-Chinese School 1 x Dunman High School	3 x Raffles JC 3 x Hwa Chong JC
2006	3 x Raffles Institution 1 x Chinese High 1 x Dunman High [both SAP schools]	3 x Raffles JC 2 x Hwa Chong Institution
2007	Not available.	4 x Raffles JC 2 x Hwa Chong Institution

with Integrated Programmes.[24] Of the two main families of schools, Raffles is clearly the dominant partner, boasting 76 per cent of President's Scholars to the Hwa Chong family's 36 per cent.[25] We do not have the equivalent break-down for SAFOS scholarship winners for 2000–2003, but Table 10.6 reveals a similar, though slightly less pronounced skewing from 2004 to 2007. Despite the caveat of having incomplete information for 2007, we can know that in these years at least 54 per cent of SAFOS winners were ex-Rafflesians and 33 per cent hailed from the Hwa Chong family. This funnelling of prospective scholars through select schools is the logical and deliberate result of the policies of stratification discussed in the previous chapters, and the introduction of the 'through train' is likely to exaggerate this pattern even further. When MOE was considering how to implement a GEP in 1982 it was torn between the Israeli model, which embedded a GEP in 'normal schools' from junior primary onwards, and the Soviet model, which set up specialised elite schools at pre-university level (*ST*, 10 January 1982). The Singapore authorities began with the Israeli model (*ST*, 8 April 1995) but it is now clear that from the mid-1980s onwards they worked towards building a hybrid system that drew on both models: specialised programmes in primary school, complemented by specialised schools in secondary and junior college.

Yet the sense of inevitability created in the three tables shown above is a slightly misleading. Many aspects of the evolution of the elite school system were fashioned on the run, rather than carefully planned. The apparently be-lated selection of the Raffles family of schools as the prime vehicle for produc-ing scholars for government service in the mid-1980s seems to have involved the personal prerogative of Lee Kuan Yew. He has always been rather fond of his *alma mater* and he drew from its history as the educator of Malaya's top students and producer of crops of civil servants and leaders for some of his self-image. The Raffles family of schools has been singled out to continue what is seen to be its historical role. Its culture has been crafted into the right mix of elements to produce the type of scholar that the government wants to see dominating the administrative and political elite – English as the 'master' language, but with strong command of the 'mother tongue'; acute conscious-ness of one's place at the top of the 'meritocracy'; deeply ingrained notions of 'service' to the community and indebtedness to society-cum-government; particular consciousness of the operation of multiracialism (even though they are mostly Chinese).

The Hwa Chong family of schools was created to produce a very different type of scholar: racially Chinese; probably stronger in Chinese language than English; supposedly steeped in 'Chinese values'. Today it is the centre of efforts to produce Chinese entrepreneurs who will enter business, particularly targeting opportunities in China, and to this end it is developing close ties with Nanyang Technological University (NTU) to create a 'through train' of its own. Trivina Kang tells part of the story:

> The Hwa Chong Programme has a five-year elective course on entrepreneurship which may take up to 30 percent of a student's assessment each year. The elective course is part of the school's IP [Integrated Programme]. In the first three years, students will study local entrepreneurs among others, and will also be taught concepts of consumer behaviour, advertising and accounting procedures. By the fourth or fifth years, students will set up their own companies and be expected to raise capital to sell their products, services and ideas. Students in the Hwa Chong Programme also have a sabbatical week every three months for enrichment activities.[26]

The cream of these students will also be graduates of the new 'Bicultural Studies Programme' and be specially trained in junior college to understand the nuances of dealing with the PRC (*ST*, 16 and 24 June 2004; *CNA*, 28 February 2005). Looking slightly to the future, many of them will already have spent time studying in China as part of exchange programmes funded by a $4.5 million fund established in 2005 (*CNA*, 13 October 2005). Even before the establishment of this fund many students of Hwa Chong JC, Chinese High School and 11- and 12-year-olds in their affiliated primary schools enjoyed enriching exchanges with schools in China, but the new funding will facilitate up to an extraordinary 9,000 exchanges a year (though not all with China) (*CNA*, 13 October 2005; *ST*, 16 November 2005). After passing through the SAP school/Hwa Chong/Bicultural Studies Programme system, the best students will be inducted into NTU – the successor to the old Chinese-language Nanyang University – through special enrichment and introductory programmes. Once in NTU, students will continue to be groomed into China-savvy business leaders (*Straits Times Interactive*, 23 June 2004). Many of these students will be scholars by this stage, though only a very small number will be considered as candidates for the administrative elite. In the mind of the government, their futures lie in business, but unleashing the entrepreneurial potential and training of these people is problematic while they are bonded to government service. Even in the likely event that government service took a lot of them to China with the Ministry of Trade and Industry it is difficult for a civil servant to be an entrepreneur in the full sense of the word. To overcome this obstacle Lee Kuan Yew has foreshadowed selectively releasing 'up to half' of all scholars from their bonds precisely to encourage them to become entrepreneurs (*CNA*, 8 June 2004). This shows the imaginative uses to which the diversification and stratification of the education system can be put, not to mention the malleability of the national myths fostered by the official nation-building project. (The transformation of the putative role of the Chinese schools and university from being supposed bastions of communism and 'chauvinism' to producers of capitalists and national elites is noted.) Precisely what the ruling elite has in store for the products of the NUS High School for Mathematics and Science will not become clear for some time, but do not be surprised if their futures are more nuanced than simply entering the civil service as top-flight scholars.

One of the direct effects of the diversification of scholarly tracks is the confirmation of the central role of the Raffles family of schools in regenerating the political and administrative elite; with Hwa Chong and SAP school scholars being siphoned into business, Raffles will remain the primary producer of scholars for the Administrative Service. Thus we return to the ever-narrowing track that we have been following in this book from pre-schooler to mandarin. There will always be exceptions to the rule (and indeed both the political and the administrative establishments take steps to encourage some new blood from outside)[27] but it appears that the Raffles family of schools is to maintain, or even strengthen its place as the predominant path into the administrative and political elite. As former Permanent Secretary Ngiam Tong Dow said in 2003,

> Each year, the PSLE creams off all the top boys and girls and dispatches them to only two schools, Raffles Institution and Raffles Girls' School. However good these schools are, the problem is you are educating your elite in only two institutions, with only two sets of mentors, and casting them in more or less the same mould (*Straits Times Interactive*, 5 October 2003).

Through Train to the Administrative Elite

It seems from our survey of both inputs and outcomes that the vast majority of the most successful candidates who make a long-term career in the administrative elite will be Chinese who have begun their socialisation into the elite during their education in the Raffles family of schools. Most will be male and nearly all will come from upper middle class, if not wealthy backgrounds. They will speak English as a first language, but will generally be very competent in Mandarin – though this particular skill may be allowed to slide since 'Mother Tongue' is no longer so important in university admission. They will be good at science and maths, but are likely to have a more rounded education than their contemporaries who went to NUS High. They will be used to privilege but also at least notionally conscious of their duty to repay society with service (for which they will expect to be well paid).

The further one looks down the administrative hierarchy, the more diverse will be the tracks followed to get there. Below the elite level one can expect to find layers of well-educated people who are paid well for responsible work, but who never had much chance to reach the heights in the Singapore system. These layers will include many more non-Chinese and many more women than one will find in the elite. There will also be many products of schools and junior colleges that are not even mentioned in this book. There will be many grievances and resentments among these groups, since a lot of these people will be acutely aware that they have not been dealt a fair hand (especially among the non-Chinese) but the grievances will be muted and balanced by an appreciation of the relative comfort and prosperity they enjoy compared to their parents' generation. For most, any tendency to complain will be subdued also by the knowledge that it could be worse, and it will be if they seriously pursue their grievances. While the Singapore system continues to deal such people a satisfactory hand, if not a fair one, it should be able to cope with some rumblings in the ranks.

Notes

1 Lee Hsien Loong, 'Staying Ahead – Scenarios and Challenges', *Ethos*, 3rd Issue 1994 [no page numbers indicated].

2 List of Cabinet Ministers and CVs found at Singapore Cabinet website, http://www.cabinet.gov.sg/. Accessed 10 October 2005.

3 Since 1993 women have been eligible to be awarded an SAF Women's Merit Scholarship, but this is a lower status award than the SAFOS scholarship, and so diminished male dominance through SAF scholarships only slightly (*ST*, 8 July 1992).

4 Tim Huxley, *Defending the Lion City: The Armed Forces of Singapore*, St Leonards, NSW: Allen & Unwin, 2000, pp. 232–240, 245, 246; Tim Huxley, 'Singapore's soldier scholars', *Asian Wall Street Journal*, 24 February 1995.

5   Ross Worthington, *Governance in Singapore*, London and New York: RoutledgeCurzon, 2003, pp. 198, 199, 208, 209, 215–217.

6   A list of President's Scholars from 1966 to 2005 with gender indicated was supplied by email to Barr by the Public Service Division, Public Service Commission on 11 October 2005. The figures for subsequent years are drawn from the Public Service Commission website at http://www.psc.gov.sg/, accessed 14 April 2008. The PSC website also indicates gender.

7   Ministry of Education website, http://moe.gov.sg/gifted/GEP_Schools.htm and http://www.moe.sg/gifted/FAQ_Schools.htm. Accessed 14 November 2005.

8   For a highly nuanced reading of the role of masculinity in the thinking of Lee Kuan Yew, see Philip Holden, 'A Man and an island: gender and nation in Lee Kuan Yew's *The Singapore Story*', *Biography*, vol. 24, no. 2, 2001, pp. 401–424.

9   Lily L. Kong, and Jasmine S. Chan, 'Patriarchy and pragmatism: ideological contradictions in state policies', *Asian Studies Review*, vol. 24, no. 4, 2000, pp. 515, 516.

10 Aline K. Wong, 'Planned development, social stratification and the sexual division of labour in Singapore', in Ong Jin Hui, Tong Chee Kiong and Tan Ern Ser (eds), *Understanding Singapore Society*, Singapore: Times Academic Press, 1997, pp. 17–32. Original article published in 1981.

11 Kong and Chan, 'Patriarchy and pragmatism', *Asian Studies Review*, vol. 24, no. 4, 2000, p. 522.

12 Worthington, *Governance in Singapore*, pp. 198, 199, 208, 209, 215–217.

13 Press Invitation, 8 August 2005, from the Office of the President, available at the http://www.istana.gov.sg. Accessed 10 October 2005; Speech by Mr Tharman Shanmugaratnam, Minister for Education, at SINDA's 14th Academic Excellence Awards Ceremony, 10 September 2005, on MOE website at http://www.moe.gov.sg/speeches/2005/sp20050910.htm. Accessed 14 October 2005.

14 *ST*, 1971–2005, various issues; and the Raffles Junior College Homepage, at http://www.rjc.edu.sg/newrjc/newsSAFOS.htm: Public Service Commission Scholarship Centre, at http://app.psc.gov.sg/scholarships/html/scholarships.asp; the MINDEF Scholarship Centre, http://www.scholar.mindef.gov.sg/safscholarships_safos_intro.asp; and the MINDEF website, http://mindef.gov.sg/imindef.html. The PSC and MINDEF websites were accessed throughout October 2005, and the MINDEF Scholarship Centre website was also accessed on 14 April 2008. The RJC Homepage was accessed on 15 April 2008. We were unable to identify any scholarship winners for the years 1977 and 1979.

15 Huxley, *Defending the Lion City*, p. 115.

16 Ibid., pp. 114, 115.

17 Lily Zubaidah Rahim, *The Singapore Dilemma: The Political and Educational Marginality of the Malay Community*, Kuala Lumpur: Oxford University Press, 1998, p. 90.

18 Huxley, *Defending the Lion City*, pp. 102–104.

19 There were also advertisements from commercial companies, but we have not considered them.

20 One of the Catholic High School students had in fact switched to RI just to sit for his HSC.

21 It might be suspected that the promotion of National JC as the preferred path into university in the early 1970s was disguising domination by Raffles schools at secondary level in the early years, but this is not the case. The four National JC students in 1972 hailed from each of Raffles Institution, St Patrick's School, Crescent Girls' School and St Nicholas Girls' School.

22 Office of the President of Singapore, http://www.istana.gov.sg/. Accessed 10 October 2005 and 14 April 2008.

23 The actual numbers vary slightly from year to year. These figures are based on the Ministry of Education's *Directory of Schools 2003* and *2005*, Singapore: Ministry of Education, 2003; 2005.

24 Of the remaining schools, the Anglo-Chinese family also has an Integrated Programme, and it caters exclusively for the sons of wealthy parents. Methodist Girl's School and Singapore Chinese Girls' School are not IP or SAP schools and are the only schools that can be regarded as 'ordinary' schools.

25 Note that some students fit into both categories, having switched between families of schools at the end of secondary school.

26 Trivina Kang, 'Diversification of Singapore's upper secondary landscape: introduction of integrated programmes, specialised independent schools and privately-funded schools', in Jason Tan and Ng Pak Tee, *Shaping Singapore's Future: Thinking Schools, Learning Nation*, Singapore: Pearson Education, 2005, p. 59.

27 For example, the Administrative Service has a mid-career entry programme. Also note that two of the three new 'rising stars' in Cabinet (Tharman Shanmugaratnam and Ng Eng Hen), did not rise through the usual scholarship path.

ELEVEN

Making a Mandarin:
Inside the Administrative Elite

There is a certain uniformity in what I would call 'the establishment'. From primary school, secondary school, junior college onwards, there is more or less a very broad similarity of experience ... .

[But] I think the very conscious elite formation starts a bit later than that. Even after the overseas merit scholar phase ... . Once you get into the Admin Service ... then there is a more conscious effort through things like the Alpha Society and Admin Service Dinner and so on. The Alpha Society is the society of Admin Service Officers. It's a social thing but it creates a certain commonality of experience. In the Civil Service there is also a fairly conscious effort to bring young Admin Service Officers in small groups under the leadership of an older civil service officer and give them projects which have nothing to do with their ordinary work, to work out their brains but also to form bonds.

Then you go through a certain basic programme together. This is all a fairly new sort of thing, from the late '80s and '90s when they became much more organised. When you join there is a Foundation Course for Admin Service Officers from all the ministries. They have a formal programme given to all ministries and they will be taken around to a good number of the ASEAN countries to visit our missions there and so on. When you go around with a bunch of fellows for 3 months a certain bonding occurs and it's meant to occur. ...

I'm just talking about the civil service now, but I will also include the military when they become majors or lieutenant colonels because there's a lot of crossing back and forth ... .

Bilahari Kausikan, Permanent Secretary, Ministry of
Foreign Affairs, in interview, Singapore, 15 April 2003

THUS FAR WE HAVE DEALT as much with elite selection as elite formation. Indeed according to the quotation given above, elite formation does not begin seriously until after the selection process is complete. In the light of the picture painted in Chapters 6–9 we have difficulty dismissing the pre-school-to-scholarship phase as having no formative value, but let us take Bilahari Kausikan's point. The real work of elite formation in the full sense of the word begins after the elite has been selected and cosseted in its new home. So let us continue following our elite as they begin their adult life. For women this means going straight into university and their professions. For men, however, there is an intervening step that can be an integral part of both elite selection and elite formation.

National Service

Compulsory National Service (NS), and subsequent service as a Reservist (or 'NSman') is an experience that sets apart male candidates for the elite from females. Notionally, however, it is a common experience that male candidates for the elite share with less educated and less privileged men. For men, NS is supposed to be a major and common element of nation building, cutting across class, education and race. In fact, we argue that the NS experience of scholars is totally different to that of the ordinary soldier; so much so that it is a shared experience only in the same way aeroplane passengers and rain-drenched pedestrians might be said to have shared the experience of looking at the same cloud formation.

The collective NS experience is intended to bolster the patriotic and nation-building impulses of the male population. A large part of this process is didactic –messages are drummed into them in formal sessions – but more significant is the NS experience broadly writ. NS is consciously intended to socialise men into an acceptance of Singapore's social order. It is a powerful experiential exercise in which the elitist and racist norms of Singapore society are reinforced and internalised, building upon the social cognition learned through school and broader society. The overall NS experience has a much deeper impact on thinking than any amount of didacticism, just as the em-bedded and lived messages of National Education and Singapore's racialised, *kiasu* education system have a greater impact than any amount of tedious history lessons and sloganeering.

We have already seen that Malays were originally excluded from NS com-pletely, and even now are almost completely excluded from responsible and sensitive positions in the military. Those Malays who are not herded into the Police Force or the Civil Defence Force mostly end up as drivers and cooks in the Army and Air Force.[1] This is an especially powerful lesson because the NS experience commonly gives many Chinese, especially but not exclusively those from SAP schools, their first experience of regular inter-racial intercourse, whether it be social or professional. Beyond these simple and unacknowledged racial divisions there is a more official demarcation between those who passed through junior college (with A-levels) and polytechnic graduates (who left school after O-levels to pursue a diploma). Before 2004, the two groups entered NS in separate cohorts, six months apart, the former for 2½ years and the latter for 2 years; today, the period is 2 years for all. A-level holders are routinely accepted into a 9-month officer training course straight after boot camp. The nineteen-year-old NS officers are then posted to the regular Army to command not just their fellow National Servicemen but professional soldiers and non-commissioned officers of many years' experience as well.

The NS experience for those who take up career options in the Army is often a positive one, but for many others it is wholly negative, and the annual call-ups and occasional mobilisations after they complete their tour of service become a burden. Said one Indian interviewee:

> After going to National Service, that is when you hate the way things are run. And SAF is part of the system and you start hating it for the way it is being run. All the officers are A-level students or have diplomas. After going through National Service you either become more patriotic or you hate the way everything is run in Singapore. A lot of Singaporean males become very disillusioned after going into the army.

For scholars, as opposed to mere A-level holders, the view of our hypothetical cloud formation is not just atmospheric, but stratospheric. The SAF scholarship system started developing in 1971, half a decade after the civilian Public Service Scholarships started to mature into the system we know today. Scholars are not left in ordinary platoons unless it is obvious that they are particularly unsuited to a military career. They are herded into the Delta Company, referred at the end of Chapter 9. They are shepherded through special training, genteel afternoon teas with senior staff officers and ministers, and once boot camp is over, largely cocooned from the world of real soldiering.[2] They are gathered into what are generically called 'scholar platoons', several former members of which have been interviewed for this book. They are often given special projects during their NS, commensurate with their academic standing – studying, preparing recommendations or even implementing some new initiative, not necessarily directly connected with the military.[3] For such scholars the added benefit is that part of their NS is often counted towards the service of their government bond, so they are fulfilling two sets of obligations concurrently. Men who are not yet SAF scholars, but are clearly in that academic league, are singled out for afternoon teas with senior officers, who encourage them to sign up as regular soldiers, instead of just as NSmen, and to take up internal SAF scholarships.[4] One short-term attraction of accepting such an offer is that they are able to study on a lieutenant's salary instead of a student's stipend.

Divergent Paths: Civilian and Military

At this point the paths followed by our putative scholars diverge. Some stay in the military while others return to the civilian service, joining a slightly younger generation of female scholars.[5] Both groups go overseas, with most of the top scholars going to American and British universities, but a fair number study in Japan, Canada or Australia. Traditionally they have studied some variety of engineering, though this pattern has begun diversifying considerably in the 2000s. Since the 1990s the traditional Public Service Commission (PSC) and SAF scholarships have also been supplemented by a host of alternatives sponsored by statutory boards (such as the Economic Development Board) and GLCs (such as the Development Bank of Singapore and A*STAR). These scholarships carry less prestige than the top PSC scholarships, but this is about the extent of the difference between them. The Administrative Service's mid-career entry programme is largely aimed at 'private' scholars such as these.

At this point we would like to focus in turn on the civilian and then the military paths into the elite before returning to a consideration of both in tandem.

❧ Civilian path

Until very recently, the civilian path has been laid out exclusively by the PSC. This body has traditionally acted as disburser of all civilian scholarships, even those offered by international bodies and the governments of other countries. It was from such humble origins that the scholarship system began to be systematised in the late 1960s (*ST*, 12 June 1967). The PSC remains the ultimate gatekeeper for entry into the Administrative Service, but just as the education system has been altered drastically since independence, so have the pathways into the Administrative Service. Until the late 1990s scholars were recruited directly into the Administrative Service. Now they enter the civil service on a 'dual career' path, whereby they are tested either in the mainstream civil service or in one of the professional services (teaching, engineering, etc.) for two or three years before being invited into the Administrative Service.[6] Some are never invited and others decide that they prefer to live a more ordinary life.

Those who do stay on track find that one of the more disquieting aspects of the Administrative Service's 'professionalism' is the deliberate practice of moving Administrative Officers around frequently between posts. Even Permanent Secretaries are not allowed to feel secure. Since 2000 they have begun their lordly tenure by opening a letter that tells them their shelf-life in this position, which can be anything up to 10 years and is often much less. Renewal of tenure is unusual and only a select few move from one PS position to another (*ST*, 8 May 2004).[7] So it is that even those members of the administrative elite who successfully reach the heights can expect to find themselves looking for a soft landing and new career in their 50s.[8]

ҙ Military path

The military path into the administrative elite is not fundamentally different to the civilian path, but there are differences in the character of the two. According to Lee Hsien Loong, SAF scholars benefit from 'rigorous SAF training, … experience analysing complex problems and managing men, and the tempering of the character of commanders responsible for the welfare, discipline and performance of their troops'.[9] If anything the SAF scholars are even more privileged than their civilian counterparts, though such benefits are offset by the necessary rigours of military discipline. They are better paid than their opposite numbers in the civil service and private sector, and they benefit from the SAF's equivalent of the Gifted Education Programme. Upon their return from studying overseas they are automatically inducted into Project Wrangler, a scheme established in 1974 to fast-track outstanding serving officers – including some non-scholars. They are rushed through a series of appointments and promotions to give them a very broad range of command experience and every opportunity to excel and rise. They are also routinely sent for further study. Lee Hsien Loong has described Project Wrangler as 'a systematic, institutionalised scheme to track and plan the careers of promising and capable officers … and ensure that they [are] assigned to appropriate posts and groomed for key appointments'.[10] Even at the most senior level, the rotation of command and staff responsibilities does not stop, ensuring that no one has a chance to settle into a comfortable niche. Perpetual privilege is balanced by the reality of continual challenges and the demand for continual achievement. These characteristics are an even more pronounced reality for SAF scholars than they are for the civilians, which is one important reason why SAF scholars are so cherished in the Administrative Service. They epitomise the ideal of the technocratic elite described in Chapter 4, with command experience over men thrown in as a bonus. It was not by chance that, when the government needed a comprehensive overhaul of the construction industry following the fatal collapse of Nicoll Highway in 2004, they turned to a soldier to do the job. The SAF scholar track is believed to be producing just the right sort of people for executing major institutional rebuilds. As we have noted before, such secondments from the military to the Administrative Service are routine and are even institutionalised though 'dual career' paths,[11] as are the recruitment of newly 'retired' SAF scholars (usually aged 40 to 45) into the Administrative Service, statutory boards, GLCs, and occasionally into politics.

Parallel Tracks and Common Problems

At this point we can resume our study of the civilian and military elites in tandem, since in many ways the similarities are more striking than the differences, and with so much cross-over we are often talking about the same personnel in any case. In each domain the scholars are placed on special training and coaching regimes, through the SAF Training Institute on the one hand, or the Civil Service College on the other. They attend both substantial and short courses on leadership, administration, creative thinking and ranges of technical skills. An integral part of these courses is testing, including tests designed to help superiors assess character and capacity for original thought. Both groups are taken on excursions, outings and study tours to build camaraderie, and an *esprit de corps*. They are invited to join exclusive clubs: the Temasek Society for very senior SAF officers and the Alpha Society for Administrative Officers.[12] Both groups are small, with a very high turnover and a very young average age. As of April 2000 there had been 206 SAF Overseas Scholars produced since 1971, and of these 162 remained in the military.[13] According to public sources the Administrative Service had only 242 officers in 1990,

247 in 1997, and 270 in 2001, but Ross Worthington has uncovered some anomalies that suggest that even these figures might be inflated.[14]

Filling positions in both services with top-quality candidates is commonly said to be a continual struggle. It is clear that throughout the 1990s the elite administrative services were scratching around, borrowing from one service to fill gaps in another. In 1994 Lee Hsien Loong bemoaned the desperate shortage of senior officers in the Administrative Service:

> We recently planned succession for the PSs. One level down, there are not enough officers. Even two levels down, we still do not have enough officers. In the cohorts who joined the service from the late 70s and early 80s, two thirds have gone. Out of the 20 recruited in 1978, there are only two left. Out of the 14 recruited in 1980, there is only one left.[15]

Note the tiny number of annual recruits and the even smaller number of survivors indicated in Lee's speech. With 10 to 20 recruits into the Administrative Service each year, and the number of SAFOS scholarships ranging from four to 12 each year (usually six to nine) the total numbers being recruited into the two core administrative elites through the usual scholarship track seem to range between 15 and 30 per annum. Since both services also suffer from high turnover and attrition rates (thanks in part to a deliberate policy of retiring most officers in the prime of their working lives) the issue of threatened or actual shortages of talent is constantly at the front of the minds of Singapore's leadership, and is still used to justify the extraordinarily high concentration of power into the hands of a small number of people through multiple directorships and board memberships.[16] During the 1990s these factors were exacerbated by low morale in the Administrative Service, leading to unsustainable levels of mid-career resignations. The frenetic character of the search for talent in the mid-1990s was indicated in a story told by Eddie Teo on the 'Scholars Speak' page of the PSC's website. In 1994, the then head of the civil service asked him to leave his position as Director of the Security and Intelligence Department of the MINDEF to join the Administrative Service. Upon declining he was then cajoled by Lim Siong Guan to come across in these terms:

> Eddie, you must come and join the Admin Service. It will be good for your career. Besides, you cannot say no. I need you to take over from me as Perm Sec of MINDEF. Otherwise I will not be able to leave.[17]

Even granting the possibility that Lim Siong Guan has a sufficiently dry sense of humour to carry this off as a joke, it was clearly intended to touch on a common perception of a problem with succession at the top of the civil service. Years later Lee Hsien Loong gave yet another indication of a general dearth of suitable candidates for the elite services when he said in 2001 that 'the opportunity cost of channelling half a dozen top notch people, plus many other good men, into the SAF every year, has been high. These officers were sorely missed elsewhere in the government and the economy, but the SAF's need was greater'.[18]

In 2005 Prime Minister Lee Hsien Loong expressed his satisfaction that 'the [Administrative] Service is stronger now, in terms of breadth and depth of talent, than it has ever been before', suggesting that the throughputs of elite supply and demand were in balance for the moment.[19] In contrast to his sense of unbecoming urgency in the mid-1990s, he seemed at this point to regard the imminent turnover of a large number of Permanent Secretaries with equanimity. The success of the renewal programme into the medium and longer term, however, must be regarded as a perpetually open question, the answer for which depends both on the rate at which the school system can produce new candidates for the elite, and on the perceived attractions of joining the elite services. Producing elites is the role of the schools, but attracting and retaining them is the responsibility of the managers of the elite services themselves, and is pursued within an environment of inter-service competition. The deliberate practice of keeping the Administrative Service and the SAF Officer Corp young has also increased the pace of turnover, even as it has created more open paths of advancement for younger officers.[20] The government's plan to release a lot of scholars from their bonds early (in an effort to release new waves of entrepreneurial energy and imagination) will stretch resources even further. In the 2000s the education system is supposed to meet the demands of not only the Administrative Service, the SAF, the security services, the Foreign Service, statutory boards, and GLCs, but it is also expected to provide elite personnel to staff many private posts in a highly sophisticated high-tech, knowledge-based economy. Part of the problem facing the government is the consequence of its successful modernisation of the economy, which has given young scholars many more options than in the past. Many positions can be filled with 'foreign talent' – a rented elite – but there are many positions in GLCs that can only be filled by Singapore nationals.

The ever-present prospect of a shortfall of elites helps to explain why – over and above Lee Kuan Yew's elitist predispositions – the government is prepared to go to almost any lengths to turn the education system into a factory for elites. No principle of fairness or equity is sacrosanct in the pragmatic struggle to fill these positions. Not even the nation's ideological cornerstones, meritocracy and multiracialism, are inviolable. Each has been corrupted in the pursuit of elite throughput. It is, however, a sad commentary on the operation of this supposed 'pragmatism' that by abandoning Singapore's founding principles so cavalierly it has actually diminished the pool of candidates for the elite on racial, religious, language, gender and class lines. Remember that nearly one quarter of Singapore's population are not Chinese, yet they are almost unrepresented at the peak of the elitist hierarchy because of systemic discrimination. Only eyes blinded by the most profound prejudice could see this as a sensible use of human resources.

Nation Building Meets Elite Formation

And why is it deemed necessary to manage Singapore's education system like a factory for elites in the first place? Any Singaporean can answer that question (and most will probably believe their answer): because of its vulnerability, its small size, because no one owes Singapore a living, because it has to be the best at everything to flourish, because they do not want to be like Malaysia, because Singapore's very existence is dependent on its economic prosperity, etc. Singapore must offer the region the best airport, the best port, the best biomedical sciences and services, the best education services and the best headquarters services and infocommunications services. This list is not exhaustive, but it should make the point. This is the message of National Education, of S-Cube and of National Service. It is the most basic premise of the elite's culture of technocratic governance. Producing the elite is the salvation of the country. The elite are the natural masters and the selfless benefactors of the grassroots.

It is a given that members of the administrative elite accept these premises without question. As the most direct beneficiaries of the 'meritocracy' it would be remarkable if they were not drenched in a culture that legitimised the system. Indeed the administrative elite has a self-referential culture of its own that generates its own sense of legitimacy. This culture is separate from those in the civil service more generally – which are usually tied to particular ministries or professions – but it extends to the elite within statutory boards and GLCs. The core is nevertheless found in the Administrative Service and the SAF Scholar Officer corps. One former head of the civil service, Sim Kee Boon, once said that joining the Administrative Service is like entering 'a royal priesthood' (*Straits Times Interactive*, 28 September 2003). In 2002 Lee Hsien Loong referred to the first 10 years of a scholar's working life as the period when 'he [sic] should be learning about the Government of Singapore and imbibing values and knowledge which should stand him in good stead over the long term'.[21] Today the culture is so strong that one senior civil servant conceded in interview that the biggest problem facing the Administrative Service is 'group think'.[22] To make it worse, it is a group think with arrogance. Former Permanent Secretary Ngiam Tong Dow sees this arrogance as a new phenomenon: 'There is a particular brand of Singapore elite arrogance creeping in. Some civil servants behave like they have a mandate from the emperor. We think we are little Lee Kuan Yews' (*Straits Times Interactive*, 28 September 2003).

Development of the Administrative Elite

The administrative elite was not always so homogenous, nor so self-confident. In 1976 Seah Chee Meow observed that the early 1970s was a period in which bureaucrats, and especially senior bureaucrats, routinely used the service as a training ground 'for better jobs in the private sector'.[23] He observed that

> the fact that the bureaucracy is subject to [a high] turnover of personnel ... shows that the bureaucratic ethos (such as pride in serving the bureaucracy) has not been effectively instilled among the bureaucrats who tended to be susceptible to purely monetary considerations. ... They have yet to internalize many of the norms of the bureaucracy.[24]

Yet even the situation of the early 1970s was preferable to that which the PAP government inherited when it first took office in 1959. Despite the fact that the PAP government drew two of its Cabinet Ministers from the civil service, it faced high levels of mistrust. At this stage the public face of the PAP was not just the Cambridge-educated Lee Kuan Yew, but also the rabble rousing Ong Eng Guan, who had made life hell for civil servants, first as Mayor of Singapore, and then as Minister for National Development. The conservative civil servants also regarded the PAP as crypto-communist because of its roots in the Chinese-educated constituency. It also did not help when the government reduced their pay and set them to work digging ditches and cleaning streets on weekends as part of their 'nation building' work.

The turnaround in civil service attitudes to the PAP came in 1961 when both Ong Eng Guan and the Left of the party split to join the opposition. These moves had the immediate effects of differentiating the remaining Lee Kuan Yew-led government from both of the forces that the civil servants held in disdain, and leaving the PAP as the only serious contender for conservative support.[25] Far from continuing its sullen attitude towards the PAP, the civil service became a virtual arm of the PAP, providing not only enthusiastic support in terms of policy advice and implementation, but engaging in politics in every sense of the word except – with a few notable exceptions – actually standing for election and speaking in public.[26]

The transformation of the civil service into a highly professional, yet fully partisan force was a slow process that was charged to particular people who were personally known and trusted by the key members of the political elite. George Bogaars, formerly of Special Branch and then an early head of the civil service, was a key person for many years. The role of personal power at that stage was an indispensable substitute for professional and more impersonal systems of elite selection because the latter did not yet exist. During the first two decades of Singapore's independence, the only way for the political or administrative leadership to find or judge talent was to seek it out by ferreting laboriously through PSC and SAF records,[27] stumble across it, or rely on existing personal relationships to form connections. Everything was personal. When true leadership was discovered in this system it was treasured and exploited. The true administrative elites were not given just one job in the civil service, but multiple roles. In 1971 a mere six bureaucrats (George Bogaars, Sim Kee Boon, Ong Kah Kok, Ngiam Tong Dow, J.Y. Pillay and Pang Tee Pow) held 40 directorships on 25 boards between them[28] – and this was apart from their day jobs. Others, such as Hon Sui Sen, were recruited directly from the Administrative Service into politics.

Such people were the cream of a much larger and more ramshackle Administrative Service than that which we see today. In the early to mid-1980s the Administrative Service had about 650 authorised posts, and nearly 500 of these were actually filled.[29] This is about twice the numbers in today's Administrative Service. This service was also leading a significantly larger civil service than we find today. In 1959 there were only 28,000 civil servants, reflecting the level of colonial disdain for involving itself very much in the affairs of its subjects.[30] By 1979 this figure had exploded to 77,400,[31] by 1985 it had been pruned back to 69,600 and stands at a relatively modest 62,000 today.[32] This is not to suggest that the government sector has shrunk. Existing and new functions have been sliced away with the creation of statutory boards and GLCs, but we make the point that the civil service itself was much more unwieldy in the 1960s, 1970s and 1980s than its contemporary manifestation.

The bureaucracy of the 1970s was not only bloated, but it was also relatively unaccountable. According to Seah, only after 1978 were matters such as performance indicators, planning (both short- and long-term) and inter-bureau co-ordination addressed in a serious fashion. The Parliamentary Estimates Committee of that year went so far as to suggest that 'the budget proposals submitted by the Ministries were not related to their work plans'.[33] A new budgeting regime was introduced in 1978 as the beginning of a serious effort to professionalize the civil service.

Elite Selection and Formation

Lee Kuan Yew put his personal stamp on the aspect of modernisation that was most central to his thinking: selection and formation of the elite. Today the selection and management of the administrative elite is a highly nuanced and sophisticated affair even after one has become a scholar, but it was not always so. Goh Chok Tong tells of his own experiences: 'After graduation in 1964, I was interviewed by the PSC. It lasted about half an hour and I was appointed to the Administrative Service.'[34] As discussed in Chapter 4, in 1982 Lee Kuan Yew introduced a model of elite selection based on that used by the Shell oil company (*ST*, 9 February and 19 April 1982).[35] Senior civil servants interviewed for this research project have argued that the 'Shell system' was nothing more than a staff appraisal system that reduced the role of personalities and luck in the hiring and promotion of staff, but even as such it was a decisive break from the ramshackle, *ad hoc* procedures of the past, where advancement depended on 'being noticed by the right people'.[36] The operation of personal power will always circumscribe the professionalism of the civil service, especially at the higher levels where permanent secretaries, ministers and prime ministers are wont to intervene unilaterally as talent spotters. (It is remarkable how many top civil servants have, like Lim Siong Guan, been the Personal Private Secretary to a Prime Minister or Senior Minister.) Yet even with such qualifications, the adaptation of the 'Shell system' provided the first principles from which the process of bureaucratisation was launched. Today, when civil servants submitting themselves to a '360 Degree Feedback Survey' (that is, appraisal by one's subordinates as well as one's peers and superiors)[37] is the norm, the lumbering appraisal committees of the 1980s must seem rather quaint, but their introduction marked the critical turn that led to the current situation.

With the foundation of the contemporary, professional civil service in place by the mid-1980s, the pace of change slowed to that of a slow drip until the shake-up of the mid-1990s, when then-Prime Minister Goh Chok Tong, his Deputy Prime Minister, Lee Hsien Loong, and the then head of the civil service, Lim Siong Guan, set about addressing new problems. These problems centred initially around low morale in junior and middle-ranking Administrative Officers and the consequent difficulty in retaining such officers, but later developed into a dynamic new project aimed at making the Administrative Service a source of true national leadership, as opposed to a mere repository of highly competent managers.[38] It is at this point that we move into what we might call the current period, when the administrative elite began to be trusted with responsibility beyond mere management.

The System in Maturity

Until the late 1990s, members of the Administrative Service were not routinely expected to show real leadership or initiative. The civil service certainly 'partnered the political leadership' but only as implementers of the political leaders' ideas.[39] According to a former head of the Public Service Division (PSD – the division that manages the civil service),

> back then, the civil servant knew exactly what his job was, and he knew that it was not the same as the politician's job. ... The civil servant was not [even] meant to manage the ground, but only to administer.[40]

It is little wonder that most of the earlier Administrative Officers were confined to the role of functionaries. Until the late 1990s scholars came into the Administrative Service straight from university. As Bilahari Kausikan said in interview,

> there used to be immense unhappiness. [There were] lots of complaints ... because when the fellow comes back [from their studies], 24 years old, or 22 years old if she is a woman, there is no way in knowing how well he would do.[41]

The problem of recruiting people 'raw' from university was probably also a major factor in the low morale besetting the Administrative Service for most of its existence. This fundamental problem was finally fixed with the introduction of the 'dual career' entry scheme in the late 1990s, which enabled the PSD to judge scholars by their work in the ordinary civil service, as well as their grades. This can perhaps be regarded as one of the more sensible modifications of the hitherto grades-driven meritocratic system of recruitment.

The introduction of the 'dual career' entry scheme in the late 1990s meant that the processes of elite selection and formation could now be relied upon to produce the 'right' sort of people to take on new leadership roles in the civil service. Over the 1990s the administrative elite was gradually required to become much more complete partners with the political elite in making decisions, gauging and taking into account public opinion and – most important of all – in convincing the public to accept government policy initiatives. From the speeches and articles emanating from the highest levels of the civil service itself, the reforms of the 1990s and 2000s appear to have been a response to the new challenges generated both by the changing economic environment in which Singapore found itself and the rising educational and aspirational levels of Singaporeans. In 2005, Lim Siong Guan, then head of the civil service, implied that the civil service changes he instituted during the 1990s were a direct response to these challenges, which collectively had led to a breakdown in the social compact that has been holding Singapore together since independence:

> Hope through opportunity is what our first generation of political leadership sought to provide for Singaporeans. ... There was an 'easy' congruence between what the people looked for and what the government could deliver: jobs for the people, education for the children and a home they could own. ...
>
> The congruence of interests between the people and the government has been replaced by dissonance. There is structural unemployment. The people ask, 'Why doesn't education result in the same job opportunities and pay as for earlier cohorts?' The government says you must look after yourself.[42]

Six years earlier, Eddie Teo (former head of PSD) indicated the extent of these changes in an in-house interview:

> The Public Service's weakness – I prefer to call it inadequacy – is that efficiency and incorruptibility may not be enough for the future. ...

No longer can they hide behind politicians. They must also engage the public, explain policies, and correct misconceptions. ... It is not enough for our public officers to be just good rule-makers or efficient in implementing current procedures. ... Civil servants must not only be able to write good papers and conceive clever plans, they must also learn how to consult with and present policies to the public in a persuasive and convincing manner. Civil servants must win over people and not talk down to them.[43]

We cannot be sure of the real balance of the impulses that led to the change in character, but the change nevertheless occurred.

Consider the following example of administrative initiative, to which we alluded in Chapter 5. In 2004, the then Ministry of Community Development and Sport began 'preparing the ground' for a new initiative to promote marriage and procreation, but the Administrative Officers discovered from the feedback that the preparatory work was having exactly the opposite effect to that which had been intended: couples were deferring conception until after the announcements in case they missed out on a new bonus. As a result of Administrative Service representations, then-Deputy Prime Minister Lee and the then MCDS Minister, Yaacob Ibrahim, both made public announcements assuring couples that there would be no advantage to deferring conception and urging them not to wait.[44] This was hardly a fundamental shift in policy and perhaps demonstrates the limits of the administrative elite's role in its new partnership with the political elite, but it does nevertheless reveal a proactive role that would have been unimaginable a decade or more earlier.

According to Teo, acquiring this sort of grassroots feedback is now a mandatory part of an Administrative Officer's job:

A policy recommendation from a civil servant that now goes up for approvals is likely to be thrown back if there is not evidence that he has sought the views of parties outside government, if the issue is one that is important enough and worthy of consultation of the public.[45]

The New Elite and New Sensibilities

The transformation of the Administrative Service has continued for over a decade and shows no signs of slowing as we write. The professionalism of the tiny group of elites that is now given grave responsibility is being continually enhanced. Even ordinary civil servants are now supposed to receive at least 100 hours of training per year. According to Eddie Teo they are expected 'to develop themselves professionally and personally through formal courses and workshops, based on a customised individual 'Learning Roadmap' that is updated annually'.[46] Yet this pales compared to the attention given to Administrative Officers:

> The training and development framework for Administrative Officers is especially comprehensive. They go through three milestone programmes and receive extended training, including postgraduate courses in top foreign universities. We send them to interesting operational attachments, such as grassroots organisations, United Nations General Assembly and government-linked companies. We are also working out a scheme for some officers to work for a few years in private sector companies so as to expose them to conditions in the private sector. Better officers are also given additional assignments outside their immediate areas of work to stretch and challenge them.[47]

We have already quoted Bilahari Kausikan at the opening of this chapter describing the basic programmes of training and bonding that await new members of the Administrative Service. This is now an appropriate place to continue that quotation, in which he described the ongoing training that continues, even for the most senior Administrative Officers:

> At another stage there's something called the Senior Management Programme which is when they reach Junior Director level. Six weeks, quite an intense programme from morning to night … .
>
> Then at the more senior level you have another one for about six weeks. You go from morning to night for about six weeks with a bunch of peers. Basically that is a far more conscious process of bonding, or elite formation if you want.[48]

Some of the training is in technocratic skills. Administrative Officers and even senior civil servants below that level are notoriously good note-takers, and routinely possess a host of technical skills that enable them to master and manage multiple briefs quickly and thoroughly. Yet the most important training appears to be in the nebulous area of encouraging independent thinking. Officers are pushed to enter a realm of ambiguity whereby they think outside the parameters of Singapore's official ideology so they can challenge it in constructive ways, while all the time remaining completely loyal in their heart and soul to it. This is a tight balancing act, but they have some fine examples to follow in Permanent Secretaries like Lim Siong Guan, Eddie Teo, Bilahari Kausikan and Yong Ying-I (Permanent Secretary at the Ministry of Manpower) – a generation that was educated without the benefits of intensive kindergarten and primary education, streaming, SAP schools, a Gifted Education Programme, Independent Schools or Integrated Programmes. Consider the example of Lim Siong Guan, who has cleverly used the ideological tool of 'pragmatism' as the point of articulation between these two conflicting demands, though without expressly identifying his theoretical approach:

> A good way of thinking through [a] subject is to ask 'Why?' five times. What do I mean by this? An example: Why did you turn down this application? Because the rule said so. Why did the rule say so? Because Cabinet had decided so. Why did Cabinet decide so? Because we recommended this to Cabinet. Why did you recommend this to Cabinet? Did you notice we asked three 'whys' without learning anything?
>
> This reminds me of an ongoing discussion the Pro-Enterprise Panel is having with the National Environment Agency. Why can't home kitchens be allowed? Because we can't inspect them whenever we want to. Why can't you inspect them whenever you want to? Because they may not open the door immediately when we knock on it. Why won't they open the door immediately? Because they may be trying to evade inspection. Why can't we set the condition that they must open the door anytime you knock, or you will remove the licence? Because they won't like us to knock on their door anytime we like. Why can't you set that as a condition? Because they won't like it. Why do the English authorities allow home kitchens? We did not know about it, perhaps English houses are different. Why can't we set the rule for home kitchens the same as them? We will think about it.
>
> Seven 'whys' and we now agree to re-examine ... .[49]

With this methodology in mind, Lim sent

> almost 100 officers from the Administrative Service and the Ministry of Finance on an exercise to develop thoughts on what *Singapore is Opportunity* should mean in terms of government thinking. ... The exercise was run with the purpose of answering the question: 'What can Singapore *not* afford *not* to do?' ...
>
> The teams were specifically asked to look at things from the viewpoint of the target groups, not from the viewpoint of the agencies. ... [They] were told to go down to the ground – to speak to the people in the stakeholder groups themselves, and not to depend on the interpretations of government agencies or the works of academics, even though these could be useful as background material.[50]

The target groups included:

- the 'average educated' or 'non-elite' Singaporeans';
- the working poor;
- entrepreneurs, small businesses and operators in the informal economy; and
- ethnic minorities.

Taking this task seriously must have been a mind-bending challenge for these officers, given the gulfs between their own life experiences and those of their target groups, but it is of the greatest significance that these challenges are being set and the then head of the civil service chose to focus attention on them. Clearly there was nothing half-hearted about this exercise, nor in Lim's efforts to push senior civil servants (not just the Administrative Officers) to open their minds beyond the parameters of orthodoxy established by the regime.

Yong Ying-I, Permanent Secretary at the Ministry of Manpower, has demonstrated a similar spirit of adventurism in her 2005 article in *Ethos*. She called for leaders 'who are comfortable with ambiguity', who are 'comfortable taking jobs that do not have fixed parameters and clear outcomes', 'who are comfortable acknowledging that they do not know the answer to the problems but can suggest how to begin to tackle it and adapt as they learn'.[51] She revealed that she has had some success in promoting a new approach to team work and leadership through a programme called 'Organisational Development and Learning Organisations', pointing to the Education Service, the SAF and the Police as the best success stories thus far. She then finishes with a warning that reveals her willingness and capacity to challenge orthodoxies:

> My last point may be a warning – as the largest organisations, the Police, SAF and the Education Service are not organisations that only have hot-shots and expensive talent. They have some of the best talent, and they have many more ordinary people – just normal hard-working, committed people who want to do a good job. My experience has been that the organisations with the most 'talent' – the hot-shots, the brightest, the most expensive – find it the hardest to go this route, because they are too smart to learn, too smart to listen and reflect.[52]

Significantly, this warning also indicates the depth of the problem being faced in breaking the mind-sets of orthodoxy among the more junior and middle-ranking members of the administrative elite.

It seems that an environment of constant change and the weakening of apparently stable and secure ideological pillars is no more comfortable for members of the administrative elite than it is for others. Arguably it is less comfortable in many ways. These people give up their personal lives for the service, but they are allowed very little sense of security until they have proved their worth to their superiors. As Eddie Teo explained:

> For the premier Administrative Service, there is a 'potential threshold'. If an officer's potential is assessed to be below that of at least Deputy Secretary when he reaches his mid-30s, he will be counselled to leave the Administrative Service.[53]

Not that 'failures' are usually out of a job. Teo went on to explain that such people routinely find lesser positions in the civil service, but as Bilahari Kausikan explained in interview, such outcomes can depend on who you know:

> If people think that you are a decent bloke they will give you a softer landing. They might say 'Mr Barr, you are not good enough for the Admin Service but I have posted you for 2 years in this institute, so go and sort your life out', instead of saying, 'Mr Barr you are not good enough for the Admin Service. Bugger off.'[54]

This account gives an indication of the limits of personal power in the administrative elite but also of the cushioning power that a connection in the elite provides. Patronage can open the door to power for young, well-connected scholars and elements of privilege play vital roles in determining who will be a scholar in the first place. As we saw in Chapter 4, patronage is also a vital element in lubricating the wheels of government, but it is not sufficient to keep an underachiever in a position of power. Comfort, yes, but not power. A 'soft landing' for the embarrassing relative of a particularly important family might be found in a Statutory Boards or GLC, but not in any place where he or she could do harm to the government's overall project.

By the same token, those in the administrative elite who are both extraordinary managers and who show leadership ability are talent-spotted and recruited into the political elite. For these high flyers, their careers in the civil service commonly bring them into personal contact with prime ministers and deputy prime ministers, usually by the deliberate design of the politicians in question. People with particularly high potential are worthy of special attention – to test them, hone them, guide and, if necessary, protect them – all of which also serves the core function of building a personal relationship between the holder of power and his potential beneficiary. Understanding this feature makes it less remarkable that the newer generations of politicians in Singapore routinely have a personal story of how they were recruited into politics. Take, for instance, Health Minister Khaw Boon Wan. Asked why he came into politics, he answered, 'I couldn't say "no" to the Prime Minister. That's the frank answer.'[55] He had been Prime Minister Goh's Principal Private Secretary for three years from 1992 to 1995.

Full Circle

Thus we come full circle, and complete our study of elite formation on the very doorstep of Chapter 4, which analysed the culture of elite governance, primarily from the perspective of the pinnacle of the political elite. With all its faults, exclusions and distortions – and this study has focused on these, giving only incidental attention to its strengths – it is a system that has delivered results of which most Singaporeans are seemingly proud – within limits. In the following, concluding chapter, we explore some of those limits.

Notes

1   The Navy is almost exclusively Chinese.

2   It would be interesting to know how much overlap there has been between the elites of the scholar platoons, and the so-called 'white horses'. Until 2000, the term 'white horse' was the official MINDEF designation of the sons of important people doing the National Service. The general opinion among former soldiers is that 'white horses' were coddled and protected from the risk of injury during their National Service, but MINDEF claims that they were identified to ensure that they would not benefit from favouritism. See, for instance, *CNA*, 14 and 19 November 2003; and *Business Times*, 22 November 2003.

3   Barr has interviewed one such scholar from the 1970s whose project was integral to a major social initiative that is still in place today. We cannot give more details without breaching Barr's commitment to de-identify this interview.

4   Barr has interviewed one such person, who turned down the offer.

5   It is difficult to say absolutely whether the 2½ years' age gap disadvantages the men or the women the most. On the one hand the men have lost 2½ years' seniority and career experience against the women of their age cohort, but on the other hand they are now matched against younger women straight from school, and they have had officer training and command experience. On balance the men – especially male scholars – seem to have come out the best in this exchange.

6   Barr's interview with Bilahari Kausikan, Singapore, 15 April 2003.

7   Ibid.

8   Ibid. Also see Teo, 'A development-oriented promotion system', p. 13.

9   DPM Lee Hsien Loong's Speech at the SAF Overseas Scholarship 30th Anniversary Dinner, 15 April 2001. Available at the Ministry of Trade and Industry website, http://www.mti.gov.sg. Accessed 27 September 2005.

10 Ibid.

11 Tim Huxley, *Defending the Lion City: The Armed Forces of Singapore*, St Leonards, NSW: Allen & Unwin, 2000, pp. 232–235.

12 The Temasek Society is not to be confused with the Temasek Club. The latter is for almost all SAF officers, while the former is the more exclusive equivalent of the Alpha Society. Barr's interview with Bilahari Kausikan, Singapore, 15 April 2003.

13 Lee Hsien Loong's speech, 15 April 2001.

14 Teo, 'A development-oriented promotion system', p. 11; Ross Worthington, *Governance in Singapore*, London and New York: RoutledgeCurzon, 2003, pp. 47, 48. Also see p. 270, note 317, where Worthington refers to a generic letter from the Prime Minister's Office in 1998 to graduate women who were married to graduate men. The letter claimed there were 'about 270' Administrative Officers but said, incredibly, that they could locate the appointment of only 195 of them. This strange letter was sent as part of the government's eugenics programme.

15 Lee Hsien Loong, 'Staying ahead – scenarios and challenges' (being his address to Administrative Officers at an Alpha Society Dinner on 25 October 1994), *Ethos*, 1994, Issue 3, page numbers not indicated.

16 Barr's interview with Bilahari Kausikan, Singapore, 15 April 2003; Worthington, *Governance in Singapore*, pp. 172–219.

17 Eddie Teo's personal story on the Public Service Commission 'Scholars Speak' website, available at http://app.psc.gov.sg/scholarships/html/scholarsspeak_eddie.asp. Accessed 26 September 2005.

18 Lee Hsien Loong's speech, 15 April 2001.

19 Lee Hsien Loong, 'Speech by PM Lee Hsien Loong at the 2005 Administrative Service Dinner, 24 March 2005'. Cited on Sprinter [Singapore Government news service] http://www.sprinter.gov.sg/. Accessed 30 March 2005.

20 Teo, 'A development-oriented promotion system', p. 13.

21 Singapore Parliamentary Debates, 15 May 2002.

22 Edgar Schein referred to the same phenomenon in 1996 when he observed that 'the real danger of elitism is that members of the elite get caught up in their own mental models to such a degree that they cease to observe accurately what is going on around them. ... The ... Singapore elites may ... have to invent ways to surmount their own biases.' Edgar H. Schein, *Strategic Pragmatism: The Culture of the Economic Development Board*, Singapore: Toppan Company and MIT Press, 1996, p. 221.

23 Seah Chee Meow, 'The Singapore bureaucracy and issues of transition', in Riaz Hassan (ed.), *Singapore: Society in Transition*, Kuala Lumpur: Oxford University Press, 1976, p. 61.

24 Ibid., pp. 61, 62.

25 Ibid., p. 56.

26 Seah Chee Meow, *Community Centres in Singapore: Their Political Involvement*, Singapore: Singapore University Press, 1973; Chan Heng Chee, 'The PAP and the structuring of the political system', in Kernial Singh Sandhu and Paul Wheatley (eds), *Management of Success: The Moulding of Modern Singapore*, Singapore: Institute of Southeast Asian Studies, 1989, pp. 79–83.

27 As Lee Kuan Yew used to do. See Lee's interview with Roy Mackie and Quek Peck Lim, of *The Business Times*, 16 September 1978, cited in Barr, *Lee Kuan Yew*, p. 122.

28 Seah, 'The bureaucracy and the issues of transition', p. 60.

29 Thomas J. Bellows, 'Bureaucracy and development in Singapore', *Asian Journal of Public Administration*, vol. 7, no. 1, 1985, p. 59.

30 Lee Boon Hiok, 'The bureaucracy', in Sandhu and Wheatley, *Management of Success*, pp. 93, 94.

31 Bellows, 'Bureaucracy and development in Singapore', p. 59.

32 Lee Boon Hiok, 'The bureaucracy', pp. 93, 94; Yee Ping Yi, 'The philosophy and strategic directions for human resource management in the civil service', *Ethos*, August 2002, p. 2. This latter figure is all the more modest when it is realised that it includes teachers and many medical staff that are often not counted as civil servants in other countries. On the other hand, it excludes another 50,000 employees in statutory boards, who are in practical terms civil servants, but are not members of the civil service *per se*. See Lim Siong Guan, 'The new public administration: global challenges, local solutions – the Singapore experience', *Ethos*, August 1996, page numbers not indicated.

33 Lee Boon Hiok, 'The bureaucracy', p. 96

34 Goh Chok Tong's personal story on the Public Service Commission 'Scholars Speak' website, available at http://app.psc.gov.sg/scholarships/html/scholarsspeak_goh.asp. Accessed 26 September 2005.

35 Lee Kuan Yew, *The Singapore Story. Memoirs of Lee Kuan Yew*, Singapore: Prentice Hall, 1998; *From Third World to First. The Singapore Story: 1965–2000. Memoirs of Lee Kuan Yew*, Singapore Press Holdings and Times Editions, 2000, pp. 740, 741.

36 For confirmation, see Eddie Teo, 'Can public servants be leaders?', *Ethos*, September 2003, p. 10.

37 Ibid., p. 11.

38 Eddie Teo dates the changes from 1995, when Lim Siong Guan became Permanent Secretary in the Prime Minister's Office. See Eddie Teo, 'Will the real civil service please stand up?', *Ethos*, November 2002, p. 3.

39 Teo, 'A development-oriented promotion system', p. 10.

40 Teo, 'Will the real civil service please stand up?', p. 2.

41 Interview with Bilahari Kausikan, Singapore, 15 April 2003.

42 Lim Siong Guan, 'Is there a new role for government?', *Ethos*, January–March, 2005, pp. 3–5.

43 Eddie Teo, 'Vision and values in Singapore's public service', *Ethos*, August 1999, page numbers not indicated.

44 Tan Yew Soon, 'Practising public consultation', *Ethos*, July 2004, p. 16.

45 Eddie Teo, 'Building an ethical civil service for the 21st century', *Ethos*, July 2000, page numbers not indicated.

46 Teo, 'A development-oriented promotion system', p. 12.

47 Ibid.

48 Barr's interview with Bilahari Kausikan, Singapore, 15 April 2003.

49 Lim Siong Guan, 'Is there a new role for government?', p. 7.

50 Ibid., p. 6.

51 Yong Ying-I, 'Singapore's leadership challenges: developing talent for a new era', *Ethos*, April–June 2005, pp. 7, 8.

52 Ibid., p. 12.

53 Teo, 'A development-oriented promotion system', p. 12.

54 Barr's interview with Bilahari Kausikan, Singapore, 15 April 2003.

55 On Buddhist Fellowship website, http://www.buddhistfellowship.org/news_link_02.hmt. Accessed 8 April 2005.

TWELVE

Conclusion:
A Tentative Assessment of Singapore's
Nation-Building Project

*The Grassroots Organisations traditionally have the responsibility of going
around to the estates and giving people nudges and reminding them to put
up their flags and even handing over flags and have them put out. This is
part of the display of support for loyalty to Singapore and also basically
support for the government.*

A former grassroots organisation member,
in interview, Singapore, 13 March 2003

IN THIS BOOK WE HAVE ARGUED a fairly simple case: that Singapore's two
main national myths – multiracialism and meritocracy – are chimeras whose
main purpose is to facilitate and legitimise rule by a self-appointed elite,
dominated by middle-class Chinese in general, and by the Lee family in particular. The system of 'meritocracy' is a sophisticated mechanism designed
to select, educate, shape, and socialise the next generation of elites. Its stated
criteria for selection is 'talent', but in fact even though intelligence and ability
are indispensable, factors such as personal and family connections, socio-
economic background, race and ethnic identity, language background and
gender are just as crucial in smoothing the path on the road to the elite. Even
more important than any of these is a willingness to be socialised into the
conformist mind-set and 'values' of the elite. The system of 'multiracialism'
has, since the early 1980s, served two distinct purposes, neither of which is
openly acknowledged. The first is to placate the minority races so that they
accept a subordinate place in society and thus ensure social peace and order.
The second is to implement a programme that we have called 'incomplete
assimilation', which involves inviting, cajoling and pressuring the minority
races to actively embrace the supposed 'values' of the dominant Chinese.

This element is intended to foster the virtues that have supposedly made Singapore prosperous, and provides the preferred path for members of the minority races to enter into almost full communion with the Chinese-centred ethno-national project. We say 'almost', because the qualifying element that we identify – 'incompleteness' – ensures that the assimilation will never be complete and the minority races will always remain just outside the core of the nation-building project, no matter how 'Chinese' they become.

Yet without shrinking from these controversial and contestable conclusions we freely acknowledge that the story is more complex than this. As we observed in our opening chapter, our study has raised many more questions

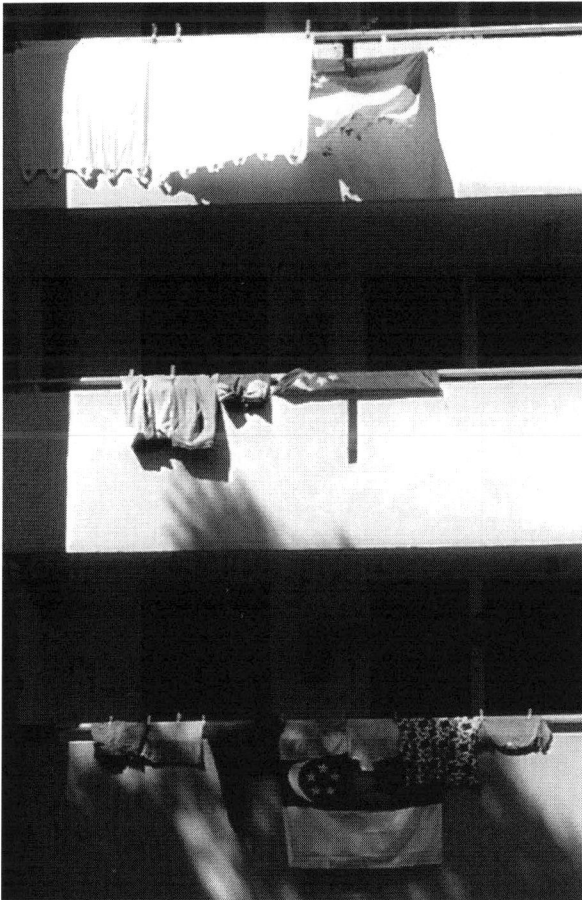

Figure 12.1: Flags in HDB estate, Bedok, July 2005.

than it has answered, and even where we do offer opinions and arguments, there are many, many nuances that we have left unexplored. This concluding chapter will try to round out the book somewhat by providing reflections of a less certain character on the costs, opportunities and tensions associated with Singapore's remarkable social experiment. We begin with two observations that we believe between them go to the heart of the Singapore enigma. The first is that, by most comparative standards, Singapore produces an effective, if not impressive, system of government. The second feature is that the system is extraordinarily brittle. Whether dealing with domestic critics, the foreign press or academic critiques (domestic or overseas), overreactions are commonly the order of the day. The reactions of the Singapore regime under Lee Kuan Yew's premiership are well documented,[1] but what is interesting is how sensitive the current crop of elites is to challenge or criticism.

This preciousness is to some extent the result of an intrinsic tension between the legitimating myths of meritocracy and pragmatism on the one hand, and the contradictions embedded in the more mundane working reality on the other. The cadres of the system ask to be judged by the highest standards of professionalism. They present themselves as the apex of the meritocratic elite, so any failure invites a critique of the basic assumptions upon which rest their claims for prestige and privilege. They are especially sensitive because, unless one enjoys special protection, the system is usually unforgiving of failure (current efforts to introduce a higher tolerance of failure notwithstanding) and the mere perception of inadequacy can bring a quick end to a career. And there are many such failures. Take, for instance, the already-mentioned Nicoll Highway disaster of 2004. This was supposed to be routine tunnelling under an existing highway to build an underground railway line, but a cave-in left four people dead and threatened to shatter confidence in government management of the whole construction industry. The official inquiry into the tragedy found 'glaring and critical shortcomings' in the safety standards of Singapore's construction industry *per se* – not just at this site. Its interim report mostly blamed the government's Land Transport Authority, though the final report predictably pointed the finger at the private contractor. Yet it remains buried in the public record that among other sins, the Authority ignored all warnings of the disaster, for instance responding to underground wall movements by adjusting the recommended safety tolerances so it could declare the movements within acceptable limits (*ST*, 14 September and 10 November 2004).[2]

The government's incompetent handling of SARS in the first five weeks of the contagion in March and April 2003 – in contrast to its highly effective response after the five-week mark – is another point of embarrassment and an indicator of the system's limitations. For the first five weeks of the SARS outbreak (13 March–20 April 2003) there were no protocols or contingency plans to deal with an epidemic, and the responses were *ad hoc* and reactive. The public marker of the ending of this rudderless period was the effective removal of the SARS response from the hands of the Minister for Health, Lim Hng Kiang, and the creation of two ministerial committees to handle the crisis. It even took five weeks before the government began supplying free ambulances to take suspected SARS cases to hospital (13 March–17 April). Until then, SARS suspects generally made their way to hospital by taxi or public transport, as was recommended by official bodies such as the Office of Student Affairs at the National University of Singapore.[3] As the new head of the civil service, Peter Ho, has since acknowledged:

> We were surprised by SARS. We were surprised by its epidemiology. We were unprepared for it. But we should have been prepared. It was not a fundamental surprise, because we knew that the risk of a highly infectious epidemic existed.[4]

It is an indication of the personal nature of power (explored in Chapter 4) that the threat was taken seriously only after SARS threatened the first family itself (*ST*, 26 April 2003).

The increasingly naked threads of personal power that lie at the heart of the Singapore system are also coming under increasing public scrutiny. The cosy system of appointing friends from one's patronage network to director-ships in GLCs and statutory boards has come under challenge from the Head of the Association of Chartered Certified Accountants, who has dismissed the existing process as an 'old boy network', and called for such vacancies to be advertised and filled transparently, or even filled by corporate head hunters (*Straits Times Interactive*, 12 December 2005 – online edition only). In its 2005 official report to the government on the gross mismanagement of the National Kidney Foundation (NKF) – a notionally independent charity that is, in fact, an integral part of the health system as the main provider of discounted kidney dialysis – auditing firm KPMG also pointed to personal power as being at the heart of the problem:

> Power was centred around one man, and was exercised in an *ad hoc* manner
> through [CEO] Mr [T.T.] Durai and his coterie of long-serving assistants. ...
> The NKF appeared to run and operate, and in fact did run and operate, on the
> ideas, whims and caprice of the chief executive (*Today*, 20 December 2005;
> *Reuters*, 19 December 2005).

Not that any government instrumentality or identity can take credit for
uncovering the NKF abuses in the first place. That honour goes to a humble
plumber who was scandalised when contracted to install gold-plated taps
and a luxurious toilet seat in Durai's office (*Today*, 26 December 2005). The
government made what is becoming an increasingly frequent admission of
failure, and thousands of regular financial donors withdrew their support
from the NKF (*Today*, 30 December 2005).[5] Yet a few *mea culpa*s do not
seem to be sufficient to quell rising disquiet over the elite's claims of the
moral and intellectual superiority, which are being swamped in the public
mind by the perception that the country is being run by a cabal that cannot
even be trusted to be competent. SARS, the Nicoll Highway collapse and the
NKF scandal were major and public incidents, but stories of government incompetence and mismanagement on a smaller scale are common fare in the
hawker centres and food courts of Singapore. One such story was recounted
in interview. The interviewee's private home was compulsorily purchased in
the mid-1990s to build the North-East MRT (train) line. The home was bull-
dozed immediately upon resumption. Only then were soil tests performed,
revealing that the site was not suitable for use by the MRT. It was turned into
a car park for some years before it was eventually redeveloped.

How do Singaporeans respond to such incidents? Do they accept the
government's top-down self-justifications unquestioningly? Are they blind to
instances of incompetence and injustices based on race and arbitrary bureaucratic judgements? The letters columns of the newspapers suggest not – especially the online Forum page in *The Straits Times*, where many of the most
critical letters (especially those related to racial issues) are able to enjoy a brief
gasp of life before being removed from the public record after eight days.[6] Yet,
insofar as we can read the entrails, perhaps the most significant indicator is
one with which the regime can take heart: that the vast majority of the people
who expressed cynicism or discontent in interviews and conversations still
harboured deep affection for Singapore and a high degree of grudging support for the Singapore system, if not explicitly for the government itself. Thus

former Civil Service Head Lim Siong Guan speaks of a sense of 'dissonance' between the government and the people rather than a proper gulf or a clear sense of disconnection or hostility.[7]

There is plenty of anecdotal evidence in newspapers – especially in the letters columns – of discontent about issues as they affect the poor (especially issues of the cost of health, housing, utilities, and education), the elderly, and particular government initiatives such as the highly unpopular decision in 2005 to build two casinos to boost tourism. The government's programme of building an elitist education system has had a very mixed reception, with many seeing it as a means of ensconcing class privilege – correctly it seems, judging by the steadily increasing fees (*Business Times*, 3 November 1989; *ST*, 11 August 1990 and 29 November 2005). The government itself has been particularly concerned that the pattern that began emerging in 2004, whereby housing estates started rejecting the government's offers of subsidised upgrades, was a sign that ordinary people were beginning to reject the government's nation-building project. Such indicators are worrying for the government, particularly because they appear to be developing into a class-based response that cuts across the government's preferred social divisions, which are based on ethnicity-cum-race. It seems to be infecting the attitudes of poor and poorly educated Chinese as much as Malays and Indians.[8] At this stage they do not indicate anything more than 'dissonance', and unless such complaints and symptoms are allowed to fester without any balm (a most unlikely contingency) they are all manageable.

The key challenge for Singapore's elite is therefore how to continue its successful balancing act so that elitist and racist policies and structures can continue to be implemented without alienating the majority of ordinary Singaporeans. The paradox of the Singapore system is that in the collective mind of the elite, these two pillars – elitism and racism – have acted as guarantors for the success of the nation-building project since the end of the 1970s, but are also responsible for the deepest forms of 'dissonance' that afflict the nation-building project. Let us examine each of these factors in turn.

Reproduction of the Elite

The question of elitism, elite formation and elite selection preoccupies the bulk of this book. In Chapter 3 we discuss elitism through its link with ethnicity and in Chapter 4 we discuss the 'culture' of elite governance. The remainder of the book provides an extensive account of the anatomy of elite formation inasmuch as this process is embedded in the institutions of the state and the system: education, National Service and Administrative Service. We are confident that no reader of our work could fail to appreciate the care and thought that is devoted to the reproduction of the elite and how much effort is demanded before one is admitted into the top echelons of power in Singapore.

The predictable result is the perpetuation of an administrative and political elite that is fiercely loyal to the regime and the system. Loyalty at this level is easy to understand because it can be explained by self-interest, but what about those lower on the social and political hierarchy? What about, for instance, the 'grassroots leaders' – the political foot soldiers of the regime who staff (often on a voluntary, unpaid basis) the grassroots organisations (GROs) by which the regime keeps in close touch with the sentiments on the ground? Three such people – two current grassroots leaders and one former grassroots activist – were interviewed in the course of researching this book, and these interviews uncovered a surprising lack of enthusiasm for the regime and a consistent sense of remoteness and disappointment about aspects of the Singapore system. Least surprising were confessions of joining the GROs for the fringe benefits. One current member of a Resident's Committee (RC) was completely transparent (under cover of anonymity) about this. Being active on an RC means that 'your' MP will brush aside bureaucratic obstructions that are interfering with your business, waive fines, and your own housing block will always have a direct line to the HDB office.[9] Another interviewee who had been a member of a Community Centre Management Committee during the 1980s confirmed that GRO activists reap advantages such as being able to get their children into better primary schools and jump HDB queues. On the other hand he also assured me that many GRO activists are genuinely altruistic.[10]

With this in mind perhaps the most telling account of life as a grassroots leader came from the most senior of the three. At the time of interview, he was the grassroots leader and self-described electoral officer for one of the most senior Cabinet ministers in the country, and was one of those altruistic grassroots leaders of whom the previous interviewee was speaking. He was also a member of the PAP, but discounted that as just a matter of form: 'I sometimes wonder why we have a party. It counts for nothing.' Yet as the interview wore on and he became more open, it became increasingly obvious that though he placed the highest value on his personal loyalty to his MP, his loyalty to the broader regime and 'the Singapore system' was paper thin. Meritocracy? After a very long pause, he said:

> It is difficult to answer that question. I mean if we look at it from the point of view of scholarship and so on, yes [Singapore] is [a meritocracy]... and the best will lead. But then sometimes there are other intervening factors that might not be too obvious to the casual person. But when you look at the structure of things and so on, after a while you think that it seems slightly wrong. There are certain aspects, you know, and you wonder whether it is meritocracy, whether there are other quiet factors which are coming into view. It could be language ... it could be race ... could be religion.[11]
>
> *Barr: Could it be whom you know?*
>
> I think there is this very strong belief in Singapore society, that if you belong to a certain group, a certain particular group and you are linked to that group, things become easier for you, things are made easier for you.
>
> *Barr: You are not talking about the party now ...*
>
> No, it is not the party, because when it comes to party is quite clear ... it doesn't matter.

His strongest words were reserved for civil servants. Upon resuming the interview after being interrupted by a telephone call, this grassroots leader spontaneously started leading the interview down a new track: complaining about senior technocrats who are isolated from the ordinary person, who talk only to each other, and who think that they know better than elected politicians, grassroots leaders and ordinary people. He regarded them as being mostly secretive and arrogant, and said that the organisations they run are often capricious and incompetent in their decisions. He alluded to incidents in which he had been involved, but that he did not want to become public. As Barr started to wonder what that telephone call had been about, the grassroots leader launched into a critique of the values embedded in the elite. His main points were:

- Nothing matters to them except money, both their own and their department's money.
- The meritocracy has made everyone more selfish because they think that they won their positions by their own efforts and they owe nothing to anyone.

- There is so much natural affection for Singapore by ordinary Singaporeans, but it is being 'squandered'.

- Human values are being 'squandered'.

- He only keeps working in his grassroots position because of his loyalty to 'his' MP, and because he still wants to serve Singapore.

Thus we return to a variation of a major theme of this study. We have already discussed how power is personal, but we have not discussed loyalty. Yet upon reflection it seems logical that loyalty is also personal, at least inasmuch as it is loyalty emanating up the social hierarchy. (There are few indications that unqualified personal loyalty is extended down the social hierarchy, except insofar as family is involved.) Thus we arrive by accident at a picture of characteristically Asian patron–client relationships in Singapore similar to that described by Clark Neher many years ago as being intrinsic to the practice of democracy in Asia.[12]

We have the word of the former head of the Civil Service that the regime's relationship with the grassroots is best characterised as 'dissonance', but it is surprising to find that this extends even to the 'grassroots leaders', whose loyalty should be guaranteed nearly as strongly as that of the elite themselves. It is doubly significant that this particular grassroots leader's strongest expressions of 'dissonance' were on the key areas of elitism and ethnicity.

The Continuing Significance of Ethnicity and Race

The question of ethnicity and race is ubiquitous in Singapore's process of nation building. Accidents of birth and upbringing determine not only access to power, but life chances more generally. The story of the Singapore nation-building project is substantially a story of the management of ethnicity – a practice which manifests itself in the construction, maintenance and essentialisation of stable racial categories. Such solidification of racial categories creates a purported reality that is open to intervention and management much more readily than the usual messiness associated with ethnic complexity.

Yet even though it has always held a central place in the nation-building project, the treatment of race has been far from constant. We noted the shift from a race-blind project of nation building that dominated the early stages of the project until around 1980, to a more or less decisive shift towards ethnicisation, and more specifically Sinicisation thereafter, the public face of which were the various programmes privileging Chinese education, language and 'values'. We discussed these processes in detail in Chapters 3 and 5.

The question that arises in the light of this history is that of the extent to which the minority races feel ownership of the nation in which they live. We note the subdued sense of alienation among Malays and Indians interviewed for this project. The emotions expressed by these interviewees were often complex, reminiscent of unrequited love. They had clearly wanted to love Singapore but often felt rejected and, particularly in the case of the Malays, mistrusted.

It is in this feature – the levels of trust exhibited by the regime – that the vulnerabilities of the national project show up most starkly and most publicly. We know, for instance, that in the early 1970s the regime had very little trust in the Chinese-educated, as was evidenced by a multitude of policies and actions designed to subdue their wayward tendencies (e.g. closing down their newspapers and detaining their editors). We know that in the same period the Malays were not trusted because the government has told us: this is why no Malays were called up for National Service until the mid-1970s. It seems very likely that in both cases the government overreacted, and confused ordinary dissent and ethnic-religious bonds with sedition and disloyalty, but this does not mean that it was wrong to think that both groups were less than enthusiastic about important aspects of the regime's rule. So what do we see today? The programme of incomplete assimilation described in Chapter 5 is an attempt to overcome this dissonance among the minorities without disturbing the post-1980 ethno-national basis of the national project – to recruit the minority communities into the national project in the interests of peace while retaining the pre-eminence of 'Chinese culture' and 'values' in the interests of prosperity.

ॐ *Indians*

To the best of our knowledge, the treatment of Indians and Indian organisations by the regime is routine and excites little attention. Yes, Indians suffer discrimination in education, scholarships and in the employment market, but it seems likely that at least for the most part this is the result of routine and perhaps even unthinking discrimination rather than outright mistrust. The Indian communities are divided in too many ways to be easy targets of mistrust: by race (light-skinned North Indians and dark-skinned South Indians), diet

(North/South, Hindu/Muslim), religion (Hindu, Muslim, Sikh, Christian) and language (Tamil, Malayalam, Bengali, Gujarati, Hindi, Punjabi, Urdu). Intelligent, hardworking, *kiasu* Indians who have assimilated themselves thoroughly into the ethos and mores of Chinese-dominated Singapore can rise to be President, senior members of Cabinet and Deputy Prime Minister. Furthermore they are trusted completely in the SAF (provided they are not Muslims).

ॐ *Malays and Muslims*

The Indians have found a comfortable, if subordinate relationship with the regime at the more benign end of the government's programme of incomplete assimilation, but the same cannot be said about the Malays, whose continuing, ongoing efforts to find a place in the nation-building project speaks volumes for the persistence of angst in the community. The regime itself is convinced beyond doubt that Malays and Muslims feel very little affinity with the regime, despite the apparently contradictory evidence of Malay voting patterns (which have generally been pro-PAP for several decades)[13] and positive Malay responses to surveys on patriotism.[14] Ironically, some of the government's own responses to this perception seem to have fed the very dissonance that it fears. This has been expressed in several ways. The first is the continuing refusal to trust Malays in the SAF. The mistrust has ameliorated to the point where it is now possible for Malays to become officers, and one has even become a fighter pilot, but we have Minister Mentor Lee Kuan Yew's word that such trust is assessed on a case-by-case basis, and that Malay candidates face particular scrutiny precisely because of their race and religion (*ST*, 11 March 2002).

We can also thank Minister Mentor Lee for a further piece of evidence that Malays feel excluded from their society. In July 2005 he volunteered an extraordinary assessment of the current state of multiracialism in the country:

> [Multiracialism has] not been completely successful because the rate of intermingling and acceptance is faster among some groups than others. The Malay community now is centred on a mosque more than the other social centres we have built. That's the end result, we live with that (*ST*, 2 July 2005).

The statement was extraordinary for several reasons. First it singled out Malays for shunning interracial activities, whereas it failed to criticise the majority of Chinese Singaporeans who mix almost exclusively with their own race.[15]

Second, there is no evidence at all to support the suggestion that Muslims are centring their lives on the mosque.

That Malays have a very low participation rate in the official grassroots organisations is beyond question and has been a subject of discussion in Parliament,[16] but we should be wary of jumping to the conclusion that Malays are heavily involved in activities centred on the mosque. Apocryphal evidence suggests that Singapore's Muslims generally shun the mosques except to facilitate their basic religious obligations and observances, and that they do this precisely because of the close association of the mosques with the government. MUIS is the government statutory board that manages the mosques and Muslim affairs in Singapore, and it has come close to confirming its failure to build links with its constituency by its current campaign to make itself relevant. MUIS and kindred Muslim organisations have been collectively and separately engaged in major efforts to increase both their professionalism and their outreach into the Muslim community. For MUIS this has meant improving (and being seen to improve) its organisation of the *hajj* (pilgrimage to Mecca) (*CyBerita*, 28 November 2005), the quality of the (centrally issued) Friday sermons,[17] and the collection of the *zakat* (tithe).[18] It has also meant improving the standard of teaching in the *madrasahs* (Islamic schools) (*Berita Harian*, 25 June 2005), increasing the integration of *madrasah* education into the mainstream system of PSLE certification (*Berita Harian*, 11 July 2005) and improving the standard of teacher training in the *madrasahs* through courses run by the National Institute of Education and Edith Cowan University in Australia (*Berita Harian*, 3 July 2005; *CyBerita*, 15 December 2005). Indeed the basic structure of MUIS and mosques has been drastically restructured to make it more professional, with the creation of a MUIS Executive Officer (*CNA*, 18 October 2005; *CyBerita*, 19 October 2005). Much more radical is the introduction of an office called 'Executive Imam' in the mosques.[19] For 14 centuries mosques have managed with mere imams, but this is no longer sufficient to provide the levels of professionalism, family counselling and outreach required in twenty-first-century Singapore (*Berita Harian*, 11 July 2005). This intensification of outreach and professionalism was particularly noticeable in MUIS, but it manifested itself in a myriad of Malay and Muslim organisations, including the educational self-help group, MENDAKI, whose CEO has found himself door-knocking so he could engage the grassroots first hand (*CyBerita*, 5 December 2005).

Yet not only are MUIS and mosques improving their performance in their core business (the delivery of religious services); they are also reaching out into areas that might appear to the casual observer to have no connection with MUIS's statutory responsibilities. MUIS has even floated the idea of a 'constituency mosque' – one that 'want[s] to play a more active and significant role in the social community surrounding it', becoming something akin to a community centre servicing all the people in the neighbourhood, rather than just serving Muslims.[20] The revision of priorities has taken MUIS and Singapore's mosques in surprising directions. For instance, since the mid-2000s, mosques and MUIS (in cooperation with the Muslim Kidney Action Council) have started working with the National Kidney Foundation to provide material and moral support for kidney patients – including business loans, counselling and subsidised vocational training classes (*Berita Minggu*, 10 July 2005; *CyBerita*, 31 October 2005). During the 2000s, a pregnant teenager in Singapore has been able to shelter in a home run by the Singapore Young Women's Muslim Association (PPIS – Persatuan Pemudi Islam Singapura) and social research into teenage pregnancy was being conducted by the mosque-based Islamic Research Association (*CyBerita*, 22 November 2005). More broadly speaking, young people could come to a mosque for sex education and young couples to join a family support network (*CyBerita*, 22 November 2005). Bored or troubled youths could also come to mosques to engage in graffiti competitions, indoor netball and soccer and even rock climbing, as part of the outreach to youth (*ST*, 29 July 2005). Families could join in the government's *Family Ties* social development programme through one of five mosques and they could call Family Help Lines based in mosques (*CyBerita*, 15 November 2005 and 14 April 2006). Volunteers began door-knocking in the housing estates to seek out those in need, thus raising the profile of mosques immeasurably (*CyBerita*, 27 October and 15 November 2005). MUIS was even using the MUIS Annual Grants under the Community Service Scheme to steer other Muslim bodies to use its preferred model of family assistance programme (*CyBerita*, 6 April 2006).Whether one is looking for Mandarin classes, for the opportunity to volunteer for community work cleaning up the local beach, or for a pregnancy helpline, the mosque became the place to go (*Berita Harian*, 27 June 2005; *CyBerita*, 22 November 2005 and 23 January 2006).

This transformation of MUIS and the mosques was being conducted under the watchful eye (and probably under the explicit direction) of Dr Yaacob

Ibrahim, Minister for Muslim Affairs, and was part of a three-year plan initiated in January 2004, which reached a critical point of determination at the July 2005 Mosque Convention.[21] According to the convention's pre-publicity, it set out with the explicit purpose of 'shaping more mosques so that they can play a more active role in the lives' of Singaporeans (*Berita Harian*, 16 July 2005) through the types of strategies outlined above. The main purpose of the exercise was to put the mosques and MUIS in a position where they could foster a 'Singapore Muslim Community of Excellence that is religiously profound and socially progressive'.[22] A major element of this was embedding deep in the minds of Singaporean Muslims an identity as Muslims living as a minority in a multiracial, 'cosmopolitan nation', and accepting the social realities of such a position 'without compromising their true stand as Muslims' (*CyBerita*, 3 November 2005). MUIS went to great lengths to promote this minority identity in a cosmopolitan society, including inviting Muslim scholars from Western countries to address local imams, and providing scholarships to send young Singaporean Muslims to study in the West.

We are not suggesting that there is anything wrong or mischievous with any of the initiatives taken by Yaacob Ibrahim or MUIS, but for our study the main significance is that such drastic surgery was deemed necessary to make MUIS and mosques relevant to the lives of Singaporean Muslims. The accumulation of this evidence suggests that not only are Muslims under-involved with state-based community organisations but also there was a strong disconnection between Muslims and their own Muslim institutions – which are, in any case, state-managed, right down to the appointment of the approximately 850 members of the Mosque Management Boards.[23]

ஆ Chinese

And what of the majority Chinese? At the risk of lapsing into trite generalisations, we would like to venture just a few tentative observations based on the relatively narrow parameters of the research conducted in the course of writing this book: essentially issues of language, education and hegemony, with particular attention to the period after the late 1970s.[24] The Chinese seem to be relatively comfortable with their dominant place at the centre of Singapore society insofar as they are aware of it, but they have such a low level of consciousness of issues of discrimination that they are generally unaware of the advantages they enjoy. This is, perhaps, typical of dominant majorities, but it is worth noting. There has been in fact a tendency to begrudge minorities the minimalist concessions of multiracialism, to assert the imagined entitlements of Chinese living in a Chinese society,[25] to indulge in hostile stereotypes of non-Chinese and to ostracise non-Chinese – particularly Malays and Muslims – in ordinary social and commercial intercourse.[26] These factors go a long way towards accounting for racial discrimination against members of minority races – especially wearers of the *tudung* – in employment, and the aggressive use of Mandarin as a basis of exclusion. They also strongly suggest that four decades of 'multiracialism' has generated only a very superficial state of racial harmony and understanding.[27] We hesitate to suggest that it is even 'skin deep'.

Beyond such a narrow line of inquiry we can make a few other disquieting observations. There has been a high level of dissatisfaction with language policy, especially as it affects educational aspirations and burdens. The generations that suffered the indignity of having their 'dialect' mother tongues stolen from them in the government's push for everyone to speak Mandarin are now an ageing and shrinking minority but the aftermath still haunts younger generations who cannot speak to their grandparents, yet still speak proudly of the 'dialect' origins of their names and their families. A survey conducted around 2002 found that 69 per cent of Chinese would prefer to wear their family's dialect heritage as their racial identifier, rather than being called 'Chinese', and 54 per cent regard a 'dialect', not Mandarin, as their 'mother tongue'.[28] Then again, many champions of Mandarin and 'Chinese culture' bemoan the decline of standards in Mandarin even as many Chinese students and their parents complain about the burdens of bilingualism. On the one hand, learning spoken and written Mandarin singles out English-speaking Chinese students for a particularly heavy workload; on the other hand, those students who have been educated in an all-Chinese, Mandarin-speaking environment often carry a similar burden when trying to learn English. The rewards for success are immense – far beyond, for instance, any rewards that an Indian could ever hope to receive for mastering both Tamil and English – but most students fail to master both languages, and often end up with a command of neither. Perhaps the educational reforms of 2004 will ease some of this pressure and reduce the levels of frustration, but this remains to be seen. If the government can defuse the contradictory frustrations over the language policy, then it will have soothed a festering sore that largely was of its own creation.

National versus Political Loyalty

The evidence that we have accumulated suggests that, in broad and important sections of the community, Singapore's official nation-building project is accepted as satisfactory, rather than endorsed enthusiastically. On the surface this appears to be an adequate arrangement, provided that the system keeps producing enough elites who believe in, and whose careers and livelihood depend on reproducing the Singapore system of governance. It also depends on the capacity of this system to ensure that the dissonance between the elite and the grassroots does not intensify. It seems unlikely that either of these threats will reach a critical point in the near future, which will allow the regime to plan with a substantial level of confidence. Yet the regime's attitude to this situation is precisely the reverse of the relative indifference exhibited at the grassroots. All the rhetoric of the nation-building project suggests that the ruling elite is seeking real commitment in its relationship with its constituency, and is continually disappointed to find itself in an indifferent marriage. Such a yearning was clearly present in the rhetoric of Lee Kuan Yew in the 1960s and 1970s, but we do not have to go back that far. Goh Chok Tong was trying to achieve precisely this effect in his 2002 National Day Rally Speech when he challenged the citizenry to define themselves as either 'stayers' or 'quitters':

> Fair-weather Singaporeans will run away whenever the country runs into stormy weather. I call them 'quitters'. Fortunately, 'quitters' are in the minority. The majority of Singaporeans are 'stayers'. 'Stayers' are committed to Singapore. Rain or shine, they will be with Singapore. ... I take issue with those fair-weather Singaporeans who, having benefited from Singapore, will pack their bags and take flight when our country runs into a little storm (*ST*, 19 August 2002).

Note the personal level at which he issued the challenge. It was rhetoric imbued in patriotic phraseology, demanding commitment to an ideal, not loyalty based on expediency.

The personal character of this call to loyalty leads us to reflect upon another key feature of Singapore's nation-building project: the intimacy with which governmental power is exercised. The regime imposes on its citizenry intimate demands, ranging from control over resources (beginning with land, housing and employment) and the minutia of private life (such as the management of religions, procreation and education) as well as demanding unquestionable loyalty to the political regime. Such all-round management of social life reflects the regime's insecurities, whereby the future and security of the nation are identified in national rhetoric, and in the minds of most Singaporeans, with the future and security of the PAP government. Indeed, the government's success is measured by the twin principles of social loyalty and national patriotism. As Goh Chok Tong said when he first became Prime Minister, the nation's 'good sons and daughters' are expected to 'dedicate themselves to help others' and 'to serve the country' (*ST*, 29 November 1990).

The close identification of regime, nation-state and national community is part of what makes Singapore's nation-building project so brittle. In short, the regime has visited its own insecurities onto the nation via its top-down nation-building efforts. Complaints and criticisms that have been voiced once-off in this book and are voiced regularly in the coffee shops and housing estates do not in the main represent disloyalty to Singapore, but merely criticism of the government – or at most criticism of 'the Singapore system' that is embodied in the regime. Yet they are taken in official circles and implicitly by many of Singaporeans as expressions of disloyalty to the nation, or at the very least of diminishing loyalty. Hence the government monitors closely the feedback it receives about the enthusiasm of 'heartlanders' in displaying the national flag from their balconies in the lead up to National Day and became seriously concerned when, in the aftermath of the 2001 recession, it discovered that 'heartlanders' were showing reluctance to hang the national flag outside their flats in the lead up to National Day, and that even the grassroots leaders were lukewarm about distributing them.[29]

In a country where the regime and the nation are conceptually almost inseparable, displaying the national flag becomes not only an exemplary manifestation of Billig's 'banal nationalism',[30] but also a partisan political statement which implicitly endorses the regime. Such a conflation of national loyalty and political preference is a conscious squandering and marginalisation of the natural affection that ordinary people have for their homeland, based on memories and associations, family, food and familiarity. It is also self-indulgent and puts the nation-building project at risk in the long term. The government would do well to turn its mind to ways in which it could start separating the issue of regime legitimation from the nation-building project. As Singapore becomes more of a cosmopolitan city with an increasingly outward-oriented and cosmopolitan population, such a move could even prove to have pragmatic benefits for the economy and the regime.

★

In the meantime, Singapore remains a project 'under construction', based upon the dynamics of perpetual experimentation and perpetual revisionism. Little is stable or settled and much is in a state of flux. The professionalism of the 'elite', and the indefinable but very real peace of mind created by the myths of meritocracy and multiracialism are the three central elements of Singaporeans' sense of security, but even these are being exposed gradually to all as fragile constructions that hide injustices and distortions based on class, ethnicity-cum-race, and personal power networks. In the meantime, flags keep flying (or at least draping) from balconies and elite schools keep producing new candidates for the elite. The construction of Singapore can therefore be expected to continue unabated for the medium term, but it remains to be seen how these contradictions within the official nation-building project will resolve themselves.

Notes

1   For instance, in 1989 Lee Kuan Yew sued the *Far Eastern Economic Review*, and reduced its circulation in Singapore to 500 because he objected to some of its reporting on Singapore affairs. This episode found an echo in the 2006 decision to ban the sale of *FEER* completely.

2   Also see 'Official Report into Singapore Tunnel Collapse Reveals Shocking Design and Construction Failings: Nicoll Highway investigators fear repeat collapse', *New Civil Engineer*, 23 September 2004; and reports at the *New Civil Engineer* website on www. nceplus.co.uk/. Accessed 7 May 2005.

3   Michael D. Barr, 'Singapore', in Robin Gauld, *Comparative Health Policy in the Asia-Pacific*, Maidenhead, UK: Open University Press, 2005, p. 168.

4   Peter Ho, 'Preparing for the Future', *Ethos*, July-September 2005, p. 3.

5   'Government failed over Kidney Foundation scandal: minister', *Agence France Presse*, 21 December 2005, cited on Singapore Window on www.singapore-window.org. Accessed on 2 January 2006.

6   See, for instance, 'Why only Chinese on McDonald's packaging? We're a multiracial society. Use neutral English', and 'Non-Malay won't get into lift with Malay. How civil are we if we can't be civil to fellow Singaporeans?', both in the online-only Forum page of *The Straits Times Interactive*, 8 November 2005.

7   See Chapter 11.

8   We have dealt with many issues related to questions of class in this book, but only as they have impinged upon themes of exclusion and inclusion in education and elite selection. For a dedicated study of class in Singapore, see Tan Ern Ser, *Does Class Matter? Social Stratification and Orientations in Singapore*, Singapore: World Scientific, 2004.

9   Barr's interview with a member of a grassroots organisation, Singapore, 15 April 2004.

10 Barr's interview with a former member of a grassroots organisation, Singapore, 13 March 2003.

11 Barr's interview with a grassroots leader, Singapore, 8 April 2003.

12 Clark D. Neher, 'Asian Style Democracy', *Asian Survey*, vol. 34, no. 11, 1994, pp. 949–961.

13 See, for instance, the 2006 General Election results, where the Malays voted for the PAP more strongly than other ethnic groups. This result can be perceived as pro-active support for the PAP, but we believe that it would be more accurate to say that it reflects the success of the government's co-option Malay community leadership and the concomitant failure of the Chinese- and Indian-dominated opposition parties to build substantial links with the Malay community.

14 See, for instance, Chee Keng John Wang, Angeline Khoo, Chor Boon Goh, Steven Tan and S. Gopinathan, 'Patriotism and National Education: Perceptions of Trainee Teachers in Singapore', *Asia Pacific Journal of Education*, vol. 26, no. 1, 2006, pp. 51–64.

15 Ooi Giok Ling, 'The Role of the Development State and Interethnic Relations in Singapore', *Asian Ethnicity*, vol. 6, no. 2, 2005, pp. 109–120.

16 *Parliamentary Debates, Singapore, Official Report, Tenth Parliament*, Thursday 23 May 2002.

17 Yaacob Ibrahim, Speech by Dr Yaacob Ibrahim, Minister-in-Charge of Muslim Affairs, at the MUIS Work Plan Seminar 2005, 5 February 2005. Available as a Singapore Government Press Release at http://app.sprinter.gov.sg/data/pr/200502-5998.htm. Accessed on 15 November 2005. MUIS has always issued Friday sermons centrally. Today they are available on the MUIS website http://www.muis.gov.sg/rservices.

18 See MUIS website at http://www.muis.gov.sg.

19 See MUIS/Mosques website at http://cmsweb.mosque.org.sg. Accessed 15 November 2005.

20 Ibid.

21 Yaacob Ibrahim, Speech at MUIS Work Plan Seminar. The government's involvement in this programme makes Lee Kuan Yew's outburst all the more extraordinary.

22 Ibid.

23 See MUIS/Mosques website.

24 Unfortunately these parameters exclude major aspects of inquiry, such as the place of Nanyang University graduates, clan associations and Chinese SMEs. These and many other aspects of Singaporean Chinese social history would be indispensable in a full

study of the place of Chinese in Singaporean nation building but must regrettably be passed over in this cursory overview. Academia has only just begun seriously exploring the place of Chinese in independent Singapore. Early products of such efforts include: Sikko Visscher, *The Business of Politics and Ethnicity: A History of the Singapore Chinese Chamber of Commerce and Industry*, Singapore: National University of Singapore Press, 2007; Eugene K.B. Tan, 'The Majority's Sacrifices and Yearnings: Chinese-Singaporeans and the Dilemmas of Nation-Building', in Leo Suryadinata (ed.), *Ethnic Relations and Nation-Building in Southeast Asia: The Case of the Ethnic Chinese*, Singapore: Singapore Society of Asian Studies and Institute of Southeast Asian Studies, 2004, pp. 168–206; Eugene K.B. Tan, 'Re-engaging Chineseness: Political, Economic and cultural imperatives of nation-building in Singapore', *China Quarterly*, vol. 175, 2003, pp. 751–774; Chiew Seen Kong, 'Chinese Singaporeans: Three Decades of Progress and Changes', in Leo Suryadinata (ed.), *Ethnic Chinese in Singapore and Malaysia: A Dialogue Between Tradition and Modernity*, Singapore: Times Academic Press, 2002, pp. 11–44.

25 Raj Vasil, *Governing Singapore: Democracy and National* Development, St Leonards, NSW: Allen and Unwin, 2000, pp. 185–89; Kwok Kian Woon, 'Singapore' in Lynn Pan (ed.), *The Encyclopaedia of the Chinese Overseas*, Singapore: Archipelago Press and Landmark Books, 1998, p. 215.

26 Rahil Ismail and Brian J. Shaw, 'Singapore's Malay-Muslim minority: social identification in a post-'9/11' world', *Asian Ethnicity*, vol. 7, no. 1, 2006, p. 41.

27 Ibid.

28 Tan, 'The Majority's Sacrifices and Yearnings', p. 189.

29 Barr's interview with a former member of a grassroots organisation, Singapore, 13 March 2003; with a member of a grassroots organisation, Singapore, 15 April 2004; and with a grassroots leader, Singapore, 8 April 2003. Also see the opening quotation and photograph at the beginning of this chapter.

30 Michael Billig, *Banal Nationalism*, London: Sage, 1995.

Bibliography

Anderson, Benedict, *Imagined Communities*, London: Verso, 1993.

———, 'Western nationalism and Eastern nationalism: is there a difference that matters?', *New Left Review*, vol. 9, 2001, pp. 31–42.

Ang Beng Choo, 'The teaching of the Chinese language in Singapore', in S. Gopinathan, Anne Pakir, Ho Wah Kam and Vaithamani Saravanan (eds), *Language, Society and Education in Singapore: Issues and Trends*, Second Edition, Singapore: Times Academic Press, 1998, pp. 335–352.

Ang Wai Hoong and Yeoh Oon Chye, '25 years of curriculum development', in John Yip Soon Kwong and Sim Wong Kooi (eds), *Evolution of Educational Excellence: 25 Years of Education in the Republic of Singapore*, Singapore: Longman, 1990, pp. 85–109.

Barr, Michael D., 'Lee Kuan Yew in Malaysia: a reappraisal of Lee Kuan Yew's role in the separation of Singapore from Malaysia', *Asian Studies Review*, vol. 21, no. 1, 1997, pp. 1–17.

———, *Lee Kuan Yew: The Beliefs Behind the Man*, Richmond, UK: Curzon, 2000.

———, 'Lee Kuan Yew and the 'Asian values' debate', *Asian Studies Review*, vol. 24, no. 3, 2000, pp. 309–334.

———, 'Lee Kuan Yew's Fabian phase', *Australian Journal of Politics and History*, vol. 46, no. 1, 2000, pp. 109–124.

———, 'Trade unions in an elitist society: the Singapore story', *Australian Journal of Politics and History*, vol. 46, no. 4, 2000, pp. 481–498.

———, 'Medical savings accounts in Singapore: a critical inquiry', *Journal of Health Politics, Policy and Law*, vol. 26, no. 3, 2001, pp. 707–724.

———, 'Perpetual Revisionism in Singapore: The Limits of Change', *The Pacific Review*, vol. 16, no. 1, 2003, pp. 77–97.

———, *Cultural Politics and Asian Values: The Tepid War*, London and New York: Routledge, 2002, 2004.

———, 'J.B. Jeyaretnam: Thirty years as Lee Kuan Yew's *bête noir*', *Journal of Contemporary Asia*, vol. 33, no. 3, 2003, pp. 299–317.

———, 'Perpetual revisionism in Singapore: the limits of change', *The Pacific Review*, vol. 6, no. 1, 2003, pp. 77–97.

———, 'Singapore', in Robin Gauld (ed.), *Comparative Health Policy in the Asia-Pacific*, Maidenhead, UK: Open University Press, 2004, pp. 146–173

———, 'Beyond technocracy: the culture of elite governance in Lee Hsien Loong's Singapore', *Asian Studies Review*, vol. 30, no. 1, 2006, pp. 1–17.

———, 'Racialised education in Singapore', *Educational Research for Policy and Practice*, vol. 5, no. 1, 2006, pp. 15–31.

Barr, Michael D. and Jevon Low, 'Assimilation as multiracialism: the case of Singapore's Malays', *Asian Ethnicity*, vol. 6, no. 3, 2005, pp. 161–182.

Barr, Michael D. and Carl A. Trocki (eds), *Index of Political Headlines of Singapore's and Malaya's Vernacular Press: December 1953–September 1961*, Brisbane: Centre for Social Change Research, Queensland University of Technology, 2002, available online at http://www.pathsnottaken.qut.edu.au/.

———, *Paths Not Taken: Political Pluralism in Postwar Singapore*, Singapore: National University of Singapore Press, 2008.

Beiner, R. (ed), *Theorizing Nationalism*, Albany: State University of New York Press, 1999.

Bellows, Thomas. J., 'Bureaucracy and development in Singapore', *Asian Journal of Public Administration*, vol. 7, no. 1, 1985, pp. 55–69.

Benjamin, Geoffrey O. 'The cultural logic of Singapore's "multiracialism"', in Ong Jin Hui *et al.* (eds), *Understanding Singapore Society.*, Singapore: Times Academic Press, 1997, pp. 67–85.

Billig, Michael, *Banal Nationalism*, London: Sage, 1995.

Brown, David, *The State and Ethnic Politics in Southeast Asia*, London, Routledge, 1994.

———, 'Contending Nationalisms in Southeast Asia', Working Paper No. 117, Asia Research Centre, Murdoch University, Perth, January 2005.

————, *Contemporary Nationalism: Civic, Ethnocultural and Multicultural Politics*, London and New York: Routledge, 2000.

Brown, Michael E. and Šumit Ganguly, *Fighting Words: Language Policy and Ethnic Relations*, Cambridge, Mass. and London: The MIT Press, 2003.

Butterworth, Herbert, *A Whig Interpretation of History*, London: G. Bell & Sons, 1931.

Chan Heng Chee, *Singapore: The Politics of Survival 1965–1967*, Singapore and Kuala Lumpur: Oxford University Press, 1971.

————, 'The PAP and the structuring of the political system', in Kernial Singh Sandhu and Paul Wheatley (eds), *Management of Success: The Moulding of Modern Singapore*, Singapore: Institute of Southeast Asian Studies, 1989, pp. 70–89.

Chayan Vaddhanaphuti, 'The Thai state and ethnic minorities: from assimilation to selective integration', in Kusuma Snitwongse and W. Scott Thompson (eds), *Ethnic Conflicts in Southeast Asia*, Singapore: Institute of Southeast Asian Studies, 2005, pp. 151–166.

Cheah Boon Kheng, 'Ethnicity in the making of Malaysia', in Wang Gungwu (ed.), *Nation-Building: Five Southeast Asian Histories*, Singapore: Institute of Southeast Asian Studies, 2005, pp. 91–115.

Chee Keng John Wang, Angeline Khoo, Chor Boon Goh, Steven Tan and S. Gopinathan, 'Patriotism and National Education: Perceptions of Trainee Teachers in Singapore', *Asia Pacific Journal of Education*, vol. 26, no. 1 2006, pp. 51–64.

Chew, Melanie (ed.), *Leaders of Singapore*, Singapore: Resource Press, 1996.

Chiew Seen Kong 'The socio-cultural framework of politics', in Ong Jin Hui *et al.* (eds), *Understanding Singapore Society*, Singapore: Times Academic Press, 1997, pp. 86–106.

————, Chinese Singaporeans: three decades of progress and changes', in Leo Suryadinata (ed.), *Ethnic Chinese in Singapore and Malaysia: A Dialogue Between Tradition and Modernity*, Singapore: Times Academic Press, 2002, pp. 11–44.

Chua Ai Lin, 'Negotiating national identity: the English-speaking domiciled communities in Singapore, 1930–1941', MA thesis, Department of History, National University of Singapore, 2001.

Chua Beng Huat, 'Racial-Singaporeans: absence after the hyphen', *Social Scientist*, vol. 24, no. 7–8, 1996, pp. 51–68.

———, *Political Legitimacy and Housing: Stakeholding in Singapore*, London and New York: Routledge, 1997.

———, 'Culture, multiracialism, and national identity in Singapore', in Kuan-Hsing Chen *et al* (eds), *Trajectories: Inter-Asia Cultural Studies*, London and New York: Routledge, 1998, pp. 186–205.

———, 'Multiculturalism in Singapore: an instrument of social control', *Race and Class*, vol. 44, no. 3, 2003, pp. 58–77.

Clammer, John, *Singapore: Ideology, Society, Culture*, Singapore: Chopmen, 1985.

Connor, Walker, 'A nation is a nation, is a state, is an ethnic group, is a … ', *Ethnic and Racial Studies*, vol. 1, 1978, pp. 377–400.

Cranston, M., *John Stuart Mill*, London: Longmans, Green & Co, 1967.

Cummings, W.K., S. Gopinathan and Y. Tomoda (eds), *The Revival of Values Education in Asia and the West*, Oxford: Pergamon Press, 1988.

Deutsch, Karl W., 'Nation-building and national development: some issues for political research', in Karl W. Deutsch and William J. Foltz (eds), *Nation-Building*, New York: Atherton Press, 1963, pp. 1–16.

Deutsch, Karl W. and William J. Foltz (eds), *Nation-Building*, New York: Atherton Press, 1963.

Drysdale, John, *Singapore: Struggle for Success*, Singapore and Kuala Lumpur: Times Editions, 1984.

Elson, R.E., 'Constructing the nation: ethnicity, race, modernity and citizenship in early Indonesian thought', *Asian Ethnicity*, vol. 6, no. 3, 2005, pp. 145–160.

Eng Soo Peck *et al.*, *Principals' and Teachers' Views on Teaching Monolingual Classes*, Singapore: Institute of Education, 1982.

Evans, Grant, 'Laos: minorities', in Colin Mackerras (ed.), *Ethnicity in Asia*, London and New York: RoutledgeCurzon, 2003, pp. 210–224.

Furnivall, J.S., *Colonial Policy and Practice: A Comparative Study of Burma and Netherlands India*, Cambridge: Cambridge University Press, 1948.

Gans, Herbert, 'Symbolic ethnicity: the future of ethnic groups and cultures in America', *Ethnic and Racial Studies*, vol. 2, no. 1, 1979, pp. 1–20.

————, 'Symbolic ethnicity and symbolic religiosity: towards a comparison of ethnic and religious acculturation', *Ethnic and Racial Studies*, vol. 17, no. 4, 1994, pp. 577–592.

Gauld, Robin (ed.), *Comparative Health Policy in the Asia-Pacific*, Maidenhead, UK: Open University Press, 2004.

Geertz, Clifford, *The Interpretation of Cultures*, London: Fontana, 1973.

George, Cherian, *Singapore – The Air-Conditioned Nation: Essays on the Politics of Comfort and Control 1990–2000*, Singapore: Landmark Books, 2000.

Giddens, Anthony, *The Nation-State and Violence*, Cambridge: Polity Press, 1985.

Glad, Ingrid, *An Identity Dilemma: A Comparative Study of Primary Education for Ethnic Chinese in the Context of National Identity and Nation-Building in Malaysia and Singapore*, Oslo, Scandinavian University Press, 1998.

Goh, Cheryl, *Chinese Enrichment for Nursery*, Singapore: Success Publications, 2002.

————, *Child Development Programme, Nursery Book 4*, Singapore: System Publishing House, 2001 (revised 2002, reprinted 2003, 2004).

————, *Learning Skills for Early Years, Numbers, Nursery*, [Singapore]: Educational Publishing, [c. 2004].

Goh Chi Lan and the principals of the Study Team, *Towards Excellence in Schools: A Report to the Minister for Education February 1987*, Singapore: Ministry of Education, 1987.

Goh Chok Tong, Speech by Goh Chok Tong, First Deputy Prime Minister and Minister for Defence, at the Opening of PAP Community Foundation Education Centre, Tampines Branch, 6 August 1987, Singapore Government Press Release. Available at http://sprinter.gov.sg/. Accessed 24 May 2005.

————, Singapore Government Press Release. Speech by Mr Goh Chok Tong, Minister for Health and Second Minister for Defence, at the Singapore General Hospital (SGH), Nite 1982, 6 March 1982. Available at National Archives of Singapore, at http://www.museum.org.sg/NAS/nas.shtml/.

Goh, Joyce, *English Kindergarten 1 Term 3*, Singapore: Oxford University Press, 1995.

Goh Keng Swee and The Education Study Team, *Report on the Ministry of Education 1978*, Singapore: [Singapore National Printers], 1979.

Gopinathan, S., 'Being and becoming: education for values in Singapore', in W.K. Cummings, S. Gopinathan and Y. Tomoda (eds), *The Revival of Values Education in Asia and the West*, Oxford: Pergamon Press: 1988, pp. 131–162.

Gopinathan, S., Anne Pakir, Ho Wah Kam and Vaithamani Saravanan (eds), *Language, Society and Education in Singapore: Issues and Trends*, Second Edition, Singapore: Times Academic Press, 1998.

Greenfeld, Liah, 'Nationalism in Western and Eastern Europe compared', in Stephen E. Hanson and Willfried Spohn (eds), *Can Europe Work? Germany and the Reconstruction of Postcommunist Societies*, Seattle and London: University of Washington Press, 1995, pp. 15–23.

Haggay, R. 'The immemorial Iranian nation? School textbooks and historical memory in post-revolutionary Iran', *Nations and Nationalism*, vol. 6, no. 1, 2000, pp. 67–90.

Han Fook Kwang, Warren Fernadez and Sumiko Tan (eds), *Lee Kuan Yew: The Man and His Ideas*, Singapore: Singapore Press Holdings and Times Editions, 1998.

Hanson, Stephen E., and Willfried Spohn (eds), *Can Europe Work? Germany and the Reconstruction of Postcommunist Societies*, Seattle and London: University of Washington Press, 1995.

Hassan, Riaz (ed.), *Singapore: Society in Transition*, Kuala Lumpur: Oxford University Press, 1976.

Hastings, A., *The Construction of Nationhood: Ethnicity, Religion, and Nationalism.*, Cambridge: Cambridge University Press, 1997.

Heng, Geraldine and Janadas Devan, 'State fatherhood: the politics of nationalism, sexuality, and race in Singapore', in Andrew Parker *et al.* (eds), *Nationalisms and Sexualities.*, London and New York: Routledge, 1992, pp. 343–364.

Hill, Michael and Lian Kwen Fee, *The Politics of Nation Building and Citizenship in Singapore*, London and New York: Routledge, 1995.

Ho, Peter, 'Preparing for the future', *Ethos*, July–September 2005, pp. 3–6.

Holden, Philip, 'A man and an island: gender and nation in Lee Kuan Yew's *The Singapore Story*', *Biography*, vol. 24, no. 2, 2001, pp. 401–424.

Hong Lysa, 'Making the history of Singapore: S. Rajaratnam and C.V. Devan Nair', in Lam Peng Er and Kevin Y.L. Tan (eds), *Lee's Lieutenants: Singapore's Old Guard*, St Leonards, NSW: Allen & Unwin, 1999, pp. 96–115.

Huff, W.G., 'What is the Singapore model of economic development?', *Cambridge Journal of Economics*, 19, 1995, pp. 735–759.

———, 'Turning the corner in Singapore's developmental state?', *Asian Survey*, vol. 39, no. 2, 1999, pp. 214–242.

Huthinson, William and Hartmut Lehmann (eds.), *Many Are Chosen: Divine Election and Western Nationalism*, Minneapolis: Fortress Press, 1994.

Huxley, Tim, 'Singapore's soldier scholars', *Asian Wall Street Journal*, 24 February 1995.

———, *Defending the Lion City: The Armed Forces of Singapore*, St Leonards, NSW: Allen & Unwin, 2000.

Ishak, A. Rahim, Speech by Senior Minister of State for Foreign Affairs, Encik A. Rahim Ishak, at the Siglap Community Centre Kindergarten, 5 November 1977, Singapore Government Press Release, located at http://www.sprinter.gov.sg/.

———, Speech by Mr A. Rahim Ishak, Senior Minister of State for Foreign Affairs and MP for Siglap Constituency, at the PAP Siglap Branch Kindergarten Presentation of Certificates, 18 November 1977, Singapore Government Press Release, located at http://www.sprinter.gov.sg/.

Ismail, Rahil and Brian J. Shaw, 'Singapore's Malay-Muslim minority: social identification in a post-'9/11' world', *Asian Ethnicity*, vol. 7, no. 1, 2006, pp. 37–51.

James, Joyce, 'Linguistic realities and pedagogical practices in Singapore: another perspective', in S. Gopinathan, Anne Pakir, Ho Wah Kam and Vaithamani Saravanan (eds), *Language, Society and Education in Singapore: Issues and Trends*, Second Edition, Singapore: Times Academic Press, 1998, pp. 99–116.

Jelavich, C. 'Serbian textbooks: toward greater Serbia or Yugoslavia?', *Slavic Review*, vol. 42, no. 4, 1983, pp. 601–619.

Johannen, Uwe and James Gomez, *Democratic Transitions in Asia*, Singapore: Select Publishing in association with Friedrich Naumann Foundation, 2001.

Johnson, Chalmers, *MITI and the Japanese Miracle: Growth of Industrial Policy, 1925–1975*, Stanford: Stanford University Press, 1982.

Josey, Alex, *Lee Kuan Yew: The Crucial Years*, Singapore and Kuala Lumpur: Times Books International, 1980.

Junko Kato, *The Problem of Bureaucratic Rationality: Tax Politics in* Japan, Princeton, NJ: Princeton University Press, 1994.

Juve, Richard G., 'Education as an integrating force in Singapore, a multi-cultural society', dissertation in the Graduate School of Education, Rutgers University, 1975.

Kamaludeen bin Mohamed Nasir, 'Disciplining Islam: a Foucauldian analysis of Islam in Singapore', Honours Thesis, Department of Sociology, National University of Singapore, 2004.

Kang, Trivina, 'Schools and post-secondary aspirations among female Chinese, Malay and Indian Normal Stream students', in Lai Ah Eng (ed.), *Beyond Rituals and Riots: Ethnic Pluralism and Social Cohesion in Singapore*, Singapore: Eastern Universities Press by Marshall Cavendish for Institute of Policy Studies, 2004, pp. 146–171.

———, 'Diversification of Singapore's upper secondary landscape: introduction of integrated programmes, specialised independent schools and privately-funded schools', in Jason Tan and Ng Pak Tee (eds), *Shaping Singapore's Future: Thinking Schools, Learning Nation*, Singapore: Pearson Education, 2005, pp. 52–67.

Kaufman, E. and O. Zimmer, '"Dominant ethnicity" and the "ethnic-civic" dichotomy in the work of A.D. Smith', *Nations and Nationalism*, vol. 10, nos. 1–2, 2004, pp. 63–78.

Keith, Patrick, *Ousted!*, Singapore: Media Masters, 2005.

Keyes, Charles F., 'The politics of language in Thailand and Laos', in Michael E. Brown and Sumit Ganguly, *Fighting Words: Language Policy and Ethnic Relations*, Cambridge, Mass. And London: The MIT Press, 2003, pp. 151–166.

Khaw Boon Wan, Ministry of Health Budget Speech (Part 1), on Wednesday, 17 March 2004 by Mr Khaw Boon Wan, then Acting Minister for Health.

Available on the Singapore Government website, http://www.moh.gov.sg/.

Khong, Lana, Joy Chew and Jonathan Goh, 'How now NE? an exploratory study of ethnic relations in three Singapore schools', in Lai Ah Eng (ed.), *Beyond Rituals and Riots: Ethnic Pluralism and Social Cohesion in Singapore*, Singapore: Eastern Universities Press by Marshall Cavendish for the Institute of Policy Studies, 2004, pp. 172–196.

Khoo, Angeline and Lim Kam Ming, 'Trainee teachers' stereotypes of ethnic groups in Singapore', in Lai Ah Eng (ed.), *Beyond Rituals and Riots: Ethnic Pluralism and Social Cohesion in Singapore*, Singapore: Eastern Universities Press by Marshall Cavendish for Institute of Policy Studies, 2004, pp. 197–227.

Koh, B.C., *Japan's Administrative Elite*, Berkeley, Los Angeles and Oxford: University of California Press, 1989.

Koh Choon Teck, *Growing Up with Lee Kuan Yew*, Singapore: Educational Publishing House, 2000, 2001.

Kong, Lily L., and Jasmine S. Chan, 'Patriarchy and pragmatism: ideological contradictions in state policies' *Asian Studies Review*, vol. 24, no. 4, 2000, pp. 501–531.

Kusuma Snitwongse and W. Scott Thompson (eds), *Ethnic Conflicts in Southeast Asia*, Singapore: Institute of Security and International Studies, and Institute of Southeast Asian Studies, 2005.

Kwa Kok Beng, 'Multiculturalism or multiracialism? a critical analysis of the portrayal of race in Primary One English textbooks in Singapore', Honours thesis in English Language, National Institute of Education, Singapore, 2004.

Kwok Kian Woon, 'Singapore' in Lynn Pan (ed.), *The Encyclopaedia of the Chinese Overseas*, Singapore: Archipelago Press and Landmark Books, 1998, pp. 200–217.

Lai Ah Eng, *Meanings of Multiethnicity: A Case Study of Ethnicity and Ethnic Relations in Singapore*, Singapore: Oxford University Press, 1995.

———, 'Introduction: beyond rituals and riots', in Lai Ah Eng (ed.), *Beyond Rituals and Riots: Ethnic Pluralism and Social Cohesion in Singapore*, Singapore: Eastern Universities Press by Marshall Cavendish for Institute of Policy Studies, 2004, pp. 1–40.

———— (ed.), *Beyond Rituals and Riots: Ethnic Pluralism and Social Cohesion in Singapore*, Singapore: Eastern Universities Press by Marshall Cavendish for the Institute of Policy Studies, 2004.

Lam Peng Er and Tan, Kevin Y.L. (eds), *Lee's Lieutenants: Singapore's Old Guard*, St Leonards, NSW: Allen & Unwin, 1999.

Lau, Albert, *A Moment of Anguish: Singapore in Malaysia and the politics of disengagement*, Singapore: Times Academic Press, 1998.

Lau, Lydia, *Pre-School, Covering Primary 1 Syllabus, Vocabulary, Book 3*, Singapore: Casco Publications, [c. 2004].

Lee Bee Geok, *Census of Population 2000: Household and Housing*, Singapore: Department of Statistics, 2001.

Lee Boon Hiok, 'The bureaucracy', in Kernial Singh Sandhu and Paul Wheatley (eds), *Management of Success: The Moulding of Modern Singapore*, Singapore: Institute of Southeast Asian Studies, 1989, pp. 90–101.

Lee Hsien Loong, 'Staying ahead – scenarios and challenges', *Ethos*, 1994, Issue 3, no page numbers indicated.

————, 'Deputy Prime Minister Lee Hsien Loong's speech at the SAF Overseas Scholarship 30th Anniversary Dinner, 15 April 2001', Ministry of Trade and Industry website, available at http://www.mti.gov.sg.

————, 'Prime Minister Lee Hsien Loong's National Day Rally 2004 Speech, Sunday 22 August 2004, at the University Cultural Centre, National University of Singapore'. Cited on Sprinter [Singapore Government news service] http://www.sprinter.gov.sg/.

————, 'Speech by Prime Minister Lee Hsien Loong at the 2005 Administrative Service Dinner, 24 March 2005'. Cited on Sprinter [Singapore Government news service] http://www.sprinter.gov.sg/.

Lee Kuan Yew, *Prime Minister's Speeches, Press Conferences, Interviews, Statements, etc.*, Singapore: Prime Minister's Office, 1965.

————, *New Bearings in Our Education System*, Singapore: Ministry of Culture, [1966–67].

————, *The Singapore Story. Memoirs of Lee Kuan Yew*, Singapore: Prentice Hall, 1998.

————, *A Selection of Lee Kuan Yew's Speeches Over 40 Years* (Chinese Edition), Singapore: Federal Publications, 1993.

————, *From Third World to First: The Singapore Story: 1965–2000: Memoirs of Lee Kuan Yew*, Singapore: Singapore Press Holdings and Times Editions, 2000.

————, *The Singapore Story: Memoirs of Lee Kuan Yew* (abridged student's edition), Singapore: Federal Publications, 2000.

————, *Lee Kuan Yew at 80: 80 quotes from a life* [in English and Mandarin], Singapore: Lianhe Zaobao, 2003.

———— (ed. Chua Chee Lay), *Keeping My Mandarin Alive: Lee Kuan Yew's Language Learning Experience*, Singapore: World Scientific and Global Publishing, 2005.

Lee, Christine, Mary Cherian, Rahil Ismail, Maureen Ng, Jasmine Sim and Chee Min Fui, 'Children's experiences of multiracial relationships in informal primary school settings', in Lai Ah Eng (ed.), *Beyond Rituals and Riots: Ethnic Pluralism and Social Cohesion in Singapore*, Singapore: Eastern Universities Press by Marshall Cavendish for Institute of Policy Studies, 2004, pp. 114–145.

Leong Yf and Zenda Leu, *From Kindergarten to P1*, [Singapore]: Teacher-Pupil Connections, [c.2000].

Li, Tania, *Malays in Singapore: Culture, Economy, and Ideology*, Singapore: Oxford University Press, 1989.

Lim Siong Guan, 'The new public administration: global challenges, local solutions – the Singapore experience', *Ethos*, August 1996, no page numbers indicated.

————, 'Is there a new role for government?', *Ethos*, January–March, 2005, pp. 3–9.

Lim Soon Tae and S. Gopinathan, '25 years of curriculum planning', in John Yip Soon Kwong and Sim Wong Kooi (eds), *Evolution of Educational Excellence: 25 Years of Education in the Republic of Singapore*, Singapore: Longman, 1990, pp. 61–83.

Lind, Andrew W., *Nanyang Perspectives: Chinese Students in Multiracial Singapore*, Honolulu, University Press of Hawaii, 1974.

Liow, Y.B., *Nursery Activity Book Term 2*, Singapore: Oxford University Press, 1995.

Low Kar Tiang and Dunlop, Peter K.G. (eds), *Who's Who in Singapore*, Singapore: Who's Who Publishing, 2000.

Mackerras, Colin (ed.), *Ethnicity in Asia*, London and New York: Routledge-Curzon, 2003.

Marx, Karl, *Eighteenth Brumaire of Louis Bonaparte*, Moscow: Progress Publishers, 1954.

Mauzy, Diane K. and R.S. Milne, *Singapore Politics Under the People's Action Party*, London and New York: Routledge, 2002.

Miksic, J.N., *Archaeological Research on the Forbidden Hill of Singapore: Excavations at Fort Canning*, Singapore: National Museum, 1985.

Mill, John Stuart (ed. S. Collin), *On Liberty with The Subjection of Women and Chapters on Socialism*, Cambridge: Cambridge University Press, 1989.

Mok, Ka-ho, 'Decentralization and marketization of education in Singapore: A case study of the School Excellence Model', *Journal of Educational Administration*, vol. 41, no. 4, 2003, pp. 348–366.

Moore, Quinn R., 'Multiracialism and meritocracy: Singapore's approach to race and inequality', *Review of Social Economy*, vol. 58, no. 3, 2000, pp. 339–360.

Neher, Clark D., 'Asian style democracy', *Asian Survey*, vol. 34, no. 11, 1994, pp. 949–961.

Ng Pak Tee, 'Students' perception of change in the Singapore education system', *Educational Research for Policy and Practice*, vol. 3, no. 1, 2004, pp. 77–92.

Ong Jin Hui *et al.* (eds), *Understanding Singapore Society*, Singapore: Times Academic Press, 1997.

Ong Jin Hui, Tong Chee Kiong and Tan Ern Ser (eds), *Understanding Singapore Society*, Singapore: Times Academic Press, 1997.

Ooi Giok Ling, 'The role of the development state and interethnic relations in Singapore', *Asian Ethnicity*, vol. 6, no. 2, 2005, pp. 109–120.

Pan, Lynn (ed.), *The Encyclopaedia of the Chinese Overseas*, Singapore: Archipelago Press and Landmark Books, 1998.

Pellizzoni, Luigi, 'The myth of the best argument: power, deliberation and reason', *British Journal of Sociology*, vol. 52, no. 1, 2001, pp. 59–86.

Pillay, J.Y., 'Reflections of a recycled bureaucrat', *Ethos*, April 2004, pp. 10–13.

Pogden, A. (ed), *The Idea of Europe: From Antiquity to the European Union*, Cambridge: Cambridge University Press, 2002.

Rahim, Lily Zubaidah, *The Singapore Dilemma: The Political and Educational Marginality of the Malay Community*, Kuala Lumpur: Oxford University Press, 1998.

———, 'The political agenda underpinning economic policy formulation in Singapore's authoritarian developmental state', in Uwe Johannen and James Gomez, *Democratic Transitions in Asia*, Singapore: Select Publishing in association with Friedrich Naumann Foundation, 2001, pp. 207–232.

Reynolds, Craig J., 'Nation and state in histories of nation-building, with special reference to Thailand', in Wang Gungwu (ed.), *Nation-Building: Five Southeast Asian Histories*, Singapore: Institute of Southeast Asian Studies, 2005, pp. 21–38.

Richard Juve, 'Education as an integrating force in Singapore, a multi-cultural society', dissertation for Doctor of Education, Graduate School of Education, Rutgers University, 1975.

Rodan, Garry, *Transparency and Authoritarian Rule in Southeast Asia: Singapore and Malaysia*, London and New York: Routledge, 2005.

Rodriguez, S.J. (ed.), *Lee Kuan Yew in His Own Words – Book 1: 1959 to 1970*, Singapore: Hurricane, 2003.

Sandhu, Kernial Singh and Paul Wheatley (eds), *Management of Success: The Moulding of Modern Singapore*, Singapore: Institute of Southeast Asian Studies, 1989.

Schein, Edgar H., *Strategic Pragmatism: The Culture of the Economic Development Board*, Singapore: Toppan Company and MIT Press, 1996.

Seah Chee Meow, *Community Centres in Singapore: Their Political Involvement*, Singapore: Singapore University Press, 1973.

———, 'The Singapore bureaucracy and issues of transition', in Riaz Hassan (ed.), *Singapore: Society in Transition*, Kuala Lumpur: Oxford University Press, 1976, pp. 52–67.

Sekulic, D., Massey, G. and Hodson, R., 'Who were the Yugoslavs? Failed sources of a common identity in the Former Yugoslavia', *American Sociological Review*, vol. 59, 1994, pp. 83–97.

Shamira Bhanu Abdul Azeez, *The Singapore–Malaysia 'Remerger' Debate of 1996*, [Hull]: Centre for South-East Asian Studies and Institute of Pacific Asia Studies, The University of Hull, 1998.

Shepherd, Janet, *Striking a Balance: The Management of Language in Singapore*, Frankfurt, Peter Lang, 2005.

Siddique, Sharon, 'The phenomenon of ethnicity: a Singapore case study', in Ong Jin Hue *et al.* (eds), *Understanding Singapore Society*, Singapore: Times Academic Press, 1997, pp. 107–124.

Silver, Rita Elaine 'The discourse of linguistic capital: language and economic policy planning in Singapore', *Language Policy*, vol. 4, 2005, pp. 47–66.

Skrbiš, Zlatko, *Long-distance Nationalism: Diasporas, Homelands and Identities*, Ashgate: Aldershot, 1999.

Smith, D. Anthony, *Chosen Peoples: Sacred Sources of National Identity*, Oxford: University Press, 2003.

Sukma, Rizal, 'Ethnic conflict in Indonesia: causes and the quest for solution', in Kusuma Snitwongse and W. Scott Thompson (eds), *Ethnic Conflicts in Southeast Asia*, Singapore: Institute of Security and International Studies, and Institute of Southeast Asian Studies, 2005, pp. 1–41.

Sukmawati bte Haji Sirat, 'Trends in Malay political leadership: the People's Action Party's Malay political leaders and the integration of the Singapore Malays', PhD thesis, Department of Government and International Studies, University of South Carolina, 1995.

Suryadinata, Leo (ed.), *Ethnic Chinese in Singapore and Malaysia: A Dialogue Between Tradition and Modernity*, Singapore: Times Academic Press, 2002.

——— (ed.), *Ethnic Relations and Nation-Building in Southeast Asia: The Case of the Ethnic Chinese*, Singapore: Singapore Society of Southeast Asian Studies and Institute of Southeast Asian Studies, 2004.

Tamney, Joseph B., *The Struggle Over Singapore's Soul: Western Modernization and Asian Culture*, Berlin and New York: Walter De Gruyter, 1996.

Tan, Charlene, 'Driven by pragmatism: issues and challenges in an ability-driven education', in Jason Tan and Ng Pak Tee (eds), *Shaping Singapore's Future: Thinking Schools, Learning Nation*, Singapore: Pearson Education, 2005, pp. 5–21.

Tan Ern Ser, *Does Class Matter? Social Stratification and Orientations in Singapore*, Singapore: World Scientific, 2004.

Tan, Eugene K.B., 'Re-engaging Chineseness: political, economic and cultural imperatives of nation-building in Singapore', *China Quarterly*, vol. 175, 2003, pp. 751–774.

———, '"We, the citizens of Singapore…": multiethnicity, its evolution and its aberrations', in Lai Ah Eng (ed.), *Beyond Rituals and Riots: Ethnic Pluralism and Social Cohesion in Singapore*, Singapore: Eastern Universities Press by Marshall Cavendish for the Institute of Policy Studies, 2004.

———, 'The majority's sacrifices and yearnings: Chinese-Singaporeans and the dilemmas of nation-building', in Leo Suryadinata (ed.), *Ethnic Relations and Nation-Building in Southeast Asia: The Case of the Ethnic Chinese*, Singapore: Singapore Society of Southeast Asian Studies and Institute of Southeast Asian Studies, 2004, pp. 168–206.

———, 'Multiracialism engineered: the limits of electoral and spatial integration in Singapore', *Ethnopolitics*, vol. 4, no. 4, 2005, pp. 413–428.

Tan, Jason, 'Independent schools in Singapore: implications for social and educational inequalities', *International Journal of Educational Development*, vol. 13, no. 3, 1993, pp. 239–251.

———, 'The marketization of education in Singapore', in Jason Tan and Ng Pak Tee (eds), *Shaping Singapore's Future: Thinking Schools, Learning Nation*, Singapore: Pearson Education, 2005, pp. 95–111.

Tan, Jason and Ng Pak Tee (eds), *Shaping Singapore's Future: Thinking Schools, Learning Nation*, Singapore: Pearson Education, 2005.

Tan, Kevin Y.L., 'The presidency in Singapore: constitutional developments', in Kevin Y.L. Tan and Lam Peng Er (eds), *Managing Political Change in Singapore*, London and New York: Routledge, 1997, pp. 52–87.

Tan, Kevin Y.L. and Lam Peng Er (eds), *Managing Political Change in Singapore*, London and New York: Routledge, 1997.

Tan, Tony, 'Speech by Dr Tony Tan, Minister for Education, at the opening of the First National Conference and Exhibition on Kindergarten Education, 15 November 1990', Singapore Government Press Release, available at http://sprinter.gov.sg/.

Tan Yew Soon, 'Practising public consultation', *Ethos*, July 2004, pp. 15–18.

Tang Qing, *Nursery, Recognising Words, B*, [Singapore]: Educational Publishing, [c. 2004].

Teo Chee Hean, 'Ministerial Statement by Teo Chee Hean, Minister-in-Charge of the Civil Service, on Civil Service Salary Revisions, 9 April 2007', Singapore Government Press Release, located at http://www.sprinter.gov.sg/.

Teo Chong Tee, 'Speech by Mr Teo Chong Tee, Parliamentary Secretary (Social Affairs), and MP for Changi, at the Kindergarten Graduation Ceremony/Variety Show for Parents at the Education Centre of PAP Changi Branch, 8 November 1981', Singapore Government Press Release, located at http://www.sprinter.gov.sg/.

Teo, Eddie, 'Vision and values in Singapore's public service', *Ethos*, August 1999, page numbers not indicated.

———, 'Building an ethical civil service for the 21ˢᵗ century', *Ethos*, July 2000, page numbers not indicated.

———, 'The Singapore public service: a development-oriented promotion system', *Ethos*, May 2002, pp. 10–15.

———, 'Will the real civil service please stand up?', *Ethos*, November 2002, pp. 2–7.

———, 'Can public servants be leaders?', *Ethos*, September 2003, pp. 8–12.

Tharman Shanmugaratnam and the Junior College/Upper Secondary Education Review Committee, *Report of the Junior College/Upper Secondary Education Review Committee*, Singapore: Ministry of Education, 2002.

———, 'Speech by Mr Tharman Shanmugaratnam, Minister for Education, at SINDA's 14ᵗʰ Academic Excellence Awards Ceremony, 10 September 2005', on MOE website at http://www.moe.gov.sg/speeches/2005/sp20050910.htm.

————, 'Speech, "Innovation and enterprise in our schools", 16 February 2004'. Cited on Sprinter [Singapore Government news service] http://www.sprinter.gov.sg/.

Tin Maung Maung Than, 'Dreams and nightmares: state building and ethnic conflict in Myanmar (Burma)', Kusuma Snitwongse and W. Scott Thompson (eds), *Ethnic Conflicts in Southeast Asia*, Singapore: Institute of Security and International Studies, and Institute of Southeast Asian Studies, 2005, pp. 65–108.

Trocki, Carl A., *Singapore: Wealth, Power and the Culture of Control*, London and New York: Routledge, 2005.

Vasil, Raj, *Governing Singapore*, First revised edition, Singapore: Mandarin, 1992.

————, *Asianising Singapore: The PAP's Management of Ethnicity*, Singapore: Heinemann Asia, 1995.

————, *Governing Singapore: Democracy and National Development*, St Leonards, NSW: Allen and Unwin, 2000.

Visscher, Sikko, *The Business of Politics and Ethnicity: A History of the Singapore Chinese Chamber of Commerce and Industry*, Singapore: National University of Singapore Press, 2007.

Vogel, Ezra, *Japan as Number One: Lessons for America*, Cambridge, Mass: Harvard University Press, 1979.

Wang Gungwu (ed.), *Nation-Building: Five Southeast Asian Histories*, Singapore: Institute of Southeast Asian Studies, 2005.

Winner, Langdon, *Autonomous Technology: Technics-out-of-control as a Theme in Political Thought*, Cambridge, Mass. and London: The MIT Press, 1977.

Wong, Aline K., 'Planned development, social stratification and the sexual division of labour in Singapore', in Ong Jin Hui, Tong Chee Kiong and Tan Ern Ser (eds), *Understanding Singapore Society*, Singapore: Times Academic Press, 1997, pp. 17–32.

Worthington, Ross, *Governance in Singapore*, London and New York: RoutledgeCurzon, 2003.

Yaacob Ibrahim, 'Speech by Dr Yaacob Ibrahim, Minister-in-Charge of Muslim Affairs, at the MUIS Work Plan Seminar 2005, 5 February 2005'.

Available as a Singapore Government Press Release at http://app.sprinter.gov.sg/data/pr/200502-5998.htm.

Yack, B., 'The myth of the civic nation', in R. Beiner (ed), *Theorizing Nationalism*, Albany: State University of New York Press, 1999, pp. 103–116.

Yee Ping Yi, 'The philosophy and strategic directions for human resource management in the civil service', *Ethos*, August 2002, pp. 2–8.

Yeoh, Brenda S.A., *Contesting Space: Power Relations and the Urban Built Environment in Colonial Singapore*, Kuala Lumpur: Oxford University Press, 1996.

Yip Soon Kwong, John and Sim Wong Kooi (eds), *Evolution of Educational Excellence: 25 Years of Education in the Republic of Singapore*, Singapore: Longman, 1990.

Yong Ying-I, 'Singapore's leadership challenges: developing talent for a new era', *Ethos*, April–June 2005, pp. 7–12.

Primary school textbooks

ॐ 1970s

English This Way – Book 1: Special Singapore Edition, London: Collier Macmillan International, 1970.

English This Way – Book 2: Special Singapore Edition, London: Collier Macmillan International, 1970.

English Today As Second Language for Singapore Primary Schools, Singapore: Academia Publications, 1976, revised edition 1977.

Enjoying English: Nelson's Primary English Course for Singapore – 1A, Singapore: Thomas Nelson, 1979.

Enjoying English – 1B, Singapore: Thomas Nelson, 1979.

Looking Ahead with English – 2A, Singapore: Longman, 1970.

Looking Ahead with English – 3, Singapore: Longman, 1970.

New Primary English – 2A, Singapore: Longman, 1972.

Primary English for Singapore – EL2, 2A, Singapore: Preston Corporation, 1976.

ॐ 1980s

New Course English – 6A/B, Singapore: Educational Publishing Bureau for Curriculum Development Institute of Singapore, 1981, 1982.

New Course English – 6D/C, Singapore: Educational Publishing Bureau for CDIS, 1982, 1983.

New English Thematic Series Course Book – 1A, Singapore: EPB Publishers and CDIS, 1991.

Primary English Programme [PEP] Textbook – 1A, Singapore: Longman and CDIS, 1982.

PEP Textbook – 4A Extended, Singapore: Longman and CDIS, 1982.

PEP Textbook – 4A, Singapore: Longman and CDIS, 1983.

PEP Textbook – 4B Extended, Singapore: Longman and CDIS, 1982.

PEP Textbook – 4B, Singapore: Longman and CDIS, 1983.

PEP Textbook – 6A Extended, Singapore: Longman and CDIS, 1984.

PEP Textbook – 6B Extended, Singapore: Longman and CDIS, 1984.

PEP Textbook – 6A, Singapore: Longman and CDIS, 1985.

PEP Textbook – 6B, Singapore: Longman and CDIS, 1985.

❧ *1980s and 1990s*

New English Series for Primary Education [NESPE] Course Book – 1A, Singapore: Pan Pacific Book Distributors and the Curriculum Development Institute of Singapore, 1981.

NESPE Course Book – 1B, Singapore: Pan Pacific and CDIS, 1981.

NESPE Teacher's Edition – 1A, Singapore: Pan Pacific and CDIS, 1981.

NESPE Course Book – 4A, Singapore: Pan Pacific and CDIS, 1982.

NESPE Course Book – 4B Extended, Singapore: Pan Pacific and CDIS, 1981.

NESPE Teacher's Edition – 4A Extended, Singapore: Pan Pacific and CDIS, 1982.

NESPE Teacher's Edition – 4B Extended, Singapore: Pan Pacific and CDIS, 1982.

NESPE Course Book – 4B, Singapore: Pan Pacific and CDIS, 1983.

NESPE Course Book – 6A, Singapore: Pan Pacific and CDIS, 1983.

NESPE Course Book – 6A Extended, Singapore: Pan Pacific and CDIS, 1983.

NESPE Course Book – 6B Extended, Singapore: Pan Pacific and CDIS, 1983.

NESPE Course Book – 6A, Singapore: Pan Pacific and CDIS, 1984–94.

NESPE Course Book – 6B, Singapore: Pan Pacific and CDIS, 1985–94.

இ *1990s*

Primary English Thematic Series [PETS] – 1A, Singapore: EPB Publishers and Curriculum Development Institute of Singapore, 1991.

PETS – 6B EM3, Singapore: EPB Publishers and CDIS, 1996.

இ *2000s*

In Step: A Course in English for Primary Schools 2B, Singapore: Pan Pacific Publications, 2001.

My Pals and Here! English Writing Skills – 1, Singapore: Times Media Private, 2002.

My Pals are Here! English – 6A, Singapore: Times Media Private, 2005.

Treks. Setting Off: Interactive English for Primary Levels Course Book – 1A, Singapore: SNP Publishing, 2000.

Other sources without personal authors

Please note that some web links listed below are no longer functional. Although some have migrated to new addresses we have retained the old addresses because they were accurate at the time the research was done and many of the new web links do not contain the information cited in the text. For instance the Scholars Speak site is now at http://www.pscscholarships.gov.sg/SCHOLARS_SPEAK/ScholarsSpeak.htm, but this new address does not contain the stories that are recounted in this book.

ACNielsen, 'More Singaporeans than ever before looking to migrate overseas', dateline 4 September 2002. Available at http://www.acnielsen.com.sg/news.asp?newsID=112/. Cited 10 September 2002.

Administrative Service website, at http://www.adminservice.gov.sg/great.htm.

Buddhist Fellowship website, http://www.buddhistfellowship.org/news_link_02.htm.

Department of Employment, Education and Training (Australia), – DEET, *Country Education Profiles: Singapore, A Comparative Study,* Canberra: Australian Government Publishing Service, 1991.

Department of Statistics website, http://www.singstat.gov.sg/.

Educational Publishing House website, http://www.eph.com.sg/.

English Language Syllabus for Lower Primary Classes (Primary 1, 2 and 3), Singapore: Ministry of Education, 1990.

English Syllabus for the New English System. Primary 1 to 6 (Normal Course), Primary 4 to 8 (Extended Course), Primary 4 to 8 (Monolingual Course), Singapore: Ministry of Education, 1981.

Ethos, http://www.cscollege.gov.sg/main.html.

History Syllabus: Secondary 1 to 2 (Special/Express Course), Secondary 1 to 2 (Normal Academic Course), Singapore: Ministry of Education, 2000.

Majlis Ugama Islam Singapura (MUIS, Islamic Religious Council of Singapore) website, at http://www.muis.gov.sg/.

Marshall, David, The David Marshall Papers, held in the Institute of Southeast Asian Studies, Singapore.

Mathematics Syllabus for the New Education System. Part A Primary 1 to 3 (Common Course), Singapore: Ministry of Education, 1980.

Methodist Girls' School (Primary), 2002 English P1 examination papers.

Ministry of Community Development, *Singapore's Family Values*, Singapore: Ministry of Community Development, 1994.

Ministry of Community Development and Sport (MCDS) website at http://www.mcds.gov.sg/. (No longer functioning. Replaced by MCYS website.)

Ministry of Community Development, Youth and Sports (MCYS) website at http://www.mcys.gov.sg/. (Formerly the MCDS website.)

Ministry of Defence (MINDEF) Scholarship Centre, available online at http://www.scholar.mindef.gov.sg/safscholarships_safos_intro.asp.

Ministry of Defence website, http://mindef.gov.sg/imindef.html.

Ministry of Education (MOE) website at http://www.moe.gov.sg/.

Ministry of Education, *Curriculum Guidelines for the Pre-Primary Programme: Development of Skills (Semester I and II)*, Singapore: Educational Publications Bureau, 1979, pp. 1, 2.

———, *Curriculum Guidelines for the Pre-Primary Programme (Semester I & II)*, Singapore: Ministry of Education, 1979.

————, *Ministry of Education Pre-Primary Programme: Suggestions for Planning Activities,* Singapore: Educational Publications Bureau, 1980.

————, *Ministry of Education Pre-Primary Programme (Revised Edition): Suggestions for Planning Activities,* Singapore: Educational Publications Bureau, 1987.

————, *Nurturing Every Child: Flexibility and Diversity in Singapore Schools,* Singapore: Ministry of Education, 2004. Available at the MOE website, http://www.moe.edu.sg/.

Ministry of Education's *Directory of Schools 2003,* Singapore: Ministry of Education, 2003.

Ministry of Education's *Directory of Schools 2005,* Singapore: Ministry of Education, 2005.

Ministry of Information and the Arts (MITA), News email service, 29 November–5 December 2003.

————, *Riding the Tiger: The Chronicle of a Nation's Battle Against Communism,* DVD, Singapore: Ministry of Information and the Arts, 2001.

————, *The Singapore Story: Overcoming the Odds. An Interactive Media,* CD-ROM, a National Education Project by the Ministry of Information and the Arts, 1999.

Mirror of Opinion: Highlights of Malay, Chinese & Tamil Press, Ministry of Culture, Singapore, 1966, 1969.

National Heritage Board, *Singapore: Journey into Nationhood,* Singapore: National Heritage Board and Landmark Books, 1998.

New Civil Engineer, 2004

New Civil Engineer website at www.nceplus.co.uk/.

Office of the President of Singapore, available online at http://www.istana. gov.sg/.

PAP Community Foundation website, at http://www.pcf.org.sg/.

PAP Community Foundation, *Book of Memories,* Singapore: PAP Community Foundation, Tampines West Education Centre, 1992.

————, *PAP Tampines East Education Centre Year Book '90,* Singapore: PAP Community Foundation Tampines East Education Centres, 1990.

————, *Project Pre-School 1991–1994,* Singapore: PAP Community Foundation Pre-School Development Unit, 1994.

Parliament of Singapore website, http://www.parliament.gov.sg/.

Parliamentary Debates, Singapore, Official Report, Tenth Parliament, Thursday 23 May 2002.

Press Invitation, 8 August 2005, from the Office of the President, available at the http://www.istana.gov.sg.

Public Service Commission 'Scholars Speak' website, available at http://app. psc.gov.sg/scholarships/html.

Public Service Commission Scholarship Centre, available online at http:// app.psc.gov.sg/scholarships/html/scholarships.asp.

Public Service Division, Public Service Commission, email communication to Michael D. Barr, 11 October 2005.

Raffles Girls' Primary School, 2002 English P1 examination papers.

Raffles Junior College Homepage, available online at http://www.rjc.edu.sg/.

Shared Values, White Paper, Singapore: Singapore National Printers, 1991.

Singapore Cabinet website, at http://www.cabinet.gov.sg/.

Singapore Government Press Release online, at http://app.sprinter.gov.sg/.

Singapore History Project Team, *History of Modern Singapore (Lower Secondary),* Singapore: Addison Wesley Longman for the Curriculum Development Institute of Singapore, 1984, 1994.

———, *History of Modern Singapore (Secondary 1),* Singapore: Addison Wesley Longman for the Curriculum Development Institute of Singapore, 1984, 1994.

Singapore Infomap at www.sg/.

Singapore Parliamentary website, 15 May 2002, available at http://www.parliament.gov.sg/Publication/Htdocs/H1505.htm.

Singapore Police Force website at http://www.spf.gov.sg/service/cer1.html.

Singapore Police Force, 'Application for Certificate of No Criminal Conviction (CNCC)'; cited December 2003.

Singapore Window, available at http://www.singapore-window.org/.

Singapore's Survival, Security and Success, prepared for a seminar for Junior College students, circa 1998, vetted by Ms Ong Chong Lian, Head National Education Office and MAJ Chin Kok Keng, Head Curriculum Branch. Compiled by Mr Alden Teo, Curriculum Staff Officer.

Syllabus for Ethics for Primary School and Secondary School, Singapore: Ministry of Education, 1961.

Syllabus for Implementation from January 1999. Mathematics Primary EM1, EM2 and EM3 Streams, Singapore: Ministry of Education, 1998.

The Weekly Digest of Non-English Press, Singapore: Singapore Public Relations, 1956.

Up Close with Khaw Boon Wan, Channel NewsAsia, aired in Singapore 28 April 2005.

Up Close with Lee Hsien Loong, Channel NewsAsia, aired in Singapore 5 May 2005.

Up Close with Ng Eng Hen, Channel NewsAsia, aired in Singapore 21 April 2005.

Up Close with Tharman Shanmugaratnam, aired on Channel NewsAsia, 14 April, 2005.

Up Close with Vivien Balakrishnan, aired on Channel NewsAsia, 7 April, 2005.

News services

Agence France Presse

Asian Political News Service

Berita Harian

Berita Minggu

The Business Times

Channel NewsAsia

CyBerita

Lianhe Wanbao

Lianhe Zaobao

Reuters News Agency

The Straits Times

The Straits Times Interactive

The Straits Times Weekly Edition

The Sunday Times

Tamil Murasa
Today

Interviews made available by the Oral History Centre, National Archives of Singapore
Interview with Anna Tham, 1994.
Interview with Chan Kai Yau, 1995.
Interview with Eugene Wijeysingha, 1995.
Interview with Mr Rudy Mosbergen, 1994.

Interviews conducted by Michael Barr
Interview with Zulkifli Baharudin, Singapore, 26 March 2003.
Interview with Eugene Wijeysingha, Singapore, 11 April 2003.
Interview with Bilahari Kausikan, Singapore, 15 April 2003.
Interview with Syed Haroon Aljunied, Singapore, 29 April 2003.
Interview with Catherine Lim, Singapore, 24 March 2004.

Another 61 interviews conducted over 2002–2005 that have been de-identified at the request of the interviewee, and in accordance with procedures approved by the Behavioural and Social Science Ethical Review Committee of the University of Queensland. These include interviews with a serving Permanent Secretary and a former Permanent Secretary. Others interviewees are described at the end of Chapter 1, and in the text and references throughout the body of the book as appropriate.

Index

Abdul Rahman, Tunku 27, 30

Administrative Service. *See* civil service

Air Force 230. *See also* SAF

Aljunied, Syed Haroon 139, 145

Anderson, Benedict 2, 3, 40

Army 197, 219, 230–231. *See also* SAF

'Asian values' 45, 65, 95, 185. *See also* values

assimilation. *See* ethnicity/race

Association of Muslim Professionals (AMP). *See* ethnicity

Azeez, Duriya 170

Baharudin, Zulkifli 79, 218

Balakrishnan, Vivien 67

Barisan Sosialis 28

Benjamin, Geoffrey 52

bilingualism. *See* education

Bogaars, George 239

Brown, David 3, 53

Burma 3

Cabinet 9, 66, 69, 71, 74, 91–92, 209–210. *See also* civil service; elite; government

Chai Chong Yii 137

Chan Heng Chee 57

Chan Kai Yau 115, 116

Chee Soon Juan 75

Chew, Melanie 29, 30

Chiam See Tong 75, 76

China 102

Chinese. *See* ethnicity/race

Chinese Development Assistance Council (CDAC). *See* ethnicity/race

'Chinese values' 5, 45, 77, 92, 94, 95, 100, 101, 104, 128, 171, 224. *See also* values

Chua Mui Hoong 199

Citizens' Consultative Committees (CCCs). *See* GROs

civil service 46, 60–62, 79, 80, 239, 240

Administrative Service 13, 64, 61, 66, 67, 70, 71, 74, 198, 201, 208, 209, 229, 230, 232–248,

Prime Minister's Office 61, 64, 79

Public Service Commission 66, 68, 78, 179, 232, 235

see also government; MCDS/MCYS; MINDEF; MITA/MICA; MOE; permanent secretaries; SAF

Clammer, John 6

Confucianism. *See* ethnicity/race; 'Confucian values'

'Confucian values' 45, 47, 185. *See also* values

Contempacion, Flor 31

Daipi, Hawazi 138

Durai, T.T. 256

EDB (Economic Development Board) 72–74

education 19–35, 60, 70, 91, 94, 101, 102, 113–123, 150–173, 179–202

bilingualism 77, 113, 118–120, 154, 155, 184–186

elite ~ . *See* elite education

history, constructions of Singaporean 19–35, 187

KiFAS (Kindergarten Financial Assistance Scheme) 128, 142–145

kindergartens; pre-primary education 93, 112, 113, 127–145, 151, 152

Nanyang Technological University 64

Nanyang University 27, 89, 95, 224

National Education 19–35, 113, 186–188, 237

National Institute of Education/ Institute of Education 129, 160, 184, 263

National University of Singapore/University of Singapore 91, 95, 185, 198

PCF (PAP Community Foundation) 128, 130–135, 138–140. *See also* PAP

SAP schools. *See* ethnicity/race

textbooks 19, 21, 23, 34, 90, 121, 128, 129, 131, 134, 135, 144, 151, 156, 157, 160, 162, 164–172, 189, 216

elections 79, 80

elite 41–50, 57–81

formation 6, 8, 60–62, 112, 113, 119, 122, 179–202, 229–248

selection 12, 60, 122, 180–184, 188–196, 208–226

Singapore 8, 9, 13, 44–50, 57–81

see also elite education; government; Lee Hsien Loong; Lee Kuan Yew; meritocracy; technocracy

elite education

class/socio-economic background of students 128, 135, 136, 161, 162, 192–194, 222–226

gender 209–214, 219, 232, 237

GEP (Gifted Education Programme) 94, 120, 160, 184, 194, 200, 212, 245

Hwa Chong family of schools 94, 122, 195, 215, 220–225

NUS High School for Mathematics and Science 122, 196, 212, 225, 226, 255

Pre-University/Junior College 25, 30, 77, 93, 102, 117, 119, 121–123, 162, 180, 181, 183–187, 190, 191, 193–195,

197, 199, 220–224, 226, 229, 231

Raffles family of schools 44, 117, 118, 122, 160, 183, 190, 193, 195, 196, 198, 199, 212, 220–223, 226

SAP schools. *See* ethnicity/race

scholarships; scholars 13, 14, 49, 60, 66, 70, 72, 73, 78, 96, 97, 179, 184, 197, 208–226, 231, 231, 241

streaming 21, 70, 101, 113–118, 120–123, 129, 130, 136, 141, 152–155, 163, 180–184, 189

see also education; ethnicity/race

ethnicity/race 3–5, 9–11, 12, 24, 33, 41, 47, 48, 50–54, 59, 88, 89, 91, 92, 94–98, 102–106, 141, 121, 122, 131, 144, 150, 151, 162–173, 188, 189, 191, 192, 214–222, 237, 259, 261–267

AMP (Association of Muslim Professionals) 49

assimilation, incomplete 97–108, 137–145, 252, 253, 261–266

CDAC (Chinese Development Assistance Council) 48

Chinese 24, 25, 27, 32, 33, 43, 45–48, 50, 89, 90, 92, 93, 98, 104–108, 114, 131, 137, 151, 152, 163–172, 214–221, 262, 265, 266

Chinese language 92–101, 105–107, 114, 133, 135, 136, 155, 158, 159, 184–186, 189, 224, 266

Chinese-educated 24, 25, 27, 43, 45, 89, 90, 92, 118–121

Eurasian Association 48

Indians 21, 33, 46, 49–52, 89, 93, 95, 96, 99, 105–108, 118, 131, 138, 152, 163, 165–169, 215, 218, 219, 257, 261, 262. *See also* SAF

Malays 24, 25,30–33, 49, 50–52, 57, 87, 88, 89, 93, 96, 97, 99, 100, 102–108, 118, 131, 138–145, 152, 163–171, 218–220, 257, 262–265. *See also* SAF

MENDAKI (Council for the Development of the Malay-Muslim Community) 49, 138, 263

multiracialism 1, 24, 30, 32, 50–54, 87–92, 101–108

SAP (Special Assistance Plan) schools 93, 94, 120, 131, 132, 162, 171, 172, 189, 195, 196, 197, 215, 220–222, 224, 225, 245

SINDA (Singapore Indian Development Association) 49, 135, 215

Speak Mandarin Campaign 120

see also education; elite; elite education; Lee Hsien Loong; Lee Kuan Yew

Eurasian Association. *See* ethnicity

Fay, Michael 31

Foo, Cedric 67

Furnivall, John S. 88

Geertz, Clifford 51

gender. *See* elite education

GEP (Gifted Education Programme). *See* elite education

George, Cherian 11, 12

Giddens, Anthony 51

Glad, Ingrid 172

GLCs (Government-Linked Companies) 61, 66, 76, 180, 208, 210, 214, 232, 236, 238

Goh Chok Tong 7, 52, 65, 66, 68, 71, 102, 107, 186, 189, 190, 194, 209, 240

Goh Keng Swee 30, 57, 58, 113–115

government 2, 5, 11, 32, 34, 44, 46, 48, 63, 67, 68, 118, 198, 209, 223, 240, 247, 254, 267. *See also* Cabinet; civil service; elite; GLCs; government ownership; ministers; PAP; permanent secretaries; President; Prime Minister

Government-Linked Companies. *See* GLCs

government ownership 7–9. *See also* GLCs

GROs (grassroots organisations) 48, 49, 100, 252, 258–260
   CCCs (Citizens' Consultative Committees) 48
   RCs (Residents' Committees) 49, 258
   trade unions 49, 57
   see also ethnicity/race

HDB (Housing and Development Board) 79

health system 65, 66, 255, 256

Heng, Geraldine and Janadas Devan 47

Hill, Michael and Lian Kwen Fee 10

Ho Kah Leong 93

Ho, Peter 255

Hon Sui Sen 239

Hong Lysa 18

housing 96–98. *See also* GROs

Housing and Development Board. *See* HDB

Huxley, Tim 218

Hwa Chong family of schools. *See* elite education

Indians. *See* ethnicity/race

Indonesia 1, 4, 5, 25, 28, 29

ISD (Internal Security Department) 80

Islam. *See* religion

Jayakumar, S. 95

junior college. *See* education

Kang, Trivina 163, 164

Kausikan, Bilahari 229, 241, 244, 247

Khaw Boon Wan 67, 69, 81

Khoo, Angeline and Lim Kam Ming 170

kiasu 96, 97, 117, 118, 127, 136, 159, 184. *See also* values

kindergartens. *See* education

Krugman, Paul 32

Kwa Kok Beng 169

Labour Front 27

Lai Ah Eng 51, 52, 191, 192

language. *See* education; ethnicity/
race

Laos 100

Lee Hsien Loong 72–81, 184, 194,
208, 243
and elite/elitism 57, 58, 62, 64,
65, 68, 69, 73, 81, 233, 235,
236, 238, 241
and ethnicity/race/multiracial-
ism 87, 105, 106, 171, 208, 219

Lee Kuan Yew 1, 6–11, 18, 19, 24,
29, 34, 43, 46, 52, 57–59, 71, 72,
87, 91, 92, 96, 100–108, 119,
137, 185, 186, 188–190, 213,
216, 219, 238, 254, 262
and elite/elitism 6, 8, 9, 44, 47,
48, 58, 59, 61, 64–67, 76–81,
115, 152, 154, 163, 179, 209,
223, 225, 237, 240
and ethnicity/race/multiracial-
ism 10, 11, 24, 43–45, 52, 77,
87, 91, 92, 94, 96, 100–104,
108, 113, 119, 163, 172, 185,
188, 189, 216, 219

Lee Yock Suan 94, 212

Lim Boon Heng 105, 106

Lim Chin Siong 43

Lim Hng Kiang 255

Lim Kim San 29

Lim Pin 185

Lim Siong Guan 208, 209, 235, 240,
242, 244, 257

Lim Yew Hock 27

Lim, Raymond 67

Malaya/Malaysia 2, 4, 24–30, 43,
46, 57–60, 90, 91, 186

Malayan Communist Party. *See* MCP

Malays. *See* ethnicity/race

Marshall, David 27, 59, 88, 90

MCDS /MCYS (Ministry of
Community Development and
Sport /Ministry of Community
Development, Youth and Sport)
143–145, 243

MCP (Malayan Communist Party)
26, 27, 29
ABL (Anti-British League) 26

media 95
MediaCorp 75, 105, 106
television 75,

MENDAKI (Council for the
Development of the Malay-
Muslim Community). *See*
ethnicity

meritocracy 41–50, 57, 59, 60, 87,
114–123, 192–195, 208–226,
259. *See also* education; elite

military. *See* SAF

MINDEF (Ministry of Defence)
61, 115, 216, 235. *See also* SAF

ministers 61, 66, 72, 74, 76, 119,
145, 197, 209, 231, 238, 240.
See also Cabinet; civil service;
elite; government

Ministry of Community
Development and Sport /
Ministry of Community
Development, Youth and Sport.
See MCDS/MCYS

Ministry of Defence. *See* MINDEF

Ministry of Education. *See* MOE

MITA/MICA (Ministry of Information and the Arts/Ministry of Information, Communication and the Arts) 75, 79

MOE (Ministry of Education) 61, 94, 129, 132, 133, 136–138, 144, 161, 162, 183, 185, 192, 201, 214

Mok, Ka-ho 190

Mosbergen, Rudy 117

MUIS (Majlis Ugama Islam Singapura, or Islamic Religious Council of Singapore). *See* religion

multiracialism. *See* ethnicity/race

Muslims. *See* religion

Nair, C.V. Devan 18

Nathan, S.R. 100, 138

nation building, Singapore 5–12, 18–35, 40–44, 47, 48, 51, 52, 60, 61, 62, 87, 90, 91, 94, 95, 98, 101, 112, 113, 119, 187, 188, 267,–269

National Kidney Foundation 255, 256

National Service (NS). *See* SAF

nationalism 39–41
Asian 1, 2, 3, 5, 34, 35, 41, 100
civic 3, 4, 5, 12, 24, 87, 90–92
ethno-; ethnocultural 3–5, 12, 24, 43, 47, 51, 87, 92–108
see also nation building, Singapore

Navy 248n. *See also* SAF

Neher, Clark 260

Ng Eng Hen 66, 105

Ngiam Tong Dow 225, 239

Nicoll Highway disaster 254

Ong Eng Guan 44, 238, 239

Ong Kah Kok 239

Ong Pang Boon 24, 91

Ooi Giok Ling 163

Pang Tee Pow 239

PAP (People's Action Party) 9, 23, 79, 80, 128, 130–135, 138–140, 258. *See also* PCF

Pellizoni, Luigi 62, 63

People's Action Party. *See* PAP

permanent secretaries 68, 72, 198, 206, 209, 210, 233, 236, 240. *See also* civil service; elite

Pillay, J.Y. 32

pre-university education. *See* elite education

President 68, 262. *See also* elite

Prime Minister 66, 113, 240, 247. *See also* Goh Chok Tong; government; Lee Hsien Loong; Lee Kuan Yew

Prime Minister's Office. *See* civil service

Public Service Commission. *See* civil service

race. *See* ethnicity/race

Raffles, Sir Stamford 24, 25

Raffles family of schools. *See* elite education

Rajaratnam, S. 18, 91

religion 52, 96, 97, 99, 100, 103,
117, 215, 259
Buddhism 3–4
Christianity 52, 262
Hinduism 52, 98, 262
Islam 52, 99, 100, 103, 104, 107,
215, 262–265
Jemaah Islamiya 107
MUIS (Islamic Religious Council
of Singapore) 139, 263–265
Sikhism 52, 262
see also ethnicity/race
Residents' Committees (RCs). *See*
GROs; housing
Reynolds, Craig 34

Sadasivan, Balaji 66, 67
SAF (Singapore Armed Forces)
60–62, 66, 70, 71, 78, 114, 180,
197, 198, 208, 210, 216–220,
223, 230–234, 236, 238, 262
in government 61, 66, 70, 71, 78,
180, 198, 209, 210, 234–236,
238, 239, 246
and Malays 31, 218, 219, 220, 262
NS (National Service) 31, 70,
112, 197, 230–232, 237, 257
scholars/scholarships 70, 78,
180, 184, 191, 197, 209, 210,
216–219, 220, 223, 231–236,
238. *See also* Air Force; Army;
MINDEF; Navy
SAP schools. *See* ethnicity/race
SARS (Severe Acute Respiratory
Syndrome) 255, 256
scholars/scholarships. *See* elite
education; SAF

schools. *See* education
Seah Chee Meow 238
security. *See* ISD
See, Martin 75
Shanmugaratnam, Tharman 67, 69,
81, 100, 201
'Shared Values' 45, 95. *See also*
values
Sia, Lawrence 93
Sim Kee Boon 238, 239
Singapore Armed Forces. *See* SAF
Singapore Democratic Party 75
'Singapore Inc.' 76, 85. *See also*
GLCs; technocracy
Singapore Indian Development
Association (SINDA). *See*
ethnicity
Sitoh Yih Pin 75, 76
Smith, Anthony 8
Special Assistance Plan (SAP)
schools. *See* elite education
streaming. *See* elite education

Tan, Eugene 102
Tan, Jason 121
Tan, Leo 184
Tan, Tony 112, 113, 120, 130, 131,
135, 137, 189–191, 196
Tay Eng Soon 93
technocracy 62–72. *See also* civil
service; SAF
Teo Chee Hean 192
Teo, Eddie 235, 242–244, 247
textbooks. *See* education

Thailand 3, 4, 34, 35, 100

Toh Chin Chye 29, 91

Town Councils 79

Toynbee, Arnold 8, 44

trade unions. *See* GROs

   leadership. *See* elite

Trocki, Carl 25

unions. *See* GROs

universities. *See* education

values 45, 94– 97, 100, 101, 137.
   See also 'Asian values'; 'Chinese
   values'; 'Confucian values';
   kiasu; 'Shared Values'

Vasil, Raj 53, 93

Vietnam 1, 2

Vogel, Ezra 63

Wijeysingha, Eugene 190

Winsemius, Albert 6

Wong Kan Seng 106

Wong, Aline 137

Worthington, Ross 210, 214, 235

Yaacob Ibrahim 138, 243, 265

Yeo Cheow Tong 66

Yeo, George 18, 39, 52, 102

Yeo, Philip 73, 74

Yong Ying-I 244, 246

NIAS Press is the autonomous publishing arm of
NIAS – Nordic Institute of Asian Studies, a research institute
located at the University of Copenhagen. NIAS is partially funded by the
governments of Denmark, Finland, Iceland, Norway and Sweden
via the Nordic Council of Ministers, and works to encourage and
support Asian studies in the Nordic countries. In so doing, NIAS
has been publishing books since 1969, with more than two
hundred titles produced in the past few years.

COPENHAGEN UNIVERSITY

norden

Nordic Council of Ministers